GEORGE WASHINGTON'S SCHOONERS

GEORGE WASHINGTON'S
SCHOONERS
THE FIRST AMERICAN NAVY

Chester G. Hearn

NAVAL INSTITUTE PRESS

Distributed by:
Airlife Publishing Ltd.
101 Longden Road, Shrewsbury SY3 9EB, England

© 1995 by Chester G. Hearn

Library of Congress Cataloging-in-Publication Data
Hearn, Chester G.
  George Washington's Schooners : the first American navy / Chester G. Hearn.
       p.   cm.
  Includes bibliographical references and index.
  ISBN 1-55750-358-3
  1. United States—History—Revolution, 1775–1783—Naval operations.
2. Schooners—United States—History—18th century.
I. Title.
E271.H43 1995
973.3'5—dc20   94-24209

Printed in the United States of America on acid-free paper ∞

02 01 00 99 98 97 96 95   9 8 7 6 5 4 3 2
First printing

To Ann and Chet,

and to the beloved memory

of Wendy

Contents

Introduction 1

1 George Washington Takes Command 5
2 The Chaotic Cruise of *Hannah* 15
3 Commodore Broughton Cruises North....................................26
4 Not So Much as a Candle 37
5 The Schooners of Plymouth 48
6 The Cruise of the "Humorous Genius" 58
7 The Capture of Sion Martindale 70
8 The Last Two Schooners Out of Beverly 80
9 Manley Sets the Stage 88
10 Manley Strikes and Graves Falls......................................99
11 The Brief Cruise of Winborn Adams...................................109
12 Reorganizing the Fleet 116
13 Echoes of Gunfire...126
14 Tucker and Waters Join the Hunt....................................135
15 The Commodore's Pestiferous Squadron...............................142
16 A Month in Transition 152
17 The Death of the Valiant Mugford...................................160
18 Greeting the Royal Highlanders.....................................174
19 Summer of Dissension...189
20 The Autumn of '76 199
21 Winter of Unrest 208
22 The Last Schooner 215
23 Fighters to the End..223

Epilogue..235
Appendix: Prizes Captured by Washington's Schooners........241
Notes 243
Bibliography 269
Index...277

GEORGE WASHINGTON'S SCHOONERS

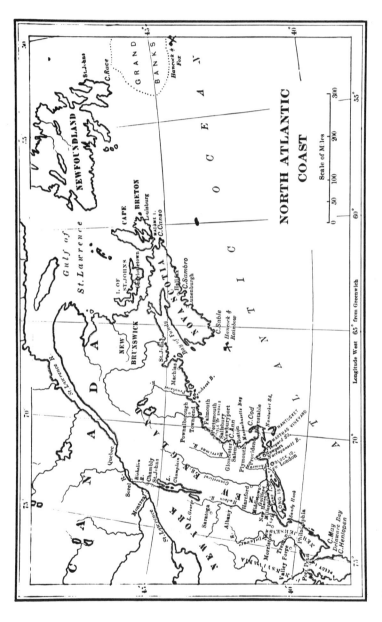

The range of Washington's armed schooners. Reprinted from Gardner W. Allen, *A Naval History of the American Revolution* (Boston: Houghton Mifflin, 1913).

Introduction

hen naval historians recall America's first battles on the high seas, they think of John Paul Jones, John Barry, Nicholas Biddle, and Abraham Whipple. Men such as these achieved fame by serving in the first navy of the United States, the Continental Navy. But the Continental Navy had a predecessor, a small flotilla of armed schooners commissioned by a Virginia planter by the name of George Washington, who came to Massachusetts to drive the British out of Boston.

The general's name never appeared on the list of the Continent's well-known naval personnel. He had never been an admiral or a commodore, or even a common sailor. During his distinguished career as commander in chief of the Continental Army, and as first president under the Constitution of the United States, he never held even the lowliest of commissions in what became the Continental Navy. Out of necessity, however, Washington created the first American navy and by doing so helped convince the Continental Congress that a prolonged war against King George III could not be won without mobilizing a naval force capable of harassing His Majesty's supply lines.

Washington was a military man—not a brilliant military man of the stature of a Napoleon or a Wellington, but one with enough foresight and tenacity to win a war neither Britain's ministers nor King George III believed they could lose. When Washington took command of the Continental Army on June 17, 1775, the main British army was safely ensconced in Boston. Although surrounded on three sides by Continentals, they enjoyed the unabated flow of supplies, munitions, and reinforcements from Great Britain. Washington had few experienced soldiers, certainly not enough to risk an attack on Gen. Thomas Gage's professionally trained regiments. Gage had fewer men than Washington, too few to storm Washington's entrenchments. The British general still

George Washington during the American Revolution.

remembered Bunker Hill, where English blood had stained the grassy, windswept knoll and where old squirrel guns, blunderbusses, and rusty muskets had cut down his regulars.

Forty-three-year-old General Washington had two problems: He needed muskets and gunpowder for his army, and he needed to stop the flow of supplies into Boston. With powder horns nearly empty the Continental Army felt almost defenseless, but they had one advantage. They could collect provisions from the countryside, forcing the British to depend on the sea. Washington worried that Gage would attempt to break out of Boston before the untrained and poorly equipped militia had the firepower and confidence to repel an attack. As long as the Continental Army did nothing but maintain the siege, Gage's regulars would only get stronger.

The solution to Washington's problems became obvious soon after he arrived at his Cambridge headquarters. From the hillsides above Boston he witnessed the steady flow of British transports entering the harbor unchallenged, and the Royal Navy's ships of war at anchor with their heavy guns protecting the landward approaches to the town. Informants from Boston rowed across the Charles River to report new regiments in town or to announce the arrival of another vessel from England laden with arms. In a land war, supply lines could be cut by cavalry, but not here. What Washington needed was a navy, but there was none, and the Continental Congress doubted if one would be needed.

Washington's orders from Congress allowed him sufficient latitude to do much as he pleased in containing the British army. Hundreds of vessels lay in nearby harbors, waiting for a resolution of the present crisis before returning to their trade. Washington wanted a few fast vessels, like the swift little schooners built by the craftsmen of Marblehead. He wanted them lightly armed but still fast enough to elude the powerful British frigates standing in Nantasket Road. And he wanted his schooners mobilized without delay. As Congress labored in chambers, debating the practicality of creating and financing a navy, the general decided the matter for them. He pressed his schooners to sea in the fall of 1775, and prizes began to flow.

The War of the Revolution could not have been won without help from the sea. The Continental Army lost most of its battles to the professionally trained soldiers of George III. The navy, as it evolved from one reorganization to another, lost frigates to the Royal Navy faster than Continental warships could be put to sea. Without help from France and, to a lesser degree, Spain and Holland, there would not have been a decisive battle fought at Yorktown, and King George III could have carried on the war at his leisure. Washington understood the value of a navy. If he needed a primer to consolidate his strategy, his armed schooners provided him with an education that helped to carry thirteen American colonies through eight years of war to final victory and lasting independence.

George Washington's schooners were unique. They fit no category either naval or military. They were not privateers sailing under letters of marque. They were not armed vessels commissioned by the navy. They were manned and armed by soldiers serving the military in a naval occupation. They were, however, the forerunners of the Continental Navy, and their existence demonstrated the need to create that branch of the service.

Although confronted with desperate military problems, Washington retained control of his schooners until Congress formulated a naval policy he could accept. A naval flotilla did not belong under the command of the

General of the Army, but Washington demonstrated the validity of providing for a navy and Congress eventually agreed. In the first year of the war, he helped to provide the foundation for this nation's naval policy. And he did it with eight small New England schooners.

This is their story.

🎟 1 🎟
George Washington Takes Command

O n *June 15, 1775,* the Continental Congress unanimously elected by ballot George Washington "to command all the continental forces raised, or to be raised, for the defence of American liberty." A committee defined "all the continental forces" as whatever force Washington deemed necessary to "destroy or make prisoners" those who "are, or hereafter shall appear in arms against the good people of the United Colonies." As a hedge, the committee added, as "all particulars cannot be foreseen, nor positive instructions for such emergencies so beforehand given . . . many things must be left to your prudent and discreet management, as occurrences may arise." The committee made no mention of naval forces and at this time gave the matter little thought. They simply authorized Washington "to order and dispose of the said Army . . . as may be most advantageous for obtaining the end for which these forces have been raised, making it your special care, in discharge of the great trust committed unto you that the liberties of America receive no detriment."[1]

Washington reached Cambridge on July 3, 1775, and there met a restless group of riflemen guarding fortifications stretching from Roxbury on the southeast to Winter Hill and Prospect Hill on the northwest. From any rise overlooking Boston, he could look down on the harbor and see a forest of spars, topped by the masts of British warships.

The selection of a Virginian to command an army composed exclusively of New Englanders seemed odd, but Washington's reputation as a soldier was recognized throughout the colonies. As a wealthy aristocrat, he knew how to deal with the influential men seated in Congress, and there was little opposition to his appointment as commander in chief.

The general, at six feet, two inches, was lean and soldierly, big boned, and padded well with muscles. He had intense, blue-gray eyes that sparkled with energy, and a pleasing way of speaking in an agreeable, rather than dictatorial, manner. His skin was quite pale and scarred from smallpox, and—because of defective teeth—he rarely smiled, but his movements and gestures were graceful. At first the men viewed him with a mixture of curiosity and doubt, likening him to a soldier who had come from a foreign country to take command of their lives. Washington quickly earned their acceptance, but independent-minded New Englanders had a habit of following their own agendas.

The British occupying Boston were hemmed in on all sides but one, and that side faced the sea. A stalemate settled around the town. Washington would not send his fourteen thousand homespun-clad irregulars against the heavy guns of the British, and General Gage seemed content to exercise his six thousand regulars by parading them around Boston Common. The town presented a natural barrier to both armies, being almost an island attached to the mainland by a slender, mile-long neck of mud flats.[2]

From the surrounding hilltops, Boston looked like a patchwork of dwellings topped by chimneys emitting a curl of smoke from cook fires. Steeples bristled here and there, punctuating the skyline with simple crosses. A jumble of piers, shipyards, distilleries, storehouses, and stages for drying fish skirted the silent and deserted waterfront. An occasional sail slipped into the harbor laden with supplies. Vice Adm. Thomas Graves's navy lay listless but watchful in Nantasket Road. If the rebels attacked, they would suffer the might of His Majesty's naval artillery.

Washington rejected any notion of attacking the British outposts or bringing on an engagement. His men were neither trained nor disciplined and knew little of war. Volunteers who had rushed to fight the British never expected to waste their days slinging dirt while the enemy enjoyed the taverns and comforts of the city. Trouble brewed in the trenches. Men wanted to fight or go home, but jobs were scarce. They were sailors, shipbuilders, fishermen, and whalers—all livelihoods interrupted by a war of no fighting. The thought of abandoning the earthworks and opening the countryside to the ravages of the enemy horrified Washington. He needed to find a way to keep the men occupied.[3]

Authorized by Congress to exercise his "prudent and discreet management, as occurrences may arise," the general considered his options.

If the British could not be driven out of Boston, perhaps they could be starved out, which meant stopping their flow of supplies. But Washington had a more immediate problem—an urgent need to equip a threadbare army grubbing for tents, clothing, muskets, gunpowder, lead, and bayonets.

James Warren of the Massachusetts General Court probably had no idea of Washington's private deliberations when he wrote John Adams on July 11 that "ten very good sloops, from 10 to 16 guns . . . would clear our coasts." Warren pressed Adams to encourage Congress to initiate discussions for financing a Continental navy. At the same time, Washington wrote reflectively, "A fortunate capture of an ordnance ship would give new life to the camp, and an immediate turn to the issue of this campaign."[4]

Among the army rank and file Washington observed an abundance of young seamen bemoaning the monotony of duty in the trenches. At night they congregated around campfires and wistfully spun yarns about the girls in Jamaica or lamented over the big cyclone that had snapped their masts off windy Cape Hatteras and left them stranded on a sandy strip of beach. The ragged seacoast had been etched in their memories since youth. Sweating behind earthworks and swatting mosquitoes was no way to fight a war. Give them the open sea. They'd show King George who owned the colonial coast.

No unit in Washington's army breathed more salt air or lived closer to the sea than Col. John Glover's blue-jacketed Marbleheaders, the 21st Massachusetts, later to be designated the 14th Continental. Most ports in Massachusetts Bay lay snug in sheltered coves and harbors, but Marblehead defiantly thrust a craggy fist out to sea, and the people of the town looked as hardy and weathered as the great rocks in their front yards. Glover was much like his Marblehead neighbors: patriotic, courageous, and resourceful. The colonel owned ships, and when they were not at sea they bumped against the pilings at Glover's Wharf.

Born in neighboring Salem on November 5, 1732, Glover understood the meaning of struggle and survival. He was four when his father died, leaving his mother with four small boys to raise. She gave them an education and moved the family to Marblehead, where John labored as a shoemaker through his early twenties. In 1756, impressed by an opportunity to make money in the rum business, he applied to the General Court for a license. To his surprise, he received a grant giving him "lib-

Col. John Glover supplied *Hannah*, the first schooner of Washington's fleet. After a drawing by John Trumbull.

erty to retail strong Liqours" in Marblehead. By 1760 he had accumulated enough capital to buy his first ship and become a merchant. His vessels plied the seas from the West Indies to Portugal and Spain, trading dried fish for fruits, fine wines, salt, sugar, and rum.

By 1774 Glover was a wealthy man by most New England standards. After moving his place of business from Marblehead to Beverly, he purchased a parcel on the waterfront, built a wharf, warehouse, and cooper's shop, and added equipment for shipping, salting, and packing fish. His home remained in Marblehead, where he lived with his wife, Hannah, and family, surrounded by all his brothers but one, who had died at the age of thirty-one.[5]

Beverly proved to be a better location for Glover to expand his business. The town numbered three thousand inhabitants and lay snugly tucked behind a seacoast extending for several miles along a north shore divided into alternating sections of sandy beach and rocky points. Prosperous Salem lay across the harbor from Beverly, and to the west lay Danvers. Small farms with livestock and pine groves dotted the landscape between the towns, but fishing dominated Beverly's commerce, with shops for making ropes and sails, yards for building ships. To keep fishermen jolly at their lines, five small distilleries converted West Indies molasses into rum.

In 1775 Beverly's fishing fleet contained thirty-five schooners manned by over three hundred men. Glover's three vessels lay among them, and he, like other shipowners, fished during the summer and, after the hurricane season passed, shipped his salted catch to the West Indies.[6]

Glover had already compiled a long list of grievances against the British. Parliament's so-called Intolerable Acts of 1774 shut down the port of Boston, and the impact rippled up the coast and spread into Marblehead, Salem, and Beverly. The Royal Navy, enforcer of the laws, overstepped its authority, stopping colonial vessels and impressing the sailors. Glover found himself in the thick of the fight, backed by every able-bodied man in Marblehead. Relations worsened when Parliament passed the Fisheries Bill and threatened to shut down Marblehead's major industry. Glover, expecting war, mobilized a boycott, but before Marblehead fishermen learned what life could be like under the Fisheries Bill the farmers of Lexington and Concord took matters into their own hands. After that, Glover began recruiting companies of minutemen from fisherfolk unwilling to chance an encounter with the king's fast frigates. When the regimental commander, Jeremiah Lee, died unexpectedly, Glover took command of Marblehead's minutemen.[7]

Glover had no fear of the British. On June 6, 1775, he had already thumbed his nose at HMS *Merlin,* a sloop of war off Marblehead Harbor. Late that afternoon he sighted his schooner *Hannah* making for port and rowed out to greet her. A boat lowered from *Merlin* was headed in the same direction. Both parties met beside the schooner, and a British officer ordered *Hannah* to bring to. Glover shouted at his captain to fill for the harbor. Running under *Merlin*'s guns, the schooner slid by unharmed. The British sloop failed to fire, but her captain wisely refrained from pursuing *Hannah* into Beverly. Glover and his neighbors had fortified the harbor, and a detail from the colonel's regiment stood at the point of Marblehead Neck, itching to try their guns. At the time, Glover had no presentiment this small schooner would become the first armed vessel fitted out for the general's fleet.[8]

When Glover met Washington, the colonel was a forty-two-year-old, short, heavy-set redhead fully charged with energy. He had clear, deep-set eyes, a broad, high forehead, and the slightly outthrust chin of a man accustomed to giving orders. Glover and the general shared a common characteristic—patriotic determination.

Exactly how Washington and Glover conceived the idea of arming *Hannah* is left to speculation. When the general arrived at Cambridge the guards detailed at headquarters were mostly Marbleheaders. He found them noisy and troublesome, but he enjoyed their spirit and the strong flavor of salt in their talk. A mind as keen as Washington's must have appreciated the possibilities of employing his guardsmen in a duty more closely associated with their seafaring skills. He discussed the idea with Glover, who just happened to have *Hannah* laid up at his Beverly wharf. Glover, both businessman and patriot, agreed to lease the vessel to the army at a cost of "one Dollar pr Ton pr Month."[9]

Hannah, named for Glover's wife, was a typical schooner of her day. At 78 tons burden she exceeded in size most other vessels in Beverly's fishing fleet, but her stubby two-masted design was distinctive of her class. At Beverly, where many vessels had been moved to get away from Marblehead's exposed harbor, carpenters went to work on her. After tying her up at Glover's Wharf, they cut gunports—two to a side—in her bulwarks and strengthened her planking. For speed, sailmakers increased her usual main, fore, and jib sails by adding topsails and a flying jib. Workmen set a whaleboat amidships and expanded the large cookstove below to serve a larger crew. Glover owned his own cache of arms and provided four 4s with carriages, a dozen swivels, and an assortment of gunnery stores. By August 24 *Hannah* was ready to sail, but she had no crew.[10]

Glover suggested Nicholson Broughton, an old salt from Marblehead serving in the 21st Massachusetts, as the man most fit to command *Hannah.* The general, inexperienced in judging seafaring men, interviewed Broughton and approved. Glover volunteered his eldest son, twenty-year-old John Jr., a lieutenant in the 21st, as *Hannah's* first officer.

To Broughton's credit, he had been a skillful shipmaster for twenty years and was thoroughly familiar with the New England coast. At the age of fifty he looked the part of a well-fed sea captain. He spoke with authority and radiated the enthusiasm of a patriot eager to strike a blow for independence. With John Jr. as first lieutenant and John Devereaux,

Broughton's son-in-law, as second lieutenant, the general held high expectations for a successful cruise.[11]

Since Glover had provided *Hannah's* officers, Washington asked the colonel to pick a crew from his own regimental privates. He believed soldiers bred to the sea would transform quickly into an effective force of marines. Glover selected another member of his family, brother-in-law Richard James, as sailing master, and added a master's mate and four able-bodied sailors hired at Beverly. The balance of the crew of forty-three came from his own regiment. He had no difficulty raising volunteers. In addition to receiving Continental pay, Washington offered officers and crew a share in the value of captured cargoes. The cruise, however, as well as the distribution of shares, manifested signs of becoming a family affair.

Instead of standard army fare, Lt. Col. Joseph Reed, Washington's military secretary, drew up a list of sea rations. He chose a month's supply of salt beef instead of fresh, hard ships' bread for flour, potatoes for peas and beans, and rum in place of spruce beer. Officers enjoyed a supplemental ration of coffee, chocolate, sugar, and the most potent West Indies rum available, no doubt tapped from Glover's own distillery.[12]

On September 2 Washington commissioned Broughton captain "in the Army of the United Colonies of North America" and handed him detailed sailing instructions. Because Broughton radiated all the independence of a ship's master accustomed to having his own way, Washington sensed his new captain needed some guidance on military matters as they pertained to naval operations. Broughton's endorsement on his instructions, however, did not guarantee he understood them.

In addition to fixing the distribution of prize shares, Washington directed Broughton to "cruize against such vessels as may be found on the high seas or elsewhere, bound inward and outward to and from Boston, in the service of the ministerial army, and to take and seize all such vessels, laden with soldiers, arms, ammunition, or provisions . . . which you shall have good reason to suspect are in such service." Prizes were to be sent "to the nearest and safest port to this camp, under a careful Prize-Master, directing him to notify me by express immediately...."

The general asked Broughton to treat all prisoners with "kindness and humanity, as far as consistent with your own safety." After prisoners were searched, Washington wanted their money and personal belongings returned to them, "and when they arrive at any port, you are to apply to the Committee [of Safety], or to any officer of the Continental Army... to bring them up to Head Quarters."

Washington may not have known much about *Hannah*, but he knew enough to caution Broughton "to avoid any engagement with any armed vessel of the enemy, though you may be equal in strength, or may have some small advantage; the design of this enterprize, being to intercept the supplies of the enemy, which will be defeated by your running into unnecessary engagements."

Aside from not wanting *Hannah* lost on her first cruise, Washington had a diplomatic motive for avoiding an engagement with the Royal Navy. Many influential Loyalists lived in the colonies. The policy of Congress had been to placate them by not warring upon good King George but by resisting his evil, tax-imposing ministers. The war was still confined to New England, and Loyalists had not taken up arms against the patriots. Washington did not want to disrupt this détente by attacking His Majesty's ships. He may have spared himself much grief had he counseled Broughton more thoroughly on the difference between the king's friendly subjects and the mercenaries of the "evil ministers."

Although Washington commissioned but one vessel, he already had plans for more. He demonstrated a fundamental understanding of commerce-raiding tactics when he added in his instructions to Broughton, "As there may be other vessels imployed in the same service with yourselves, you are to fix upon proper signals, and your stations being settled so as to . . . avoid cruizing on the same ground. If you should happen to take prizes in sight of each other; the rules which take place among private ships of war, are to be observed in the distribution of Prize-Money."[13]

When Washington issued his instructions to Broughton, neither Massachusetts nor the Continental Congress had formalized any legislation on privateering. Massachusetts legalized privateering on November 1, 1775, and Congress on November 25. The general, operating from Cambridge, could not have anticipated the details of this later legislation.

Massachusetts awarded privateers the entire prize—vessel, cargo, and all—regardless of the character of its contents. If a vessel was recaptured from the enemy, the owner, on repossessing the vessel, was obligated to pay the privateer one-third of the value of the ship and her cargo. In Massachusetts, the owner of a privateer who enjoyed a small amount of good fortune became immensely wealthy.

Congress was equally generous to privateers but followed a policy similar to Washington's for vessels financed with public funds. One-third of the value of the prize went to the captor and the remainder to the state or Continental government. If the prize was armed, one-half of its value went to the captor. In both instances, however, the prize had to be brought to a home port and libeled in a district court. Courts, however, did not exist and many months passed before Congress established them.

Washington's distribution of prize money looked niggardly compared with later legislation. Broughton and his crew were entitled to only one-third of the value of the cargo, except "military and naval stores . . . which with vessels and apparell are reserved for publick service." Of this third, Broughton would get six shares, two lieutenants five and four, respectively, all the way down to privates, who received one share each. If *Hannah*'s crew recaptured a prize, the vessel's owner had no legal obligation to pay Broughton a cent. Washington merely promised to "recommend it to such person to make a suitable compensation."

The general concluded his instructions to Broughton by admonishing him "to be extremely careful and frugal of [his] ammunition, by no means to waste any of it in salutes, or for any purpose, but what is absolutely necessary."[14]

Broughton paid little attention to Washington's instructions. The captain of *Hannah* was not a military man but a sailor accustomed to receiving simple sailing orders from shipowners like John Glover, who might have said, "Well, Nicholson, we've got a nice cargo of fish tucked in the hold. Take the boys and get on down to Havana before the market drops. Bring back all the rum she'll hold, and if there be space left, fill her with sugar and molasses. There's a pretty penny in it for you if you get back by October." Marbleheaders knew all about incentives, and if nothing else in Washington's letter tweaked Broughton's consciousness, the opportunity for prize money did. And a similar pecuniary eagerness percolated throughout the crew.

Broughton concealed a personality quirk that surfaced shortly after he went to sea. The newly commissioned captain of *Hannah* emerged as an overzealous treasure hunter whose behavior toward British subjects surpassed what the general may have considered sound and rational in an undeclared war confined to Boston. At Cambridge, under the purview of Glover and Washington, Broughton had occupied his infantry captain's post with fitting behavior. Now cast loose and bubbling with avarice, Broughton stuffed the general's directives into the ship's chest and proceeded to sea in search of booty. He reasoned that any British vessel laden with ordnance would be armed, and since the general had admonished him to avoid such vessels, he created his own sailing agenda.

John Glover was probably not at the Beverly wharf on September 5 when *Hannah,* crammed to the bulkheads with forty-three men, slipped out of the harbor for her first cruise. Thirty-six privates had been recruited from the colonel's regiment. Oddly, only twelve signed up from Broughton's company. One might wonder why only a dozen of Broughton's men chose to sail with him. Perhaps they knew each other too well.

Hannah's captain had waited three extra days for his crew to arrive. They were "absent without leave," having decided to go home for a three-day visit before crossing over to Beverly.[15] Marbleheaders were like that—tough, a little clannish, and independent. And Nicholson Broughton, a pretentious and acquisitive man, was a Marbleheader, too.

🎕 2 🎕
The Chaotic Cruise
of Hannah

t 10:00 on the morning of September 5, with the aid of a
fair breeze, *Hannah* spread her sails and stood forth
from Beverly Harbor. The schooner was crowded and
cramped, but visions of quick cash prevailed among
the men who squeezed on deck to wave good-bye to loved ones. As the
vessel cleared the harbor, Broughton posted two lookouts in the tops,
rounded Marblehead Point, and set a southeasterly course, keeping
Halfway Rock well to starboard.

With land still in sight, the lookouts nervously reported two men-
of-war bearing toward them. Broughton came about and, with westerlies blowing a few points to the south, sped for Cape Ann. As he passed
Marblehead, the thought perhaps occurred to him that the safety of
Beverly Harbor lay but a short distance away, but how would it look to
all those people who had just bid him good-bye if he came running back
to port with his tiller between his legs?

By dusk Broughton lay off Cape Ann, where he remained until
dark. His pursuers, the 20-gun frigate *Lively,* Capt. Thomas Bishop, and
the 8-gun sloop *Savage,* Capt. Hugh Bromedge, paused offshore,
unwilling to test unfamiliar water at night. *Savage* abandoned the chase,
but *Lively* remained off Eastern Point, lingering until morning.

Broughton, sighting no enemy offshore, crept out of his hiding
place and started back down the coast. As he rounded the Point, *Lively*
hove in view. Taking advantage of a fair wind, Broughton beat into
Gloucester Harbor. At nightfall he found *Lively* gone and stood south.

After two close calls the crew grew nervous, and when a large vessel loomed under the lee quarter at daybreak Broughton braced his sails
and sped away. But this time there was no pursuit. Fear dwindled.

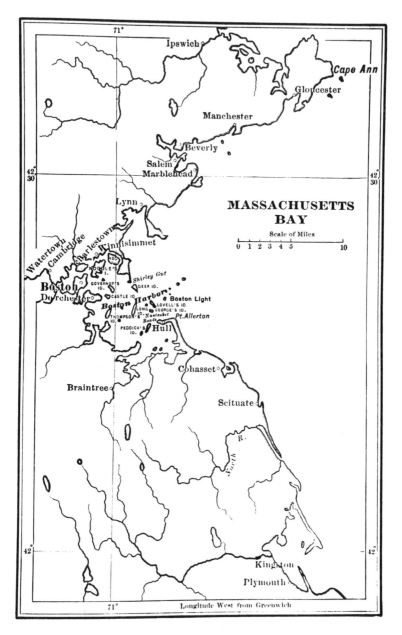

The main cruising grounds of Washington's schooners, 1775–1776. Reprinted from Gardner W. Allen, *A Naval History of the American Revolution* (Boston: Houghton Mifflin, 1913).

Visions of prize money flashed afresh. *Hannah* came about and closed cautiously on the larger vessel. Lookouts scanned the ship and reported no evidence of arms. Broughton felt more courageous and ordered the schooner forward. Standing off a short distance, he hailed, asking her name and where she was from. Captain Flagg answered back, "*Unity* from Piscataqua and bound for Boston." Broughton probably leaped with joy. To his way of thinking, any vessel bound for Boston had to be a fair prize. "I told him he must bear away and go into Cape Ann," Broughton later reported, "but being very loth, I told him if he did not I should fire on him."[1]

Boarding officer John Glover Jr. lowered the whaleboat and rowed over to examine *Unity*'s papers. What Glover discovered deflated Broughton's euphoria. The 260-ton *Unity* belonged to John Langdon of Portsmouth, a shipowner widely known as a patriot and delegate to the Continental Congress. *Unity*, recently captured by *Lively*, was being escorted by a prize crew to Boston. Flagg claimed his original destination had been the West Indies, where he intended to sell a cargo of fish, beef, and lumber. Flagg was telling the truth. Broughton could have removed the British prize crew and returned the vessel to Flagg, but he wanted compensation for his trouble and deceived himself into believing the prize worth bringing to port. He transferred everyone to *Hannah*, put a prize crew on *Unity*, and escorted the vessel to Cape Ann.

Later in the day Broughton sailed to Gloucester and deposited the British prize crew with the town's Committee of Safety. Young Glover had been accidently wounded during the capture and needed medical attention. For some reason Broughton kept Flagg on board, perhaps in a frail effort to solidify his prize money by proving that *Unity*'s master was secretly trading with the British. Unable to shake a confession from Flagg, Broughton reported the capture to Washington and added: "Have sent the Captain of the ship we took for your Excellency's examination, and I shall proceed immediately in the further execution of your . . . orders."[2]

Broughton extended his stay at Gloucester, using as his excuse Glover's wound. Since Broughton never mentioned the nature of the injury, it could not have been serious enough to prevent *Hannah* from sailing. Broughton left no record of how he spent his time, but he decided to wait for Washington's ruling on prize money. Without a court to libel prizes, lofty admiralty decisions devolved upon the general.

While the Committee of Safety marched the prisoners to Cambridge headquarters for questioning, Broughton concocted his own rationale for why *Unity* should be declared a fair prize. Instead of confining deliberations to his quarters, he discussed the prospects of prize money with the crew, thereby elevating everyone's expectations. Broughton's letter to Washington on September 9 suggests as much: "On my sending of an Officer on board said ship, his treatment was such as I would rather have expected from a polite enemy than a friend to our cause as Americans." Having dubbed Flagg a possible traitor, Broughton explained that *Unity* contained "a much greater Quantity of Naval Stores than is customary to export from our ports" but failed to identify what they were. To add more strength to his allegations, he accused Flagg of carrying a "considerable quantity of raw fish" and deemed this conclusive evidence that the cargo was "designed for the Port of Boston, instead of for the West Indies Isles." The so-called fresh fish were well-salted cod and haddock, but Broughton hoped the general might think fresh fish would spoil before reaching a West Indies port. After all, what would a planter from Virginia know of the fisheries trade?

Broughton suggested *Unity* be moved to Beverly, a harbor of greater security than Gloucester. To justify the move, and perhaps to appeal to His Excellency's concern over material shortages, Broughton reminded him that *Unity*'s cargo of lumber would be more difficult to cart to headquarters from Gloucester. He closed his report by informing the general that he would leave the prize with the Committee of Safety pending further orders. Instead of sailing, he and the crew waited at Gloucester for instructions. They wanted to be handy when an express arrived with their shares.[3]

Broughton's letter, the British prize crew, and Captain Flagg arrived at headquarters together. After placing the prisoners under guard, Washington had a pleasant chat with Flagg, perhaps apologizing for any spoilage of Langdon's "fresh fish." The general released *Unity* and dismissed Broughton's letter as incredulous—undeserving of an answer. He did, however, ask Langdon to grant *Hannah*'s officers a reward for recapturing the vessel but denied the crew so much as a cent.[4]

Broughton, either by his own avarice or by having *Unity*'s cargo examined so microscopically, telegraphed to his Marbleheaders expecta-

Washington's first armed schooner, *Hannah,* commanded by Capt. Nicholson Broughton. Model by Harold M. Hahn. Courtesy U.S. Naval Historical Center.

tions of quick cash. Masters of eighteenth-century sailing vessels usually kept their own counsels, sharing little information with crews. In keeping with tradition, Broughton probably never explained the difference between a fair prize and a recapture, but from his actions he certainly knew the difference.

When Washington's order releasing the vessel reached Gloucester, *Hannah* was still there. The outraged crew designated Joseph Searle, a private in Broughton's own company, to carry a protest to the captain. Backed by friends and neighbors, Searle confronted the captain on the deck of the schooner and demanded an explanation. The reply must have sounded hollow, because Searle flew into a rage. Broughton ordered Searle's arrest, and a scuffle followed as Searle squirmed to free himself from the officers' clutches. To the other thirty-five members of the crew, Searle's arrest had all the trimmings of a conspiracy. Broughton, they concluded, intended to divide the money among his officers, with perhaps a share or two going to His Excellency. They rushed forward to liberate their shipmate from the small circle of officers supporting the captain. Broughton ordered the mutineers arrested, but someone broke into the arms chest and began passing weapons to the front. The crew stormed the deck, freed Searle, and then shuffled about the vessel, waiting for some higher power to deliver their prize money.

On receiving news of the mutiny, Gloucester's Committee of Safety dispatched a messenger on a fast horse to Cambridge. Washington reacted quickly and expressed a rider to Beverly-based Lt. William Groves of Moses Brown's company, instructing him to take his command to Gloucester and arrest the Marblehead mutineers. When Groves arrived on September 11, the Marbleheaders sheepishly surrendered their arms and started the long march to headquarters. Along the road, ringleader Searle received special attention, but the other prisoners accepted their fate with typical Yankee optimism. Word spread through Cambridge that the troublemakers were on their way: "The Rascals are brought down here," a local diarist wrote, "and I hope they will meet their deserts [*sic*] . . . had it not been for a mutiny among the crew," he speculated, "they might have taken eight more [prizes] and captured the [*Lively*]."[5]

In a letter to *Unity*'s owner, Washington requested compensation for Broughton and his officers. Regarding the crew, he wrote, "I should have done the same thing in behalf of the men . . . but for their exceeding ill behaviour upon that occasion—I was obliged to send for, and bring them here Prisoners instead of prosecuting a scheme I had in view for the people of Halifax & I hope to bestow a different kind of a reward upon them for their mutinous behaviour."[6]

On September 22 thirty-six privates were tried by court-martial for "Mutiny, Riot, and Disobedience of orders." The general was not so mean-spirited as to want the Marbleheaders shot. Searle, the acknowledged ringleader, received thirty-nine lashes and was drummed out of the army. The court ordered twenty lashes for the thirteen men who had attempted to rescue Searle. The others received fines of twenty shillings apiece, but the court ruled they were "proper objects of mercy" and remitted their fines. Searle felt the lashes the following morning, but the others escaped the whip and were let down easily. They filed back into the ranks, no doubt praising His Excellency as a merciful man.[7]

Washington's problems with *Hannah* might have discouraged another general from continuing the experiment, but he refused to allow a halfhearted mutiny to spoil a good plan. After all, Broughton's recapture of *Unity* had saved Langdon's vessel. Washington considered the incident good experience for all and decided to give Broughton another chance. He dipped into Glover's Marblehead regiment for another crew and sent them packing to Gloucester. On September 21 they reported aboard, stowed their baggage, and waited for the captain's sailing orders.

A week later Broughton tacked out of Gloucester Harbor and headed down the coast to Marblehead. When he arrived he granted the crew shore leave, instructing them to return in the morning. After a comfortable night's sleep and a warm breakfast, the men sauntered down to the schooner, raised sail, cruised offshore for a few hours, and returned to the somniferous pleasures of feather beds, warm rum, and a crackling fireside for another night. For ten days Broughton seldom ventured far from Marblehead, awaiting the rare chance of intercepting a Boston-bound supply ship whose skipper had wandered off course through indifferent seamanship.

This casual and comfortable routine continued until the general sent Glover to stop it, and on the night of October 7 Broughton ranged down the coast under easy canvas. By dawn *Hannah* stood two miles off Eastern Point when lookouts reported a small vessel dead ahead. Broughton ordered pursuit. *Hannah* closed quickly, but the quarry made a spirited dash for Nantasket Road. Disregarding the general's orders to not waste gunpowder, Broughton fired four shots. All fell short. The sound of gunfire rumbled across the bay and into the spacious cabin of Vice Admiral Graves, who ordered out the 16-gun *Nautilus,* Capt. John Collins.[8] Broughton, unaware that his schooner had been targeted for destruction, idly sailed for home.

For the next two days Broughton discontinued his nighttime cruises, unable to resist the pleasures of home-cooked meals. At dawn on October 10 he sailed north, keeping away from the warships stationed at Boston. The watch had not sighted a sail all day, and the crew lolled dreamily on deck, anticipating another quiet night ashore. At noon they came about and headed leisurely for home, coasting through the passage between Baker's Island and Little Misery Island. As they cleared the latter the lookout broke the serenity, shouting, "Sail aport!" Broughton took one look and knew he would never reach Marblehead. *Nautilus,* bearing down with a full spread of sail, was closing fast and maneuvering to cut him off from the harbor.

For two days Collins had been running along the coast under easy sail in search of the schooner. *Hannah* was to the north when he sighted her, but Collins masked his approach by shielding his vessel behind Baker's Island. Broughton ordered all sail for Beverly Harbor, and while the privates muddled in the tops *Nautilus* continued to gain.

Broughton stayed close to shore, running through the shallows. A scant half mile east of the harbor his luck ran out. He sheered hard to starboard and drove the schooner onto a bar of mud off Beverly Cove. When *Hannah* grounded, the heavier *Nautilus* came about and stood off.

Collins fired a few rounds of grape, but it splattered short. With the ebb tide running he moved into deeper water, presented his broadside, and dropped anchor. After firing several shots, his gunners found the range and drove Broughton's men ashore. With *Hannah* aground and deserted, Collins withheld fire and ordered the schooner set afire. His men hoisted out the boats and brought combustibles topside, but before the incendiaries could man the oars *Hannah* lay high and dry on the flats. Having not reckoned with the swiftness of the ebb, Collins found his own vessel aground. In the meantime, *Hannah's* crew, with help from the townsfolk, scampered over the flats and began to remove guns and supplies. Unable to move, Collins ordered his men back to the guns and began peppering the schooner with a steady barrage of shot, driving Broughton's privates back to shore.

If not for malice, perhaps for a little diversion, some of the gunners could not resist the temptation to lob a few shots over the cove and into Beverly. In plain sight, not half a mile away, stood the church steeple, and scattered nearby were the town's better homes, with small, well-kept gardens of fall flowers and a few unharvested vegetables. Shots from *Nautilus* missed the church but fell in town, penetrating the chaise house of Thomas Stephens, splintering his fine chaise, and knocking apart the chimney of a house across the street. When the first shots fell, women and children fled to the countryside. Stephens picked up his musket, ran down to the beach, and blasted a few useless rounds at the interloper who had smashed his carriage.

Col. Henry Herrick, an active member of the Committee of Correspondence, raised the alarm and led his own small force to the beach, where they found Stephens angrily ramming another ball into his musket. Before gathering his men, Herrick took a few moments to

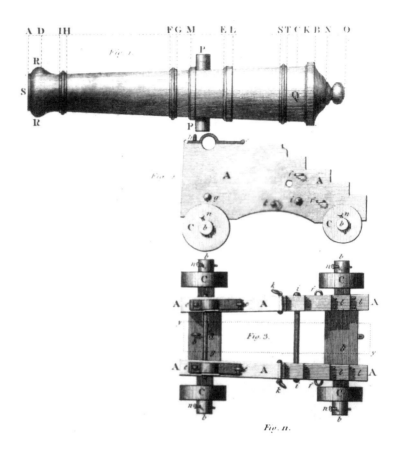

Sketch of typical carriage gun used on Washington's schooners. Courtesy U.S. Naval Historical Center.

change clothes and appeared on the beach dressed in military attire saved from the Seven Years War. He sauntered back and forth across the sand, issuing orders and presenting a tantalizing target to the enemy, but at that moment the grounded *Nautilus* careened out of position and could not bring a gun to bear.[9]

Across the harbor, at Hospital Point, Salem citizens gathered on the hilltop to witness the fight. Collins ordered a shot fired to disperse them, but it fell short. To his surprise, Salem militia opened with several long 4s and 6s, sending several shots ripping through the tops and plunging into the hull of His Majesty's sloop. At the same time, Herrick's Beverly troops hunkered down behind rocks, elevated their muskets, and drove Collins's deckhands below. Broughton's privates, who had been lurking in the woods beyond the beach, raced back across the flats to the schooner. With help from the townsfolk, they carried *Hannah*'s guns ashore, along with swivels, ammunition, loose gear, and most of the remaining provisions. Moments later three of *Hannah*'s 4s opened on *Nautilus*. Collins could do little but watch.

The guns of Salem, joined by continuous fire from Beverly's beach, played upon *Nautilus* for four hours. From time to time the sloop fired back, but without effect. One shot fell among a crowd of two hundred who had gathered on Salem Neck, but no one was injured. The only casualty was David Newell, who had his hand "blowed off" while loading a gun. Had the firing from the Neck been more accurate *Nautilus* would have been cut to pieces, but the sloop was too far away for the gunners to make proper adjustments and most of the shots went high.

Collins tried to bring more guns to bear on the Neck, but the firing "from Salem Side with three Pieces of Cannon, at different Stations, [was] so well chosen that I could not see them with my Glass." Collins, now caught in a cross fire, continued to serve his guns in an effort to not give the impression of being badly damaged, but what he wanted in the worst way was the evening flood tide to lift his vessel off the mud and carry him out of the hornet's nest.

At 7:30 P.M. *Nautilus* floated free. Leaving her bow anchor behind, she stood out to sea with tattered sails and broken spars. Collins reached open water and steered for Boston. One gun had been dismounted and a swivel shot in two. One man had lost a leg, and another died of wounds. Collins counted twenty holes in the hull and through the hammocks. He reported to Graves, "Tis very lucky they fired so high."[10]

The *New England Chronicle* reported that when the tide rose, *Nautilus* cut her cable and got off before the Beverly militia—presumably with the help of Broughton's privates—could board her. No doubt the plan had been discussed, and certainly boarding at night was preferred to daylight, but *Nautilus* represented a formidable adversary. The deck of the sloop measured ninety-eight feet, with a breadth of twenty-seven feet, and a depth in the hold of twelve feet, eight inches. At 316 tons burden, she was four times *Hannah*'s size, and her crew of 125 men were well trained to repel boarders. The provincials would have faced stiff resistance and found the names of many of their beloved townsmen carved on markers in the Beverly cemetery.[11]

Damage to *Hannah* from enemy gunfire was negligible. Nicholson Broughton, the only unofficial casualty, caught a bad cold when he fell overboard in a frantic dash for shore. The schooner, however, had struck the bar hard and strained her keel. She would never sail again, but Broughton's career had only begun, despite his inauspicious beginning.

Washington continued to be intrigued by the benefits of raising his own navy. Although Broughton had not captured any ordnance or disrupted the flow of ministerial transports during his five weeks at sea, his recapture of *Unity* gave the general encouragement. Even before Broughton toppled into the water on the Beverly bar the general was adding to his fleet. As his naval enterprise grew, he expected everyone to benefit from Broughton's mistakes.[12]

Washington's understanding of human nature, however, did not include the mind of Nicholson Broughton. The general obviously liked his first captain enough to grant him a second chance. He discounted the squabble over prize money as being an unfortunate misunderstanding and placed the entire blame on the mutinous crew.

The general had an important mission in mind, one requiring solid sailing experience and sound judgment. Broughton looked like a man with the right credentials. He had good sailing skills and detailed knowledge of the seaboard. Washington took a chance, perhaps with some misgivings, and sent Broughton on another mission. His Excellency could not have made a worse decision.

🕉 3 🕉
Commodore Broughton Cruises North

*N*o *article of war* consumed Washington's attention more than the acquisition of arms and gunpowder. At the time *Hannah* sailed, 110 pieces of correspondence dealing with the scarcity of gunpowder had passed between Congress and the provinces, and another 58 letters mentioned it. Every ounce of powder within the thirteen colonies had been located and shipped to Cambridge or conserved for provincial militias. When Washington arrived at Cambridge he observed pickets guarding the roads to Boston with spears and pikes instead of muskets. Benjamin Franklin suggested that men be armed with bows and arrows, reasoning that a man could shoot four arrows in the time it took to load and fire a musket.

When intelligence was received of a store of ammunition on the island of Bermuda, Congress "begged" to have the Rhode Island sloop *Katy,* Capt. Abraham Whipple, sent to "possess" it. Whipple left no record of his cruise, but two weeks after *Katy* returned Admiral Graves complained that "One Hundred Barrels of Gunpowder are forcibly taken from the Magazine at [the] Bermudas and carried away."[1]

Congress soon realized that begging armed vessels from the colonies was a poor way to direct naval missions, but it still hesitated to authorize funds for a navy. Although the Continental Army held all the roads leading into Boston, some members of Congress still favored reconciliation with George III. Establishing a navy implied sovereignty, and therefore independence from the Crown. While John Adams pressed the issue of building a navy at every congressional session, others watched the British lethargically mobilize their forces.

Despite Congress's efforts to raise money for arms, the general feared delays. Sensing a strong sentiment in Canada toward the American struggle for liberty, he organized an expedition to Quebec City, to be led by Col. Benedict Arnold, stipulating that "whatever

King's stores you shall be so fortunate as to possess . . . are to be secured for the Continental use."[2] Washington needed Arnold's mission to succeed because he believed the arsenal at Quebec held the largest stock of ammunition ever collected in North America.

To accelerate the mobilization of his own fleet, nothing piqued the general's interest more than a letter from John Hancock advising him that two vessels had sailed from England on August 11, 1775, "loaded with six thousand stand of arms, a large quantity of powder [and] other stores for Quebec." According to Hancock the vessels sailed without any protection, and he asked Washington to immediately "apply to the Council of the Massachusetts Bay for two arm'd vessells in this service and dispatch the same . . . to intercept said brigantines." With Arnold on his way to Quebec, the last thing Washington wanted was to have more arms and reinforcements reach the fortified city.[3] At the time, neither Hancock nor Congress knew Washington had armed a schooner and hired two more for his Continental fleet. The general confessed his plans the same day Hancock's letter arrived.[4]

Washington did not need a suggestion from Hancock to "apply" to the Massachusetts Provincial Congress for additional ships. He had already done so, but with unsatisfactory results. At the time of *Hannah*'s mutiny, two British supply ships stumbled into the colony's possession. The brig *Dolphin,* caught in a gale off Cape Ann, sought refuge at Thatcher's Island. Gloucester fisherman spotted her standing offshore, armed themselves, shoved off in their boats, and captured her. They took the vessel into Sandy Bay, bringing off over a hundred head of livestock.[5]

On the same day, the schooner *Industry,* Capt. Francis Butler, blew into Marblehead from the Bahamas with twenty-three casks of turtles and a cargo of fresh fruit. When Butler began his voyage, he had been told that if he came into Salem there would be a British man-of-war off Marblehead Harbor. He carried a tidy sum of money and fumed over being captured. "I would have run the vessel upon the rocks," he growled, "rather than fall into the hands of rebels." Marbleheaders sailed the vessel around to Salem and deposited Butler and his crew with the local Committee of Safety.[6]

The disposition of both vessels landed in the laps of the Provincial Congress, which decided to auction the cargoes and offer the ships to Washington. To inspect this windfall, the general dispatched Glover to Salem and Gloucester, where *Industry* and *Dolphin* waited at anchor with provincial price tags. The prices surprised Washington. He did not want to tap the Continental war chest to buy the vessels outright. He felt the ships should be given without conditions attached. He recalled Glover, choosing "not to meddle with either of the vessels," and sent him back to Marblehead with orders to obtain two different vessels on better terms. "Let them be prime sailers, put them into the best order & lose no time."[7] Glover returned to Marblehead, where friends had fishing schooners laid up in Continental mothballs.

The loss of both vessels troubled Washington. Informants had warned that "a great number of transports are hourly expected at Boston from England." Furthermore, the two vessels en route to the St. Lawrence had not yet arrived but were expected daily. Even an appeal from Hancock, their favorite son, failed to induce the Massachusetts Council to liberalize their terms and give Washington the vessels.[8]

In mobilizing his fleet, Washington involved two officers from his personal staff: thirty-four-year-old Philadelphia lawyer Lt. Col. Joseph Reed, his personal military secretary, and thirty-eight-year-old Col. Stephen Moylan, mustermaster general of the army. In addition to empowering Glover to negotiate for two vessels, the general asked for independent appraisals. Moylan accompanied Glover as a second set of eyes. He understood His Excellency's wishes and soon became as useful as Glover in fitting out the fleet.

The choice of Moylan was a good one. Born in Cork, Ireland, Moylan had been a Philadelphia merchant-shipowner and knew his way around the waterfront. A man of wealth and social standing with a good head for business matters, he could deal with ship chandlers, sailmakers, carpenters, and blacksmiths. He pitched into problems whenever Glover needed another set of hands. The general did not want to spend any money and asked Glover and Moylan to appeal to the patriotism of the owners by inquiring if the vessel could be borrowed. If not, the pair could negotiate a simple lease, providing they haggled the cost down to "the cheapest rate per month." Washington was getting wise to the ways of Marbleheaders. And with Moylan at his side, Glover would be less likely to give kindhearted terms to his friends and relatives.

The general, however, empowered Glover to select suitable men in the port towns along the coast to act as agents to care for and dispose of prizes. He wanted "persons of approved good character, and known substance," individuals capable of keeping good records. "Substance" held special meaning for Washington. He needed men willing to advance funds to the Continent when the war chest was empty, and he demonstrated his faith in Glover by agreeing to ratify and confirm all contracts entered into by either the colonel or his agents. Glover took advantage of the general's offer and selected his brother Jonathan as Marblehead agent and a close friend, William Bartlett, as Beverly agent. Despite Washington's misgivings of Glover patronizing friends, the colonel's selections were sensible.[9]

With Moylan in tow, Glover persuaded two of his fishing friends to lease their vessels to the army. Archibald Selman chartered his 60-ton schooner, *Eliza,* and Thomas Grant his 72-ton schooner, *Speedwell.* The ink had barely dried on the agreement when a dispute erupted between Glover and the owners. Glover wanted the vessels rigged like *Hannah,* with topsails added for speed. The owners argued that their vessels were designed for fishing with three sails only—a mainsail, foresail, and jib— and "were they to purchase the other sails necessary for the present purpose, the hire of the vessels would be inadequate to the expence." They demanded the army pay for the extras. Glover yielded and on October 5 leased the vessels for 5s. 4d. per ton per month in the "lawful money" of Massachusetts. He promised the general one vessel would be ready by October 12.[10]

Glover moved *Eliza* and *Speedwell*—to be rechristened *Franklin* and *Hancock,* respectively—to his Beverly wharf to be refitted. Nothing went smoothly. Shipwrights and sailmakers had left town to seek work elsewhere. Arms and ammunition had to be scavenged from Salem and Danvers. In the meantime, Broughton, after his flight from *Nautilus,* returned *Hannah* with a strained keel.

Moylan had been sent to Plymouth by Washington and was not available when needed. A week later he returned to find Glover immensely frustrated by his problems and somewhat bullied by a scalding letter from Reed, quoting the general as being "much dissatisfied" with progress. "I cannot but think," Reed wrote, "a desire to secure particular friends or particular interests does mingle in the management of these vessels." Two weeks passed and the schooners were still not ready, but Moylan saw the situation for what it was and penned an assuaging letter to Reed:[11]

Col. Glover showed me a letter of yours which has mortified him much. I really & sincerely believe he has the cause much at heart, & that he has done his best for the publick service. You cannot conceive the difficulty . . . & the delay there is in procuring the thousand things necessary for one of these vessels . . . I dare say one of them could be fitted in Philadelphia or New York in three days, because you would know where to apply for the different articles but here you must search all over Salem, Marblehead, Danvers & Beverly for every little thing. . . . The Carpenters are to be sure the idlest scoundrels in nature. If I could have procured others, I should have dismissed the whole gang of them last Friday, & such religious rascalls are they, that we could not prevail upon them to work on the Sabbath. I have stuck very close to them since, & what by scolding & crying shame for their torylike disposition in retarding the work, I think they mend some.

Moylan suggested liberating Glover from further dealings with his friends and family. He thought a person born in the same town or neighborhood should not be employed in public affairs within the same locality. "The spirit of equality which reigns through this country," Moylan explained, "will make him afraid of exerting that authority necessary [for] expediting his business. He must shake eve[ry] man by the hand, & desire, beg, & pray, do brother, do my friend, do such a thing, whereas a few hearty damns from a person who did not care a damn for them would have a much better effect. This I know by experience."[12]

Moylan's advice was partially correct. When Reed later left the army and returned to his home town of Philadelphia to build the Continental fleet, a few damns there worked no better than at Beverly. Reed's criticism of Glover returned to haunt him, as he encountered exactly the same problems in Philadelphia but on a scale far surpassing those at Beverly.[13]

Glover and Moylan refit *Franklin* and *Hancock* in two and one-half weeks rather than the promised seven days. Unable to muster a crew for either vessel, Moylan deferred to Glover, who again tapped the 21st Massachusetts for officers and crew. John Selman, a captain in Glover's regiment and son of the vessel's owner, took command of the armed schooner *Franklin*. Broughton, fully recovered from his dip in Beverly's harbor, preferred the larger *Hancock*.[14]

If Washington had reservations about the possible mismanagement of *Hannah,* he threw caution aside and placed both schooners under Broughton's command. Once again he issued written orders. He wanted no misunderstanding and expected Selman to benefit from the senior commander's experience. The orders cited a specific target; the two brigantines carrying six thousand stands of arms and large amounts of powder to Quebec. The mission must proceed with "all possible dispatch" and straight to the mouth of the St. Lawrence. If the ordnance ships had passed up the river, both schooners were to stay in the mouth, capturing all commerce in the service of the ministerial army. By then, Washington hoped, Arnold would have captured Quebec City, driving every British transport back down the river and into the clutches of Broughton's waiting schooners.

Washington instructed Broughton and Selman to send all prizes laden with ammunition, clothing, or other stores to the nearest colonial port. Armed vessels must be avoided, and every effort made to "prevent being discovered." They must stay away from areas where their presence could be reported, such as the small ports along coastal Nova Scotia.

As an added incentive, Washington increased prize shares to coincide with pending legislation, a third share going to the crew and encompassing everything from military stores to the vessel herself. Washington warned against molesting the personal belongings of prisoners, but, as the cruise of *Franklin* and *Hancock* reached its pinnacle a few weeks later, one wonders whether either Broughton or Selman read beyond the general's clause covering prize shares. Washington wanted Canadians as allies and treated "with all kindness," but Broughton had different motives.[15]

Selman's letter read like Broughton's, except Washington elevated the older skipper to the quasi-military post of acting commodore. Selman did not object to serving under Broughton. They were much alike in every way but age, Selman being thirty-one and Broughton having just passed his fifty-first birthday. Like his boss, Selman became a Marblehead shipmaster at a young age and soon acquired all the trimmings of a quarterdeck despot, along with a good nose for sniffing opportunities for financial gain. He had been master just long enough to form the intractable habits of a demigod with the power to modify directives not consistent with his personal interests. Broughton had already demonstrated a penchant for disregarding orders, and putting the two of them together promised to be a cruise capable of shattering His Excellency's well-known patience.

Washington's orders, sealed and endorsed, read "Not to be opened till out of sight of land." Had the pair read the orders beforehand, they might have asked questions. Reed enclosed a companion message to Glover and with a little anxiety wrote, "Capt Broughton & Capt Selliman [Selman] have their orders & must be immediately dispatched." Six days later *Franklin* and *Hancock* cleared Beverly Harbor and headed for sea.[16]

For the first few days the schooners bobbed about in rough seas, adding to the discomfort of the men, who already felt squeezed for elbow room. *Hancock*, at sixty feet in length and twenty in breadth, was roomy compared with *Franklin*, at fifty by seventeen. The captain occupied a small cabin under the half deck, and officers shared a small enclosure nearby. The rest of the vessel contained cargo space, now filled with over sixty privates, extra sails, rigging, spars, muskets, pistols, ammunition, provisions, water, casks of rum, and a few personal belongings. The decks, where summer fishermen spent much of their time in relative comfort, now contained a large whaleboat and an arsenal of guns. *Hancock* carried six 4s and ten swivels, *Franklin* two 4s, four 2s, and ten swivels. The cramped conditions were not unlike those experienced by the coolies brought to America eighty years later, but on this mission the discomfort was justified, especially if Arnold succeeded and the two powder vessels were captured.[17] But the men grumbled, and Broughton decided to acquire more spacious accommodations by taking a prize. Instead of good fortune, however, *Franklin* nearly swamped off the southeastern coast of Nova Scotia. The schooner leaked badly, and Selman ran into Country Harbour.[18]

While *Franklin* received repairs and men stretched their legs ashore, Broughton and Selman discussed their orders. The entrance to the St. Lawrence lay five hundred miles away. With the storms of November ahead it seemed silly to travel so far while prizes coasted the eastern seaboard of Nova Scotia. Besides, if Quebec City fell, where would British shipping go if not to Halifax? And the shortest route to Halifax would be down the Gulf of St. Lawrence and through the Gut of Canso. With Canso but a few miles up the coast and easily accessible, a long voyage to the St. Lawrence made no sense to Broughton. He may not be able to give the crew nightly shore leave as he had with *Hannah,* but the comfort of having land in sight made personal discomfort less odious. Broughton decided the two powder vessels had already reached Quebec. If so, Arnold would flush them down the river with the rest of the shipping headed for Halifax. Much of Broughton's planning depended on Arnold, who was still mired in the swamps of the upper Kennebec River and many torturous miles from Quebec.

On October 29 Broughton and Selman set sail for Canso, convinced their plan was superior to His Excellency's and confident of vindication if they took a few prizes. Already Broughton might have wondered what life would be like as the first admiral in the Continental Army. As they rounded into the Atlantic, the watch reported two small schooners. Broughton stopped one, Selman the other. *Prince William,* William Standley, master, and *Mary,* Thomas Russell, master, enjoyed a good laugh as they surrendered. At first the whole affair seemed like a bad joke. Canadians were not at war with the colonies. Both vessels carried fish and oil, all privately owned, but Broughton ruled they were bound for Boston. Prizemaster John Devereaux, Broughton's son-in-law, boarded *Prince William,* and Edward Homan of *Franklin* took charge of *Mary.* Broughton poked through the cargoes, confiscating fishing tackle, sugar, and molasses. Selman dipped into the spoils for his share, taking seven books for his Marblehead library. Content with executing his patriotic duty and flush with expectations of prize money, Broughton dispatched his two prizemasters to Marblehead with orders to keep company with each other until they got there.[19]

With two prizes to their credit, Broughton and Selman sailed for Canso, a rocky point off Guysborough Harbour. A gale threatened from the northeast when a lookout, tottering precariously from the masthead, hollered down, "Sail aport!" Broughton observed a lone vessel pressing hard for the safety of Whitehead Harbour. Anxious to get out of the wind himself, he followed her in and captured the sloop *Phoebe,* laden with fish and oil. Her master, James Hawkins, admitted the sloop belonged to Enoch Rust of Boston, who had cleared her for Halifax and Quebec in the spring. Actual ownership of the vessel rested with James Aborn of Rhode Island, who made her over to Rust in an effort to enjoy a little illicit trade. Since then she had ranged from Louisburg to the

West Indies. Broughton ruled that any cargo, albeit privately owned, could be confiscated if the vessel hailed from Boston. Trade with British subjects had been banned by the Continental Congress. If Broughton needed a better excuse to make *Phoebe* a prize, Hawkins supplied it by mentioning that the owner, now at Canso, was currently considering a return trip to Boston.

Before sending *Phoebe* off with a prize crew, Broughton penned a confusing report to Washington. Referring to Enoch Rust's return to Boston, he wrote, "The smallest intention of going to that den of mischievous violators of the rights of humanity, must carry in the bosom of it as we conceive our selfes bound in obedience to your Excellencys instructions to send the vessel to a friendly port in New England." Because Washington might wonder why, on November 2, his schooners had progressed no farther than Canso, Broughton added, Hawkins "informs [us] that there was no vessel of force at Quebec the beginning of September & that he knows of none going up there since."

If Broughton thought he could convince Washington that a trip to the St. Lawrence was a waste of time, he probably produced the opposite effect. With no warship at Quebec, the armed schooners would have had sole command of the river and access to all her shipping. Instead, Broughton learned from Hawkins of a brigantine loading coal at Louisburg for the ministerial army and declared, "We shall hoist sail directly, the wind [breasting] rather favorably & pursue our course," thereby leaving the general little clue as to where that "course" might lead. Prizemaster Benjamin Doak sailed *Phoebe* directly into Beverly and turned the vessel over to William Bartlett, Glover's newly designated prize agent.[20]

Contrary winds kept Broughton and Selman confined to the Gut of Canso. Instead to going north in search of the brig, they sailed up the Gut as far as St. George's Bay. Broughton called the bay the "entrance to the Gulph of St. Laurence," which was literally accurate but about as far from the St. Lawrence River as one could get and still expect credit for entering the gulf.

Broughton learned of a vessel at the northern entrance to the Gut and sent *Franklin* to investigate. Selman captured the New Haven sloop *Warren,* which John Denny, owner and master, had loaded with a cargo of lumber at Gaspe, Quebec, for sale at Nantucket. By bad seamanship Selman lost his mainmast and sent both crews ashore for a new one.

Fifty privates stumbled through swamps and thickets for a mile and cut down five trees before they found one suitable as a mast. They lost several days dragging the trunk through the swamp and trimming it to fit. By mid-November the crew stepped *Franklin's* new mast and had the schooner ready to continue her cruise.

While men repaired *Franklin*, Broughton interviewed Denny and a man named Buddington, *Warren's* supercargo. Relying on his usual guile, Broughton decreed Denny a Tory deviously supplying the British at Boston. "Buddington himself dares not speak in favor of Dennys political authodoxy," Broughton explained. After baiting both men by using terms such as "Yankeys & Punkings [Pumpkins] with apparent Jerings" and getting equal measure in return, Broughton disclosed his credentials. He claimed neither Denny nor Buddington made "such apologies as true sons of Liberty" strongly attached to the cause, as good patriots "might naturally be expected to do." After concocting his rationale, he wrote Washington that "upon the whole we think ourselves bound to send the vessel, cargo & her papers to your Excellency for your decision." Before sending the prize he helped himself to half a barrel of Denny's flour and two half barrels of Buddington's pork. "Immediately upon the wind suiting," Broughton added, omitting any specifics as to his plans, "we endeavour to conform to the spirit of your Excellency's orders."[21]

Despite the spirit of His Excellency's orders, Broughton remained at the Gut of Canso. On November 13 his indolence was rewarded by the capture of the sloop *Speedwell*, Frances Corey, master, as she entered the Gut. Jacob Greene of Rhode Island owned the vessel. He had contracted for a cargo of dry goods to be loaded in England and delivered to Canada. Although the vessel carried no powder, Broughton believed Washington would be pleased to share the dry goods with his threadbare Continentals. He had no more basis for holding *Speedwell* than any of his other prizes, but he erroneously attributed to Washington his own conniving mentality. After Broughton and Selman raided *Speedwell's* larder, Joseph Gregory of *Hancock* took possession of the sloop and sailed her to Gloucester. Broughton sent no letter with Gregory to report his whereabouts, as the acting commodore had given no thought to them himself.[22]

According to the *London Chronicle*, in November Broughton detained and later released several unidentified vessels. He stopped two merchantmen, *Unity*, Captain Chevalier, and *Clementina*, Captain Air, as they came through the Gut, both bound for the Island of Jersey and laden with lumber. Prize crews searched the vessels but found nothing of value. When Chevalier reached Jersey, he reported that Broughton and Selman "had in their possession many vessels, chiefly loaded with cod fish, and were waiting for others to send them all to New England." His statement was supported by Simeon Perkins of Nova Scotia, who claimed to have observed two armed vessels with twenty-two prizes, all lying at Canso. Neither Broughton or Selman ever mentioned this, perhaps knowing His Excellency disapproved of molesting the property of Canadians. The commodore released the Jerseymen but removed two pilots who claimed they knew the way to the Island of St. John. The allure of the isolated island standing fifty nautical miles from the northern outlet of the Gut of Canso may have piqued Broughton's curiosity to the extent that Canso's fishing fleet apprehended at the opposite end of the Gut lost its appeal. Besides, the commodore planned to pass back through the Gut on his way home, and the fishermen would still be there.

Broughton interviewed the two French Canadian pilots and learned of several cannon in a fortress at Charlottetown, the island's capital, and of recent recruiting activity to reinforce Quebec. After discussing the matter with Selman, he ruled a short voyage to the island within the scope of their orders. Here was an opportunity to "break up a nest of recruits" on their way to reinforce Quebec. An immediate attack on Charlottetown might save Arnold's army from possible defeat, thereby forcing the rapid departure of all British shipping. They could pick off the transports as they fled through the Gut. "The winds came southerly, we went through the Gut of Canso with the two pilots . . . declaring to them should they run us ashore death to them would be inevitable, they behaved true and honest."[23]

And for the virtue of truth and honesty, the quiet inhabitants of the Island of St. John were about to receive a visit from Nicholson Broughton and his armed Marbleheaders.

🎕 4 🎕
Not So Much as a Candle

*C*harlottetown lay about one hundred nautical miles west of the Gut of Canso, and on November 16 the armed schooners *Hancock* and *Franklin* sailed across St. George's Bay, rounded Cape George, passed Pictou Island, and entered Northumberland Strait. The next day they doubled Point Prim and moved cautiously into Hillsborough Bay, passing to port the remnants of old Fort Amherst. Charlottetown rested on the north bank of the Hillsborough River, and the schooners anchored about a mile and a half from the town.

From *Hancock's* deck Broughton scanned the buildings of the small town spread out on flat, gradually rising ground between the confluence of the Hillsborough and York Rivers. To the left rose a solitary flagstaff marking the location of the town's only fort. Guns were there, the pilots said, but no one in town knew how to fire them. This, however, called for caution. Broughton plotted a pincer movement, using the schooner's two fourteen-foot whaleboats. He would take a crew of five and a pilot and approach the fort from the northwest. Selman, with a pilot and crew, would attack from the south. With a brace of pistols tucked in their belts, the invaders squeezed into the boats and rowed toward shore.[1]

The citizens of Charlottetown had no idea why two armed schooners had entered their harbor, and they watched with mounting apprehension the approach of Selman's oarsmen. Gov. Walter Patterson had recently departed to winter in England, leaving affairs in the hands of Philip Callbeck, pro tem "Commander in Chief of the Island of St. John." Callbeck trudged down to the wharf at the foot of Queen Street. "Not having heard that the Colonys had fitted out Privateers," he recalled, "I judged them to be pirates. . . . To preserve the Town from being burn'd, I determin'd (not having force of any kind to make resistance) to face them singly." As Selman's boat approached, Thomas Wright, the town's justice of the peace, and John Budd, clerk of courts, joined Callbeck at the wharf, but the rest of the town wisely spread out along the shore and remained at a safe distance.

The pilot turned to Selman and pointed out Callbeck and Wright, the two most influential men in town. Callbeck had enlisted a few volunteers for the defense of Quebec, and Wright, according to the pilot, had sworn them in. Selman grabbed Callbeck, Wright, and Budd, herded all three into the boat, and rowed them out to *Franklin*. A half dozen armed mariners held the townspeople at bay. They flourished pistols and eyeballed the small row of stores advertising English woolen goods.

Broughton landed near the fort, found several unattended cannon, spiked them, and then joined the discussions on *Franklin*. After counseling with Selman, Broughton decreed that the woolen goods in the stores "were for the recruiting service" and should be taken on board the schooners. Selman demanded the keys to Callbeck's and Patterson's homes, or "he would break the doors open." Budd held keys to most buildings in town and with a pistol in his ribs agreed to open any door Broughton wished. Selman snatched the keys out of his hands. Leaving Callbeck on *Franklin*, Selman and Broughton returned to town with Wright and Budd.

With a half dozen marines, Broughton and Selman strolled toward the town's largest store. Rather than waste time looking for the right key, they smashed in the door and stripped the shelves of shoes and clothing. Marines carried goods down to the whaleboat and rowed her, piled to the gunwales, back to *Franklin*. After emptying the first store, they moved to the next, battered down the door, and hauled another load of booty to the wharf. Townsfolk remained at a safe distance and watched in amazement. They drifted back to their homes, locked the doors, and made a furtive effort to hide their few valuables.

Broughton eyed the tidy bundles piled outside the stores and asked his looters if they thought the articles were intended for the recruiting service. With wry smiles on their faces, the sailors replied, "Aye, sir, that they are." Broughton agreed and sent another load of goods to the wharf. Clerk Budd, accustomed to keeping records, suggested an inventory be taken, but Broughton vetoed the idea. Someone back in Cambridge might ask where all the booty went.

After a taste of successful plundering, the looters could not be stopped. Broughton led the way. Going first to Callbeck's home, they smashed through doors, broke open Mrs. Callbeck's drawers and trunks, scattered her clothes about, took her bed and bedding, and then helped themselves to her jewelry and trinkets. Moving to the parlor, they bundled up curtains, carpets, and plate and then raided the cellar, collecting wine, porter, rum, and geneva. To celebrate they stove in one cask of wine, and while drinking it dry they helped themselves to fruit, sweetmeats, hams, and bacon. Before leaving, they packed all of Callbeck's clothes and shoes into two trunks and for good measure threw in the provincial seal. Callbeck later recounted:

> These unfeeling monsters, not satiated with their flagitious depredations on the whole of my property, & the common Rights of Mankind, blood-thirstily sought Mrs. Callbeck for the purpose of cutting her throat, because she was the daughter of a Mr. Coffin at Boston, who is remarkable for his attachment to [the] Government. Fortunately, she was at my farm, four miles distant, else it is likely her treatment would have been equal to their savage declarations. . . . These brutal violators of domestic felicity have left her without a single glass of wine, without a candle to burn or a sufficiency of provisions.

Both schooners stood close in to the wharf, and as goods flowed out to the vessels more of the crew joined the fun ashore. They broke down the door of the governor's home and stripped out the valuables. After warming their gullets liberally with libations, they brought their bundles to the wharf.

When Judge Wright returned to shore he hurried home, locked his door, and tried to quiet his wife. After the looters finished ransacking the governor's home, they snatched Wright "from the arms of his wife and sister, and insultingly smiled at the tears and lamentations of women who were in the greatest distress." Broughton's buccaneers took nothing from the Wright home but the judge, probably because it was late afternoon and they had been warned a rider had left town to raise reinforcements. With only the clothes on his back, Wright joined Callbeck on board *Franklin*.

When the two officials discovered that Broughton and Selman were not pirates but officers in the Continental Army, they asked who had authorized the raid on His Majesty's Island of St. John. Broughton, who had given little thought to the general's orders since opening them at sea, produced his set of instructions and read them aloud with flourishes of grandiloquence.

Callbeck and Wright listened carefully, noting that nothing in the orders mentioned an attack on their town. To the contrary, Washington had specifically cautioned against abuse of private property. The two prisoners attempted to assist Broughton in properly interpreting the general's instructions, but with his hold already filled with Callbeck's belongings, Broughton refused to listen. Callbeck and Wright then pleaded to be allowed to return to their homes, if just for one more night. Having "worked up the human pashions in the breast in their behalf," Selman declared, "they were allowed to go on shore that night and come on board the next morning."

Broughton reluctantly put them ashore, doubting he would see them again. After the recent review of his orders, leaving the officials on their lonely island should have made sense to Broughton. Back in Massachusetts they could make trouble for him, but he had recklessly read the general's secret orders and disclosed the entire mission. That night in the lamplight of his cabin, Broughton may have felt a little foolish, but not fool enough to empty the vessel of its precious loot, or make room for the cannon he had spiked at the fort. Selman later claimed the guns had been left behind because he "could not obtain any scows" to bring them away.

If Broughton harbored misgivings about the disposition of his two prisoners, he lost his opportunity to sail away without them. At dawn Callbeck and Wright waited at the town's wharf with small bundles in their hands. A whaleboat picked them up and brought them on board *Hancock*. The two schooners sailed early in the morning and headed for the Gut of Canso.

On the night of November 19 they came to anchor off the tiny hamlet of Canso. Facing the cold Atlantic and the uncertain prospect of imprisonment, Callbeck and Wright renewed their pleas for freedom. If set ashore at Canso, they could still get home before winter. If carried to Massachusetts, they would not see their families until spring, if ever.

Wright referred once more to Broughton's orders, warning the commodore he had overstepped his authority. Soon he would have to answer to his government. Selman angrily replied—he would never consent to giving them freedom. "If we come acrost a Brittish Frigate," Wright warned, "I will have you hung to the yard arm." "Take care you are not hanged," Selman replied, adding that if soldiers like Arnold failed to capture Quebec, Callbeck and Wright would make excellent hostages.[2]

On November 20, as daylight streaked the southeastern sky at Canso, Broughton peered over the rail of *Hancock* and found himself among a fleet of fishing vessels. Instead of sailing as planned, he herded all the masters on board the schooners to examine their papers. Because every vessel carried nothing but fish and a few supplies, Broughton released all but one. Each fisherman, however, returned to his vessel knowing that George Washington had sent armed schooners to Nova Scotia to prevent the delivery of supplies to any of the "Dominions of Great Britain." Canadians were free to trade with France or Spain, but nothing could be shipped to Boston.

Broughton detained the 170-ton schooner *Lively,* not because she was going to Boston but because she was headed for Charlottetown, that heinous recruiting port so recently plundered. If he released the vessel, surely Callbeck and Wright would demand a ride home. Furthermore, *Lively,* owned by a Mr. Higgins, carried a cargo of forty "Tubbs of Butter" and dozens of crates filled with English dry goods. Since he had just stripped Charlottetown's stores of clothing, Broughton could not allow replenishments to reach there so soon. He took possession of the prize and Higgins became a "guest" of *Hancock,* where he remained separated from Callbeck and Wright.[3]

Broughton, however, missed an opportunity to snare another of the island's officials. John Russell Spence had been traveling with his wife and servants as passengers on *Lively.* Although they lost most of their personal belongings to the looters, Broughton put them ashore. "If they had known," Spence reported, "that I had the honour of being one of the Councill of St Johns and that consequently the Government of said island devolved upon me, they would undoubtedly have carried me with the rest."[4]

On a favorable wind, Broughton and Selman headed home, bringing with them *Lively* and her forty tubs of butter. Stiff northerlies, mixed with a spitting of wet snowflakes, became a daily reminder that winter was coming. The crew had been reduced in size by prizes, but prisoners filled the hold. The quarters below were cramped, cold, and filled with smoke and plunder. Men grumbled over the daily fare of salt rations and were eager to get home to collect their prize money.

On November 26 the shivering lookout, camped on the masthead, hollered down a halfhearted "Sail to starboard!" Broughton came on deck, sized up the vessel, and ordered her capture. The brig *Kingston Packet*, Samuel Ingersoll, master, had just cleared Barrington Bay with a cargo of dried fish for Cape Francois, Hispaniola. After having explained a few days earlier to befuddled fishermen that he did not molest vessels with Spanish or French destinations, Broughton claimed the brig a fair prize because she was owned by Richard Derby of Salem and violated the Continental Association's trade boycott against Great Britain. Broughton probably knew Derby, a wealthy Salem merchant and an active patriot, but the commodore had a less noble mission in mind. Opportunities for amassing prize money subordinated such mundane matters as good fellowship and past friendship.

Once again Broughton did not send his prisoners to Beverly but deposited them, along with the vessels, with the Committee of Safety at the remote port of Winter Harbor, Maine. Perhaps Broughton envisioned swinging from the yardarm of a "Brittish frigate" if he were captured with the judge on board, but he probably wanted a head start to stake his claims with Washington before Callbeck, Wright, and all the others straggled into Cambridge headquarters with their protests.[5]

In early December, as Broughton and Selman sailed into Beverly as self-proclaimed heroes, Sgt. John Lewis of *Hancock* began his long march down the coast with seven armed men and fourteen prisoners. On December 3 they reached Portsmouth, where Joshua Wentworth, the Continental agent, provided funds for their journey to headquarters, an expense Broughton had overlooked. Wentworth advised Washington he could use *Kingston Packet*'s fish, as they were "much wanted here," but recommended moving the prizes because the exposed nature of the port invited trouble from the enemy.[6]

Even before Lewis arrived at headquarters, the general had a disconsoling impression of what to expect from prizes captured by his two Marbleheaders. If Broughton had not made reference to the "spirit of your Excellency's orders" in his November 6 report, Washington may have wondered if his captains had ever opened their sealed instructions.

Broughton's first two prizes, *Mary* and *Prince William,* had just been delivered to Marblehead, and their detention carried the same fishy smell as their cargoes. Washington issued orders to free "those persons who belong to the two schooners" and to carefully lay up the vessels and their cargoes until the owners could be contacted. On December 19 he released both vessels with an apology.[7]

The sloop *Phoebe,* captured on October 31, was owned by James Aborn of Rhode Island, another "sincere friend of the liberties of this Country." Aborn claimed he had resorted to a small subterfuge by sending his vessel "to the Eastward to trade and fish, and to cover his interest from the enemy [had] made use of a friend in Nova-Scotia," to whom he issued a sham bill of sale. Because of this arrangement Washington might have excused his two skippers on the grounds of overzealous patriotism, but a troublesome pattern had emerged. On December 2 he released *Phoebe* at the request of Gov. Nicholas Cooke of Rhode Island, who had supplied the Continental Army with two thousand troops.[8]

When word reached Washington that *Speedwell* had arrived at Cape Ann, he expected another letter of protest. Instead, Gen. Nathaniel Greene paid him a visit and asked for the vessel to be released. Jacob Greene and Company of Providence owned the sloop, and Nathaniel was a partner in the firm. Washington apologized to one of his more able generals and ordered the vessel returned, as he did "not wish to have anything to do with her." On second thought he admonished Beverly agent William Bartlett to keep the cargo from being "injured or embezzled." Broughton had educated Washington well. This marked the first time the general applied the word "embezzled" to cargoes captured by his skippers.[9]

After releasing *Speedwell,* Washington sat at his desk and expressed his thoughts to John Hancock. "By the last accounts from the armed schooners sent to the River St. Lawrence, I fear we have but little to expect from them. They were falling short of provisions and [mentioned] that they would be obliged to return, which at this time is particularly unfortunate." But the general remained hopeful, adding, "If they . . . chose a proper station, all the vessells coming down the river must have fallen into their hands." Washington did not know his two captains had just arrived at Beverly, and as he handed the sealed letter to an express rider he did not know that Sergeant Lewis and fourteen prisoners were slogging through the mud and snow to his headquarters.[10]

Lewis arrived the following day and deposited Callbeck and company at headquarters, along with a bundle of papers. By this time Washington's volunteers had grown tired of life in the earthworks around Boston and were threatening to go home. Their enlistments were up, and the weather had turned cold. Keeping the volunteers at their posts required all the general's influence; if the army dispersed, only a few regulars would be left to guard the approaches to Boston. He did not need further distractions, but one look at *Kingston Packet*'s papers must have made his stomach roll. The owner, Richard Derby, was well known for his many contributions in support of the present war, yet Broughton claimed that the Salem merchant illegally traded with the enemy. If Broughton was correct Derby could be tried for treason, and at this stage of the war Washington knew that many so-called patriots had placed their financial interests ahead of the cause. He turned the problem over to the Salem Committee of Safety, admitting he was not "a Competent judge of such matters" and presently had no "time to attend to them." Salem wanted no part of the problem and declined "to give [its] judgment in a matter of this importance." John Pickering, answering for the Salem Committee, added, "Many merchants have considered the prohibition in the same light [as Derby]—many vessels being thus employed."[11]

On December 8 Washington returned *Kingston Packet,* not out of deference to Derby's fidelity but because, after interviewing Callbeck and Wright, he had lost faith in Broughton and Selman. Moylan turned the matter over to Glover, who had borrowed carriage guns from the Derby family to arm one of the schooners. "The General," Moylan added, "is determined to have no further trouble with this vessel." Moylan also added a few instructions from the general regarding the prisoners from Charlottetown. "I beg you will be attentive to Mr. Callbeck's goods," Moylan wrote. "Let him have every thing he had been so cruelly pillaged of."[12]

If any doubt remained regarding Derby's patriotism, the Salem merchant erased it by declaring "that I have not the most distant thought of the Brigg's returning again to Nova-Scotia, nor is it my intention to have any . . . connection with that Province until matters are settled, or liberty granted." Derby spoke honestly.[13] Massachusetts had just passed a resolution providing letters of marque, and he was among the first to convert his vessels to privateers.

Washington could find no basis for detaining *Lively* and ordered the schooner and her assorted dry goods released. In doing this, the general may have acceded to a request from Callbeck. On reaching Cambridge, Callbeck had penned a lengthy petition describing outrages upon his property, totaling "two thousand pounds sterling." The claim staggered Washington. There is no official record of *Lively's* release, but on December 29 the vessel stopped at Halifax with Callbeck, Wright, and the provincial seal on board. She had sailed from Winter Harbor on December 24, but not before Callbeck had written a letter of thanks to Washington for "the generous treatment Your Excellency has been pleased to shew me."[14]

The last of Broughton's and Selman's prizes to be adjudicated at headquarters was the sloop *Warren,* and because Washington had no agents in Maine he referred the matter to the Stonington Committee of Safety. Unaccustomed to dealing with such heady affairs, the committee deliberated for a month before ruling, after a "full hearing and careful examination," that the vessel and cargo should be restored without further delay. Broughton had branded Denny, the master, and Buddington, the supercargo, flagrant Tories, which lengthened the investigation, but the committee found that neither man had adopted or pursued any measure "toryistical."[15]

When Washington learned his two captains had reached Beverly he sent for them. The pair anticipated trouble, as most of their prizes had been stripped away. Nonetheless, they rode over to Cambridge and knocked on the general's door. Selman's account of the meeting shows how calm, thoughtful, and attentive Washington could be under difficult circumstances:

> This year being nearly up, Commodore Broughton and myself went to head quarters at Cambridge to see the General—he met us on the steps of the door. We let his Excellency understand we had called to see him touching [upon] the cruise. He appeared not pleased—he wanted not to hear anything about it and broke off

abruptly to me. "Sir," says he, "will you stand again in Col. Glover's regiment?" My answer to him was, "I will not, sir." He then accosted Commodore Broughton: "You, sir, have said you would stand." Com. Broughton said, "I will not stand." Thus ended the matter relative to the cruise.[16]

"My fears," Washington lamented to John Hancock, "that Broughton and Selman would not effect any good purpose were too well founded."[17] He cashiered them as skippers but generously offered to reassign them to Glover's regiment. For such total disregard of orders officers in the Royal Navy would have been shot for disobedience. But Washington was a forgiving man and needed every true patriot in the fight for independence. As for Washington's choice of captains, Moylan summed it up in a letter to Reed: "Broughton and Selman are indolent and inactive souls, Their time was out yesterday, and from frequent rubs they got from me (under the General's wings) they feel sore, and decline serving longer. I hope we shall pick . . . more active men."[18]

Selman returned to Marblehead and lapsed into obscurity. Broughton, however, had a change of heart, rejoined the army, and rose to the rank of major.

There is no way to estimate the cost to the Continental treasury of Broughton and Selman's cruise to Nova Scotia. Callbeck claimed losses of £2,000, but there is no record of restitution. Goods and provisions had been "embezzled" from every prize, personal belongings absconded, cargoes detained and spoiled, and vessels interrupted from their voyages. In addition to owners' claims, there was the cost to the Continent of leasing, refitting, manning, and provisioning the vessels. In terms of the currency of the day, William Bell Clark has estimated the cost of the expedition at £500.[19]

By marching Callbeck and Wright to Cambridge, Broughton gave his prisoners an opportunity to observe Washington's military and naval preparations from the inside. When Callbeck reached Halifax he penned a lengthy letter to Vice Adm. Molyneux Shuldham, who had arrived at Boston on December 30. After reiterating all the "wanton and flagrant outrages" on their persons and property, Callbeck attempted to stimulate greater vigilance and activity on the part of the Royal Navy. He expressed surprise at the volume of colonial trade, reporting that "at most of the ports east of Boston, while I passed and repassed, there were daily arrivals from the West Indies, but most from Saint Eustatia: everyone brings more or less gun-powder. Some vessels had sailed, numbers were being fitted out, loaded with fish, lumber and some with specie, all I believe bound for the West Indies." Callbeck observed guns emplaced at Cape Ann, Marblehead, and Beverly and saw supplies of gunpowder moving across the countryside. At Newberry and Salem he noticed hulks had been sunk to narrow the channels, and at Portsmouth a boom placed across the channel, with three forts around it. He also reported "rebels are in possession of [our] Signals," a nice windfall for Washington's skippers had the signal book not been seen by Callbeck. In response to Callbeck's letter, Shuldham stepped up the pressure on American traffic to the West Indies. Hereafter, Washington's schooners would find the quest for British supply ships a more treacherous occupation.[20]

If Washington had waited for Broughton's return to expand his navy, he might never have leased another vessel. The experience would have been too painful to explain to Congress and too wasteful to be continued. But Washington did not wait. Even as Broughton and Selman took to sea in mid-October, the general sent Glover and Moylan to shop for more schooners. Vessels lay idle in every harbor, along with young sailors and old salts to man them. The general had begun to learn that seamen were different from landsmen. Marbleheaders had started his training, but he still had more to learn. Now the British tarried in winter quarters, snugged comfortably in their Boston barracks. The general had no big battles to fight, which gave him plenty of time for study. Unfortunately, there were others like Broughton. The cream had not risen to the top.

5

The Schooners of Plymouth

On *October 23, 1775,* Washington met with a congressional delegation consisting of Benjamin Franklin, Thomas Lynch, and Benjamin Harrison to obtain approval for his dabblings in naval matters. "Six vessels are now fitted out & fitting upon the best terms to intercept the enemy's supplies," he declared. "Will this be agreeable to Congress?" One vessel, named after Franklin, had already sailed on a mission of mischief with Broughton's *Hancock.* Another vessel soon to stretch her sheets had been named *Harrison,* and to recognize each delegate equally, another vessel would be named *Lynch.* There would even be a vessel named for the general, and one for the patriot Dr. James Warren, who had fallen at Bunker Hill, but neither *Washington* nor *Warren* was ready to sail. And for those who kept count, the general commissioned a seventh vessel, *Lee,* whose name could have been pluralized because there were two Lees, Richard Henry Lee, of Congress, and Charles Lee, Washington's second in command, neither of whom knew which was being honored. Since the general had already committed to six of the seven vessels, the committee approved of "this scheme," shook the general's hand, and promised to recommend it to Congress. Upon departing, they probably wished His Excellency good hunting, especially with their respective namesakes.[1]

At Beverly, Glover exerted every effort to refit, arm, and man four vessels. *Hancock* and *Franklin* had already sailed, but *Lee* and *Warren* were still in the hands of the carpenters. To expedite the completion of his flotilla, the general sent Moylan to Plymouth to hurry along *Washington* and *Harrison.*

Through Colonel Reed, Washington kept pressure on Glover and Moylan to get the schooners to sea. Besides needing gunpowder, Washington, whose own ranks had begun to thin, wanted to stop reinforcements from reaching Boston. Maj. Gen. William Howe had replaced General Gage early in October, and Washington was unsure of what to expect from this new general. But one thing was certain. With winter approaching, the British would be rushing supplies to Boston, and the sooner the schooners got to sea, the better their chances of capturing the transports.

On October 11 Washington learned of a large convoy sailing from England. Reed wrote to Glover and Moylan, "It is some disappointment to us that the vessels cannot be got ready sooner, as we have just received very important advices respecting the dispatch of a number of transports from England which may be hourly expected on the coast ... set every hand to work that can be procured & [let] not a moment of time be lost in getting them ready." Four days later he added, "We are very anxious to hear of the armed vessels being ready for sea. Every day, nay every hour is precious." On October 17 he warned, "The General is much dissatisfied."[2]

In an effort to ease His Excellency's anxiety, Reed reported the schooner *Harrison,* Capt. William Coit, had sailed on October 26, and that *Washington,* Capt. Sion Martindale, would sail at the end of the month. On the dates reported by Reed, however, neither vessel left Plymouth's harbor.[3]

Fitting out the schooners *Harrison* and *Washington* at Plymouth had been Washington's idea, although doing so meant involving different people. With the exception of Moylan, who made a hurried trip to Plymouth and then returned to Beverly to help Glover, no one clearly understood the general's wishes but Capt. Ephraim Bowen Jr., an energetic young officer who departed from headquarters on October 13 with Washington's orders stuffed in a leather pouch and wrapped in oilskin.

Forty miles and a sunset later, Bowen reached Plymouth as tired as his old horse and secured lodgings at Thomas Howland's Inn. There he obtained a room for himself and a stall for his horse. Because of the late hour he treated himself to a tankard of ale and a hot supper of beef and boiled potatoes before reopening his orders.

Bowen's first directive sent him to the Plymouth wharf to locate Capt. Daniel Adams, who, according to the general's information, had already set carpenters to work modifying his schooner. Evidently no deal had been struck, because Bowen had the authority to engage another vessel if he was not satisfied with the looks of the 64-ton *Triton.*

In the morning Bowen hastened to the wharf and asked for Adams. He learned the captain and his vessel were at Kingston, which he had passed on his way to Plymouth. If Bowen considered this waste of time an omen of things to come, he did not record it in his journal. Mounting his ailing horse, he rode to Kingston and obtained Adams's promise that *Triton* would be at Plymouth for inspection by 5:00 P.M. Bowen, in an effort to recover lost time, rode back to Plymouth to fulfill the general's second order—to designate "proper persons to appraise the vessel."

Heeding another of the general's directives, Bowen stopped at Watertown on his way to Plymouth and asked Col. James Warren to nominate as Continental agent a man capable of providing such things as provisions for the crew and proper management of prizes. Warren recommended William Watson, a member of the Plymouth Committee of Correspondence and senior member of the mercantile firm of Watson and Spooner. While waiting for Adams to arrive, Bowen located Watson, who readily agreed to accept the post.

Watson's role as agent was identical to William Bartlett's at Beverly and Jonathan Glover's at Marblehead. He provisioned the crew one month at a time, maintained an accounting of all transactions, and appraised and documented the value of all prizes sent into Plymouth. His authority was limited to vessels fitted out at Continental expense and their prizes. He was expected to retain all captured military stores for the use of the army and to be especially watchful for vessels suitable for the general's fleet. Washington trusted no one but himself to make final disposition of captured property and asked his agents to send all papers to him and await further directions. Since Broughton had demonstrated the Marblehead penchant for practicing self-interest, the general suspected the trait afflicted all New England mariners. He even went a step further and asked agents to report any irregularity or misconduct on the part of his chosen officers. For this service the agent would receive an emolument: 2.5 percent of the value of all expenditures made in provisioning and fitting the schooners, and another 2.5 percent of the value of all prizes and cargoes sold.[4]

On October 17 Bowen notified Washington that the people of Plymouth gave *Triton* "an excellent character as a sailor," and carpenters had set to work on her. Adams promised to have the vessel ready in four or five days if, Bowen warned, "he is not obliged to wait for guns." With

Watson's help, Bowen located guns in Plymouth—an assortment of 3s, cohorns, and swivels—but nothing uniform enough to suit the needs of a fighting ship. Bowen sought permission from headquarters to go to Providence or Bristol to obtain "proper guns."[5] Remembering the general's recent experience with Marbleheaders, Reed replied, "If it is absolutely necessary [then] you must go, but we have always found that when gentlemen sent upon this business go among their friends, they are apt to stay too long & are induced to favour their friends in such articles. … I therefore think it necessary to give you this caution."[6]

Bowen took offense at the slur on his honor and retorted, "I have no friends in Providence or Bristol who can reap any advantage in this business [through] my means & be assur'd that I would not lose one moment's time to the detriment of the cause in which I am engaged."[7]

In addition to the "caution," Reed handed Bowen another project, the fitting out of the schooner *Endeavor,* owned three-fourths by George Erving and one-fourth by her master, Benjamin Wormwell. Erving's share had been confiscated by the Plymouth Committee of Correspondence when he left town to join his Loyalist friends at Boston.

"Captain Martindale is to command," Reed wrote, "but Wormwell may sail as master if he chooses." This peculiar arrangement bothered Bowen. Wormwell had dual objectives in mind, one being the protection of his vessel, the other being the allure of a master's share of prize money.[8]

Before Bowen could start to refit *Endeavor* (renamed *Washington*) he had to finish work on *Triton* (renamed *Harrison*). Rather than lose time looking for guns elsewhere, or perhaps because Reed had politely cautioned against doing so, Bowen accepted Plymouth's four 3s and seven swivels. Adams cooperated by agreeing to add topsails, a good longboat, rigging, cables, anchors, tackle, and all "appertinances, strong & sufficient to perform a cruise any where between Cape Cod & Cape Ann, or elsewhere." Bowen felt good about his progress. The general had instructed him to hire the vessel for five shillings per ton per month, and Adams had settled for a slight increase of only four pence more.[9]

On October 16 work started on *Washington,* and three days later Bowen optimistically notified Reed that *Harrison* would be ready for sea in four days. He borrowed ammunition from the town and asked Reed to send the crew to Plymouth by the twentieth. In the meantime,

Martindale arrived in town to help supervise work on *Washington*. Word reached Adams that Wormwell, part owner of the schooner, had signed on as master. Almost as an aside, Bowen informed Reed that "Capt Adams accepts the berth of Master [on *Harrison*] & expects the same terms as other masters," a matter given no thought by headquarters.[10]

Before Martindale's arrival, Bowen's progress on *Harrison* flowed unimpeded by side issues or unexpected distractions. Adams seemed quite happy with the contract and industriously upheld his end of the agreement. Even the carpenters showed energy. New sails had been cut, tackles rigged, and the vessel provisioned with barrels of beef and pork, casks of bread, water tanks, canvas bags of coffee, and rations of rum. A longboat lay ready to be lifted on board as soon as workmen installed the guns. Captain Coit had not arrived to take command or to cloud any issues, and Bowen reported the vessel nearly ready to sail.

Martindale rode into town just as work started on the 160-ton *Washington*. He took one look at his vessel and demanded twelve carriage guns and twenty swivels. Then Wormwell refused to sign his contract, demanding six shillings, a trifle more than the 5s. 4d. per ton offered Adams. Work stopped on *Washington* while Bowen conferred with Watson. The decision exceeded his authority. He would be forced to drop everything and go to Bristol or Providence in search of guns. He could not spare the time. When Adams got wind of Wormwell's dispute over monthly terms, he felt his vessel was worth just as much. Bowen's work suddenly came to a standstill, and he appealed to Reed.[11]

Reed asked the Plymouth Committee of Correspondence to remind Wormwell that he did not hold the majority interest in *Washington* and that the terms offered by Bowen had been accepted by the committee. Wormwell agreed to drop his demand for more money in exchange for a lieutenant's berth on the schooner. Bowen had no authority to grant commissions and applied to Reed, recommending that a lieutenancy be given Wormwell, as it would "greatly oblige Capt Martindale, as he [Wormwell] is well acquainted with the vessel & bears a good character." The general offered a second lieutenancy, which Wormwell indignantly refused, preferring his present status as master. Wormwell, however, asked what wages went with the job. No terms had been set, but Wormwell was promised the same amount as Adams. This satisfied Wormwell and enabled Bowen to reconcentrate his attention on the schooners.[12]

Reed agonized over Martindale's demand for so many guns. The general did not want his vessels armed for venturesome captains to risk fights with British warships. Tell Martindale, Reed wrote Bowen, "there can be no occasion for such a number of guns, unless he means to go without powder for them as we cannot spare so much of that article. . . . We think 8 or at the most 10 six pounders quite sufficient with 10 or 12 swivels."[13]

In a steady rain, Bowen and Martindale mounted their horses and rode to Bristol, where the latter wished to visit his family before sailing, but he also wanted to make certain Bowen purchased the best guns His Excellency's money could buy. Bowen never mentioned the matter of Martindale's unauthorized interference, but to the young man's credit, he followed the general's orders with exceptional care. On reaching Bristol the following day, Martindale rode home and Bowen took a room at Smith's Inn. Tired and wet, Bowen nonetheless looked up the Bristol Committee of Safety that night and asked its aid. They could offer him nothing and sent him to Simeon Potter, who owned all the guns in town.

Potter had just what Bowen needed, ten 4s and ten swivels, but the arms merchant recognized an opportunity to pocket a nice profit. "He refused to lend or let [them]," Bowen reported, "& asked 1,000 Dollars for the guns exclusive of the swivels, which price I thought too extravagant."

Disgusted, Bowen rode to Providence and searched around the harbor. He found several guns in the possession of Gen. Esek Hopkins, who would not, however, part with them without an order from the governor. Discouraged but still undaunted, Bowen rode back to Bristol for one last look. Finding nothing but Potter's guns, Bowen returned to Providence for the night. In the morning he called on the governor, who was out of town. Bowen wasted the day resting his horse but was encouraged the following morning when Governor Cooke promised him ten 4s. However, the governor refused to part with any of Rhode Island's swivels, as he needed them for harbor defense. Bowen thought he knew where he could get swivels and in a rainstorm rode back to Bristol to buy them from Potter.

"Sorry," Potter said, sensing another opportunity to salvage a lost sale from a young man unaccustomed to the wiles of bargaining. "I will not sell the swivels without the carriage guns."

Once again Bowen left, each thinking they had seen the last of the other. Bowen spent the night in Bristol, planning to return to Providence in the morning to secure the 4s before the governor changed his mind. But he still needed ten swivels. As he finished his supper at Smith's Inn, Potter walked into the room and dropped a piece of paper on the table. The look on Potter's face reminded Bowen of a man ready to make his final sacrifice.

"Look here, lad," Potter said, "I'll give you ten swivels and carriage guns with ten cartridges for each, 200 shot, with what rammers, spunges, ladles, wormers, and everything else that goes with them for 700 dollars. If the price suits you," Potter added, "you may have them delivered immediately. If not, we say no more about them."

Bowen politely declined and Potter left, mumbling that this was his final offer, but Bowen still had a problem. If he took the governor's 4s, he still needed Potter's swivels. In the morning he stopped to haggle with Potter one last time. To his surprise, Potter dropped his price to £220 if Bowen would arrange for the freighting. Bowen accepted and spent the next three days carting the guns to Plymouth.[14]

To add a military flair for the arsenal on *Washington*, Martindale asked for a drum and a fifer. Moylan, who had been tapping Rhode Island regiments to fill the crew of eighty, replied with disgust. "I don't know the use of a drum & fife on board, nor do I imagine that any other vessels get them, but if it will give Capt. Martindale any pleasure he shall be indulged with them."[15]

Martindale's demand to convert the schooner to a brig-rigged vessel caused further consternation. Washington probably did not know one rig from another, but if Martindale thought a brig-rig would increase the vessel's speed, then a brig-rig she would have. On November 3 Bowen promised the vessel would be ready as soon as possible. Two weeks later he blamed *Washington*'s delayed departure on the weather being "extremely bad." Bowen returned to Cambridge on November 18, convinced the vessel would sail that day. But Martindale did not sail, and when all the bills were assembled for refitting her, invoices exceeded £1,000. The extravagance staggered the cost-conscious general, as no other vessel came close to that cost. The brig-rigged schooner, however, was the largest vessel in Washington's fleet, and the general hoped she would become his finest commerce raider.[16]

On October 25 Captain Coit and his Connecticut volunteers rollicked into Plymouth. Coit, from New Haven, was a tall, portly man with a ruddy face, "soldierly in bearing, frank, jovial, somewhat eccentric, and very liberal." Thirty-three-year-old Coit had graduated from Yale at the age of nineteen. He studied law, but feeling the need for adventure spent a few years at sea earning a master's berth. Bored with the isolation of weeks afloat, he returned home to practice law, but shots rattling across Lexington Common lured him into the war. Like Broughton and Selman, Coit rode into headquarters with good credentials.[17]

With William Watson at his side and his command in tow, Coit marched down to Thomas Lathrop's wharf where *Harrison* lay ready to sail. Whatever Coit expected in an armed schooner was far different from the stubby, dirty-black vessel tied to the wharf. She featured an old, tallowed bottom, two topsails, a long boat, four small popguns, and oars at her quarters. Coit thought the vessel "rather old & weak," and word of his grumbling got back to Reed. The colonel tried to be placating. "[Coit] has leave to take one of the late captures if he can do it without loss of time," Reed replied, "but is advised rather to keep in the vessel fitted out till he can take a better [one]."[18]

What Coit restrained himself from saying to Watson he mirthfully shared with his friend Maj. Samuel B. Webb. "To see me strutting about on the quarter-deck of my schooner!" he jibed, for there was no quarter-deck, only a top deck "ashamed of being old. . . . The first time we made use of a clawed handspike, it broke a hole through . . . directly over the magazine. Ah, and more than that too—4 [three] pounders, brought into this country by the Lords Say and Seal, to *Saybrook* when they first came. A pair of cohorns that Noah had in the Ark; one of which lacks a touch-hole, having hardened steel drove therein. . . . Six swivels, the first that were ever landed at Plymouth, and never fired since. Now, that is my *plague*."

"Her accommodations," Coit wrote, "are fine; five of us in the cabin, and when there, are obliged to stow spoon fashion. Besides, she has a chimney in it, and the smoke serves for bedding, victuals, drink and choking." The vessel had two masts, but Coit preferred to think of her as having one, "which is her foremast; she had a mainmast, but it was put in so long ago, that it has rotted off in the hounds."

Coit concluded his diatribe by saying that when peace came, he would "recommend her and her apparatus to be sent to the Royal Society; and I dare eat a red-hot gridiron if ever they have had, or will have, until the day of judgment, a curiosuty equal to her. In short, she is the devil. If obliged to fire both guns of a side at a time, it would split her open from her gunwale to her keelson."[19]

Martindale's demand for modifications to *Washington* resulted from seeing the armament and rig of *Harrison.* Coit did not have the advantage of being on-site while his ship was fitted. His annoyance with the vessel affected his cruise to the extent that he blamed every misfortune on the schooner rather than on his nautical skills. Martindale had no reason to blame any of his misfortunes on *Washington,* but his luck would prove even worse than Coit's.

One item both skippers took to sea was the provincial flag of Massachusetts. Broughton and Selman had no such banner to puzzle the inhabitants of Nova Scotia or the Island of St. John. Lucy Hammet fashioned the flag at the request of Watson, who foresaw a need for Washington's vessels to be able to identify each other. Reed liked the idea of a flag consisting of a white background with a green pine tree in the center and the words *Appeal to Heaven* inscribed below. Coit and Martindale displayed the same flag, but of different materials. Coit's, made of a thin, inexpensive woolen fabric, cost 1s. 6d. per yard, while Martindale's tastes demanded a durable kersey cloth at 4s. 8d. per yard. Lucy Hammet's labor narrowed the cost differential, eight shillings for *Harrison's* banner and twelve shillings for *Washington's.* She also earned a tidy sum making eighteen pounds of bullets for Coit. Martindale bought his bullets elsewhere and, of course, paid more for them.[20]

Coit sailed on October 26, but four weeks passed before Martindale got to sea. Besides lengthy modifications to *Washington,* Coit had taken all the powder Plymouth could spare, and Martindale, with ten guns to Coit's four, wanted forty rounds of shot for each gun and an ample supply for his swivels. Two weeks later Moylan and Watson still begged from one town to another to satisfy Martindale's demands for powder. "The General is apprehensive," Moylan wrote. "Martindale is going upon too large a scale." He asked Watson to remind Martindale that the intention of fitting out his vessel was not to attack armed enemy vessels but to capture unarmed transports. "Captain Martindale," he added, "seems to have lost sight of this."[21]

On November 3 Ephraim Bowen signed *Washington*'s lease on behalf of the Continental Army, and John Torrey co-signed for the Plymouth Committee of Correspondence. If the vessel was lost to the enemy, the Continent would reimburse the owners the "penal sum of two hundred Pounds," or about one-fifth the cost to outfit the brig. Martindale's responsibility was to make her pay for herself, and His Excellency paced anxiously about headquarters waiting for this to happen.[22]

It was just as well that Bowen, who had worked so hard to fit Coit's vessel for sea, was not in Plymouth the day she sailed. *Harrison* filled her sheets and went aground in the harbor. Coit exercised a captain's prerogative and blamed the mishap on the "Stupidity and Unskilfulness of the Pilot."[23]

Before Coit and Martindale finished their brief careers as George Washington's skippers, there would be plenty of "Stupidity and Unskilfulness," and an occasional glimmer of good seamanship.

6

The Cruise of the "Humorous Genius"

ashington's instructions to Coit read like a carbon copy of his orders to Broughton and Selman. His emphasis on stopping the flow of provisions "to or from Boston" had not changed, and he clamored for the capture of vessels laden with powder, arms, and lead. He ordered Coit to not bring on an engagement with an armed enemy vessel, but on this issue he had no need to worry. Coit believed his schooner would split open "from her gunwale to her keelson" by firing a broadside, and he did not plan to sink his own vessel. But first he needed to indoctrinate his privates on the finer points of sailing.[1]

Of Washington's fleet, *Harrison* was the smallest. After fitting her with four 3s, ten swivels, and a longboat, finding space for fifty men and a month's provisions deprived the crew of any sense of comfort. They had not seen the vessel before Coit marched them to Plymouth, and what they saw they did not like. Nonetheless, they climbed on board with typical Yankee grumbling.

Harrison sailed on October 26 with Daniel Adams at the steerage. Watson had assured Coit that Adams knew every inch of the harbor. Nonetheless, the vessel struck a shoal and remained fast until the next tide. Grounding shook her old mainmast, and Coit returned to Plymouth, where a close examination revealed a rotten base. Coit notified headquarters and all was forgiven. "I am very sorry for the accident," Reed replied, "but we hope more care will be taken in the future."

Washington still considered *Harrison* a good sailor. Bowen and Watson had told him so, and after investing £500 in refitting her he expected handsome returns. The general, however, formed the impression Coit disapproved of the vessel, but with the sailing season coming

58

to a close he wanted no more time lost. He forgave Coit's accident and acknowledged the crew had sailed without having an opportunity to acquaint themselves with the vessel or the harbor.

The general waved a carrot. Two vessels had been captured at Martha's Vineyard and would be in Plymouth shortly. Coit could have one of them if he could "shift into her without loss of time, but we rather wish," Reed added, "you should proceed in the *Harrison* as she is fitted out & sails well. There are a great many vessels on the coasts so that you may do your country great service & acquire much honour yourself if you proceed immediately." The offer of a better vessel gave Coit encouragement, but he knew he must settle for *Harrison* until he bagged a few prizes.[2]

Capt. John Manley sailed into Plymouth with the schooner *Lee,* fitted at Beverly by Glover. The general had hoped to have *Washington* ready so all three vessels could sail together, but Martindale still fussed with his brig-rig. Manley waited with Coit for a bad spell of weather to pass. If Martindale was not ready, they would leave without him.[3]

On November 4 the weather cleared, and on a bright, sunlit morning with a fresh southerly breeze, Manley and Coit headed for sea. Once again Coit filled his sails, encouraged by the prospect of replacing his dingy old schooner. *Lee* got off first, and *Harrison* plowed into another shoal. Manley went ahead and sailed out of sight. Coit followed six hours later, heading north toward Boston Bay, but he never caught up with Manley.

At dawn *Harrison* cruised with shortened sails off the outer edge of Boston Bay. Two miles to the north stood the Boston lighthouse. As daylight flooded the bay, the lookout hailed from aloft, "Sail ho! Two vessels dead ahead!" Coit came topside with his glass. Both vessels approached, keeping within speaking distance of each other. They glided toward the harbor, serene in the belief they had reached their destination. They manifested the markings of simple traders, so Coit loaded his 3s with shot and stopped both vessels. The 75-ton sloop *Polly,* Sibeline White, master, and the 85-ton schooner *Industry,* Charles Coffin, master, carried no guns. Both surrendered without an argument.

The vessels hailed from Nova Scotia and carried livestock and provisions for Boston. Hogs, sheep, cattle, and poultry controlled the deck. Both holds contained fish, potatoes, cheese and baled hay—exactly the type of provisions needed by Howe's army. The cacophony of cattle bellowing, geese squawking, and sheep bleating greeted the prize crews and probably resonated halfway across Boston Bay. "Capt. Coit (a humorous genius)," wrote an observer from Roxbury, "made the prisoners land upon the same rock our ancestors first trode when they landed in America, where they gave three cheers, and wished success to American arms." Bowen described the prizes to Washington as not of much consequence but quite valuable to the enemy.[4]

Coit complimented himself to a friend, referring to his conquests as a "blackguard snatch." One outing of thirty-six hours had netted two fair prizes—not bad for a night's work. "I took them with an old dull schooner," he declared, "with her beams as long as her keel, with but 4 guns—& if his Excellency sees fit to give me a good vessel that will carry 14 guns, he will [realize] all his expectations, or he will stand at the North Pole to all eternity." Coit never got his 14-gun dreadnought, nor did the general ever stand at the North Pole, but before leaving Plymouth for her next cruise the "old dull schooner" stepped a new mainmast.[5]

Coit turned the prizes over to Watson, who pastured the livestock and sent the provisions to his storehouse. He herded the prisoners together and sent them under guard to headquarters. Coit, however, gave special attention to the pockets of Coffin, White, and Jabez Hatch, owner of *Polly*. He justified his "blackguard snatch" by proclaiming Hatch an infamous Tory who had purposely sailed to Halifax to obtain supplies for himself and for Howe's "Ministerial Butchers in Boston." Coffin, from whom Coit liberated eight half Joes (about £14 8s.), later had his money returned, but one half Joe turned up missing.

Washington found no reason to detain the prisoners and turned them over to the Watertown Committee of Safety. Under bonds of £500 for Coffin, White, and the mates and £1,000 for Hatch, the prisoners were permitted "to go at large through this Colony" as long as they did not return to Boston or correspond with the enemy. Washington demanded all personal belongings be returned to the prisoners, including any cash still residing in Coit's pockets. Moylan did not think the prisoners warranted "any indulgence," but the war had not progressed to the stage where anything of value became fair plunder for the captors.[6]

Lt. Henry Champion carried the papers taken from Coit's two captures to headquarters, along with Watson's inventory. Washington, encouraged by Coit's success, was penning a letter to Reed when Champion burst into the room, dropped his reports on the general's writing desk, and tipped over a candle. "I had just finished my letter," Washington postscripted reflectively, "when a blundering Lieutenant of the blundering Captain Coit, who had just blundered upon two vessels from Nova Scotia, came in with the account of it, and before I could rescue my letter . . . [the lieutenant] picked up a candle and sprinkled [the letter] with grease . . . but these are the kind of blunders one can readily excuse." Washington excused the accident, but "blunder" became a mental fixation whenever he thought of Coit or Broughton. The two skippers were not at all alike, but Coit had earned a share of the general's mirth on the day he grounded his schooner.[7]

Bowen inspected Coit's prizes and suggested *Industry* be refitted as a cruiser, "as she sails well . . . and might be fitted out at very little expence." The general agreed. It would be a shameful waste not to arm and man a good sailing vessel, but the disposition of prizes had not been resolved by Congress. Paperwork had begun to pile up on his Continental fleet. Once again Washington appealed to Hancock, asking that admiralty courts be established to libel prizes. "Otherwise," he said, "I may be involved in inextricable difficulties." And for many months more, he was.[8]

On news that a suspicious vessel had been observed off Cape Cod, Coit sailed to investigate. Two days later he returned. His men had refused to continue the cruise, and he asked permission to replace them with civilians. Moylan replied to Watson, "For Gods sake indulge him," but he had begun to doubt Coit's efforts and added, "If he has misinformed his Excellency, let us know immediately." Watson understood the problem, answering, "Coit has had much difficulty, & has been greatly perplexed with an uneasy set of fellows, who have got [soured] by the severity of the season & are longing for the leeks and onions of Connecticut." Watson added, protectively, "I think no man could have managed better." With Watson's help, Coit returned his malcontents to their Connecticut regiment and enlisted replacements at Plymouth.[9]

While Coit recruited, Martindale finished work on *Washington*. His crew consisted of 1st Lt. Moses Turner and 2nd Lt. James Childs, both of Rhode Island; Consider Howland, master, and Jacob Taylor, master's mate, both of Plymouth; and about seventy-five privates. The men, who had been encamped in an empty Plymouth store for two weeks, filed on board with their muskets and personal belongings. Compared with *Harrison*, the men found quarters on *Washington* spacious.[10]

Martindale scanned His Excellency's sailing instructions but on the matter of prize money felt entitled to a greater share than Coit. Congress was studying the matter, Reed replied, adding that he hoped the delay would not deter the captain from exerting himself for the "good of the common country." Martindale also demanded and obtained a surgeon, John Manvide of Quebec, an addition he declared essential for a vessel of *Washington*'s complement.[11]

At daybreak on November 23, *Washington* and *Harrison* headed to sea in unseasonably pristine sailing weather. From the wharf Watson watched them disappear over the horizon with effusive optimism. "It is fine weather," he said, drawing in a deep breath of salt air. Several pilots had joined Coit's crew to help convey prizes back to port. The general will be pleased, Watson promised Moylan. When the vessels return from their cruise there will be "good accounts of their success," Watson predicted.[12]

Watson was a trifle too optimistic of Martindale's and Coit's ability to keep out of trouble. A few miles beyond the bay, the lookout on *Washington* sighted three vessels that Manvide reported "were waiting for us." One of them, the 28-gun frigate *Tartar*, Capt. Edward Medows, was not waiting but engaged in convoying two transports to Boston laden with forage from the Bay of Fundy. Coit and Martindale pressed forward for a closer look. Keeping abeam of each other, they agreed that *Tartar* was closing on them. Coit reversed course and sped toward the safety of the shallows. Martindale followed moments later. From the deck of *Washington*, Manvide observed that all three enemy vessels "seemed determined to defeat us and make us prisoners . . . the frigate chased us from three o'clock in the afternoon until the black of night."

At 3:30 A.M. Martindale feared he had gotten too close to shore and dropped anchor, expecting at dawn to see the frigate standing nearby. The sea remained calm. At daylight no breeze ruffled the water. *Tartar* had gone on about her business, escorting the transports into Boston Bay. The only vessel in sight was *Harrison*, which had spent the night off Plymouth Harbor. Martindale's privates clamored to get back to land on the first morning breeze, but the weather remained calm. Hardly a breath of air stirred. "God alone knows what will happen,"

Manvide moaned, adding his worry to the voices of the shaken crew, but at 10:00 A.M. he relaxed when Martindale anchored off Plymouth and sent a boat ashore.[13]

While *Washington* dallied off Plymouth, Coit left his consort behind and struck northward in search of action. He crept along the coast to Alderton (now Allerton) Point and drifted about, waiting for a straggler to come in sight. The lookout reported two vessels at anchor about a mile off the lighthouse but inside Boston Bay. They were the same two vessels, a brig and a ship, convoyed into the harbor by *Tartar* early that morning.

Coit sailed into Graves's naval stronghold, shoved out two 3s, and closed on the brig. Her master observed Coit's guns and ordered the topsail halyards, gears, and lines cut. As Coit's men boarded from one side, the crew of the brig departed from the other. With lines cut Coit could not carry off the brig. The prize crew spread burning coals on the cabin floor, set her on fire, and rowed back to the schooner. If they could not carry off the brig, perhaps they could take the ship.

Coit noticed two large vessels anchored in the passage between Alderton shoal and the lighthouse. Through his glass he observed men cutting cables and raising sail on the armed transport *Empress of Russia*, Lt. John Bourmaster, and on the 14-gun HM sloop *Raven*, Capt. John Stanhope. Watching from the deck of HMS *Phoenix*, also anchored in Nantasket Road, Capt. Hyde Parker Jr. ordered a pair of boats lowered to assist in the rescue of the brig. Before the boats got off, *Raven* and *Empress of Russia* luffed and lobbed a few long-range shots at *Harrison*. Instead of pursuing Coit, Bourmaster stopped to recapture the deserted brig and extinguish the fire. Stanhope, coming up in *Raven*, entered the action slowly, his guns firing a barrage of grape that whistled about Coit's ears.

Stanhope pursued the schooner for three hours, but Coit had the weather gauge and, with help from his sturdy new mast and a full spread of sail, kept out of range. When the wind died late in the day, Stanhope came about. Coit ordered sweeps topside, and the strong backs of his shaken crew rowed the vessel to safety. Stanhope stood by and watched.[14]

Whether Coit's invasion of the Royal Navy's stronghold with an aged schooner was an act of foolishness or audacity is anyone's guess, but good luck favored the "humorous genius." After dodging *Raven*, cold northwesterlies kicked up the seas and set Coit scrambling for Plymouth. He spotted *Mercury*, 20, and *Nautilus*, 16, standing off the port as if waiting for him. Running with the wind, he headed into Cape Cod Bay, forcing his pursuers, now joined by *Raven* and *Hinchinbrook*, into a long stern chase. By nightfall he could go no further and ducked into Barnstable Harbor. There he waited until morning, surrounded by sheets of sleet and snow, unaware that during the night his pursuers had become disoriented. In the storm, *Raven* chased and fired on *Hinchinbrook*, and *Mercury*, smothered by snow, left the bay in chase of *Raven*.[15]

For the next four days *Harrison* remained snugged inside the harbor at Barnstable. Headquarters heard nothing from Coit until Champion arrived on a borrowed horse. Tired and cold, the lieutenant left an exaggerated account of how the schooner was "so old & crazy as to be unfit" for service.

Despite his misgivings about Coit, Washington agreed to fit out another vessel if Watson could make one ready, guns and all, in six to eight days. From Prospect Hill the general could see stray transports slipping into Boston Harbor. Why his schooners made so little effort to intercept them baffled and discouraged him. The general's attitude slumped to a new low when Watson reported a mutiny brewing on board *Washington*. He informed Watson that Coit must either repair the schooner or lay it up—ammunition, stores, and all. If the latter, Coit could gather up his men when he returned from Barnstable and march them back to camp.[16]

What puzzled Washington was Martindale's mutinous crew. No one could explain the trouble, and, from Watson's reports, Martindale had accomplished nothing. Why, then, Washington wondered, would the men disobey orders?

On November 24, Martindale had spent most of the day off Plymouth waiting for *Harrison*, but Coit had gone to Boston Bay to taunt the British navy. Unable to find his sailing companion, Martindale waited until the suspense was broken by lookouts reporting two vessels and a schooner a few miles to sea. Martindale ordered all hands, sallied forth, and captured two of the three vessels. Moses Turner boarded both vessels, examined their papers, and released them. One vessel contained a cargo of oil, and the other was in ballast for Philadelphia. Neither appeared to be a fair prize.

Martindale anchored off Plymouth and sent the brig's longboat east "two leagues to see if any vessel was about." Turner stopped two traders loaded with wood. Since they were headed into Plymouth, he followed them back to *Washington*. Martindale hoisted the boat aboard and, because there was still daylight, weighed anchor and cruised a few miles off Plymouth. At sea a storm brewed, the same northwester that sent Coit bounding down Cape Cod Bay with four enemy warships nipping at his heels. "We saw one frigate," Manvide recorded, "which apparently wanted to give us battle; but could not overtake us." Martindale returned to his original anchorage and resumed his vigil for the missing Coit. "We spent a very bad night at sea," Manvide scrawled in his journal. "There was a strong westerly wind all day and some snow." That was enough for Martindale. He was as cold as his crew and headed into Plymouth to ride out the gale.[17]

The two-day storm erupted with violence, dumping rain, hail, and finally snow on *Washington*'s deck. The men shivered in their light clothing and grumbled around the smoky stove below. Out on the bay the last of *Tartar*'s convoy of twenty-two transports limped toward Boston, fighting gale-force crosswinds. Lightning struck the transport *Jupiter* and ignited her cargo of hay. Wind blew the flames to a fury, exploding a magazine of powder and destroying the ship. The sloop *Britannia*, Joseph Hall, master, took another bolt, which burned through the rigging. Disabled, Hall sought the closest landfall. The wind carried him toward Gurnet Point, a short distance from where *Washington* lay, and Martindale sent Turner and a few hands to investigate. Manvide observed the capture from the deck. "At one o'clock in the afternoon," he wrote, "our longboat came back with a vessel of about 80 tons laden with wood, hay, cheese, potatoes, turnips, cabbage . . . and other goods. All this was of little value," he added, forgetting that to the British troops occupying Boston, every morsel of food or stick of fuel added to their comfort.

After Martindale and the surgeon went ashore to turn *Britannia* over to Watson, Manvide returned to *Washington* and complained to his shipmates that his share of prize money had not been disbursed on the spot. Evidently Martindale, like Broughton, had either failed to explain the distribution of prize money or did not understand it himself, and Manvide's grumblings mixed with the crew's growing dissatisfaction toward their captain.[18]

Never straying far from Plymouth, *Washington* faced a stiff head-wind and on November 28 ventured a few miles to sea. The lookout reported a strange object floating offshore. Martindale sent a boat to investigate and found a partly submerged vessel. "We took it," Manvide said, "and we assumed that it belonged to the warship that had exploded at sea from her powder-magazine." Martindale hauled the hulk into Plymouth, hoping it might bring a small amount of prize money. "The night was very bad," Manvide grumbled. "Strong winds, rain and snow."[19]

Washington's crew spent another cold and miserable night bobbing about off Plymouth, but on the morning of November 29 the weather improved and Martindale, conscious that Watson had been observing his inactivity, decided to make a thrust northward. "As we were about to get under way and make for Cape Hand [Ann]," Manvide wrote, "our crew mutinied unanimously. . . . They were willing to lend a hand to weigh anchor but . . . refused to do any more." Martindale called his officers together for a conference. Rather than attempt to understand the under-lying cause of the mutiny, Martindale sent Turner to Cambridge to inform Washington "of this wicked behavior." Turner promised to return the following day.

In the meantime the crew agreed to take the brig into Plymouth, thereby putting themselves in better juxtaposition to shore, but Martindale would not let them leave the vessel. On December 1 Manvide scribbled his last journal entry: "Fair weather still. Same wind. At about eleven o'clock in the morning we saw five sails. We sent our longboat with seven armed men to investigate. They have not come back."[20]

While Turner trotted to Cambridge with bad tidings for the general, Coit sailed out of Barnstable. As *Harrison* rounded the northern tip of Cape Cod, the lookout reported a schooner skimming through the caps toward Boston. Coit cut her off and sent an officer to inspect her papers. *Thomas,* another vessel owned by Richard Derby, carried a cargo of wine from Fayal to Derby's hometown of Salem. Over the protests of the schooner's master, Coit decreed the wine contraband and sent the vessel into Plymouth.

When Derby learned *Thomas* had been captured, he complained bitterly to Washington. Moylan dispatched a rider to Plymouth notifying Watson that His Excellency "commands" the vessel be immediately returned to Derby's master, and "Capt Coit pay for any thing that the schooner may be robbed of." Moylan wanted Coit to be reminded that interrupting "good citizens in their trade . . . was not the intention of fixing out these armed vessels at the Continental expence. This Capt. Coit would know well if he consulted the instructions given him."[21]

During the same junket, Coit captured a nameless 15-ton fishing schooner on December 1 with a cargo far more valuable than Derby's stock of wine. He nabbed four Tory pilots sent by Graves to escort into Boston all the transports scattered by the recent storm. Coit clapped the pilots in irons, removed Jeremiah Downey, master, and ordered the vessel into Plymouth. With a set of old, battered sails and barely enough gear to steer her, the rickety prize hobbled into Plymouth far behind Coit's "old dull schooner." Watson released Downey under bond but kept the pilots well guarded.[22]

Dull schooner or not, Coit had done well despite his complaining. When he reached Plymouth he put the vessel on the ways for a quick overhaul. For the little graving and refitting she needed, he would be back to sea in two days. But Coit had complained too much, and his seizure of *Thomas,* coming as it did on the heels of Broughton's misadventures, convinced Washington the time had come to clean house. Despite Watson's report that Coit was determined to make another cruise, and that, unlike Martindale's mutinous crew, his men were contented and well behaved, Washington ordered the "humorous genius" to Cambridge along with his crew of volunteers.[23]

Coit's career as *Washington*'s skipper was over, but Martindale remained in command of *Washington*. Oddly enough, Coit's crew wanted to resume the hunt, but Martindale's men would neither sail nor vacate their vessel. Watson, who had not investigated the dispute, advised Washington that the men had enlisted to serve in the army and not the marines. "I believe Capt. Martindale has done all in his power to make things easy," he declared. "His people really appear to be a set of the most unprincipled, abandoned fellows [I] ever saw. . . . I am very apprehensive that little is to be expected from fellows drawn from the army for this business, but . . . if people were enlisted for the purpose of privateering much might be expected of them."[24]

Unlike Broughton's mutineers, His Excellency offered Martindale's men an opportunity to reconsider their actions. Much money had been invested in *Washington,* and with it expectations of many rich prizes. The general asked Watson to go to the ship and talk with the crew directly. If the men refused to work the vessel because they envisioned themselves soldiers, they were to be sent back to their regiment. If the problem concerned compensation, Watson could up their pay to forty shillings a month and "one third of all prizes they may have the good luck to make." Whatever the outcome of Watson's negotiations, the general wanted the vessel manned and sent to sea. "Should you . . . find it impossible to get men on these terms in a reasonable time," he added, "I must only say that the deficiency of public spirit in this country is much more than I could possibly have ever imagined."[25]

Although Coit and his men had been recalled to Cambridge, the general was willing to transfer them to *Washington* if Martindale failed to quell his mutiny. Somewhere at sea were fourteen British transports. Coit, however, had condemned the sailing qualities of his schooner to the extent that Washington had given up on her when, in reality, she was comparable to two of the Beverly vessels.

Watson went on board *Washington* to confer with the crew and found to his surprise that the men were half frozen. They simply lacked warm clothing, a detail Martindale had chosen to ignore. "After supplying them with what they wanted," Watson reported merrily, "the whole crew to a man gave three cheers & declared their readiness to go to sea."[26]

Coit returned to Connecticut, taking with him what laurels his imagination could educe from his adventures. He loved the sea, preferring it to the practice of law, and when the Connecticut Council of Safety sought a skipper to command the new provincial ship *Oliver Cromwell,* he asked for it. For a while the council deliberated. They had many deserving officers to consider, but Coit had experience. The council invited him to their chambers for an interview. Gov. Jonathan Trumbull gave Coit advice, instruction, and admonition as to his conduct. Perhaps Washington had warned the governor that with Coit precautionary "instruction and admonition" were necessary. The governor left no record of his advice, which would be of interest if the cruises of the 10-gun *Oliver Cromwell* were to be followed.[27]

Coit's performance fell far short of the expectations of the governor and his council, and they dismissed him eight months later. Coit demanded an explanation. The governor responded curtly, "My Council of Safety have been greatly mortified for a long time to find it out of their power to push the ship out on a cruise." Problems of desertion and unrest among the crew had kept Coit in port. Watson had been right. Sailors much preferred life on privateers, where pay was more certain and discipline less harsh.[28]

Coit fished about for employment of a nautical nature, and on September 20, 1777, he obtained command of the 12-gun privateer *America* and its crew of sixty-seven. He captured a British brig and a ship. On September 6, 1781, he was wounded and taken prisoner. He died in North Carolina in 1802.

Washington made the right decision when he let Coit down easily. What to do with Martindale was another matter. He gave the man another chance to prove his ability. Somewhere out beyond Boston Bay were His Majesty's transports, loaded with men and munitions, and Washington wanted them.

🎄 7 🎄
The Capture of Sion Martindale

atson's prompt delivery of warm clothing made the Rhode Islanders feel they had won a concession from their captain, who evidently did not listen to their complaints. News of enhanced prize shares rekindled their enthusiasm, and since thirteen British transports were headed for Boston, the crew unanimously agreed to another cruise.

On the day they sailed, the sun radiated from a clear blue sky and sparkled on a white-capped sea. A soft spray splashed over the bow, and men went about their work with fresh energy. For a rare moment, life on board *Washington* felt good. The sails stretched full and tight in an Indian summer breeze that carried the brig north, out beyond Massachusetts Bay, further from Plymouth than ever before, to where British warships prowled in search of rebel prizes.[1]

As the brig passed Boston Bay, a bank of dark clouds drove in from the west, spitting rain. The storm passed to the east, followed by another, even worse than the last. All that night wind howled through the rigging, blowing the brig north against an angry, crossing sea. Heavy flakes of snow, mixed with rain, washed across the deck. In the morning *Washington* stood well off Cape Ann with lookouts tied to the tops. Another squall roared out of the northwest, blowing hard and driving the watch below, but as the storm passed lookouts climbed back to their posts.

"Two sail to windward," came a cry from aloft. Martindale brought a glass topside and studied the vessels. Were they two plump prizes or a pair of frigates keeping company with each other? The vessels were coasting under light sail, keeping well apart, but on one Martindale observed a topsail blossom, followed by another. She carried a cloud of canvas, and Martindale, now about thirty hours out of Plymouth, sus-

70

pected trouble. One vessel sheered in chase, but the other stood away. Martindale put on his fastest heels and sailed for Gloucester, twelve leagues away. Turner and Childs looked to the guns.

Earlier in the day, the 20-gun HMS *Fowey*, Capt. George Montagu, had been chased by HMS *Lively*, Capt. Thomas Bishop, both sixth-rate frigates ordered by Admiral Graves to cruise between Cape Ann and Cape Cod. During the squall, Bishop failed to recognize *Fowey*. He came alongside at 1:00 P.M. and, after exchanging greetings and perhaps a good laugh, sailed to the northeast, leaving Montagu to chase a distant sail.

Before *Lively* passed out of sight, Montagu crowded on more sail and for more than three hours pursued Martindale in a stiff wind blowing hard from the starboard quarter. Gaining slowly, he came in range at 8:00 P.M. and fired eight shots. *Washington* luffed and came about, but the seas were piled too high for Montagu to lower the cutter. Wind howled through the rigging, and seas crashed across the deck. Shouts from the frigate could not be heard on *Washington*'s deck. The sky blackened and Martindale stood off, steadying the brig against the wind. *Fowey* stayed abeam, her lanterns dimly outlined in the distance. *Lively* came about late in the chase and joined *Fowey* at 10:00 P.M. Both frigates kept a close vigil on the wallowing prize, and at daybreak Montagu lowered the cutter and took possession of *Washington*. Martindale never fired a single shot from any of the ten guns Bowen had searched so hard to find and paid so much to buy. Montagu reported the brig armed with six 6s and four 4s and manned by a crew of seventy-four. "We took her people out," he reported, "and sent the Lieutenant, a Mate & 12 men on board her."[2]

The prize crew took the brig to Boston, where Graves spent eight days questioning Martindale. After obtaining detailed information on Washington's maverick navy, he put the soldier-sailors on board *Tartar* and sent them to England. General Howe, who grimaced every time his inbound supply vessels were intercepted by Washington's fleet, favored the prisoners' deportation to England. He hoped that giving Martindale and his men a dose of life on board one of His Majesty's prison ships might discourage other rebels from sporting about in privateers.[3] On the trip to England, Martindale's men joined Col. Ethan Allen and some of his Green Mountain Boys, who had been captured during the attack on Quebec.[4]

Diarist Ezekiel Price, in an outburst of patriotic propaganda, reported the capture of *Washington* as he imagined it. "The brig being commanded by one Captain Mansfield [Martindale], who, being attacked by a twenty-gun ship, which boarded them several times and was beat off. At last the privateer was overpowered by their great force, but not before they had every officer on board killed, and all men to eighteen out of seventy-five." Anyone reading Price's account would have difficulty identifying Martindale as the heroic Mansfield.[5]

Governor Cooke of Rhode Island evidently bought Price's story, because a few days later he reported to Provincial delegates, "There is no doubt but that Capt. Martindale in a fine cruizer fitted out by General Washington from Plymouth is taken by one of the enemy's ships of war disguised as a transport. . . . It is reported that he had 55 men killed and wounded out of 70."[6] *Fowey* carried a complement of 130 men, but not a single casualty occurred on either side.

Before *Lively* joined *Fowey*, Martindale may have missed an opportunity to save his brig by attempting to escape in the gale. Another commander might have jettisoned his guns to lighten the vessel. Instead, Martindale spiked the guns and destroyed his small arms. After disarming himself, he may not have considered escape an option.

Graves ordered *Washington* surveyed the moment she reached Boston. He mustered a crew, hoping the prize would decoy other rebel vessels. Lt. George Dawson and seventy men waited with muskets, pistols, pikes, and baggage to go on board. Evidently the brig-rigged schooner was never worth what the general paid in Continental dollars to have her fitted for commerce raiding. "It was my intention to have manned the Brig and send her out again, but her unfitness was so strongly represented," Graves declared, that "I ordered three Captains to survey and report the state she was in." Not one inspector considered her seaworthy. Graves took one last look and agreed, remarking, "She exceeds their description of her badness."

The surveyors found rot in the main and foremost beams and on sections of the main deck, and the "whole of the timber under the deck—rotten and totally decayed." The bowsprit had sprung in two places and the main boom in one, and the hull was "not fit for sea." One might wonder what Bowen's Plymouth inspectors had found so acceptable about a vessel the British recommended trashing two months later.

In view of the surveyors' assessment, Martindale may not have gotten far with his rotten timbers.[7]

Graves took interest in documents Martindale neglected to throw overboard. Among them were Washington's instructions, which gave the Royal Navy the first intimate look at the general's naval strategy.

Whatever fine fare Graves fed Martindale loosened the captain's tongue. He gave a full description of *Harrison,* down to her ugly black sides, topsails, and tallowed bottom. When Graves picked up an odd banner and asked, "What flag is this?" Martindale probably ran his fingers through the fine fabric spun by Lucy Hammet and replied, "Why that's ours, a green pine tree on a white field, with the motto 'Appeal to Heaven.' All our vessels carry it." As Martindale talked, Graves probably handed the banner to an aide and ordered several copies made. Whatever loosened Martindale's tongue continued to work. "The signal to know each other was to hoist the colors at the fore topmast head, and lower the main sail half down." To the question "How many of these schooners are there?" Martindale admitted knowing of three fitted out at Beverly, but he was uncertain of their armament. "Two are of four carriage guns each," he replied, as he had seen both *Lee* and *Harrison.*

After Graves siphoned Martindale dry of information, he sent him to the frigate *Tartar,* Captain Medows, to be shipped off to England with the rest of the crew. The admiral knew he had an important prisoner. "As there is no Commission in Boston to try persons guilty of acts of rebellion of high treason committed on the high seas," Graves wrote London, "I have sent home the whole crew of the brig." He wanted Martindale to repeat his story to the king's ministers. "When you get to Spithead," Graves told Medows, "take Capt. Martindale by express to Town." No doubt Howe had issued similar orders regarding Ethan Allen.[8]

Tartar made the crossing in twenty-one days, but if Pvt. Israel Potter's scheme to capture the vessel had not been betrayed, the imprisoned crew of *Washington,* with help from Allen's men, may have made her a prize. Three days out of Boston, Potter and his fellow prisoners hatched a scheme to overpower the guards and take the ship. One of *Washington'*s crew, whom Potter referred to as "a renegade Englishman," betrayed them. For his mischief, Potter endured the balance of the voyage in irons. When the frigate reached Portsmouth, Potter was ques-

tioned. By then he had learned more about the "renegade," a British
deserter attempting to save his own neck. The interrogator looked into
the antecedents of the alleged deserter and decided Potter had told the
truth. Potter's irons came off, but his problems had only begun.[9]

Once *Tartar* reached England, Sir Hugh Palliser became the first of
many to read Washington's instructions to Martindale. During his long
career in the Admiralty, Sir Hugh had never seen anything quite like
those documents. He sent the papers to Lord Sandwich, First Lord of
the Admiralty, with the comment, "Their proceedings at sea is at present
limited against ships and vessels employed in the service of the fleet and
army in America. Their regulations for their army is curious," Palliser
added, perhaps wondering why a general was directing naval operations.
He suggested the pine tree flag be given to Adm. John Montagu, "as it
was taken by his son." After the flag reached the Admiralty Montagu
displayed it for the public.[10]

Palliser also sought the king's pleasure regarding the captives still
locked in the hold of *Tartar*. Because no policy existed for dealing with
American prisoners, Lord George Germain suggested they be distributed among His Majesty's undermanned warships but kept under close
observation. The Admiralty took the matter under consideration and
sent all the prisoners to a guardship at Spithead, to be victualed at
two-thirds allowance until further orders.[11]

Unlike a typical British prison ship, consignment to a guardship
meant impressment into His Majesty's navy. As Martindale's men were
the first captured mariners to reach "jolly old England," citizens from all
over the countryside flocked to Portsmouth to get a glimpse of the
rebels, all of whom looked incredibly filthy. A reporter for the *London
Chronicle* noted "that a great deal of money had been collected for their
support."[12]

The Admiralty discovered that *Tartar* brought more than prisoners
to England when an outbreak of smallpox and "other disorders" flared
among *Washington's* crew. If moved to other ships, the Admiralty
warned, prisoners would carry their disorders with them and "infest"
others. The problem had been caused by filth and lack of proper clothing. Prisoners had been stripped of their winter woolens, and the remnants teemed with vermin. Palliser and Sandwich ordered the rebels
moved to Haslar Hospital, placed in the smallpox ward, cleaned up, and

provided with proper clothing. In exchange for clean clothes and a better life, seventy prisoners brought over by *Tartar* agreed to enter the king's service and, according to Vice Adm. Sir James Douglas, "would not choose to be sent back to America." Thirty-two of the men hailed from Rhode Island, twenty from other parts of New England, and the others everywhere from Virginia to Lisbon, Portugal. With a fresh set of slop clothes, the new recruits threw their old clothing overboard and, clutching their little bundles, mustered aboard the guardship *Centaur*. There they enjoyed greater liberty while awaiting reassignment. Only one officer, Surgeon John Manvide, agreed to serve His Majesty. Martindale and his other officers preferred incarceration in their single, but comfortable, room.[13]

John Walkar, a Rhode Islander, accused Martindale of dealing his crew to the British in exchange for his own freedom. "When we got to England," Walkar claimed, "our Captain petitioned to the Court that his men were willing to serve voluntarily, which was false, and by that he was sent home to America again. . . . I was put on board the *Royal Oak* & from thence on board the *Ostrich* & sent away to the West Indies."[14]

Martindale may have been looking out for himself. He left the impression with British officials that he was an "intelligent man" who had been commanded by Washington "to fit out the vessel, although he saw the impropriety of embarking in such hazardous enterprize." He claimed to have expressed his views to the general, but to no avail. After the vessel had been fitted, he also claimed a petition had been drawn up by the entire crew and sent to headquarters, begging the general to return them to camp. Washington refused to listen, Martindale declared, and if the men had not sailed immediately, "they were to be sent to him in irons, and would have been hanged as traitors to America for daring to refuse his orders." The appeal made nice copy for the local papers. Martindale may have believed half of what he said, as he had surrendered to *Fowey* without firing a shot.[15]

Most of *Washington's* crew convalesced at Haslar Hospital. John Vail, gunner's mate on the brig, was among those who recovered. "We were put into the hospital," he wrote, "the greater part of the crew being sick in consequence of confinement during the voyage, where many died. I remained in imprisonment about sixteen months when I made my escape."

Potter did not become infected until he entered the hospital, where, he wrote, "many of us took the small-pox the natural way from some we found in the hospital effected with that disease . . . which proved fatal to nearly one half our number." A reporter for the *Public Advertiser* agreed: "Nothing could exceed the extreme wretchedness of the crew of the privateer lately taken from the Americans."[16]

Potter, who lived most of the balance of his life in England, never submitted to impressment. After surviving smallpox he returned to a guardship at Spithead, where a month later an officer ordered him out of the hold to help row the ship's lieutenant ashore. Members of the boat's crew, of which he was the only prisoner, stopped in a local alehouse for a few pots of beer. Potter was forced to join them, and as the crew entered the tavern he asked permission to relieve himself. "As soon as I saw them all snugly in and the door closed, I gave speed to my legs, and ran . . . about four miles without halting."

He escaped but spent the next forty-eight years of his life in England scratching out an existence for himself and his family by crying "Old Chairs to Mend" through the streets of London. Finally, in 1823, with help from the American consul, seventy-nine-year-old Israel Potter returned home. Had he not escaped, he would probably have joined many of his comrades in the West Indies, serving in one of the Royal American regiments sent there to perform guard duty.[17]

In February all the loyal officers of *Washington* were shipped on board HMS *Greyhound*, Capt. Archibald Dickson, and delivered in late May to Halifax for exchange. Of the original crew, only Martindale, Lieutenants Moses Turner and James Childs, Master Consider Howland, Master's Mate Jacob Taylor, and about sixteen others remained. As soon as they stepped off the vessel, a detachment of soldiers marched them to the town jail. According to Martindale's account, he was in good spirits and expected "to be set at liberty soon."[18]

Soon did not come fast enough for Martindale. On June 19 he and thirteen others escaped from prison. A search party recaptured six of the men, including Howland and Taylor, but Martindale and his two lieutenants fled down the coast of Nova Scotia, stole a fishing smack, and sailed safely into Casco Bay. Howland and Taylor, however, returned to Halifax in irons, where they remained for many months under lock and key in a single room shared with Ethan Allen and a dozen sundry "felons, thieves, robbers, negroes, soldiers, etc."[19]

Instead of going to Washington's headquarters, Martindale went directly to Plymouth. During his captivity he had kept his mental cash register running, and at Plymouth he confronted agent Watson with a long list of personal expenses. Watson, who had since been superseded by John Bradford, gave the captain an empty-handed shrug and sent him to Washington with a letter of explanation. Martindale's account included £80 for clothing the men, a list of personal expenses, and nine months' back pay for himself and his officers.

At this time Washington was at New York, where his army had just suffered a serious defeat. The last thing he needed was another problem with his navy. He had no more cash available than Watson or Bradford. When Martindale and Turner appeared at his field office he suggested the account be processed by Congress and sent them to see Hancock. Childs returned to Providence, leaving such heady matters as back pay in the hands of his boss. Martindale and Turner rode to Philadelphia and met with Hancock, who sent them home with promises but not a cent for their trouble. Eventually, Congress awarded their pay and expenses in Continental dollars. By then a bucket full of paper money could not buy a good pair of shoes.[20]

Consider Howland and Jacob Taylor languished in their Halifax cell until the end of 1776, waiting for the general to negotiate their exchange. A full year had passed since *Fowey* captured *Washington*. It was then that agent Watson had first brought the matter of exchange to the general's attention. On December 23, 1775, Capt. Samuel Jackson had recaptured the brigantine *Peter* and taken six British prisoners—a midshipman and five sailors. Jackson knew Taylor had been captured, and he offered his six prisoners in exchange for his friend's release. In a letter to Washington, Watson also put in a bid for Martindale, who at the time was still Graves's guest at Boston. "Capt. Martindale . . . has a large family in poor circumstances which must suffer much unless some way can be devised for his redemption. I am very unwilling to give your Excellency trouble," Watson added, "and must ask your pardon, when at the very earnest request of Taylor's friends & unhappy family, ask your Excellency whether it an't possible to exchange for Taylor."[21]

Congress neglected the matter of prisoner exchange until inundated with appeals from the public. In a series of resolutions on December 2, prompted in part by the capture of Ethan Allen, Congress passed legislation providing for an exchange of "citizens for citizens, officers for officers of equal rank, and soldier for soldier." But they failed to recognize the existence of sailors. All of Washington's sailors were soldiers, but as far as the British were concerned they were sailors because they served on board sailing vessels.

On December 18, 1775, Washington had Ethan Allen in mind when he wrote Howe suggesting an exchange be made.[22] Howe remained silent on the matter, although the British had acquired a glut of prisoners taken from privateers and provincial ships. In the absence of a Continental navy, few British sailors had been captured by Americans. Those taken on prizes were civilians who sailed British transports, and Washington released them on parole or bond, assuming they had little or no exchange value. The British navy, however, impressed many of its captives because of the Admiralty's chronic lack of manpower. For many months occasional exchanges of prisoners occurred without any organized program. As late as May 10, 1776, Congress still argued among themselves over the protocol of exchange, losing much valuable time refereeing the process. Finally, on August 19, 1776, Vice Adm. Richard Lord Howe, General Howe's brother, speaking for the Royal Navy, agreed to exchange "officers for those of equal rank, and sailors for sailors."[23]

Howland and Taylor were moved from their Halifax cell and sent to a prison ship in New York Harbor. On December 25 Howland was released on parole, contingent on Mr. John Loring's delivery to the British Commissary of Prisoners. In the typical confusion of prisoner exchange, Loring had already been exchanged for another prisoner, thereby making Howland a British prisoner at large. For nine months he enjoyed his freedom, subject at any time to be recalled to the prison ship. Finally, on September 17, 1776, Capt. Gideon White was officially exchanged for Howland, who, like his prison mate Jacob Taylor, had found civilian work less odious than occupying a berth on one of Washington's schooners.[24]

When the British vacated Boston and consolidated their forces in the vicinity of New York, they left behind the brig *Washington*, no longer a clumsy sailer with ten guns but a stripped-down hulk of no earthly value.

As for the captains who sailed from Plymouth in George Washington's schooners, Stephen Moylan expressed his opinion in a few choice words. "Poor Martindale . . . his vessel was not at all calculated for the service; she was fitted out at enormous expence, did nothing, and struck without firing a gun. Coit I look upon to be a mere blubber." Remembering the bothersome duo of Broughton and Selman, Moylan added reflectively, "They all are indolent and inactive souls." Moylan made one exception, adding, "Manley is truly our hero of the sea." And John Manley was one of the few reasons Washington still had faith in his schooners.[25]

🎐 8 🎐
The Last Two Schooners Out of Beverly

hen Broughton and Selman sailed out of Beverly on October 22, 1775, in *Hancock* and *Franklin,* Glover and Moylan may have toasted themselves with a cup of warm rum, but they had no reason to relax. The general had ordered four vessels outfitted for war, not two, so they still had much work to do. Glover selected the next two schooners and brought them from Marblehead to his Beverly wharf. He also picked one of the captains, John Manley, whose name, unlike those who preceded him, would not be so readily lost in anonymity.

Manley had as much salt pumping through his veins as any man who ever followed the sea, but much of his early life remains obscure. Robert E. Peabody, who spent years searching for Manley's roots, places his birth in 1733 at the village of St. Marychurch, on the outskirts of Torquay near Tor Bay in Devonshire, England. Manley adopted life at sea from boyhood and while a young man crossed the Atlantic and settled at Marblehead. On September 27, 1764, he married Martha Hickman, also of Marblehead, but according to the town's records he married using the name John Russell. If Manley had a reason for changing his name, he did not share it with the public. To confuse matters further, all his children born before 1775—at least two sons and three daughters—were also named Russell, leaving the person of John Manley an enigmatic specter who floated into the naval history of the Revolution without clear antecedents. Outside of Marblehead he used the name Manley, and when he moved his family to Boston after the war he continued to use it.[1]

Unlike other captains Washington had pulled from the ranks, Manley had not joined the army. John Glover knew the man and

Map of islands of Boston Harbor. Based on a map found in the Yale University Library.

recommended him to the general. Washington granted Manley a captaincy and assigned him to the schooner *Lee*.

At the time of his commission, Manley was about forty-two years of age and considered by most people who knew him as a rough-and-ready individual capable of making quick but sometimes unpopular decisions. His familiarity with naval discipline and gunnery gives credence to the belief that he had served in the British navy. As a young man he may have jumped ship in New England; this would explain both his name change and his resumption of the name Manley when the war started. Prior to 1775 he had become a well-established merchant skipper with an excellent reputation for honesty and hard work. Whatever name he preferred to be called by, he was exactly the type of skipper Washington needed.[2]

About the time Broughton and Selman departed for the Gulf of St. Lawrence, Glover and Moylan were hard at work fitting out and arming the 74-ton *Two Brothers* and the 64-ton *Hawk* at Beverly. Thomas

Stevens of Marblehead owned *Two Brothers,* which he sailed to Beverly on October 12, 1775, for her conversion to *Lee.* Glover immediately started work, ordering what had now become standard modifications to her rigging and deck. Another Marbleheader, John Twisden, owned *Hawk* and brought her into Beverly the following day. Renamed *Warren,* she would be commanded by Winborn Adams. Both vessels characterized the typical short, bulky design of the day with large holds and a wide deck. Moylan and Glover leased each vessel at the going rate of 5s. 4d. per ton per month.

Unlike Manley, Winborn Adams came from the ranks, highly recommended by Brig. Gen. John Sullivan, commander of New Hampshire's troops. Adams's background is obscured by dozens of genealogists who, working with poor records, erroneously mingled his name with the many Adamses associated with the Revolution. He was about forty-five years old when he took command of *Warren,* having spent most of his career as a master working out of Durham, across the bay from Portsmouth. In December 1774 he participated in the seizure of military stores at Fort William and Mary in Portsmouth Harbor. Soon afterward, Sullivan commissioned him captain of the first company of volunteers raised at Durham—among the first from New Hampshire to join the Continental Army.

On October 12, Jonathan Glover and Edward Fettyplace, chairman of Marblehead's Committee of Safety, appraised *Two Brothers* at £315 8s., about par for schooners of her size. They thought *Hawk* a better, although smaller, vessel and rated her value at £340 10s. Washington wanted a schooner to sea quickly, so Glover and Moylan concentrated their resources on fitting out *Lee.* This decision was influenced by the availability of the crew from *Hannah,* which had rejoined Glover's regiment. Thinking the schooner would be salvaged, Broughton and Selman had recruited new crews, but *Hannah* was out of the war.[3]

Modifications to *Lee* progressed more rapidly than work on *Warren,* in part because *Lee* already had a big square sail on the fore topmast. But work never progressed fast enough for Washington, and from headquarters came the message, "Every day, nay every hour is precious."[4]

To alleviate some of the pressure on themselves, Moylan and Glover asked headquarters to send Manley and Adams to Beverly to help superintend the finishing touches. Having the commanders on site would prevent another problem, Glover cautioned, citing the crews' penchant for taking unauthorized leave. "The Marblehead gentry will go home," Glover warned. "Send them off tomorrow, and we shall stand a better chance of being able to collect them on Thursday [October 26]."[5]

Glover's private stock of guns had been sorely depleted by *Hancock* and *Franklin,* but John Derby of Salem, whose brother's vessels had not yet been molested, lent Glover four 4s and two 2s for *Lee* and four 4s for *Warren.* Glover collected ten swivels for each vessel and then began a lengthy search to locate twenty rounds of ammunition for each gun. Before *Lee* or *Warren* could sail, Glover advised headquarters he needed 300 swivel shot, 40 spears, match rope, 2 signal flags, 50 pounds of chocolate, 50 pounds of coffee, and a firkin of butter. Reed assigned the collection of supplies to John Jr., the colonel's son.

Young Glover wanted his own command, but Washington considered him too young. "Perhaps another vessel," he said, and John Jr. agreed to sail on *Lee* as second in command to Manley. "The experience he will gain," Reed explained to John Sr., "will enable him to take the first command afterwards with more honour."[6] Eager to prove himself, twenty-year-old John Jr. busied himself with the chore of filling his father's grocery list.

Glover purchased most of the supplies in Cambridge, but he could not find swivel shot. Instead, he located one hundred pounds of four-ounce bullets, which he left behind. Moylan considered the oversight incredible. "Young Glover has returned without the most important article," Moylan grumbled, "the 300 swivel shot. He says there was none but he says there was plenty of four ounce bullets. If he had one ounce of sense, [he] must have known [they] would answer for all the purposes." Reed forwarded the shot; half went to Manley and half to Adams.

While collecting supplies, John Jr. tried to scavenge something else from headquarters—twenty more men for the crew of *Lee.* Washington had no idea how many men a schooner could hold and referred the request to Moylan. Annoyed that someone had meddled with his careful sizing of the crew, Moylan made inquiries and discovered that young Glover had an officer friend in camp whom he wanted to have on board. The friend agreed to come if he could bring his command. Moylan had provisioned the vessel for fifty and wanted nothing to do with twenty more. He discussed the problem with John Sr., who "chose not to interfere." Rather than create a family squabble, Moylan told young Glover "he may have his friend if he pleased," but no one else. The friend declined to leave his command.[7]

Manley's crew straggled over to Beverly after stopping, as Glover feared, for a few days' respite at their Marblehead homes. *Lee* lay idle at the wharf. "Manley's vessel is all ready," Moylan reported to Cambridge. "We now only wait the collecting together of his hopefull crew to send him off. I have declared that if there are even 30 men on board tomorrow morning & the wind proves fair that he shall hoist sail."

With delays in obtaining ammunition and supplies, *Warren* was also within a day, or two of completion. Scheduled to sail on October 27, the schooner lay beside the wharf as another day passed. Not a single marine arrived from camp. "Pray what keeps Capt. Adams and his company?" Moylan asked. "His vessel has got all her guns, provisions, etc., on board and I know there will be many things wanting which we cannot possibly think of until he comes."[8]

On October 28 carts loaded with ammunition clattered into Beverly with shot and cartridges for the carriage guns and powder and ball for the swivels. Manley collected his share and pushed off the wharf in late afternoon. He gave Glover and Moylan a quick salute as he rode the tide out of the harbor. A pine tree flag with the motto "Appeal to Heaven" fluttered defiantly from the mainmast. Off Tuck Point he lay to, waiting for morning.[9]

Glover dispatched a message to headquarters, "Capt. Manley is off & only waits a fair wind to proceed to sea," but with regard to Adams and his men from New Hampshire, he added dolefully, "We will be glad to see him soon. His vessel is ready. It is now five o'clock p.m. & no appearance of him or his men."[10]

Before Manley sailed, Glover and Moylan had intended to hold a conference with the two captains. Manley knew every inch of the coast around Cape Ann, and they wanted Adams to cruise further to the eastward, lying in the track of shipping rounding Cape Sable.[11] Broughton and Selman were supposed to be in the Gulf of St. Lawrence, and Coit and Martindale east of Boston Bay. With six vessels cruising the approaches to Boston and Quebec, Glover and Moylan hoped to intercept a valuable munitions vessel. Their strategy made sense, but they had no way of knowing that Broughton and Selman had stopped at Canso and that neither Coit nor Martindale had sailed from Plymouth.

When Adams failed to arrive they sent Manley on his way, sharing with him an important dispatch from headquarters. A transport with twelve hundred barrels of powder had departed England without a convoy and had not arrived at Boston. General Howe feared the shipment had fallen into the hands of the rebels, but Washington knew better. Unless Broughton and Selman had captured the vessel, which His Excellency doubted, she was still out there. When Manley cast off Glover's Wharf and headed out of the harbor, Moylan's words probably rang in his ears, "That would be a glorious prize indeed."[12]

Since October 25 Moylan and Glover had watched for the arrival of Adams and his volunteers from New Hampshire. The men were to come from General Sullivan's camp at Cambridge, but Portsmouth had been threatened by enemy warships and the general had departed for home to help fortify the town. When the attack proved to be a false alarm, Portsmouth's local militia drifted back to their homes, leaving the fortifications unfinished, but Sullivan remained behind to finish the work. Then came the order from headquarters to send Adams and his crew to Beverly, thereby stripping Sullivan's command of fifty of its most reliable soldiers. Sullivan ignored the order until another came on October 27 expressing urgency. He then sent word back to Cambridge to let the men go.

Adams and his privates took their time marching from Medford to Beverly, arriving on the afternoon of October 30. They crowded on board *Warren*, stowed their baggage, and looked about for elbow room. Early in the morning a fair wind filled the sails of the schooner and sent her bounding to sea. Fifty men loitered on the deck as the vessel passed Baker's Island. They talked and joked like a bunch of lads out on a frolic. Two men hung from the mastheads, scanning the sea for the first white glimmer of a distant prize.

Glover and Moylan congratulated each other as they packed their bags. They had fitted out four ships and sent them off to sea in one day short of four weeks. Unlike the people who stood on the hill to watch *Warren* pass out of sight, Glover and Moylan had other work to do. They mounted their horses and rode off to Cambridge. They still had a war to fight.[13]

ON SEPTEMBER 8, 1775, twelve vessels departed St. Helens under convoy of the 44-gun HMS *Phoenix,* Capt. Hyde Parker Jr. Two transports carried a small amount of ordnance and two companies of artillery. Seven of the vessels carried supplies and provisions for the British army at Boston. Three vessels carried only ordnance stores, but one among them, the brig *Nancy*, was laden end to end and top to bottom with enough arms and military supplies to equip over two thousand troops with the best weapons manufactured in Great Britain.

A few days after the convoy sailed a gale swept through the fleet, and at night three victuallers became separated. As the convoy proceeded westward the weather worsened. Strong headwinds continued to break up the convoy, scattering vessels all over the northern Atlantic. The pack grew smaller, but Parker stayed with it, occasionally circling out of sight to look for strays.

After the storm passed, Parker had the sea to himself. For a day or two he cruised about looking for the convoy. The transport *Charming Nancy*, with two companies of artillery, and *Williamson*, an ordnance vessel, had been blown to the north and passed Cape Ann on November 8. On November 9, as Parker headed for Boston, he finally sighted them but could not locate the others.[14]

Graves worried about the missing convoy and dispatched the 20-gun *Mercury*, Captain Graeme, to look for it. Graeme, who had just arrived from a short cruise along the coast, had not seen a ship. "Go out again," Graves ordered, "and keep the sea a fortnight longer for their protection."[15] The admiral had not heard from *Nancy*, but General Howe told him she must be found. Unfortunately, petty differences existed between Graves and Howe, and the admiral considered the missing *Nancy* more an incident than an emergency.

Late on November 9 another ordnance vessel—the brig *Juno*—made Nantasket Road in a rainstorm, followed by two more of the victuallers, but as they came to anchor another gale whipped out of the northwest and blew fiercely all night. A week passed before more of the convoy dribbled into the bay, the worrisome *Nancy* still conspicuous by her absence. Graves began to fear the worst. He sent out *Hinchinbrook* and *Nautilus* and on November 18 added *Canceaux* to the search. When *Fowey* straggled into the Road from Halifax, Graves sent her back to sea. If *Nancy* had been taken by a privateer, Graves wanted every rebel vessel eradicated from the coast of New England. His orders were clear: "You are to take, sink, burn and destroy all pirates and rebels you meet with, and seize and bring to Boston all merchant ships and vessels belonging to any of the colonies either bound to or from the Continent." For Graves the cat-and-mouse game had ended, with the consequence that Coit and his schooner got chased to Barnstable and *Washington* fell victim to *Fowey.* Too many British warships ranged offshore.[16]

Graves did not know that Adm. Molyneux Shuldham was at sea and on his way from London to replace him. Had Graves overcome his remarkable indolence a few weeks earlier, his recall may have been delayed. His fighting spirit, dampened by worn-out crews manning vessels in need of repairs, had germinated too late. He never considered Washington's siege of Boston more than a nuisance, and he never understood why first Gage and then Howe tolerated it. His wake-up call had come with word of the missing *Nancy.* Wherever she was, he must find her.

Graves had been at war for nearly eight months, but he mistook it for a foolish rebellion of a few mutinous New Englanders who would eventually exhaust themselves and pray forgiveness from the king. Graves, an unreconstructible despot, was wrong, and because he was also lazy, pompous, and unimaginative, his war was nearing an end.

Capt. John Manley's war, however, had just begun.

❧ 9 ❧
Manley Sets the Stage

O n the morning of October 29, John Manley weighed anchor, passed Baker's Island, and set a course for Cape Ann. For two days he drilled the crew, and when he found the right men to man *Lee*'s guns he changed course, working slowly to the south. Ranging off Boston Harbor on November 1, a northeaster forced him into Plymouth. Ephraim Bowen, who had worried over Martindale's extravagances in fitting out *Washington*, rowed out to examine *Lee*. "Since seeing her," he declared, "I have been very happy, as I thought before that the expence Capt. Martindale was at would be disliked by the general."[1]

For three days neither Manley nor Coit could clear for sea. The two captains chatted with each other and decided to cruise together. On the evening of November 3 the northeaster died, and the next morning *Lee* and *Harrison* cleared for Alderton Point. Coit struck a shoal, and Manley went on alone. He did not have time to waste on bad sailing.[2]

At dusk Manley crossed Boston Harbor, skirting Deer Island. He could see the crosstrees of Graves's warships idle at anchor. At dark he stood off Nahant Bay, keeping well to sea. Since leaving Plymouth he had not seen a single sail, but his first prize was about to be arranged for him by HMS *Cerberus*, Captain Symons.

In the light airs of early morning on November 5, Symons stopped and boarded the sloop *Ranger*, William McGlathry, master, off Piscataqua lighthouse. The vessel carried an inexpensive cargo of wood, a valuable commodity to His Majesty's regulars facing the chilly onset of winter. Symons removed part of the crew and replaced them with a midshipman, two marines, and four sailors. The prizemaster came about and headed for Boston.[3]

On November 6, working toward Cape Ann, *Lee*'s lookouts spotted the captured sloop. Manley scanned the vessel and ordered all hands. The speedy *Lee* closed on *Ranger* and came quickly abeam. Manley spoke to McGlathry, who was still on board and feeling stress. With a British pistol shoved against his ribs, McGlathry replied he was bound for Gloucester, perhaps hoping Manley had a keen enough eye to notice the vessel was beyond that point. The ploy worked and Manley dispatched a boarding party. John Glover Jr. bounded over the bulwarks and confronted a disgruntled midshipman, who gave up his pistol without a fight. Manley transferred the prisoners to *Lee* and sent *Ranger* into Marblehead.[4]

The recaptured *Ranger* should have gone back to McGlathry, but because of the absence of libeling courts Marblehead agent Jonathan Glover laid up the vessel, sold off the wood, and awaited a decision. Washington used the capture as a reminder to Hancock that a legal mechanism needed to be established to adjudicate prizes, "for I cannot spare time from military affairs to give proper attention to these matters." The overall problem of prize disposition was about to expand, as privateers were going to sea. Expecting no response from Congress, Washington asked Glover to settle the compensation between Manley and McGlathry amicably, as he wanted no "further trouble about her."[5]

Glover must have imposed heavy demands for Manley's compensation, as the Salem Committee of Safety begged relief from "hard terms." Evidently, the vessel and her cargo were worth little more than Glover's proposed settlement, from which, of course, he received a commission. On November 11 Glover released the vessel at Washington's request with accounts to be settled later.[6]

On November 6, after leaving *Ranger* in the care of a prize crew, Manley cruised between Marblehead and Cape Ann. Two days later, as *Lee* routinely passed Misery Island, the watch spotted a schooner lying off the entrance to Beverly Harbor. By the vessel's actions, Manley could not determine whether the skipper intended to go inside or whether he was confused and looking for landmarks. Manley wanted a closer look, and Robert Robbins, master of the schooner *Two Sisters,* observed *Lee* approaching and headed down the coast toward Beverly.

A small crowd of observers collected on shore, and when *Lee* gave chase fifteen armed and opportunistic fishermen piled into a boat and rowed out to intercept the schooner. The fishermen arrived first and jumped aboard *Two Sisters*. When *Lee* edged alongside, they gave her a snub and claimed the prize for themselves. Manley came about and headed back to sea. Entitlement to the prize could wait until later.

Two Sisters had sailed from Ireland on September 24, laden for Boston with beef, tongues, butter, potatoes, and eggs. Robbins carried a packet of correspondence he neglected to toss overboard. Eight vessels carrying five fresh regiments had departed for Boston six weeks ago. Included in the correspondence, the fishermen found an official-looking document from George III, his August 23 *Proclamation for Suppressing Rebellion and Sedition* among the colonists. By spring the king planned to build his army to 22,500 men.

When the fishermen brought the prize to Beverly, William Bartlett attempted to perform his agency duties by impounding the vessel and cargo, securing the papers, and confining the prisoners. The fishermen refused. What they captured they kept. Bartlett appealed to Washington, who, no matter how hard he tried, could not extricate himself from naval affairs. "When she came in," Bartlett wrote, "I made a demand for her papers, etc., but the people refused me. As I am willing and desirous to live in peace with all men, [I] should be extremely glad if your Excellency would give me some particular direction . . . for if I have no power to make such demands, I make myself appear ridiculous to the eye of the world, which is far from being my desire."[7]

Moylan took a squad to Beverly, retrieved the papers, and rode back to Cambridge for a joint meeting of Washington's generals. The king had declared war on his colonies. No longer should it be necessary for the armed schooners to be selective in their captures. Any vessel flying the British flag was fair game. When the meeting ended, Washington sent the letters by express to Hancock, carried by none other than Paul Revere. The general enclosed a brief message, asking Hancock to take the matter before Congress, "who will now see the absolute necessity . . . of exerting all their wisdom to withstand the mighty efforts of our enemies."[8]

Moylan responded to Bartlett's question of entitlement to *Two Sisters*, but he did not resolve the matter. He warned that if the prize became a nuisance to the general, Bartlett should have nothing to do with her. However, if Manley held a valid claim to the vessel, Bartlett must take her, but "if it is not very apparent, don't you trouble yourself or the General with a litigious dispute. . . . get rid of the trouble in the best manner you can, and let us hear nothing further thereon."⁹

Manley settled the issue in his own manner. On November 9, sailing out of Marblehead, he sighted a convoy of twenty vessels bound for Boston and laden with firewood trimmed from the shores of Penobscot Bay. *Lively* hovered nearby, herding the slow-moving fleet together.¹⁰ Manley stayed close to the convoy's heels, picking off a small schooner east of the Boston lighthouse. Her master claimed he was bound for Newburyport with a cargo of lumber but, lacking a pilot, had lost his bearings. Manley remained doubtful and took the schooner into Marblehead. Glover took possession of her and sent the skipper and a passenger to Cambridge to present their case to Washington.¹¹

The general took half an hour away from his military duties and ordered the vessel released. "Manley is not to blame for taking the schooner," Moylan wrote, "she was in a suspicious place." Fearing that Manley might be falling into the same annoying habits as Broughton and Selman, Moylan confided to Glover that he hoped Manley would "soon send in some prize that will be of more consequence to you and the public."¹²

During *Lee*'s stop at Marblehead, Glover informed Manley that Beverly's fishermen refused to give up *Two Sisters*. Manley sailed to Beverly to repossess the vessel and, if necessary, move her to Marblehead and turn her over to Glover. Bartlett pleaded against such an action, promising that *Lee* would be credited with the prize. Bartlett explained that he and Glover had formed a partnership wherein they would assist each other and share equally in the interests of any vessel sent into Marblehead or Beverly.¹³ Manley drew up his claim and handed it to Bartlett, who sent it to headquarters. The fishermen complained over the loss of their prize money, and Robert Robbins, master of *Two Sisters*, was released on a £500 bond allowing him to go at large throughout the colony provided he stayed away from Boston.¹⁴

Bad weather kept Manley at Beverly for a week. When he sailed, signs of winter hung heavy over the ocean. Gray clouds scudded overhead, spitting rain and snow, with seldom a ray of sunshine to give warmth and color to the shortened days. Marines huddled around the small stove in the smoky hold as the schooner bobbed and creaked under short sail. Seven days passed and men grumbled, but Manley kept them busy working down the coast toward Boston Harbor. The monotony broke on November 27 with a cry from the masthead, "Sail, ho!"

Manley sailed into Boston's main shipping channel to intercept the 80-ton sloop *Polly,* S. Smith, master. Laden with freshly dug Nova Scotia turnips and a chest of Spanish milled dollars, Manley observed from her papers that she was irrefutably "in the Ministerial service." Certain *Lee* had been sighted from Boston, he sent *Polly* into Beverly and headed north to cruise off Nahant.[15]

Weeks earlier Washington had looked disconsolately at his ragged volunteers and noted that "a fortunate capture of an ordnance vessel would give new life to camp, and an immediate turn to the issue of the campaign." His powder was weak from age and exposure and his cannons few. He had no bayonets other than relics from the Seven Years War, and muskets ranged from ancient blunderbusses to Pennsylvania rifles. By late November, capturing a munitions vessel had become a forlorn hope, but when word leaked out of Boston that Graves had his fleet looking for a missing ordnance brig, Washington dispatched the information on a fast horse to Beverly.[16] "If either the *Lee* or the *Warren* are in port," Moylan wrote, "it is his Excellency's expressed orders they put to sea as soon as possible and keep a sharp lookout for this brig." Manley and Adams were both at sea. Neither got the message, but Manley got the brig.[17]

After capturing *Polly,* Manley cruised off Boston, keeping well out to sea. He had confidence in *Lee's* ability to outrun Graves's warships, and late afternoon on the 28th the lookout sighted a big brig standing to windward.

"All hands," Manley ordered. "We'll take her."

If the brig was armed, like many vessels her size, Manley courted disaster. From the distance she appeared to carry a peculiar apparatus amidships, pointed over her port rail and configured like a very large gun. *Lee* lay athwart her course, and Manley kept a glass to his eye as the two vessels closed. If *Lee* engaged in a running fight, the sound would carry into the harbor. The situation demanded clever tactics. He must contrive a way to capture the brig without firing a shot.

Robert Hunter, master of the 250-ton *Nancy,* unwittingly solved Manley's problem. For three weeks he had been blown up and down the eastern seaboard by the same gales confining *Lee* to port. As far back as November 8, *Nancy* had been located by *Cerberus* off Cape Cod, but headwinds stalled both vessels. *Nancy* came within five leagues of the Boston lighthouse when a gale struck and blew her out to sea. In the storm, which raged all night, *Cerberus* lost her sails and then *Nancy*.[18] After separating from *Cerberus,* Hunter fell in with *Mercury* off Cape Ann and again parted in a squall.[19] Now, at long last, an hour before nightfall, Hunter felt comfort in knowing he had finally reached the outer fringes of friendly Boston Bay. From the deck of the brig he could see the town and the clutter of shipping close inshore, but he was not familiar with the harbor. When he observed a small schooner edging toward him, he convinced himself she was a pilot. He luffed to receive her and ran up his signal flags.

Manley played the game to the end. He sent his longboat with eight armed marines, who greeted the master cheerfully, clambered on board, and with pistols cocked took possession of the prize. The manifest of military stores shocked Manley into the realization that this prize, apart from all others, must be delivered to a safe port before British warships found her. Her huge cargo of military stores lay her so low in the water that she wallowed under the weight. Manley transferred his most experienced sailors to the prize and brought the prisoners on board *Lee*. As darkness settled over Boston Bay, the two vessels stood northward for Beverly. Prevailing winds pushed the vessels to the east. Early in the morning Manley changed course and by daylight on the 29th arrived at Fresh Water Cove on the west shore of Gloucester's outer harbor.[20]

Unlike Beverly Harbor, Gloucester had not been fortified. If Manley expected to keep his prize, he must move fast. He sent an express to Cambridge with *Nancy*'s manifest and turned the prisoners over to the local Committee of Safety.

The rider located the general sipping tea at headquarters with Dr. John Morgan, the new director general of hospitals, Morgan's wife, and Gen. Horatio Gates. "What delighted me excessively," Mrs. Morgan recalled, "was seeing the pleasure which shown in every countenance, particularly General Gates; he was in ecstasy. And as General Washington was reading the invoice there was scarce an article he did not comment upon, and that with so much warmth as diverted everyone present."[21]

After a brief celebration, Washington dispatched Glover and Maj. William Palfrey on two fast horses with orders to ride to Gloucester and "raise the Minutemen and Militia of that part of the country." He ordered Palfrey to unload the cargo and waste no time removing it from Gloucester. Without an agent or an armed force in Gloucester, Washington worried as much about looting as he did the enemy. The lone platoon in Gloucester had marched to Cambridge with *Nancy's* prisoners and not returned, leaving only Manley's men to safeguard the cargo. On the way to Gloucester, Glover stopped at Salem and ordered out the Essex County Minutemen, and as he passed through Manchester he picked up a small company organized to protect the seacoast. On reaching Gloucester, he found hundreds of people milling about the waterfront and probing the contents of the captured brig.

By December 1 Glover had 450 minutemen and militia under his command, and he needed them all. When Gloucester ran out of wagons, he sent details into the countryside to impress anything on wheels. Two days later a long, heavily laden, flag-bedecked train of wagons began rolling into Cambridge.

The troops shouted their exultation. Cheer after cheer went up in camp. "The huzzas on the occasion," an officer wrote, "I dare say were heard through all the territories of our most gracious sovereign in this Province. Such universal joy ran through the whole as if each grasped victory in his hand." The British heard the cheering from across the Charles River, but a week passed before they fully understood its meaning.[22]

If Washington harbored disappointment over the absence of powder on *Nancy,* he kept it to himself. The prize netted the army 2,000 sets of muskets, bayonets, cartridge boxes, slings, 100,000 flints, 31 tons of musket shot, and 1,200 pounds of buckshot. He had just requisitioned flints, and here they were. The brig also provided 3,200 round shot for 24s, 3,000 for 12s, 4,000 for 6s, and 8,440 fuses. The balance of the cargo consisted of equipment for fielding a force of over two thousand regulars with every item from seven ammunition wagons to camp kettles and frying pans.

The odd, gunlike apparatus on *Nancy's* deck that had worried Manley turned out to be a huge 13-inch brass mortar, complete on its bed and inscribed to honor George III. An enthusiastic gunner, noticing the initials "G.R." engraved near the touch hole, chiseled out the "R" and replaced it with a "W" for Washington. When the monster went on display, everyone agreed "it was the finest piece of ordnance ever landed in America." If Washington enjoyed small ironies, he probably looked forward to bombing His Majesty's troops with a few ponderous rounds from the king's own mortar. Mortar and all, the value of the prize soared to estimates topping £30,000.[23]

General Howe admitted that if he had composed a list of ordnance for the Continental Army, he could not have added one article more. The absence of *Nancy* had put him at his "wits end" for more than ten days. The poor working relationship between Howe and Graves reached a new low when the general learned the brig's fate. On December 3 he vented his anger to Lord Dartmouth, complaining the rebels were "now furnished with all the requisites to setting [Boston] on fire, having got a large quantity of round carcasses and other stores, with which they could not have been otherwise supplied"—and all because of the navy's apathetic attitude toward the safety of His Majesty's transports. "I submit to your Lordship," Howe added, "the necessity there may be of supplying the loss of arms, flints, etc., suffered on this occasion." Treasury secretary Sir Grey Cooper confided to a friend that the "very carcasses and bombs" captured by Manley had been shipped for the purpose of burning Roxbury and Cambridge, and now the "Saints & Predestination will have it to say that the Lord hath delivered them into [the rebels'] hands." From Boston's garrison, one of Howe's subordinates agreed, adding, "and we are likely to be complimented with the contents."[24]

When Manley delivered *Nancy* to Gloucester, Graves made no effort to recover her, although another vessel entered Boston Harbor just ahead of her and reported the capture. Without ever leaving his armchair to survey New England's coastal defenses, Graves assumed the prize had been taken to Beverly or Marblehead and declared that fortifications there could not be passed. He drew his conclusions from "diligent enquiries" made about "Marblehead and Cape Ann harbours." He had almost lost *Nautilus* off Beverly, and since then a battery of twelve guns had been added, including two 18s. Graves claimed Cape Ann and Gloucester had been "partly fortified" and advised Howe that "the outer road is foul, narrow and greatly exposed, and a ship once in the inner road cannot get out again without a leading wind. Frigates cannot be in either," he added, "without being exposed to certain destruction."

In a puzzling bit of rhetoric, Graves named four vessels he had ordered to go into Cape Ann and Marblehead harbors and destroy every vessel they found there, but on drawing a second breath confided to

Howe he had no hope of success. The admiral never issued those orders, and the logs of the cruisers normally on station there do not indicate having received such orders. Graves's dishonesty with Howe attests to why the two men could not work together.

In another conversation with the admiral, Howe suggested a blockade of the Marblehead-Salem-Beverly area and of the Cape Ann–Gloucester area. Graves disliked the idea of his warships lying constantly off some port. He countered by suggesting the army "destroy both towns as soon as possible" rather than camp in their Boston barracks and do nothing. Graves knew Howe could not fight his way out of Boston. An attack on Gloucester would require naval support, and Graves had already stated the inability of his vessels to navigate in the "foul" inner and outer roads. He concluded his reply by recommending that Howe take a thousand men and seize Cape Ann. The harbors, he argued, would then be theirs. Howe took the suggestion for what it was—Graves's excuse for doing nothing.[25]

Graves received criticism from a captain on an English transport, who complained to his London owners of poor cooperation from the Boston fleet. He had just come to the end of a horrible crossing where the "sea continually washed over us, and froze so excessively hard, that had it not been for our masts, we might have been taken for an island of ice." After being buffeted up and down the coast for three weeks by contrary gales, the captain finally made Boston and wrote home of ten British warships snugged in the bay, but when he asked for guidance into the harbor from an outbound frigate no ship would help. "At last I got a pilot from Boston," he complained, "who tells me that a ship with ordnance stores is taken by the Rebels, and that likewise, several coal and porter ships are taken which I find, now, to be likely, for there are only eight sail of the forty arrived yet, and they had no force to resist."[26]

An observer writing from Halifax to a friend in London had the admiral pegged pretty well. "Graves seems very well contented, being boomed in to keep the whale boats from taking him, as well as a large number of ships round him, to keep off the Marblehead fishermen, whilst the coasts of N.E. are ravaged by two mast[ed] boats and other craft."[27]

Lord Sandwich blamed the loss of *Nancy* on her captain. "She went from England under convoy," he declared, "parted company at sea, was then picked [up] by another frigate on the coast who took charge of her, parted from her also, and then suffered herself to be taken, most probably on purpose." Washington may have added substance to Sandwich's theory when he generously released Hunter and his crew and ordered their personal property returned, asking that "they be treated with all humanity" and permitting them to live on board *Nancy* "until further orders." The "further orders" had less to do with the disposition of the prisoners than with disposition of the prize, as the general still waited on Congress to establish libeling courts.[28]

In a report to the Admiralty, Graves concocted his own excuse, blaming the recent tempestuous weather. He reminded his superiors that during the winter, "prevailing winds [are] S E and N W, hard gales each way, and with the former thick weather, rain, snow, and ice without a friendly port to push for except Boston. . . . In this situation our cruisers have been greatly harassed to prevent being wrecked or blown off the coast." He kept ships at sea only "at a great risque . . . to protect the transports, victuallers, storeships and other vessels coming in with supplies. Notwithstanding our utmost endeavors to the contrary, *Nancy* had been taken by the rebels." In his lamentations, the admiral condemned whoever sent "a cargo of such consequence . . . from England in a vessel [so] destitute of arms even to protect her from a rowboat."

Sandwich's idea of putting a naval officer on board munitions-laden transports probably came from Graves. The notion that *Nancy* had been deliberately delivered to the colonists also came from Graves, who suggested that the pilot was an American who "betrayed the master or enticed him" to surrender the vessel "with the promise of great rewards."[29]

On December 8, 1775, Loyalist Peter Oliver Jr. wrote from Boston to former Massachusetts governor Thomas Hutchinson in London his assessment of the navy's failures. Oliver also suggested treachery in the capture of *Nancy:* "To send an ordnance brig of such value out so poorly manned and armed looks very odd. We have 8 or 10 pirate vessels out between the Capes, and yet our men-of-war are chiefly in the harbour. Two thirds of the troop and provision vessels are [yet] out . . . we expect they will be taken, many of them."[30]

Oliver's prediction had been fulfilled a week before he made it. When Glover took possession of *Nancy* on December 1, Manley recalled his prize crew and sailed back to sea before his men became too accustomed to public praise. More transports were on the way, and Manley knew exactly where he would find them—right under the drooping eyelids of Admiral Graves and his weary warships.

✺ 10 ✺
Manley Strikes and Graves Falls

hile Graves complained about the weather and made excuses for his idle warships, Manley sailed from Gloucester on November 30 and set a course for Boston Bay. In contrast to the grumbling crews of *Washington* and *Harrison,* men on board *Lee* envisioned great wealth. Moylan, now performing the function of Washington's secretary, wrote to Watson on December 1, predicting that the men of *Lee* "will make their fortunes by Manley's activity."[1] About the time the ink dried on Moylan's letter, the lookout on *Lee* sighted a large vessel bending toward Boston Harbor.

The 300-ton ship *Concord,* four times the size of *Lee,* had been at sea for eleven weeks.[2] Storms and contrary winds had blown her up and down the coast for half that time. James Lowrie, her master, studied an approaching schooner through his glass. He stood toward her, anxious to reach Boston before the next gale blew him back to sea. Like the skipper of *Nancy,* he expected a pilot boat. By the time he discovered his error, Manley's armed marines had clambered on board and taken possession of the ship.

Determining ownership of the cargo created a dilemma for Manley. *Concord* carried clothing and coal shipped from Glasgow by Crawford, Anderson and Company of Greenock to Boston merchant James Anderson. Washington's orders still excluded from capture vessels not employed by the ministerial government, although a resolution was pending in Congress to include any vessel flying British colors. Technically, the privately employed *Concord* enjoyed exemption from capture. Her cargo, however, would bring great comfort to the enemy during the harsh winter months ahead. Manley continued to scan a packet of documents taken from the ship. As he searched he found letter after letter condemning the rebellion and promising future employment of *Concord* on behalf of the king. Manley could neither release the vessel nor be confident she was a fair prize, but he could detain her. He took off her crew and escorted *Concord* into Marblehead.

Jonathan Glover rowed out to the vessel, inspected the documents, and ordered her around to Beverly. The prizemaster lacked knowledge of the harbor and ran *Concord* aground. The vessel was unharmed, but the accident settled the problem of the cargo. To get her off the shoal she had to be lightened, and the men removed everything but the coal. Glover possessed enough "Yankee ingenuity" to have colluded with the prizemaster to put her aground, but conspiracies such as these seldom get into the records.[3] Glover promised the general he would "take all the care of the ship & cargo possible" until final disposition could be made.[4]

Washington studied *Concord*'s baffling documents and referred the matter to Congress. The general found many letters confirming that the cargo "was for the use of the Army," but the manifest clearly designated as consignee the shipper and owner, James Anderson, a captain in the Loyal Scotch Americans. "Every letter on board," Washington wrote Hancock, "breathes nothing but enmity to this Country, and a vast number of them there are." Here was another prize, he warned, with a cargo worth £3,600, waiting for Congress to authorize admiralty courts. *Concord* was new and suitable as a cruiser. Was she to be wasted and permitted to rot? Urging immediate action on the matter, he asked, "Pray what is to be done with this ship and cargo?"[5]

Moylan read the letters and expressed himself with less reserve. "What is really extraordinary," he told Reed, is that every letter breathes "enmity, death and destruction to this fair land, G-d damn them."[6]

The capture of *Concord* and her bundle of abusive letters prompted Congress to declare that "all transport vessels having on board any troops, arms, ammunition, clothing, provisions, or military or naval stores of what kind soever . . . and all vessels employed in carrying provisions or other necessaries to the British Army . . . shall be liable to seizure, and, with their cargoes, shall be confiscated." The resolution gave Washington's agents more latitude to dispose of captured prizes, but it still failed to provide for a court system where issues of ownership could be legally contested.[7] Bartlett, however, ignored pending battles over ownership and sent twenty-four casks of shoes and several bales of blankets, linens, and clothing to Cambridge.[8]

Lt. Col. Robert Hanson Harrison, who questioned *Concord's* prisoners, learned that five of them wished to enlist in the service of
Washington's armed schooners. The frugal Scots observed that if captains like Manley could nab prizes as easily as he captured *Concord,* there
must be lots of money for those serving with the rebels. Washington
approved the plan but advised against mustering them all on the same
vessel.[9]

After delivering *Concord* to Glover, Manley wasted no time in
returning to sea. On December 9 he sailed back to his self-appointed
post off Boston Bay and waited for the next transport to show her topsails above the eastern horizon. If he thought the 300-ton *Concord* big,
his eyes must have popped out when the 400-ton ship *Jenny,* Robert
Foster, master, ranged into sight. He let her approach, posing once again
as a friendly pilot coasting five leagues off the bay to guide His Majesty's
transports safely into Boston. *Jenny* carried two 6s, but by the time
Foster discovered the deception Manley's men had grappled onto the
prize and taken possession of the deck.

Seven weeks earlier Foster had sailed from London with a packet of
secret signals and instructions from Britain's treasurer to "not go into
Boston until you shall meet with some of his Majesty's ships who can
conduct you in."[10] As Foster approached the coast he expected to find a
small vessel lying off Boston Bay, but he did not expect her to be the
enemy. Discovering his error, Foster recalled his instructions and tossed
the signal book and papers, weighted by six blunderbusses, over the side.
The papers followed the guns to the bottom, but the signal book floated free. Two days later a beachcomber found it onshore.[11]

While the prize crew inspected *Jenny's* cargo, Robert Adams, master of the 140-ton brig *Little Hannah,* sailed into sight after a long voyage from Antigua and noticed Manley's schooner standing abeam an
English transport. Adams made the mistake of assuming *Lee* a tender
and sailed over for assistance. *Little Hannah* carried two 2s, which
Adams never gave a thought to loading. Manley obliged Adams's request
for a pilot by sending over a boatload of marines. With two fat prizes in
his clutches, Manley trumpeted sailing orders and struck a course for
Beverly.

Both vessels carried huge cargoes intended for the British garrison.
Jenny's invoice listed 186 cauldrons of coal, 100 casks of porter, 439
bushels of potatoes, and 40 live hogs.[12] *Little Hannah's* lading was for the

benefit of Graves's sailors and consisted mostly of intoxicants—139 hogsheads of rum, 96 cases of geneva, and 123 gallons of spirits. A few bags of cocoa, a cask of oranges, and numerous other delicacies had been squeezed on board by former Boston Tories as a present to deposed General Gage. Bartlett moved the goods into storage and wrote headquarters for instructions.

Stephen Cabot, a volunteer from Beverly, carried an express to Cambridge announcing Manley's double capture. The house where Washington lived was in turmoil when the messenger arrived. The general's wife and servants were expected on December 11. Extricating himself from the commotion, His Excellency absorbed the news cheerfully, read Bartlett's report, and scanned the list of delicacies captured on *Little Hannah*. He made a few notations and passed the list to Moylan, who wrote Bartlett, "There are limes, lemons & oranges on board, which being perishable, you must sell immediately—the general will want some of each, as well as the sweetmeats and pickles . . . as his Lady will be here today or tomorrow. Will you please pick up such things on board as you think will be acceptable to her & send them as soon as possible."

Moylan also condemned Foster for throwing his papers overboard. "He deserves to be severely punished. In any other war than the present, he would suffer death for such an action." Having cast out these harsh feelings, Moylan asked Bartlett to treat the prisoners with "tenderness" to show them "Americans are humane as well as brave."

At times Moylan issued confusing instructions, and agents like Bartlett and Glover often puzzled over their orders from headquarters. Bartlett held thirty prisoners from Manley's four prizes and asked Moylan for instructions. Moylan first suggested confining the prisoners to the captured vessels, "but don't run the least risk of their doing mischief by so many being together." Then he suggested they be confined in some "inland town" and left in the care of the Committee of Safety. His third option was to give them paroles. Two weeks later Bartlett still held the prisoners under guard at Beverly. Unable to decide what Moylan really wanted, he sent them all to Cambridge.[13]

Satisfying Martha Washington's palate from captured stores became a perplexing chore for Bartlett, who had acquired possession of over a thousand tons of arms, dry goods, provisions, wines, liquors, and livestock. Jonathan Glover helped him sift through the cargoes, posting a journal entry for every transaction. Four days later, December 14, Bartlett forwarded to Cambridge three casks of porter, a barrel of lemons, two cases of wine, one barrel of tea, a barrel of oranges, a keg of sweetmeats, a box of pickles, four loaves of sugar, and his compliments.[14]

When the cart rolled up to the door of Mrs. Washington's kitchen, she eyed the barrels and kegs with disdain and complained to the general. The fruit looked nothing like the plump, fresh articles back home. Moylan, who had arranged for the transfer of delicacies, absorbed the complaints and passed them on to Bartlett. The barrel of lemons arrived not half full, he wrote, and a barrel of loaf sugar had disappeared in shipment. Mrs. Washington would have preferred the porter in bottles rather than casks, Moylan added, forgetting that Bartlett's agency did not include bottling facilities. Finally, he scolded Bartlett for not forwarding the preserved ginger the general had noticed on *Little Hannah*'s invoice.[15]

Two passengers stopping at Cambridge to obtain paroles informed the general that cargoes at Beverly were being pilfered by the crews and then opened to crowds of people lingering at the wharf. This explained the missing loaves of sugar and the half barrel of lemons. The general collared Moylan and in a few curt words demanded the looting stopped. "The General was much surprised at the rapacity of the crews in stripping the prizes of every little thing they could lay their hands upon," Moylan noted angrily to Bartlett. "It is . . . his positive command that you make strict enquiry for the different articles which have been taken, & such as can be got returned to the proper owners." He ordered Bartlett to deduct the value of stolen goods from the shares of the pillagers, and "if they cannot be found out, it must be a charge of one third . . . to the captors." Moylan closed with the customary reminder that His Excellency expected strict attention to this order, as he did not want to be "plagued with any more applications of this sort."[16]

One passenger informed the general his personal effects and those of the crew had been confiscated. Moylan demanded every article be returned and receipts obtained. The crews, however, had been sent to Cambridge. Two weeks passed, and Bartlett did not know where to forward the dunnage. The men are here, Moylan replied. "They are in very dirty condition. Send up the baggage immediately."

In January Manley's prisoners arrived with their baggage in Worcester. The Committee of Safety issued paroles and set them free.

They were given the option of remaining in the colonies, and many found work and decided to stay.[17]

Manley belonged at sea, not meddling in the affairs of the agents. He retrieved his crew and sailed back to Boston Bay. The weather soured, but he kept the crew occupied cruising offshore. Rumor circulated of *Washington's* capture. He did not want his crew contemplating the same dismal fate. So far they had been lucky, but, like the weather, luck could change.

Manley never considered luck a factor, and on December 18, the first good sailing day in a week, he captured the 60-ton sloop *Betsey*, laden with foodstuffs, a gift from Virginia's Royal Gov. Lord Dunmore to the British cavalry at Boston. Midshipman John Atkinson of HM sloop *Otter* commanded the vessel and carried five passengers of far more value than the cargo. Moses Kirkland, a Tory colonel, held a bundle of confidential letters for General Howe. From his plantation in South Carolina, Kirkland had enlisted three hundred slaves and convicts to raid the farms of his rebel neighbors but had been driven out. Dunmore advised him to go to Boston and apply to Howe for a commission. Kirkland forgot to toss the incriminating papers overboard when Manley's prize crew came bounding over the bulwarks.

The other four passengers were prisoners Dunmore intended to ship to London for interrogation. Capt. Thomas Matthews had lost his freedom defending Norfolk; William Robinson, a delegate to the Virginia Assembly, had been snatched at his home during a raid; and two shipmasters, William Deane and Oliver Porter, had been captured by a British tender off the coast of North Carolina and charged by Dunmore with smuggling salt, rum, and gunpowder.

Manley sent the prize to Beverly, adding to the numerous hulls already in Bartlett's custody. John Glover, stopping on his way to headquarters, marched the prisoners to Cambridge. Washington read the documents and expressed them to Hancock. Thirty letters, now weeks old, had come from as far south as St. Augustine. They contained detailed plans for a British attack on Charleston, South Carolina. Another bit of news concerned John Stuart, British Indian agent for the southeastern colonies. Stuart had been arming the Indians and encouraging atrocities against the scattered inland farms. The war in the north showed signs of moving south.

Washington had not seen his Virginia plantation for many months and took more than a casual interest in Dunmore's schemes, which, he told Hancock, "are fully laid open in these letters. I need not point out to Congress," he added, "the necessity there is . . . to dispossess his Lordship of the strong hold he has got in Virginia. I do not mean to dictate, but I am sure they will pardon me for giving them freely my opinion, which is that the fate of America . . . depends on [Dunmore] being obliged to evacuate Norfolk this winter." Regarding Kirkland, "I have [him] well secured," Washington declared. "By most of the letters relative to him, he is a dangerous fellow."

In closing, the general added a word of praise for his favorite captain, whose capture of the diminutive *Betsey* looked small compared with the others. "Indeed these papers are of so great consequence," Washington remarked, "that I think this, but little inferior to any prize our famous Manley has taken."[18]

Under heavy guard, Kirkland and his documents reached Philadelphia at the end of December and created consternation in Congress. "The letters took up most of the day," New Jersey delegate Richard Smith reported. "South Carolina delegates pressed strongly to have the originals delivered to them." Virginia demanded a copy, as William Robinson, one of their own delegates, had been a prisoner on board *Betsey*. Instead, the letters were referred to a committee of five for recommendations. Robinson, along with Captain Matthews, had accompanied Kirkland to Philadelphia and received a hero's welcome from his colleagues. Kirkland's reception was less convivial. The guards marched him to the city jail.[19]

Unlike most issues pending congressional consideration, the letters received prompt attention. In 1775 the war had been mostly confined to New England. Now it threatened to expand. On January 1 Congress passed four resolutions. Two called for the capture of the garrison at St. Augustine "without delay" and "at the expence of the united colonies." The other two pertained to the defense of Charleston and several other locations in Virginia and the Carolinas targeted by the British for capture. Without the packet of letters captured by Manley, months may have passed before southern colonists recognized their vulnerability.[20]

As the first year of the war came to an end, an English soldier in Boston sent home a long letter castigating Graves. Referring to the raids of Washington's schooners and the increase of American privateering, he wrote, "We are now almost as much blocked up by the sea as we have been for these eight months by land," with transports taken "within sight of our Admiral's ship. . . . There is nothing to prevent the rebels from taking every vessel bound for this port; for though there are near twenty pennants flying in this harbour, I cannot find . . . one vessel cruising in the bay. Surely our admiral cannot be allowed to remain here much longer a curse upon the garrison."

The writer's criticism of Graves was justified. After the Battle of Bunker Hill, sick and wounded British soldiers died at an alarming rate for want of fresh provisions, but Graves did not allow a boat to fish in the harbor. In defiance of the admiral's orders, soldiers built their own boats, but Graves demanded a fishing pass be purchased from his office or he would impound the boats. "General Gage's desiring a pass was sufficient reason for a refusal," the correspondent concluded, "for the Admiral and his spouse entertained a mortal antipathy against the General and his lady." Although the general and the admiral attempted to function with an outward semblance of decorum, the wives made public capital of each other's husband's mistakes, beginning, no doubt, when Gage's regulars retreated woefully from Concord. Toward the end of summer George Gefferina, the admiral's secretary, issued a few fishing passes but charged a dollar for each, perhaps sharing the fee with the admiral.

The writer's letter appeared in the London papers on January 17, 1776, and warned, "If our sea commander is not speedily recalled no service can be expected from our fleet. He has quarrelled with the General, the army, with all his own officers except his own hangers-on . . . and with all who had any business with him." The admiral must have quarreled with his wife, also, as she grumbled that "a fit which he had on his arrival here has rendered him good for nothing."

London's *Public Advertiser* received its share of complaints from the colonies, also. "By the last letters from America we are informed that the Provincials are very successful in their naval enterprises . . . the British flag has already received every sort of insult; some of our vessels being almost daily taken under the eyes of the fleet."[21]

On December 10, one day after Manley captured *Jenny* and *Little Hannah*, Graves ordered his frigates to cruise between Cape Ann and Cape Cod. During this period bad weather kept Manley away from his usual hunting grounds. About the time the weather cleared and Manley captured *Betsey*, Graves's fleet returned to Boston Harbor empty-handed.[22]

Molyneux Shuldham, rear admiral of the White, arrived at Boston in the 50-gun *Chatham* on December 30 to take command of His Majesty's Royal Navy in North America. Graves, a vice admiral, considered it undignified to be replaced by a junior officer "who had not a flag" when Graves came to America. The deposed admiral believed Shuldham should have come to aid him, not replace him. His self-esteem received another blow when he noticed Shuldham's orders dated from September 29—three months earlier—and he had not received the slightest intimation "from the Admiralty or any part of the Government" of dissatisfaction with his performance.[23]

Evidently Graves did not possess the ability to recognize criticism when couched in the verbiage of the day, except when expressed by his army antagonists. Nevertheless, he concealed his indignation and attempted to suppress his resentment. He credited himself "with the merit of unusual activity and circumspection . . . having anticipated and exceeded every order that came to him."

Graves felt rejected, and the pain stabbed like a sharp knife inserted into his bloated ego. No one in the Admiralty understood his problems. Seamen were sick, and their misery and hardships added to his own self-pity. He seemed unable to cope with the problems around him. Washington's schooners had embarrassed him, Gage and Howe had irritated him, and now Shuldham had replaced him. Graves believed no one in London understood his problems or cared about them. His fleet had been battered about by winter storms. Every vessel needed repairs. The storms were so severe, he wrote, that "it cannot be looked against, and by the snow freezing as fast as it falls, baffles all resistance, for the blocks become choked, the tackle incrusted, the ropes and sails quite congealed, and the whole ship before long one cake of ice." As Graves became depressed, his problems became insurmountable.

Some members of Parliament sympathized with the fallen admiral and laid the naval problems on Lord Sandwich. They asked whether Graves had ever received "positive orders" he did not obey. Sandwich had enemies in Parliament who accused him of issuing instructions "so artfully discretional" that any misfortune among the fleet could be "laid upon the admiral." Was Graves's reputation as an officer to be sacrificed, they asked, "to shelter the wicked proceedings of these ministers?" Evidently so, because Sandwich remained unmoved by the debate.

Jonathan Sewall, a Loyalist and former attorney general of Massachusetts, expressed the public's attitude toward Graves. From London he wrote to a friend in Boston: "I am out of all patience at hearing, from you & others, the accounts of your sufferings. What excuse can be found for a British Admiral, who with 30 or 40 ships under his command, suffers a garrison to starve though surrounded with plenty of every necessary within the reach of his ships, [and] who tamely & supinely looks on & sees fishing schooners, whale-boats and canoes riding triumphant under the muzzles of his guns, & carrying off every supply destined for your relief."[24]

Sewall's missive was typical of the flow of complaints pouring into the Admiralty from the numerous letter bags crossing from Boston. For some reason, Graves neither understood the number of his growing enemies nor accepted the responsibility for provisioning Howe's besieged garrison.

Perhaps to give himself time to heal his pride, Graves retained his command for nearly a month—until January 27—before officially relinquishing it to Shuldham. For six days he languished on board *Preston*, rocking in Boston Harbor, and on February 2, having no business to detain him longer, sailed for London. George Washington's schooners and fishing passes for Howe's hungry garrison were no longer his problems.[25] And Shuldham, after two weeks in Boston, began sending messages to the Admiralty that sounded like replicas of those scratched from the pen of his London-bound predecessor.[26]

Neither Sandwich in faraway London nor Shuldham in Boston understood the likes of John Manley. At Cambridge, Moylan made every effort to inspire other commanders to cash in on prize money by emulating Manley. His correspondence was relentless, always urging skippers to be "as attentive to their duty and interest as Manley is." Moylan expressed his praise freely, broadcasting from headquarters to all who listened, "Manley is truly our hero of the sea."[27]

But there would be others, and in time they would come.

✥ 11 ✥
The Brief Cruise of Winborn Adams

apt. Winborn Adams sailed from Beverly on the morning of October 31 and spent as much time at sea in *Warren* as Manley had spent in *Lee,* but with much different results. He cruised northeast of Cape Ann for almost two months. Manley had orders to cruise there also, as headquarters believed enemy transports would stop at Halifax before continuing on to Boston. None of them did, and when Manley realized he was wasting time he took his schooner into Boston Bay. Adams, however, followed orders and missed the scattered convoys carrying munitions and provisions.

Unlike some of Washington's other captains, Adams cared little for fancy cabins or the privileges usually conferred on masters who spent their lives at sea. He refused to carry a one-month's supply of provisions because he never expected to be gone for more than ten days at a time. On his initial cruise he rejected extra sails because he believed the old ones would do. Each time Adams stopped at Portsmouth, agent Wentworth tried—with varying success—to trickle on board those extras he considered essential to the safety of the vessel. One hard gale could shred *Warren*'s old sails and reduce her to a floating hulk with only sweeps to take her ashore, but Adams counted on his skill as a skipper to not cost the Continent a penny of extra expense.[1]

On November 1, on the way to his cruising grounds, Adams fell in with an unnamed sloop laden with wood, boarded her, and took her as a prize.[2] Her incomplete documents and Boston destination looked suspicious, and Adams sent her into Portsmouth. Wentworth, still vague about his agency duties, referred the sloop to an equally baffled New Hampshire Provincial Congress, which passed a resolution to detain the vessel until someone could decide what to do with her. Four weeks passed before the investigation ended, and on November 26 the province returned the vessel to her skipper, whom one committee member believed "to be a friend."[3]

After capturing the sloop, Adams returned to his cruising grounds off Cape Ann and doggedly battled the elements without sighting a vessel within range of *Warren's* limited pursuing capabilities. Slowed by old sails and frayed rigging, Adams hesitated to strain the vessel. Half the crew fell sick as the schooner bobbed about on a windswept sea. On November 25 only a dozen healthy marines reported on deck when lookouts reported a lone schooner. Adams stood in her path and captured the 45-ton *Rainbow,* John McMonagle, master, laden with turnips and potatoes for Boston. Nearly out of potatoes and turnips himself, Adams carried the prize into Portsmouth and turned her over to Wentworth.[4] News of Adams's conquest reached Cambridge on the heels of the express announcing Manley's capture of *Nancy.* During the celebration that followed, *Rainbow* and her turnips were nearly forgotten. In his report to Hancock praising Manley, Washington remembered Adams's capture only as an afterthought, adding a single-sentence postscript to his message.[5]

The arrival of *Rainbow's* prisoners at Cambridge served as a reminder to Moylan that Adams's prize had been overlooked. He apologized through Wentworth, saying he did not think "Adams's *bon fortune* so despicable. Though of little value to us, it is depriving the enemy of what to them would be of consequence." Moylan no longer wanted prisoners sent to Cambridge unless they brought intelligence. He wanted them deposited with the local Committee of Safety and "kept or discharged" according to the committee's wishes. Commenting on Adams's frugality, Moylan told Wentworth to supply him liberally with whatever "he calls for," adding, "I hope Adams will soon take such a prize as Manley has . . . to us it is invaluable."

Wentworth sold *Rainbow's* cargo to local interests and laid up the vessel at Portsmouth. "If a reasonable price can be got for her," Moylan declared, "dispose of her." Several days later Moylan recanted on the sale of the vessel. Congress had failed to include the disposition of prize vessels in their recent legislation.[6]

Adams spent most of his time at sea, and because of continuous exposure to storms his crew declined to thirty. After two men died, he sent the sick ashore. He apologized for asking for a new set of sails, admitting the old ones would not last much longer. He also discovered that two of his 4s could not be safely fired. Another captain would have waited for replacements, but not Adams. He gathered the remnants of his crew and headed back to sea.[7]

Bartlett questioned spending more money to repair the battered *Warren* or replace the men on the sick list, but Washington could not deny Adams's determination to cruise. The general instructed Bartlett to give Adams whatever he needed, promising to forward another twenty volunteers from the New Hampshire regiment of Col. Enoch Poor.[8]

By mid-December Adams had a full crew, but the barren waters off Cape Ann contained no prizes. During one of his trips into Beverly he spoke with Manley and learned his best chance for a prize lay right off Boston Bay. Years of sailing for others had trained Adams to follow instructions, but if Manley could disregard His Excellency's cruising directions, perhaps he could, also. With *Lee* tied to Glover's Wharf for repairs, Manley suggested Adams sail south and told him exactly where to go and what to do.

On December 23 Adams rounded Marblehead Neck and worked down the coast. The British fleet had been out for two weeks looking for Washington's schooners and had just returned to Boston for a day or two of relaxation before Christmas. Had *Warren* arrived off the lighthouse one day sooner, she would have been sighted by British warships coming to anchor inside the road. Adams waited off the lighthouse for several hours with one eye toward the harbor and the other seaward.

As the 70-ton sloop *Sally* approached landfall, Robert Basden, master's mate, probably released a grateful sigh of relief when he spotted a small schooner waiting at the lighthouse. Adams kept the men below and sailed out to meet her. As he came abeam, marines clambered out of the hold and let the grappling hooks fly. Basden surrendered without an argument. *Sally* had been captured by HMS *Niger* off Fayal in early December, but she had separated from the frigate on December 21. Basden had come off *Niger* as prizemaster with a half dozen hands.[9]

Peter Barberie of Perth Amboy, New Jersey, owned the sloop and had sent her to Lisbon, where she picked up 153 quarter casks of Portuguese wine. Her master, John Van Emburgh, had been removed from the sloop and made a prisoner on board *Niger*. Instead of a handful of common sailors, Adams captured the prize crew from the frigate.[10]

Adams carried *Sally* into Marblehead and deposited her with Jonathan Glover, a Christmas present for His Excellency. Washington, however, recognized the prize as a recapture and worried about her safety in Marblehead's exposed harbor. "If in danger, land the cargo," he wrote. Knowing the contents as well as the season, he added, "Avoid embezzlement."[11]

For Barberie, recovering his vessel required a trip to Philadelphia and a resolution from Congress, which told him to make "his claim before the court appointed, or to be appointed, by the government of the colony to which the sloop and cargo were carried." A trip to Essex County in winter to reclaim his vessel did not appeal to Barberie. Had he ridden to Massachusetts on his fastest horse, he could not have reclaimed his vessel. No courts had been appointed for him to "pray" to for the return of his property. He never visited his vessel in Beverly Harbor. For four months she lay dormant. Finally, on April 17, Judge Thomas Pickering Jr. libeled the prize and ordered the sheriff to sell the vessel and cargo "at public vendue," deducting from the proceeds his own fees and "eight pounds three shillings and a half penny" for Glover. By then the wine had aged a little longer—becoming more valuable, perhaps, than the old, weathered hull of the sloop. "Of the residue," Pickering ordered, referring to cash receipts, "you are to deliver one third part to . . . Winborn Adams and his company . . . and the other two third parts to Peter Barberie the claimant."[12]

The capture of *Sally* ended Winborn Adams's career as captain of *Warren*. The enlistments of the crew expired on December 31, and after two months of misery and no prize money they all went home. Their enthusiasm had been frostbitten by howling northeasters and numbed by ice-cold spray washing over the deck. They had watched two friends die and wanted no more. Even Adams was discouraged and in no mood for winter cruising. He had given the general his best effort, but he had failed to meet his own expectations. Adams returned to Cambridge, rejoined his Rhode Island regiment, and rose to the rank of lieutenant colonel.

As Christmas passed and the year 1775 came to a close, the grumbling of Washington's marines pervaded Beverly's sheltered harbor. Broughton's and Selman's men had led the chorus of complaints earlier in the month, infecting Adams's crew as well as Manley's. Hostility mounted. Grumbling and discontent assumed a common cry. The men felt cheated and wanted justice. Washington had lied to them. Every schooner had taken a prize, many with rich cargoes, but the men had seen nary a penny of their cherished prize money. Worse, they had not even been paid their wages.

Unlike Adams and Manley, Broughton and Selman had never captured a fair prize, and their men could not distinguish legitimacy any better than their captains. Neither Broughton nor Selman explained the difference, or perhaps never understood it. Rather than laying their disappointment on the deserving shoulders of their captains, the men blamed the general and the government for withholding their shares. Discontent spread rapidly, reaching into the ranks of the officers, and by the end of the year most of the men were gone.

On December 26 Bartlett secured the four Beverly schooners to Glover's Wharf, and at Plymouth Watson assigned a watch to the lonely *Harrison*. A few soldiers strolled on board the empty prizes and guarded the warehouses where cargoes were stored. Bartlett peddled some of the produce before it spoiled, but Washington wanted it advertised. Rules changed daily. Bartlett suspended his sales and wrote the ads, giving his perishables a few more weeks to deteriorate.[13] There had been no orders to advertise when Mrs. Washington demanded lemons, oranges, and loaves of sugar.

If Washington was not a great general, he was at least a general of great patience. After devoting four months of time, resources, and money to outfitting seven vessels, he found his key personnel reduced to one captain, John Manley. To begin the new year he had five vessels without crews, five agents with jumbled accounts, and seven prizes awaiting the creation of admiralty courts. Any other general might have liquidated the lot, cut his losses, and refocused his precious time on military matters, but not Washington. He still had five vessels, and he still had John Manley. His original idea had been sound. A Continental navy was now being built in the harbors and up the rivers of America, but the first frigate would not be ready to sail for months. He needed to keep the fight at sea alive a little while longer, carry the siege into Massachusetts Bay, and drive Howe's army out of Boston.

After Shuldham arrived, Washington expected changes. Captured letters warned of more frigates being sent from England to blockade rebel ports and stop the flow of military supplies from friendly European nations who used their colonies in the West Indies as transfer points. Already a man-of-war had parked off the entrance to Beverly and Marblehead. Washington feared a blockade. His lifeline for military supplies came from across the ocean.

On New Year's Day an officer on picket duty rode to headquarters bearing copies of King George's speech opening the October 26 session of Parliament. No longer would the rebellion be a sham war against the ministerial government. Hereafter, the war must be fought against the king himself. George III's declaration read:

> The rebellious war now levied is become more general, and is manifestly carried on for the purpose of establishing an independent empire. I need not dwell upon the fatal effects of the success of such a plan. The object is too important, the spirit of the British nation too high, the resources with which God hath blessed her too numerous, to give up so many colonies which she has planted with great industry, nursed with great tenderness, encouraged with many commercial advantages, and protected and defended at much expence of blood and treasure.
>
> It is now become the part of wisdom and (in its effects) of clemency, to put a speedy end to these disorders by the most decisive exertions. For this purpose I have increased my naval establishment, and greatly augmented my land forces; but in such a manner as may be the least burthensome to my kingdoms. . . . When the unhappy and deluded multitude, against whom this force will be directed, shall become sensible of their error, I shall be ready to receive the misled with tenderness and mercy.[14]

The king's pronouncements came as no surprise to Washington. The general replied by raising the Continent's first national flag, a circle of thirteen white stars on a blue field, with thirteen alternating stripes of red and white, one for each of the united colonies of America. As the banner unfurled, thirteen guns thundered across the hills above Boston, wasting a little of His Excellency's precious powder. The sound reverberated through the streets of the town and out across the bay. Soldiers on both sides of the general's fortifications looked into the hills, baffled by the sudden eruption. Washington had sent his unwritten reply to

King George, but as he watched enlistments expire and men pack for home, he wondered if such displays were little more than furtive acts of useless bravado. So much now depended on filling those depleted ranks.

Washington's thoughts returned to his idle schooners. They all needed repairs, some more than others, and they required good commanders. In a span of three months, twenty-five prizes had been taken, but because of Broughton's and Selman's indiscriminate plundering, thirteen vessels reverted to their owners. Washington discussed the problems with Moylan, who promised new crews could be raised.[15]

"I hope," Moylan reflected on the second day of 1776, "we shall pick out some more active men."

At dawn he climbed into his heavy wool coat, saddled his horse, and headed for Beverly. "I shall try to get some of the schooners to sea," he told the general, "while the weather continues mild."[16]

Moylan understood the general's wishes—and so did Manley. George Washington's Continental schooners still had work to do, and a sea full of His Majesty's prizes to keep them busy.

𝕸 12 𝕸
Reorganizing the Fleet

hen Moylan reached Beverly he met with Bartlett and Manley to assess the condition of the fleet. Manley suggested improvements—a new longboat for *Lee,* guns for *Warren,* and a new set of square sails for *Hancock* and *Franklin.* Some of *Franklin's* swivels had cracked, and the list of necessities—from speaking trumpets to stew pans, blunderbusses, and candle sticks—continued to grow.[1] Bartlett searched as far as Gloucester for a pair of 4s and a bank of swivels for *Warren* but found none. Privateers had stripped the countryside bare. Moylan kept a list for each schooner and compiled the cost, as Bartlett had no money.

Manley seemed in no hurry, and perhaps for good reason. Foul weather slowed work on the schooners, and ice formed in the harbor. Another hazard, HMS *Fowey,* camped a league or two offshore. The warship was no stranger to the area. Barely a month had passed since she captured Martindale's brig off Cape Ann.[2]

Moylan brought good news to Beverly, news conceived to entice local seamen to reenlist. On December 19 Congress broadened commerce raiding, making any vessel flying the British flag "liable to seizure, and with their cargoes . . . confiscated." Under the new rules, even Broughton would have made money. Also, a graduated reward was structured for recaptures, mandating specific shares based on the value of the prize and its length of time in enemy hands. This meant more prize money for everyone.[3]

For the numerous malcontents waiting for their promised prize money, Congress also passed a resolution establishing admiralty courts. Cargoes stored in warehouses, monies received by agents from the sale of perishables, and hulls floating in the harbor could finally be adjudicated and shares distributed. Washington understood the impatience of the men and urged the agents to act swiftly in bringing prizes to trial. He felt honor bound to see the men paid and asked the agents to make distributions as soon as possible.[4]

On December 28 the Massachusetts legislature divided the colony into three districts and appointed a judge of admiralty for each. Nathan Cushing administered the Southern District, which included Plymouth and Coit's prizes. James Sullivan's Eastern District had no business to conduct because all the other prizes had been taken to Timothy Pickering Jr.'s Middle District. This arrangement promised a speedier response in determining prize money and made Colonel Glover's task of enlisting new crews a little easier. However, neither the colonel nor the men he recruited could have guessed that Pickering would waste more than three months before processing his first case.[5]

To aid his captains, Washington expanded the number of agents to five, appointing Winthrop Sargent to Cape Ann and Gloucester. When Broughton had deposited *Speedwell* at Gloucester, Safety Committee Chairman Sargent had processed the delicate matter of ownership to Washington's satisfaction and earned the agency.[6] The general instructed Sargent to keep sufficient provisions on hand to replenish the schooners but to transfer all prizes to Beverly, as Cape Ann was "not looked upon as safe." Sargent could work with Bartlett and share commissions. In addition to Gloucester and Cape Ann, the general now had agents in Plymouth, Marblehead, Beverly, and Portsmouth.

After adding Sargent, Washington expanded the agents' responsibilities in an effort to reduce the involvement of headquarters. The trial period had ended, and the hope of prizes had evolved into the expectation of more. Matters concerning the disposition of prisoners, the care and safekeeping of vessels and their cargoes, protection against theft, the sale of perishable goods, and the importance of keeping accurate inventories and disbursements were embodied in the agents' new instructions. As a carryover from his original orders, the general still wanted to know if his captains were hard at work or if guilty of any misconduct or hesitance "to proceed forthwith to sea."[7]

Before Glover recruited new crews, captains needed to be selected for the four vessels at Beverly. Every officer had quit but Manley. Only two masters remained—William Burke of *Warren* and Richard Stiles of *Hancock*. Burke had a better record than Stiles, whom Moylan considered tainted by his service with Broughton. For the other two schooners at Beverly, Glover recommended Samuel Tucker of Marblehead and Daniel Waters of Malden, both shipmates with good records. Tucker visited headquarters with a letter of recommendation from Robert Morris of the Marine Committee, and Washington was favorably impressed. Seeing Tucker's name on Glover's short list gave him enough confidence to accept both Waters and Burke, sight unseen. Stiles felt slighted but accepted the post of first lieutenant under Manley. In the shuffling of command, Manley asked for *Hancock,* perhaps at the suggestion of Stiles, who knew her sailing qualities. As senior commander, Manley had earned his choice of vessels. *Lee* reverted to Waters, Tucker took command of *Franklin,* and Burke, former master of *Warren,* became her captain.

With the recent formation of the Continental Navy, Washington received a supply of blank commissions designed for officers joining the new nation's fleet. Previously the general had simply pulled officers out of the ranks and sent them to sea with army commissions. Washington discarded the new naval forms because they subjected his commanders to orders from sources other than himself. He did not want his armed vessels tied to a congressional committee or his captains in communication with Esek Hopkins, commodore of the fleet. Washington considered Hopkins a poor choice to command the navy but kept his feelings to himself. Not wanting outside interference from anyone, he designed his own certificate of commission. Henceforth his officers were in neither the army nor the navy but subject exclusively to himself "or any future Commander in Chief."[8]

Glover worked against stiff competition as he tried to reenlist veterans. Massachusetts had passed legislation in November authorizing privateering, and the greater distribution of prize money lured seamen away from Washington's fleet. Glover attributed slow recruitment to the men's not being paid off for their past services, which was the only objection they had. "Could that be done, I apprehend they would readily engage again." But he promised the general that one way or another he would have two crews ready to sail "in a few days."

To attract recruits, Manley and Burke promised to advance a month's pay to every man enlisting for the cruise. The idea had probably been suggested by Glover as a means of meeting his "in a few days" promise to the general. The bill came to a little over £95 for *Hancock,* which carried a crew of thirty-nine officers and men. Everyone received an advance, which ranged from £8 for the captain to £2 for each marine. No provision had been made for Glover's advance-pay scheme at headquarters, where Moylan reported the treasury very low.

Authority for the schooners now rested with the Marine Committee, although the command remained with Washington. With the bureaucracy growing, wages and expenses were to be paid out of naval funds. "You must therefore wait," Moylan told Bartlett, "until a remittance comes from Philadelphia." Moylan wanted the advance revoked unless men enlisted for a full year. On further reflection he envisioned the men promptly decamping to their former occupations and advised Bartlett, "If it will retard the sailing of the vessels, I wish you would raise money & advance it to them yourself," as the general no longer wished to have naval obligations commingled with the accounts of the army.[9]

In the midst of delays over advance pay, John Derby of Salem demanded the return of *Lee's* six carriage guns, which had been lent to Glover. John and Richard Derby were fitting out privateers and needed firepower for their own vessels. Bartlett pleaded to keep the guns "for one cruise more," but they refused. At the time, the Derbys may have been miffed at Washington's skippers for capturing and detaining two of their vessels for no reason other than to pry a little prize money from the family. Moylan told Bartlett to purchase the guns, but if the Derbys refused to sell, the guns must be returned. There was still a pair of 2s on *Nancy* and another pair on *Concord.* If Bartlett could not obtain 4s, Moylan suggested he take the smaller guns, as they would be good enough for commerce raiding.[10]

As Bartlett and Glover circulated through nearby towns to enlist men and grub for guns, Washington grew impatient. Four masters, returning from London to Portsmouth, delivered a bundle of old papers to agent Wentworth. Just before sailing they had heard news of a large convoy scheduled to leave for Boston within a few days. In it were three large ships, formerly in the service of the East India Company, loaded with munitions and entirely defenseless. Wentworth sent an express to headquarters, hinting that he hoped the schooners could prevent the convoy from reaching Boston. Once more Moylan packed his saddlebags and rode to Beverly. This time Washington told him to stay there until he personally witnessed every vessel out to sea.[11]

Moylan rode into Beverly anticipating the usual turmoil, but to his surprise Glover, Bartlett, and Manley had made good progress. *Hancock* had her new set of square sails, a half dozen freshly cut oars, and twenty rounds of ammunition for every gun. The men stood by, ready to sail, grimly aware of the constant presence of *Fowey* standing off the harbor. Manley toyed with the idea of attacking her at night with all four schooners, aided by Glover's regiment, but Moylan would not accept the risk. If the attack failed, the general could lose his schooners. Headquarters agreed. With transports en route from England, Washington wanted their cargoes worse than he wanted the frigate.[12]

The harbor leading out of Beverly was wide and scattered with small islands, and *Fowey* lay in the middle with both ends open. On the night of January 20, Manley sailed out of Beverly unseen by the enemy. Moylan stood on the Point and watched *Hancock* fade into the night, and when he heard no gunfire he knew she was safe. He returned to town to finish work on *Franklin* and *Lee*.[13]

In the morning Tucker reported *Franklin* ready and her arms and ammunition on the way. He planned to sail in two or three days. For first lieutenant, Tucker chose Edward Fettyplace, a Marblehead mariner whose father served as the town's vice chairman of the Committee of Correspondence. Second Lieutenant Francis Salter hailed from Newburyport, and twenty-six-year-old James Mugford Jr., master, from Marblehead. Mugford, a young man highly regarded by his seafaring associates, showed much promise as a leader.

John Bradford, who later became an unpopular Continental prize agent for Massachusetts, referred to Tucker as "the most volatile empty body I ever met with."[14] Tucker, like most shipmates, wanted his own way and had little patience for bureaucracy. Besides picking his officers, he recruited most of his crew. When small arms failed to arrived from Cambridge, he purchased them out of his own pocket.

On January 20 Tucker received Washington's sailing orders and discovered that Bartlett had neglected to furnish him with the required banner. He enlisted his wife, who stitched the green pine tree flag "made of cloth of her own purchasing." Tucker later submitted his wife's bill, along with his own, to Bartlett for reimbursement.[15]

Tucker waited an extra day for Waters, who needed time to replace *Lee*'s 4s. Glover returned Derby's guns but found four more. Waters also demanded the pair of 2s from *Concord*, which brought *Lee*'s firepower back to her original complement. He already had his crew of thirty-five standing by, including 1st Lt. William Kissick, 2nd Lt. John Gill, and Master John Diamond, all new men. A few nights later, with a copy of Washington's sailing instructions tucked in his pocket, Waters slipped out of the harbor in company with Tucker and passed *Fowey* undetected.

On January 26 Montagu learned from informants that three of Washington's schooners had eluded his frigate and the fourth had not yet sailed. Anticipating censure, Montagu reminded Graves of *Fowey*'s poor sailing condition. He could not "put a stop to the insolence of the privateers without more force." Montagu claimed a day did not pass without several rebel vessels in sight. By exerting his best efforts, he still could not catch them. For Graves, this was his last day on the job. On the 27th he passed the problem of snaring Washington's schooners to Shuldham.[16]

With three schooners at sea, Moylan puzzled over the condition of *Warren*. He hesitated to let her go with only two 4s and a bank of defective swivels. Burke had enlisted a crew by doling out one month's advance pay and adding two lieutenants, William Ryan of Marblehead and Thomas Lewis. Burke remained ashore while Glover shopped for more guns, and Moylan rode to headquarters to make his report.

Pleased that three schooners had sailed, Washington did not send Moylan back to finish work on *Warren*. In Moylan's absence the general had located a vessel to replace *Washington*. Jeremiah Lee, Glover's Marblehead neighbor, mentioned that his brother's schooner might be available for Continental hire. Glover looked up John Lee and, over a cup of hot rum, struck a deal.

The schooner *Lynch*—named for Thomas Lynch, South Carolina delegate to the Continental Congress—lay fast in the ice at Manchester. Glover told the general not to worry, as he would send a detail to chop her out. When he reached Beverly he located John Roche, *Lynch*'s first lieutenant, and asked him to muster as many men as he could. On February 3 Roche marched to Manchester with sixteen men. They filed into John Allen's inn for supper and lodging but found quarters for only eleven men. The others downed their suppers, walked across the ice to the schooner, and bedded down on the ship.

When Lee offered to lease *Lynch* to the army, he also recommended John Ayres, a former Boston shipmaster, as her commander.
Washington interviewed Ayres and considered him knowledgeable,
energetic, and patriotic—a good combination for a skipper. Ayres left
Cambridge on February 1 with his commission, a set of instructions, and
orders to report to Bartlett.[17]

When Ayres arrived at Beverly with 2nd Lt. John Tiley, he met a
messenger from Roche asking for men to help repair *Lynch*'s hull. Ayres
applied to Bartlett for carpenters and, while waiting, held a brief conversation with Burke. Washington had decided to let *Warren* wait for
Lynch, thereby enabling the vessels to sail together, but he did not want
Warren unduly delayed. Ayres, not wanting the onus of holding up
Warren, left instructions for Tiley to muster extra men and forward them
to Manchester. Before dawn on February 3, Ayres hunkered into his
greatcoat and rode over to John Allen's inn in time to join the crew for
breakfast.

For three days the men chopped ice, and each night the tempera-
ture dropped below zero, refreezing the path cut to open water. Damage
to the hull kept carpenters busy sealing leaks and adding braces. On the
afternoon of February 6 the weather warmed, and the tide carried the
cut chunks of ice out to sea. Early the next morning Roche woke to a
dark and squally sky. A heavy mist lay thick along shore, making an ideal
backdrop for the schooner's trip down the coast to Beverly. Roche raised
sail and, with the crew on board, bumped through the ice to open
water.[18]

Ayres sat on his horse and watched from shore until *Lynch* passed
out of sight. Riding slowly back to Beverly, his thoughts focused on
Fowey, camped somewhere off Beverly about six miles to the south. Was
the frigate at Cat Island, or standing off Misery Island waiting for
Lynch? Ayres followed the road paralleling the bay, but he could not see
a thing.

Once Roche cleared the harbor, he added sail and sped down the
coast with help from a fair wind. As he quartered inside Baker's Island,
the watch reported *Fowey* standing to the southeast. Roche had the wind
and, steering a few points to starboard, skirted Misery Island.

Fowey lay at anchor off the entrance to Salem. When the watch
sighted *Lynch* on the port quarter, Montagu shifted about on his moor-

ing to engage his 9s. With the wind in his face, pursuit was useless. From shore, Ayres heard seventeen shots fired. As he reached Curtis Point he could see the outline of *Lynch* doubling into Beverly Harbor and knew she was safe. Her progress slowed as she rounded into the wind, and when she bumped against Glover's Wharf Ayres met the crew with hearty handshakes for all.[19]

By adding another schooner, Glover complicated his task. He now had more guns to buy—two for *Warren*, four for *Lynch*, and a second battery of swivels. Privateering forced prices up. Glover located a 4-pounder at Cape Ann, and Bartlett paid twenty pounds for another. Unable to buy, beg, or borrow another pair of 4s, Glover offered Ayres four old 2s in his warehouse, and the captain agreed to take them.

On February 8 carpenters began stripping *Lynch* of her old rigging. Every sail needed to be altered, mended, or replaced. Daniel Glover rerigged the vessel from top to bottom, adding square sail yards, topsail yards, crosstrees, a topmast, blocks, trucks, cleats, and every article down to handspikes and belaying pins. Along with a new set of oars, two new topsails, and a square sail, Bartlett stocked the vessel with forty gallons of rum, ten barrels of beef, and enough bread and provisions for a one-month cruise. On February 25 *Lynch* took on her water and was ready for sea, but *Warren*, whose captain seemed to lack Ayres's energy and motivation, still lingered off Glover's Wharf without all her guns.[20]

While mobilizing the Beverly schooners, Washington did not forget about *Harrison*, Coit's old vessel, at Plymouth. She still lay at the wharf without captain or crew. To keep themselves warm, four guards meandered back and forth from the garret, leisurely carrying bricks and mortar down to the wharf to rebuild the schooner's crumbling chimney. If the general needed a reminder, he received one on December 19 when he signed a warrant for slightly over £1,015 to cover Watson's accounts for outfitting two schooners. *Washington*, of course, had been captured, attaching extra importance to getting good service out of *Harrison*.

In early January Moylan ordered Watson to "examine into the condition of Captn Coits schooner." If she were fit, he said, look around for some person to command her, appoint officers, and recruit men. Even if she were not fit, Moylan would be satisfied if Watson could find a "clever set of officers and men" willing to sail her. Otherwise, Moylan added, the guns and ammunition must be removed and another vessel hired.[21]

After weeks of listening to Coit's complaints about the vessel, Moylan and the general received a pleasant surprise when Watson declared the schooner "an excellent sailer" and "sufficiently strong . . . although not very well accommodated for the officers." Watson strongly recommended the vessel be retained and nominated Charles Dyar as her new captain. "Dyar," Watson added, "was with Capt. Coit [on] his last cruise" and could vouch for the condition of the schooner.

Dyar personally delivered the message to Washington, unaware that Watson had warned the general to not expect Dyar to make a good impression, as "at first interview . . . he is no orator and seems rather softly, but his character [stands] high as a good officer, & as an active smart sailor." Watson did not help Dyar's case by adding, "Capt. Coit has recommended him in high terms & will give your Excellency his true character." Washington's expedient, however, was to recruit a crew, and he accepted Dyar because the new skipper promised to enlist men for six months. "Our people are very fond of knowing their officers," Watson explained, and would be reluctant to commit their service to a stranger. Washington appreciated the advice, perhaps wishing Watson had mentioned it three months earlier.

On January 20 Dyar returned to Plymouth as commander of *Harrison* with a set of the general's sailing instructions.[22] The general also approved his request for "a square sail & some other small sails" and instructed Watson to provide them as long as the benefits justified the expense. However, Dyar must not wait; he must sail as soon as the crew is mustered, "with such sails as he has. . . . Those he wants may be made while he is out."[23]

Three days later Watson dispatched John Wigglesworth to headquarters with a letter recommending Thomas Doten as first lieutenant and the messenger second lieutenant. "Wigglesworth had conducted this matter with great dignity," Watson explained. "I had appointed him as 1st Lieut. but Mr. Doten offering his service, Wigglesworth generously gave way to Doten as being the more experienced sailor, & as having been some years commander of a good vessel." During a brief interview, Wigglesworth's straightforward comportment impressed the general. Because Wigglesworth had given up his first lieutenancy, Washington promised to give him consideration "on a future occasion." On January 25 Wigglesworth returned to Plymouth with the commissions, a supply of cartridge paper, and an urgent appeal from the general "to get the *Harrison* out as soon as possible."[24]

The same severe weather that locked *Lynch* in the ice at Manchester played havoc on Dyar's efforts to get to sea. *Harrison* lost her anchor and cable, and part of the crew fished for it while others chopped ice. Dyar finally sailed at the end of January and stood north for Cape Ann.[25]

To shed more of his day-to-day responsibilities for the schooners, Washington named Manley commodore of the fleet, a well-deserved promotion to the man who had captured *Nancy* and a signal to other commanders that the general rewarded performance. But word of the promotion arrived at Beverly too late. Manley had sailed, and his notification to take command of his squadron was about to suffer an unexpected delay.[26]

🦋 13 🦋
Echoes of Gunfire

O n *January 20, 1776,* with a crew thinned to thirty, *Hancock* was the first of Washington's fleet to sail on a cruise since Winborn Adams delivered the last prize to Beverly on Christmas Eve. Sailors considered winter a time to avoid the dangers of perilous seas, a time to lay up vessels in safe harbors, but when Wentworth reported another convoy en route from England, Manley could not wait for *Lee, Franklin,* or the half-armed *Warren* to join him. With ice, sleet, and freezing temperatures approaching their absolute worst, he expected to see few vessels from England until spring, and his best chance of taking a prize was to intercept that last convoy before it reached Boston.[1]

Skirting Misery Island, Manley skimmed along the coast until he passed Manchester. With Eastern Point on his port, he headed out to sea, changed course to the south, and worked down Massachusets Bay. Midway to Cape Cod a squall struck, blanketing the decks with snow and covering the rigging with a thin layer of ice. The watch shivered in their oilskins and turned their eyes leeward. When the blizzard passed, a frigate stood off starboard, her canvas stretched in pursuit. The men added sail, rollicked into another squall, and quartered with the wind until the frigate faded out of sight.

HMS *Nautilus,* Lieutenant Mason, had been under orders from Admiral Graves since January 5 to cruise in the bay, making routine stops off Marblehead and Cape Ann. Graves ordered Mason to "sink, burn and destroy the Rebels" and, as the weather permitted, "to protect all vessels coming to Boston, and see them safely within the lighthouse."[2] On the 22nd Mason sighted *Hancock* but lost her in thick weather. About thirty leagues off Boston Harbor he met the first vessels of the convoy, led them into port, and, needing provisions himself, docked *Nautilus* and reported to Graves. With Shuldham looking over his shoulder, Graves moved with uncommon speed. He ordered Mason to "to push out again as fast as possible." "As fast as possible" carried no deadline, and Mason spent a few days ashore stretching his legs.[3]

After the weather cleared, Manley tacked toward Boston, nosing the schooner into the rollers. As dawn broke through low-slung clouds on the morning of the 25th, the lighthouse lay but two leagues away. Scanning Nantasket Road with his glass, Manley observed the spars of His Majesty's ships standing like a forest of tall timber, swaying back and forth in the icy breeze. Among the crosstrees rising above the Road was Mason's *Nautilus*. Assuming *Nautilus* had returned to sea, Graves failed to post another vessel off the harbor. A solitary schooner stood off the lighthouse, but her flag was white with a green pine tree in the center.[4]

At daybreak the watch reported a sail two leagues to the southeast and tacking into gusty westerlies. Manley cast a wary eye toward Nantasket Road. If Graves dispatched a frigate, she would have the wind, but the fleet had not stirred since he came in sight. So far he had been lucky—cautious, but lucky. He sliced deeply into his ration of good luck when he gave orders to come about and intercept the transport. Oddly enough, not a skipper in the Road had given thought to keeping a watch in the tops, and Manley's escapades off Boston Bay went unnoticed.

Hancock closed quickly, again posing as a friendly pilot. Using his new speaking trumpet, Manley ordered the skipper to heave to. The vessel proved to be the 130-ton ship *Happy Return*, James Hall, master, a supply ship from Whitehaven with coal and provisions for Howe's army. While Manley scanned the manifest and questioned Hall, the watch reported another vessel standing in about two leagues off. Manley came to the deck with his glass and scanned her. After ordering *Happy Return* into Plymouth, he declared the distant vessel a transport and ordered pursuit.

Jonathan Grendal, master of the 120-ton ship *Norfolk*, had just passed Cohasset Rocks when he sighted *Happy Return* abeam a schooner. He had sailed in company with Hall for most of the crossing and considered it curious when his companion turned away from Boston. Grendal thought the schooner carried important news for incoming transports. He eased to port to meet the vessel flying the strange white banner with the blot of green. To his horror, he spotted three carriage guns leveled on *Norfolk*'s beam and a man in a dark suit of clothes ordering the ship's surrender through a shiny speaking trumpet. Taken by surprise, Grendal struck.

Grendal had almost completed one of the most difficult voyages of his career. Eyeing the warships lying in Boston Harbor, he stalled for time. If just one of those vessels would fill her sails and come to his rescue, his ship would be saved. Even as Grendal climbed on board *Hancock,* he still looked longingly at the outline of those distant, friendly spars, but not a sail unfurled. Not until Manley's prize crew sailed away on his ship and headed for Plymouth did Grendal finally give up hope of rescue.

After manning both prizes, Manley counted but sixteen men left on board *Hancock* to watch as many prisoners. But when the watch reported three vessels on course for Boston, Manley came about and set a heading for the foremost, a large sloop trimming her sails. The vessel sheered toward him. This unexpected maneuver gave Manley second thoughts about the character of his quarry. If she carried arms, he must fight her or else risk losing both transports. If she was lightly armed, he planned to engage her and snatch another prize, perhaps all three. How to get them into port was a secondary matter. Uncertain of what lay ahead but game for a fight, he stayed on course, every carriage gun ready, every swivel loaded. As the two vessels closed Manley counted four gunports on her starboard beam and knew then she carried at least eight.

HM sloop *General Gage,* George Sibles, master, had been at Halifax, where he joined two small provision vessels as they left for Boston. He assumed responsibility for their safety and brought them as far as the bay when he observed *Hancock* diverting two transports away from the harbor. He could see the schooner was armed, but with his own eight guns, a dozen swivels, and a large crew, Sibles felt he could take her. He certainly had sufficient incentive. If he could capture the schooner and retake her prizes, there would be a nice piece of change in it for himself and his crew.

Sibles and Manley closed warily, the roar of their 4s carried to sea by a westerly wind. With one eye on his prizes and the other on *General Gage,* Manley ordered the men to fire as fast as *Hancock* could reload and come about. The fire from both vessels went high, ripping through rigging and damaging sails. A gunner on *Hancock* was hit in the chest. After a sharp fight, both vessels stood off and measured each other.

Manley counted his ammunition—six cartridges left. His two prizes were well down the bay when Sibles sheered off and tacked toward Boston. Manley wanted to pursue, but he had neither the men nor the ammunition. He noticed movement in Nantasket Road and, with his sails already damaged, filled for Plymouth.[5]

During Manley's action off Boston Harbor, four 50-gun ships-of-the-line lay at anchor in Nantasket Road: *Preston, Chatham, Renown,* and *Centurion. Lively,* 20, and *Adventure,* 8, bobbed off the town, and three vessels fitting out bumped against Long Wharf. *Nautilus* also lay at the wharf, but her captain had not returned from town. Two other vessels—the schooner *Halifax,* 6, and the brig *Hope,* 14—cruised to the north, several leagues off Cape Ann. When Manley captured *Happy Return, Hancock* could be seen from the deck of *Renown,* but her captain made no effort to rescue the transports, even though the wind was at his quarter.[6]

Manley deposited both prizes with Watson and on January 26 advised Washington he had captured two transports but exhausted his ammunition. After the fight with *General Gage,* Manley decided he needed a vessel commodious enough to carry more guns and a larger crew. He made the request without knowledge of his promotion. That news came on the twenty-eighth, when Washington replied with compliments, writing, "your general good behavior since you first engaged in the service merits mine, & your countrys thanks." He promised Manley a better ship and invited him to headquarters as soon as he completed his cruise. Washington wanted the schooner out to sea as soon as Manley replenished his ammunition and wrote, "I need not recommend to you to proceed again & pursue your good fortune. I wish you could inspire the captains of the other armed schooners under your command with some of your activity and industry." He asked Manley to enlist more men at Plymouth to raise his complement to forty but reminded him to avoid engagements until he had a ship of "more equal footing with your enemy."[7]

Manley's request for a larger vessel may have been influenced by Congress's passage, on December 15, 1775, of an appropriation to build thirteen frigates, two of them in Massachusetts. However, his request may have simply emanated from his promotion to commodore and the symbolic expectation of a more prestigious flagship.

In his letter to Washington, Manley failed to mention an incident he shared with Watson. During his fight with *General Gage*, he claimed, all three vessels would have been captured "had it not been for the cowardice of one of our Continental armed schooners" that was close by but sailed away. Washington asked for the immediate identification of the schooner to enable him to inquire into the conduct of her commander, but Manley had sailed by the time the general's message reached Plymouth. Other schooners had been armed as privateers, but Watson's terminology linked the coward to Washington's fleet. Manley remained mute on the matter.

In a strange turnabout, Manley also confided to Watson that during the fight his crew of sixteen received help from the prisoners, whose vessels he had just captured. "More particularly from the captains," Watson added, "who did as much as they dared do in such circumstances."

On January 29 Watson engaged a detail to chop through the ice locking *Hancock* and *Harrison* in the harbor. At 8:00 A.M. on the 30th *Hancock* sailed, but Dyar remained behind to fish for his anchor and cable. Manley replenished his ammunition and collected his crew, but he failed to recruit more hands.[8]

Flushed with his promotion and pleased with the promise of a stronger vessel, Manley set sail for Boston Bay. He wanted to return to Beverly, but not without a prize. At 10:00 A.M. he rounded Gurnet Point and, once at sea, settled into his cabin, leaving control of the vessel in Stiles's hands. Smitten by fever, Manley left instructions to not be bothered except in an emergency. With a light westerly blowing, Stiles guided the vessel a few miles to sea, working slowly up the coast. The wind had shifted a few points to the south when the watch reported an armed brig flying the king's colors approaching from astern.

HM brig *Hope*, Lt. George Dawson, had just come into Cape Cod Bay, aware that a rebel schooner had carried two prizes into Plymouth. Graves had recently added *Hope* to his fleet and considered her "one of the best fitted and appointed vessels of her size in the King's service." The brig carried eight 4s, six 3s, and a complement of fifty men. Dawson had sailed on January 26 with orders from the admiral to "cruize against the Rebels within the Bay of Boston"—which was, by Graves's definition, from Cape Ann to Cape Cod.[9]

Dawson sighted *Hancock* when she rounded Gurnet Point, but Stiles did not notice the enemy brig until he had sailed too far up the coast to return to Plymouth. At 2:00 P.M. *Hope* began to close on *Hancock.* Stiles waited until the last minute to notify Manley, who came on deck and realized instantly his schooner was no match for the brig. If he came about, the wind would be in his face. He had no choice but to beat to the northwest, following a sandy strip of beach offering no protection and no safe harbor, in the forlorn hope of outrunning the enemy. Manley steered for shore, using the wind to his best advantage as he headed for the cove at Marshfield. Another inlet lay further up the coast at the mouth of North River, south of Scituate, but shifting sands baffled the channel and made the approach treacherous. After tacking through a three-hour chase, Manley nosed the schooner into the shallows and grounded just below North River. With guns loaded, he waited on deck for *Hope* to come inshore.

At 4:00 P.M. Dawson anchored within gunshot and for the next four hours fired "not less than 400 times" at the beached schooner. Most of the shots hissed over *Hancock* and landed on shore. Curious militiamen combed the beach the following day and counted 130 balls embedded in the sand. *Hope*'s poor marksmanship could be attributed to a sudden gale that tipped the sloop to leeward and elevated her fire. With his vessel undamaged, Manley retired once again to his cabin and asked not to be disturbed unless the enemy attempted to board. He had just covered himself with blankets when the only ball to find its target "entered the stern and passed but six inches" from his head. The scare worked wonders on his ailment, as no more was heard about his fever.

After dark Dawson tried to move inshore, but his men could not raise the anchor. At high tide *Hancock* floated free, and in the darkness Manley worked the schooner into North River. According to Dawson's report, Manley attempted to get the schooner off at "seven in the evening . . . and endeavoring to push into North River, sunk." Manley, however, did not sink. He simply ran further inshore before grounding again. He took the men ashore, worked all night, and, with help from the local militia, built breastworks and mounted cannon.

At dawn, with moderating weather, Dawson dispatched a detail in two boats to set fire to the schooner. Manley's marines and the guns of the militia opened with a furious fire, driving off the firebrands. The detail returned to *Hope* and reported *Hancock* filled with water. Dawson considered the mission accomplished. In his report he assured the admiral that "the Rebel schooner being then almost full of water, he thought it best to quit her, and not risque his people further, the privateer being effectually disabled from ever cruising again."[10]

Dawson's evidence of boarding *Hancock* consisted of one swivel gun and an old red ensign. If Dawson had traced the origin of the swivel gun, he would have discovered it had been taken by Manley from one of *Hancock's* prizes.[11] However, if Dawson had remained at anchor another two days, he would have observed the schooner sailing into Scituate for repairs. On February 8 a reporter for the *New England Chronicle* reported *Hancock* "nearly ready for another cruize."

News of the "sinking" of *Hancock* reached Boston with enhanced distortions. Deputy Q.M. Gen. Francis Hutcheson reported the sinking of *Hancock* to a friend in England but erroneously credited *Hope* with killing many of Manley's marines. Hutcheson's account was no less garbled than Dawson's. A month passed before Dawson again came face to face with Manley and the resurrected *Hancock*.[12]

Manley's two prizes, *Norfolk* and *Happy Return,* passed through the libeling process on April 15, 1776, and were condemned. Washington instructed Gen. Artemus Ward to advertise the vessels two weeks prior to the sale. James Hall of *Happy Return* and Jonathan Grendal of *Norfolk* pooled their money and, with other paroled masters, acquired one of the condemned schooners. Forty-eight men squeezed on board and on May 14 sailed from Cape Ann for England. Three men drowned in the passage, and HMS *Centurion* stopped the vessel off Newfoundland and pressed eleven hands into the Royal Navy. The survivors reached Whitehaven about June 14, relating vivid accounts of American shipbuilding activity. They had seen the Continental frigates *Boston* and *Hancock* on the stocks at Newburyport and later witnessed the launching of *Raleigh* at Portsmouth. If the British Admiralty had any doubts about America's determination to win their independence at sea as well as on land, they now knew otherwise.[13]

While Manley repaired *Hancock* at Scituate, Dyar recovered his lost anchor and led *Harrison* to sea. He left no record of his cruise but on February 22 returned to Plymouth without a prize. Since taking command of the British navy in North America, Shuldham had placed his ships off rebel ports. Watson reported, "our enemies are very vigilant, and in good weather are seen every day from this shore."[14]

Dyar complained about *Harrison*'s poor sailing qualities. Vessels he chased outsailed him, the crew became dissatisfied, and Dyar asked for a better vessel. Washington probably received the news philosophically. The "blundering Capt. Coit" had been right after all. Once again the general decommissioned *Harrison,* instructing Watson to secure the weapons and save the supplies.[15]

Dyar, however, had sailed in company with the privateer sloop *Yankee,* Corbin Barnes, master, before Washington's orders reached Watson. The 75-ton *Yankee* had been commissioned by the colony of Massachusetts on December 17, 1775. Using Plymouth as her home port, she cruised at different times with both Manley and Dyar. *Yankee* carried nine guns and could outsail most of Washington's schooners.[16]

At noon on February 23, Dyar and Barnes cleared Plymouth and headed to sea. *Hope* lay offshore, and Dawson's lookouts reported two rebel vessels running out of the harbor. With a full press of sail, *Hope* closed rapidly. To Barnes and Dyar the British sloop had become a familiar sight, and they wasted no time running back to the harbor. *Yankee* got there first, leaving *Harrison* behind but well inside the Gurnet. Much to Dyar's surprise, *Hope* came into the harbor and opened with her forward guns. Dyar found himself cornered and with two options—use his guns or surrender. Barnes came about and brought *Yankee* into the fight, giving Dawson more of a battle than he expected. From his parlor window, Watson watched the action, which lasted about three hours. Barnes and Dyar maneuvered around shoals, making a determined effort to ground *Hope* on one of Plymouth Bay's many bars. Dawson disengaged and, according to Watson, spent an hour "stopping the shot holes when he bore away." Dawson reported mostly damage to yards, shrouds, and rigging. For two hours he lay off the entrance to Plymouth waiting "for the Rebels to come out" and then sailed away in chase of a small schooner.[17]

There is no record of the damage to either *Harrison* or *Yankee,* but if Washington had decided to decommission the schooner before the fight, he had more reason to lay her up afterward. The crew removed the guns and ammunition—and every other item, down to a tea kettle and a brass candlestick—and carted the inventory to Watson's warehouse.[18]

Dyar, however, remained faithful to his enlistment and wrote Washington he still had "36 men for the sea service" and would wait "on his Excellency for orders." No record exists of how long Dyar waited for the general's reply, as he was heard from no more.[19]

By the end of February, only five of the eight vessels commissioned by Washington remained active. Four of Manley's fleet—*Lee, Lynch, Franklin,* and *Warren*—had been operating out of Beverly while Manley made repairs at Scituate. Not much had happened during the commodore's absence, but this was about to change. There would be no idleness in Manley's command.

❧ 14 ❧
Tucker and Waters Join the Hunt

On *January 25, Franklin,* Samuel Tucker, and *Lee,* Daniel Waters, sailed from Glover's Wharf and set a northeasterly course, eluding two British warships stationed off Cat Island.[1] Winter gales pounded both schooners, but the captains stayed well to sea. With the exception of the watch on deck, the men huddled around the stove, wiped smoke from their bloodshot eyes, and spun yarns of yesteryear.

For four days the schooners ranged between Cape Ann and the Boston lighthouse, keeping apart but within sight of each other. Tucker and Waters had agreed on a set of signals, and lookouts on both vessels remained watchful of each other's mastheads. On the morning of the 29th, *Franklin* sighted a small sloop standing southward. Tucker signaled Waters and stood in chase, *Lee* following a mile behind. Tucker came abeam the 60-ton *Rainbow* and sent Lieutenant Fettyplace on board to obtain the vessel's papers. Samuel Perkins, with a crew of two, had sailed from Damariscotta (Maine) laden with forty-five cords of wood, ten bushels of potatoes, two bushels of turnips, a quantity of spruce for beer, and a little meat. Perkins flourished a certificate of clearance from Damariscotta for either Newburyport or Salem.

Tucker considered Perkins suspicious. *Rainbow* had passed both destinations and now lay close to Boston. Perkins explained he had been favored by a strong northerly and decided to try for Plymouth. When Tucker acted doubtful, Perkins hastened to add he was just then "thinking about putting about for Salem" when stopped by *Franklin.* To Tucker, Perkins's reply made even less sense. Facing about would put the vessel into the wind and make her an easy prize for the warships off Beverly. With *Rainbow* within four leagues of the Boston lighthouse at

Capt. Samuel Tucker commanded the armed schooners *Franklin* and *Hancock*. From an engraving by H. W. Smith. Courtesy U.S. Naval Historical Center.

the time of her capture, Perkins's credibility slumped to the bottom of his bilge. Tucker put a prize crew on board with orders to take her into Gloucester.

Beating north in company with *Lee* and *Rainbow,* Tucker took advantage of thick weather and made no effort to give Baker's Island wide berth. The fog lifted suddenly, the sun came out, and all three vessels passed Beverly in plain sight of the noon watch on *Fowey.* Cut off from Gloucester, Tucker changed course to the east, trimmed his sails, and, with *Lee* and *Rainbow* following close on his heels, slipped into Cape Ann just ahead of *Fowey.* Tucker explained his reasons for detaining the prize to agent Sargent, who was about to experience his first encounter with such heady matters. After leaving Perkins with Sargent for questioning, Tucker and Waters sailed that night, setting a northeasterly course to avoid a second encounter with *Fowey.*[2]

On February 1, while ranging in the track of shipping from Halifax, Tucker and Waters captured the 300-ton brig *Henry and Esther,* one Nellis, master, en route from Le Havre to Boston. The vessel carried 62 cords of wood, 150 butts with water, and 40 sets of soldiers' bedding.

Nellis admitted the cargo was for Boston and submitted to his bad luck quietly. Tucker and Waters escorted the prize into Cape Ann's Squam Harbor and sailed for Gloucester. On the short passage around the cape, they again encountered *Fowey*, which always seemed to be nearby but never close enough to catch them. After firing "5 guns" at the vanishing schooners, Captain Montagu anchored off Gloucester to wait for the rebels to come out in the morning.[3]

In the meantime, Sargent and the Committee of Safety questioned Perkins, found his papers in order, and released the vessel. The trip to Cape Ann had given Perkins time to reconstruct his story, at least to Sargent's satisfaction. But Perkins seemed to be in no hurry to sail, advising those who asked that he was merely waiting for a favorable wind to carry him to Salem. Benjamin Gale, master of a vessel bound for Salem, offered to guide Perkins through a passage that would enable *Rainbow* to avoid the enemy warship laying off Marblehead. Perkins followed Gale a half hour later, but as Gale exited the pass and cleared for sea, the wind changed. Gale came about and started back to Cape Ann. Sidling abeam *Rainbow*, he told Perkins the wind was too strong ahead and to go back. Perkins pretended he could not hear and continued to the westward.

At this moment Tucker and Waters ran into Gloucester with *Fowey* standing off and firing her "5 guns." If Perkins did not see the encounter, he probably heard it. At nightfall *Fowey* anchored, and at 10:00 P.M. Montagu observed *Rainbow* coming abeam.

Months passed before Perkins's activities that night came to light. John Cochran, then a seaman on *Fowey* and later boatswain's mate on the schooner *Lynch*, told the rest of the story. After anchoring within hail of *Fowey*, Perkins pushed off from *Rainbow* and came aboard the frigate. Cochran recognized him as the same man who on past occasions had delivered several quarters of beef and other provisions to Montagu, for which he was paid. On their last visit, Cochran had distinctly heard Perkins say he planned to go to the eastward for wood and carry it to Boston. At midnight Perkins transferred fifty pounds of beef and one goose to the frigate, explaining he had been delayed by privateers "and would have then met the *Fowey* but that Capt. Manley [Tucker] ordered him into Cape Ann."

On the morning of February 3, Montagu put six men aboard *Rainbow* and escorted her into Boston.[4] After unloading his cargo, Perkins received a passport to sail in ballast, signed and authorized by none other than Admiral Shuldham.[5] The venturesome Perkins headed home but encountered heavy weather and sought refuge in Salem Harbor. Guards detained Perkins while they searched the vessel. The Committee of Safety considered Perkins somewhat suspiciously, but once again *Rainbow*'s wily master demonstrated a nimble intellect. Mentioning nothing of his capture by Tucker and Waters, he explained that two weeks earlier he had been taken by *Fowey* while attempting to reach Salem. A prize crew landed him in Boston, took his wood, and sold it. In order to recover his vessel, Perkins claimed he was forced to promise to deliver more fuel. To account for the money in his possession, he told the committee he had been given three dollars per cord "to enable him to buy another load." Howe and Shuldham had promised to give him the entire proceeds if he returned. The committee evidently thanked Perkins for stopping at Salem to explain his misfortune. They then remembered that foul weather had driven *Rainbow* into their harbor, not a patriotic willingness on Perkins's part to share his adventures with the authorities. They held the vessel long enough to discover the deceit and took her as a prize.[6]

On March 11 *Rainbow* was libeled on behalf of the town. Tucker and Waters did not learn of the sloop's release at Cape Ann until they sailed into Squam Harbor with *Henry and Esther*. Irritated with Sargent for being duped by a fast-talking smuggler, Tucker sailed down to Marblehead and complained to Jonathan Glover. Acting as agent for Tucker and Waters, Glover made inquiries and apologized for not being able to reach Cape Ann before Sargent set the vessel free. He felt Perkins had effectuated a great hoax on a new and inexperienced agent's gullibility. The court condemned *Rainbow* on March 28, but not a farthing went to Tucker or Waters. *Henry and Esther* went on trial at the same time, and *Lee* and *Franklin* received credit for their first fair prize.[7]

As of February 1, 1776, none of Washington's five agents had collected a cent from the disposal of prizes. The delays in establishing a libeling process hit Glover's pocketbook especially hard, as he had paid out funds to cover a variety of expenditures. Reimbursements from Cambridge had been slow, and not a penny covered Glover's commission.

Because most of the valuable cargoes had been transferred to the army with no exchange of money, the agents waited for the vessels to be condemned and sold. Some of the larger vessels could be armed, either to satisfy Manley's request for a stronger ship or for sale to investors looking for privateers. Five months had passed since *Hannah* sailed, but not one prize had moved since being deposited with an agent. Both *Jenny* and *Little Hannah* showed good sailing qualities, and upon their release Manley could choose between them. However, the Massachusetts courts took time to get organized, and by late March the list of prizes awaiting adjudication had grown to twenty-eight. Of those, Washington's schooners claimed thirteen.[8]

Bartlett also needed capital, and on February 3 he sent an urgent message to headquarters: "As I am in great need of money I send herewith . . . the young man who lives with me for it."[9] Moylan sent the messenger back to Beverly without a cent. "His Excellency was much surprised at your fresh demand for 2000 dollars," he replied. "Indeed, so was I. There is now upwards of 10,000 dollars advanced upon these vessels, and very few accounts brought in." Instead of money, Moylan asked Bartlett for an accounting. Bartlett's records, like Glover's, needed work. Too much time had been spent provisioning the schooners and caring for the prizes. Moylan promised to pay creditors with warrants, not money, as soon as he received an accounting. He provided Glover and Bartlett with forms, assuring each that "by this means you will not want money to pay them & when you send your accounts, if money is necessary, it will be given you."[10]

Moylan was not being entirely truthful. Washington had just borrowed £25,000 from Massachusetts to carry him until Congress forwarded the next remittance. In addition, the general had tapped the prizes for anything of use to the army, articles ranging from coal and clothing to writing paper, sealing wax, and quills. His frustration continued to be the court system. Delays prevented him from generating enough cash from the sale of the vessels to pay the crews or keep the agents out of debt.[11]

Bartlett accomplished what Moylan least expected. On March 1 he rushed his accounts to headquarters. Outfitting, provisioning, and one month's pay for the four crews hired at Beverly totaled more than £2,500. Bartlett's tidy records arrived at Cambridge at an inopportune time, as headquarters still owed Watson £1,000 for arming two schooners at Plymouth. Washington's quietly planned bombardment of British positions in Boston was scheduled to begin. Bartlett and his creditors would have to wait.[12]

Since February, Washington's staff had been making secret preparations to occupy Dorchester Heights. Once fortified, the Heights commanded much of the town and a portion of the harbor. Spies slipping out of Boston had reported unusual military activity, suggesting a movement of the British army. Heavy ordnance had been withdrawn from Bunker Hill and taken on board vessels in the harbor. Bedding, water, and provisions had been observed being loaded on transports, and the inhabitants of the town suspected an embarkation of troops to either New York or Virginia. If Howe wished to change his base, Washington wanted to accommodate him. By the end of February, the Continental Army had batteries emplaced on Lechmere Point, Cobble Hill, and Lamb's Dam, with enough gunpowder to give Howe a good scare. Washington hoped to draw off enough of the British force on Dorchester Heights to enable his own artillery to move up their guns.[13]

On the night of March 2, Continental gunners opened from Roxbury and Cambridge and for three successive days blasted British positions with shot and shell. Among the mortars lobbing shells into the town was *Congress*, the 13-inch brass mortar taken from *Nancy*. On its third firing the mortar blew up with a deafening roar and injured two gunners. The artillery barrage accomplished Washington's purpose. Howe pulled men off Dorchester Heights to reinforce his lines, and on the night of the 4th Continental troops captured the few remaining defenders and moved up artillery.[14]

On the morning of the 5th, Howe was shocked to discover rebel batteries posted in his own redoubts. Gunfire from Nook's Hill began to fall among his lines and disrupt the loading of vessels at the wharf. Howe wanted the batteries dislodged and the shelling stopped. During the afternoon he moved troops across the harbor to Castle William and prepared for a grand assault on the Heights.

From atop Dorchester, Samuel Richards, captain of the Connecticut Line, noticed long ranks of British soldiers filing onto Shuldham's vessels. "Being urged to exertion by a full expectation of being attacked," Richards wrote, "we had no time to spare for reflecting on . . . the expected battle." Men dug until their arms fell limp by their sides. Three thousand British soldiers crowded into Castle William with the expectation of crossing at dawn. They had their orders. Dorchester Heights must be retaken at all costs. As night approached a fierce wind whipped out of the south, bringing torrents of rain. Trenches turned to slime, but still the men worked on, slinging mud atop their earthworks. Below, off Castle William, the same hurricane-force wind blew Howe's hopes asunder. At dawn, Richards looked down on the British position and observed a snarl of British vessels in hopeless disorder. Like the upturned earth on Dorchester Heights, Howe's grand assault had been washed away by the tempest.[15]

Washington learned on March 9 of British preparations to leave Boston "in a day or two." The Continental artillery kept up the pressure, giving Howe no reason to change his mind. The question of where the army was going troubled the general. Informants in Boston said Halifax, but Washington suspected the intelligence had been planted. He believed Howe's destination was New York. As a precaution, he prepared the Continentals for a forced march to the south.

Washington could not stop Howe's evacuation, he could only hurry it. He pushed Howe hard, forcing him to leave supplies behind. In addition to abandoned war material, he hoped to capture straggling supply ships when the main convoy headed for sea. Transports crossing from England would not know Boston had been evacuated. The general posted lookouts up and down the coast to watch for Shuldham's fleet. He sent an express to Manley, ordering him to assemble the schooners, follow the convoy, and "dog them."[16]

The message arrived at Beverly too late. The commodore did not need instructions from headquarters to hunt the enemy. After his brush with *Hope*, his blood was up, and he had primed his pugnacious little squadron for trouble. Prize money may have provided an incentive for some men to risk their lives, but no one enjoyed a fight better than John Manley. His squadron lay off Beverly Harbor, waiting for a fair wind. Two British warships stood offshore. Manley ordered the squadron to wait. He would take the lead. If they heard no gunfire from the frigates, they should follow.

🎄 15 🎄

The Commodore's
Pestiferous Squadron

*A*fter reprovisioning at Boston, *Fowey* returned to her post off Little Misery Island on February 22 and joined *Nautilus*, Captain Collins, off Cat Island. Collins remembered the sandy shoals off Beverly and wisely anchored in nine fathoms. Both vessels had a clear view of Marblehead, Smith's Island, and the steeple of Beverly's church. *Fowey* watched the main channel and the one to the east running inside of Baker's Island. *Nautilus* stood between the entrance to Marblehead Harbor and Baker's Island. On a clear day, no vessel could pass into or out of the harbor without being seen.

Once a day *Hope* joined the two blockaders, exchanged information, and circled back to Cape Cod Bay to maintain a vigil to the south. Shuldham wanted the marauding of His Majesty's transports stopped. He remembered the scalding criticism leveled at Graves in London's papers, and he wanted none of it for himself. If rebel schooners could not be captured, he wanted them confined to port where they could do no damage. For ten days *Fowey* and *Nautilus* lay off Beverly. They did not observe *Hancock* slip into port at the end of February—or any other activity—until the beginning of March.[1]

Manley departed from Scituate on February 25 and sailed into Beverly to consolidate his squadron, but Tucker and Waters were at Cape Ann. Ayres was ready to sail in *Lynch*, but no progress had been made on *Warren*. Bartlett supplied Manley with cartridges and, on the commodore's instruction, sent an express to Tucker and Waters directing them to rendezvous at Gloucester. At dark on March 1 Manley skimmed by *Fowey* unnoticed. Ayres lingered another day. At midnight on the 2nd, with spurts of rain falling from passing squalls, Ayres guided *Lynch* out of the harbor. At 1:00 A.M. the watch on *Fowey* sighted the vessel and fired a few shots from her 9-pounder. Because of thick weather, the frigate failed to pursue, and at daybreak *Lynch* sailed into Gloucester.[2]

Franklin, Lee, and *Hancock* lay anchored off Gloucester when Ayres came abeam. Brisk southwesterlies beat up the harbor, blocking them inside. When *Lynch* arrived, Manley was glad he had waited. Twenty-four miles away Continental guns roared above Boston, and when news of the bombardment reached Gloucester, the men on the schooners cocked their ears to hear the distant rumble. They sailed the night of March 2, speculating on the outcome of Washington's cannonade, but they had their own mission to consider. Three schooners fanned out behind *Hancock* and followed the commodore around Eastern Point and into the stormy Atlantic.

Six leagues off Cape Ann, Manley sighted a sail to the south, his old nemesis, HM brig *Hope,* Lieutenant Dawson. As she drew in range, he recognized the vessel and prepared to settle an old score. *Hope* was a good match for the four schooners, her eight 4s and six 3s against the schooners' combined firepower of sixteen 4s eight 2s. Manley, however, had a distinct advantage in being able to maneuver. He could close and rake *Hope* two vessels at a time. Unimpressed by Manley's schooners, Dawson steered directly for the squadron, guns loaded and ports knocked open. Manley wisely eased the squadron toward Cape Ann. If any of his schooners sustained damage, he wanted them close to land. It was not worth risking his fleet for the capture of one armed brig.

The running fight lasted about thirty minutes, with *Hope* firing the first shot at 5:30 P.M. Manley reported little damage to the schooners and remained at sea. Dawson disengaged about three leagues off Cape Ann, reporting "one man wounded, several ropes shot away, and [a] shot in the hull." On March 10 diarist John Rowe, a merchant with patriotic sentiments, observed from Boston: "Dawson is returned … he has had a severe brush with four privateers."[3]

Hope's return to Boston had nothing to do with the fight. On March 6 Shuldham dispatched *Nautilus* with orders to locate all the warships in Massachusetts Bay and send them into Boston for an emergency evacuation of the army. On the following day *Fowey* came in from Marblehead, leaving Beverly's harbor open for the first time in many weeks. By the 10th not one British warship patrolled anywhere near

Manley's cruising ground. To further complicate Howe's evacuation, Shuldham's provisions had reached the bottom of the barrel. He had just requisitioned a month's supply from naval stores at Halifax. Victuallers were on their way to Boston, and he could not stop them. He assured the Admiralty that he would leave all the force he could spare "for the protection of the supplies intended for this place," but his letter manifested the bone-deep doubt he felt.[4]

After his brief fight with *Hope,* Manley cruised off Cape Ann, unaware of the enemy's planned withdrawal from Boston. On March 6 one of the missing transports from London came in sight. Manley's flotilla loaded on canvas and sailed in chase. John Frazer, master of the 300-ton ship *Susannah,* expressed shock when surrounded by four armed schooners. He had been at sea all winter, the sixth of eight vessels that had left Whitehaven in early December with Howe's winter provisions. *Susannah* carried a handsome cargo of coal, peas, potatoes, cheese, sauerkraut, and plenty of porter. A cargo of pork had been on the hoof, but of sixty-four live hogs only twenty survived the journey. *Susannah* also carried six guns, four swivels, and three barrels of gunpowder, a treasure trove for the powder-poor schooners, and ten packages of medicine, a commodity scarcer than hard money.[5] The cargo also contained packages from home for the besieged officers in Boston. Manley escorted the prize into Portsmouth.[6]

Frazer had hidden a hefty sum of cash, which some of the commodore's men pilfered during a search of the captain's cabin. Consumed by their quest for treasure, they missed several letters sewn into the lining of Frazer's clothes. Wentworth discovered the documents—as well as the theft—after Manley landed the prisoners. Unknown hands had scooped up £63, and Washington demanded that all, down to the last farthing, be returned. The general had given positive orders to his commanders "to guard against this . . . ignominious behavior." To compensate Frazer for his loss, Washington ordered Wentworth to return the money out of Continental funds and have Manley punish the looters. If the money could not be found, Wentworth was to deduct a like amount from the squadron's prize shares. Manley sailed before Washington's message reached Portsmouth, and Wentworth reimbursed Frazer from the proceeds of the cargo. Whoever pilfered the cash kept it. Wentworth paroled the prisoners to go at liberty as they pleased.[7]

The captured letters made interesting reading for the general. The British ministry was trying to raise twenty thousand troops for service in America, but the treasury could not afford it. France had discouraged other European countries, among them Russia and Sweden, from supplying mercenaries, declaring that "if foreign troops are sent, she [France] cannot be an idle spectator." This, of course, was exactly the type of intelligence Washington needed to bolster the spirits of his volunteer army.[8]

After capturing *Susannah*, Manley lingered at Portsmouth for two days repairing damage from his battle with *Hope*. Looking forward to another engagement, he sailed the schooners right back to the cruising grounds of the British brig. Not a single enemy warship appeared off the coast, but Manley did not know why.

On the afternoon of March 10, the last of the big brigs from Whitehaven hove into sight off the Isle of Shoals. The schooners surrounded the 300-ton ship *Stakesby*, James Watt, master, laden with more coal and provisions. Mortality among the hogs on the shaken *Stakesby* provided evidence of her troublesome seventeen-week crossing. Of 164 hogs, only 3 survived the passage. With a fair wind from the east, Manley attempted to carry the prize into Gloucester. As he passed Cape Ann, darkness descended, and with it a spreading fog. Without a pilot, Manley steered by dead reckoning. Three miles south of Gloucester, *Stakesby* piled up on the rocks and *Hancock* struck a shoal, tearing up her bottom. Manley got out his speaking trumpet and warned off Tucker, Ayres, and Waters. With frequent soundings they guided their schooners inshore. By attaching a hawser to the wounded *Hancock*, they pulled her off the shoal and, through the fog, nursed her into port.

Unfortunately, *Stakesby* bilged and water damaged part of her cargo. Women and children passengers found the grounding terrifying. Sargent brought them off during the night and placed them in temporary homes. In the morning he sent a number of boats with a detail from Manley's schooners to get *Stakesby* off the rocks, but she would not budge. Boats from Gloucester clustered about the vessel, and for three days men worked around the clock to salvage the cargo and every stitch of sail they could pull down from the tops.[9]

On the evening of March 15, *Hope* made a surprise appearance. Shuldham learned of the wrecked *Stakesby* and sent Dawson to investigate. *Hope,* the only cruiser released from Nantasket Road since the admiral's recall on March 8, made a determined effort to recapture the grounded ship. Dawson chased away the salvagers with his 4s and sent a boat to investigate. The men poked around the cargo and found nothing of value but three casks of porter, which they smashed. At 9:00 P.M. they sprinkled small piles of kindling with oil and set *Stakesby* on fire. High winds struck the coast, and *Hope* departed. The storm raged for twenty-four hours, and when it passed beachcombers found broken casks and barrels strewn for miles along the shore. Nothing more could be saved. In reporting the loss to Washington, Sargent wrote, "poor Captn Watts has lost all his venter [capital], being about 150 pounds sterling." Whether the money went down with the ship or found its way into the pockets of Manley's mariners, no one knows.[10]

Manley's squadron lay at Gloucester for several days, waiting for carpenters to fit *Hancock* with a new bowsprit. While they waited, a letter came from the general predicting the evacuation of Boston. Still uncertain of Howe's destination, Washington ordered Manley to find Shuldham's fleet and "dog them."[11]

For Manley, getting the squadron out to sea was becoming unexpectedly problematic. When Dawson located *Stakesby* on the 15th he also discovered the schooners' current hiding place. Driven back to Boston by the storm, Dawson informed Shuldham. The admiral anticipated trouble and dispatched *Renown* and *Niger* with orders to cruise in the bay, protect and intercept incoming transports, and see them safely off to Halifax. Before leaving Boston, Shuldham added five more vessels to Banks's command, including *Lively* and *Fowey,* with orders to keep to sea between Cape Cod and Cape Ann and to search for vessels from the broken convoy. Protecting His Majesty's shipping meant bottling up Manley's command, as well as numerous privateers operating out of Salem and other ports. To Banks's orders, Shuldham added, "You are to take, sink, burn, or destroy all Rebel Armed Vessels you may meet with, and to continue upon this service till further orders." Banks stationed *Hope* off Cape Ann and ordered *Niger* to cruise within easy reach of Marblehead and Gloucester.[12]

On the night of March 20, Howe ordered Castle William blown up and the blockhouses and barracks burned. Flames rose high above the harbor, tingeing low-hanging clouds with shades of red. Dozens of vessels lay in King Road, their decks crowded with eleven hundred Tories seeking passage to England. They witnessed the spectacle with sorrow. Their homes and possessions had been left behind. As they watched flames leap in fiery coils upon the black backdrop of night, they wondered why King George III, their omnipotent protector, the regent to whom they had sworn fidelity, had allowed the unthinkable to happen— the evacuation of Boston.[13]

Manley observed the flames from Gloucester as he and his squadron slipped out of the harbor and headed for sea. The red beacon in the sky held his attention. Had Howe set fire to Boston? Manley once had a home there, and the glow caused him to reflect. He had no definite plans, just orders to "dog" the fleet, so he sailed toward the glare in the heavens, drawn, like many others, by his own curiosity.

At daylight the schooners worked to sea with every man crowded on deck, all watching the thick, black smoke rising from the direction of Boston. Not a vessel lay in sight as they sailed slowly to the south. Late afternoon, three or four leagues off the Boston lighthouse, the watch reported a vessel making for port. She had the cut of *Hope,* but when she stayed her course they gave chase. As the schooners closed, the lighthouse tender signaled ashore "attack at sea," and at 5:00 P.M. the sloop *Savage,* 8, and brig *Diligent,* 6, slipped cable and made sail. Manley did not see the enemy coming and continued to chase the brig. At 6:00 P.M. he fired a gun and brought her to. As he came abeam, the watch sighted *Savage* and *Diligent* coming fast. Manley gave them a quick scan and opted for the safety of his squadron. Shouting orders through his speaking trumpet, he led the schooners south, his commodore's ensign flapping defiantly from the maintopmast gallant. Hands on the rescued brig reset their sails and hurried into Nantasket Road. Two weeks later she unloaded her cargo at Halifax.[14]

Savage and *Diligent* chased Manley's schooners toward Plymouth, and as they approached, men manning a battery on Gurnet Point lit two signal fires and discharged alarm guns. Sarah Sever of Kingston, who believed Boston was burning, observed the flames and speculated that the enemy had landed and set fire to the lighthouse. She went to bed "tolerably well composed" that night but worried about her friends in nearby Plymouth. In the morning she drank coffee with a friend and heard the rest of the story. There was no enemy, just Manley's four schooners running into Plymouth, but the vessels had loomed large and demonic in the darkness. A boat sent out to see if they could discover the enemy "returned with terrible accounts" of "four large ships within the Gurnet and . . . landing men very fast." The Committee of Safety ignited a huge alarm fire atop the "burying hill." Express riders rode to Wareham and Middleboro, twenty miles away, to call out the militia. Families packed up their children and, with "as much furniture as they could get away," headed for the interior. Others waited "with their chairs at the door and cloaks on from half past ten until after four, ready to fly in a moment." In the morning, "to their great joy," they learned that the panic had been caused by Manley—"and so," Sarah Sever wrote cheerfully, "ended this mighty affair."[15]

Manley's attack on the brig and his escape to Plymouth had also been observed by Col. Francis Hutcheson, who expressed his disgust by writing, "The Rebel privateers continue to insult us. Five [four] of them appeared off the lighthouse yesterday in sight of our fleet, and they have taken several ships within this last month. In short, I do not see any great alteration for the better since the departure of Admiral G[rave]s, who was so obnoxious."[16]

Manley sailed two days later and headed around Boston Bay for Beverly. Burke had just finished installing *Warren*'s four 4s, a windfall from the prize *Susannah*. Bartlett reported forty cartridges for every gun, and he still had in storage two half barrels of powder taken from the prize.[17]

Manley passed off Alderton Point on his way to Beverly and observed Shuldham's fleet inside the harbor, waiting for a favorable wind. Three days later Sargent reported that "seventy sail passed our Cape [Ann] steering about east by south."[18] If Washington had any doubts regarding Howe's intentions, he could now sleep better knowing the enemy was bound for Halifax. For two days the balance of Shuldham's fleet remained in King Road, and then it, too, sailed. Among the last vessels leaving Boston was the brig *Elizabeth*, crowded with Tories and piled high with goods pilfered from Boston patriots. A last-minute reshuffling of passengers delayed her departure.[19]

Manley decided more might be accomplished by dividing his command. *Franklin* and *Warren* stood off Cape Ann, waiting to fall in with the second convoy. Manley raised his banner on *Hancock* and sailed south with *Lee* and *Lynch*, posting the schooners off Boston Bay in clear view of Shuldham's fleet.

At 3:00 P.M. on March 27, HMS *Chatham*, 50, made sail and edged slowly out of Nantasket Road. As she drew toward the lighthouse, Manley could see the admiral's pennant flying from her tops. Behind her sailed several armed vessels accompanied by a seemingly endless number of transports, sixty-six in all. *Centurion*, 50, followed last, having fallen out of sailing order when she ran afoul of *Niger*, lost her main yard, and split the mizzen topsail. Manley "dogged" the convoy but stayed clear of *Centurion*, whose lookouts had a clear view of his three schooners.[20]

In a season of frequent storms, the convoy enjoyed delightful sailing weather, pressing steadily forward by the grace of accommodating southerlies. Manley followed the convoy well up the coast of Nova Scotia, but not a straggler fell out. Disgusted with the unseasonably balmy breezes, he brought the schooners about and headed for Boston, curious to see if Washington had occupied the town.

On April 2, lookouts on *Hancock* reported a lone brig fifteen leagues off Cape Ann and on course for Nova Scotia. She looked like a straggler, and Manley ordered the squadron to take her. The brig moved off under a full spread of sail but, with her heavy lading, pounded cumbersomely through the rollers. The swift *Hancock* gained rapidly, and Manley, poised on the forward deck, ordered her to strike.

The wallowing vessel proved to be the brig *Elizabeth*, Peter Ramsey, master, the same vessel that had dallied at Boston to scoop up the last crumbs of occupation. Tory Crean Brush and his consorts had lost precious time loading tons of plunder gathered from the town's citizens. Neither Ramsey nor Brush seemed worried about the safety of their loot. HMS *Niger* had lost her fore topgallant mast, jib, and jib stays when running afoul of *Centurion*. She remained behind for repairs and sailed on March 29 as escort for the last six transports, one being *Elizabeth*. *Niger* lost sight of the brig on the 30th during a gale followed by snow and hazy weather. In the morning *Niger* located most of her convoy, but *Elizabeth* had fallen far behind.[21]

Ramsey ignored Manley's command to strike and for his insolence received a sharp broadside. A sergeant and twelve soldiers appeared on deck with muskets and poured a volley into *Hancock*. With ports slung open, *Lee* and *Lynch* came up as Manley reloaded his 4s. Ramsey had seen enough and let loose his sails.

Manley could see that the brig was deeply laden, but he had no idea of her contents until he took her into Portsmouth. In addition to tons of merchandise, Ramsey had crowded sixty-three passengers on board.

William Jackson, a noted Tory importer, claimed property valued at £24,000. Brush, formerly of New York "but lately a most bitter refugee in Boston," acted as Howe's agent. Wentworth considered Brush a mean man who behaved very insolently and with great rapacity during the looting binge. Other passengers, like Phineas Jones and Caleb Wheaton (also Whitten) and his two sons, John and Joseph, were renowned "bad men."[22]

In sorting through the cargo, Wentworth uncovered great bundles of goods stripped from Boston storehouses and dumped into the brig's hold without any attempt to protect them from damage. Sailors had collected piles of loot and scattered it helter-skelter, wherever space could be found. "There appeared from the pillage of this cargo," Wentworth reported, "the property was in him that could secret the most."

Howe had encouraged the pilfering. After learning of the capture of *Elizabeth*, he wrote Lord Germain at the Admiralty, "We feel this loss the more at present as there was a quantity of shoes on board which are much wanted for the soldiery, as well as woolen articles that would have been very useful to them."

Wentworth sent the prisoners to Marblehead, including thirteen soldiers from the King's Own Regiment. Among the "souls" were four blacks, two men and two women. Wentworth could not establish the antecedents of the blacks and confined them in jail, "concluding they may be esteemed a part of the prize." He also impounded £260 from the personal belongings of Jackson.[23]

During Wentworth's investigation, Portsmouth merchant Richard Hart spied *Elizabeth* in the harbor and claimed her, stating she had been captured in October on her return from the West Indies and carried into Boston. Hart described her cargo, and in rooting through the hold Wentworth uncovered seventeen hogsheads of rum and four of sugar that had never been removed by her captors. The brig had not been condemned in a British admiralty court, thus leaving in question her status as a fair prize. With no court in New Hampshire to study the matter, Manley and Wentworth set off for Cambridge to seek Washington's advice.[24]

Jonathan Glover also interviewed the prisoners and determined that twenty-two of them were "bad" enough to be held for questioning by the Massachusetts Council. Because the annual infestation of smallpox was raging throughout the colony, he placed women and children in

Marblehead homes "in [a] manner that shall be the least charge to the Government." The council, however, decided the best place to keep Tories like Brush, Jackson, and Ramsey was the Boston jail, which was now empty. James Otis of the council confined Brush and his companions to separate cells "without the privilege of pen, ink, paper or candle." Caleb Wheaton and sons, the "bad men," obtained their release by giving bonds of £500 each. Otis discovered that the Wheatons, along with Phineas Jones, had stolen a fishing boat from Marbleheader Eleazer Ingalls on the night of February 28 and escaped to a British warship. The Wheatons promised to make restitution in exchange for their freedom. During the court hearings, Phineas Jones "eloped . . . notwithstanding he was under the care of the guards."[25]

A few days before Manley's three schooners intercepted *Elizabeth*, Tucker and Burke had fallen in behind the convoy as it passed Cape Ann. When no gale disturbed the sailing formation, the two captains parted and headed back to their sailing grounds off Cape Ann, *Warren* staying well to the northeast and *Franklin* closer inshore. On April 3, with rain falling and visibility declining, Tucker left his post off Thatcher's Island and headed for Gloucester. As he rounded the island, the watch reported a frigate bearing toward them. Tucker had all his sails set and not too far to go, but the race was on. The 28-gun HMS *Milford*, Capt. John Burr, had just arrived at Boston on March 27, and Shuldham had attached the frigate to Banks's squadron. Burr closed rapidly on *Franklin*, but when he realized the schooner could not be headed he fired eight shots. Tucker rounded into Gloucester Harbor and proceeded up to the town. Late in the afternoon a squall swept across the cape and drove *Milford* out to sea.[26]

Once again Manley had his squadron together, but the crews had become restless. They had not been paid, neither Continental pay nor a penny from their prizes. Bartlett wrote an urgent note to General Ward begging for funds. Red tape intervened. Before issuing warrants, Washington wanted the captains to produce "their rolls upon oath."

For His Excellency, another problem had been brewing around the commodore's coffeepot. On May 3 it boiled to the surface and flustered General Ward. "Commodore Manley declines going on another cruise until he has a larger ship." Washington may not have been surprised, but the one man he could ill afford to lose was John Manley.[27]

❧ 16 ❧
A Month in Transition

hen *Shuldham's last convoy reached Halifax,* Washington believed Howe would never return to Boston and issued orders to his commanders for a change of base to New York, leaving four or five regiments behind to "fortify the town and erect such works for its defence." He had already developed his plans, including the disposition of the schooners. The small squadron could still be useful, and when he turned the command of New England troops over to Maj. Gen. Artemus Ward, he included Manley's mariners.[1]

Artemus Ward, at the age of forty-eight, had many years of military experience but a weak constitution. A descendent of William Ward, an early Puritan settler, young Artemus grew up on a large farm in Worcester County. He received a simple, country education in Shrewsbury, and with supplemental tutoring under the direction of a local preacher he finally entered—and eventually graduated from—Harvard.

Like most country boys of his day, he joined the local militia and served in the Seven Years War. At the age of twenty-eight, Major Ward marched with Maj. Gen. James Abercromby's army against Ticonderoga, and within a year rose to the rank of lieutenant colonel. He returned home still a young man but with his health broken. Ward turned to politics and distinguished himself as a patriot, serving as delegate to the First and Second Provincial Congresses. After the skirmish at Lexington and Concord, he offered his services to the colony and resumed a military role. Washington added him to his staff of generals but thought Ward best suited to administrative duties. Ward, however, believed he should have been named commander in chief and resentment continued to fester.

After twenty years of rich food and little physical activity, Ward had grown "too stout for his years." He developed a bladder stone, not inca-

Maj. Gen. Artemus Ward took command of the armed schooners after Washington departed from Boston. Portrait by Charles Wilson Peale (ca. 1794–95). Courtesy Independence National Historical Park, Philadelphia.

pacitating but distressing enough to drain his vitality. An elegantly dressed man of medium height, Ward had a long, sharp nose and a pointed chin as rigid as his disposition. In speaking, he rambled through his thoughts, often baffling his listeners. If Washington observed these characteristics in his new commander, he set them aside in deference to Ward's devotion to the American cause. As His Excellency soon discovered, Ward was far better suited to the banter of politics than to military matters, especially in situations requiring crisp decisions, bold planning, and quick action. Moreover, Ward's brief military experience provided him with no insight into managing the affairs of Manley's schooners.[2]

On April 4, before departing for New York, Washington had a long discussion with the new commander. He left written instructions with Ward regarding the schooners and penned a short list of naval problems requiring immediate attention. Prizes must be libeled by admiralty courts in the district into which they were carried as soon as petitioned by the agent, a matter Washington had been unable to accomplish to his own satisfaction. British officers and enlisted men must be questioned by local

authorities and thereafter confined or paroled as the committee dictat-
ed. No condemned property could be auctioned until the articles for sale
had been described and advertised three times in local papers, and the
Continental commissary and quartermaster must be given first refusal
rights on every captured cargo.

When Shuldham evacuated Boston, he left behind dozens of vessels captured as prizes and some still laden with cargoes. Ward inherited the puzzle of determining ownership. Washington ordered him to
hold all vessels until an exact inventory was taken and claimants bonded
to abide by "the [final] determination of Congress" regarding ownership.
The general said good-bye to Ward, joined his headquarters' entourage,
and headed for New York.[3]

After capturing *Elizabeth*, Manley borrowed a horse and rode to
Cambridge with Wentworth to discuss several issues with His
Excellency. By the time they arrived Washington had left, so they rode
into Boston to locate Ward. They did not wish to detain the general,
who was nursing his ailing bladder stones, but they had several questions. Since most of *Elizabeth*'s cargo had been looted from Boston merchants, who owned the goods? Since the brig had not been adjudicated
in a British admiralty court, who owned her? Wentworth advised Ward
of a recent ruling that "all vessels & goods retaken previous to a condemnation by a British Court of Admiralty were liable to a partial
decree," awarding not more than one-third or less than one-quarter of
the value to the captors. Did this rule apply to *Elizabeth*? Wentworth
also understood that all enemy property was subject to full confiscation,
but he wanted Ward's official concurrence before taking action.

In his first test of leadership, Ward admitted he did not know, "having received no instruction on this point." He supposed the vessel and
cargo would have to be libeled. Wentworth, of course, knew this. His
reason for bringing the problem to headquarters was that New
Hampshire had not established admiralty courts, and he must act quickly to prevent the deterioration of her cargo. Ward shrugged apathetical-
ly and offered no further advice. Manley and Wentworth must wait for
courts to be established.

Before returning to Portsmouth, Wentworth spoke with Boston
merchants whose property had been looted by Howe's agents. If Ward
could not help him, perhaps he could reach an agreement with the
claimants to share a portion of the value of their recovered goods with

Manley's prize crew. Showing no sign of gratitude, the merchants demanded an immediate return of their property and threatened a suit to recover it. Wentworth left Boston no wiser. Out of duty and frustration he wrote Washington and asked for his "opinion & direction."

Two months passed before Wentworth was able to release *Elizabeth*'s cargo. Ward never answered any of the questions Wentworth asked. This incident occurred at the outset of Ward's ascent to the command and typified his responsiveness during his administration. Preoccupation with his physical incapacities had the effect of demobilizing the use of his intellect. He chose not to make difficult decisions.[4]

Manley discussed another matter with Ward. Five months had passed since *Hancock* captured the ordnance brig *Nancy*. Shares had been set for the crew but no prize money distributed. Other prizes awaited action in admiralty courts, but not the *Nancy*. The Continental Army had stripped her cargo months ago. Manley wanted to know—Where's the money?

His men were dissatisfied, Manley warned Ward, and threatening to leave. For three weeks they had lounged in the rented barracks near Beverly's wharf and stared glumly at their prizes in the harbor, unattended but for a small guard. From time to time they watched Bartlett bring off cargo, filling carts with provisions and clothing, but no money ever came with the orders to fill the carts. And while the crew waited, they talked to men who sailed on privateers where money flowed like honey—good, hard money, not Continental dollars. If the general expected to keep the squadron at sea, Manley warned, he had better do something about the men's pay, and do it fast.

Colonel Glover and Bartlett also paid Ward a visit, pressing him for money to pay the marines. Ward shrugged. Washington had not left him enough funds to cover the expenses of his own small command. Besides, His Excellency's instructions did not mention pay for the men of the schooners. Ward's answer to Glover was to "supply the places of such men as might leave the privateers out of his own regiment." Glover did not think his men would be interested and returned to Beverly with Bartlett, convinced their trip had been wasted.

Ward, however, did write Washington seeking direction. On the matter of *Nancy*, Washington asked Congress for an authorization of prize money. He also advised Ward that "all accounts respecting the armed vessels should be paid by the agents." This could only be accomplished if the agents borrowed more money. However, Washington reminded Ward that "the trial of the prizes cannot be much longer deferred. They will have cash for the goods," Washington thought, more than enough to cover their current demands. If not, Ward must issue warrants for the wages due. Quoting Washington's letter, Ward advised the agents to pay the men's wages, but he edited out the section authorizing him to issue warrants.[5] As a consequence of Washington's departure, a shortage of money, and Ward's assumption of command, the armed schooners languished in port for over a month.

Condemnation proceedings began on April 16 at Ipswich, Essex County, and during the next three days the court condemned *Jenny, Little Hannah, Sally, Betsey, Polly, Concord,* and *Nancy.* Judge Timothy Pickering Jr. instructed the Essex County sheriff to sell the vessels at public auction and from the proceeds pay court costs and deduct "your own fees." The balance of the proceeds was to be delivered to John Manley et al. for the distribution of shares to the men. The court declared Peter Barberie of New Jersey the rightful owner of *Sally,* leaving Winborn Adams and his company with only a one-third share of the proceeds.

Judge Nathan Cushing held court at Plymouth and condemned *Polly, Industry, Happy Return, Norfolk, Sally,* and an unnamed schooner captured by Coit. Papers for Coit's captures had been lost at headquarters, thereby delaying the proceedings and proving that the "humorous genius" did not have an exclusive patent on blundering. Ward ordered the agents to advertise the condemned vessels for sale on May 20. Another five prizes still awaited court action, including *Henry and Esther, Susannah, Stakesby,* and *Elizabeth.*[6]

On April 16, while crews of the schooners waited for pay, Maj. Joseph Ward, nephew and aide-de-camp to the general, learned "unofficially" that Manley had been designated to command one of the two Continental frigates being built at Newburyport.[7] If the major informed his uncle, the general failed to notify Manley. Perhaps Ward was waiting for official word from Washington, as Manley's nomination did not pass Congress until the following day.[8]

On April 18 Washington asked Ward to determine whether the prize ship *Jenny* and the brig *Little Hannah* could be fitted out as cruisers. He mentioned nothing of Manley's promotion, as word had not reached him from Philadelphia, but he did ask Ward to send a person of "knowledge and trust" to inspect the two prizes. Recalling his promise to Manley, he added, "If Commodore Manley is in your neighborhood, his opinion of them must have weight, and if they are fit for the purpose . . . he will have his choice of them. . . . The sooner this is put in execution the better."

A week passed without further word of Manley's rumored transfer. On April 25 Washington again pressed Congress to place a value on *Nancy's* cargo so a "dividend" could be paid to Manley and his crew. "It will give them spirit," he declared, "and encourage them to be alert in looking out for other prizes." The general expressed annoyance that, under Ward's management, all the schooners lay inactive.[9]

Bartlett found Manley at Marblehead and informed him that Ward wanted *Jenny* and *Little Hannah* inspected as potential cruisers.[10] Manley displayed no enthusiasm for the task, but Bartlett assured him the best vessel would be fitted out as the commodore's new flagship. By now Manley must have heard of his "unofficial" captaincy in the Continental Navy and felt annoyed that neither Ward nor Washington had mentioned it. Manley and Gustavus Fellows, another old salt, trekked down to Beverly Harbor and spent the day finding fault with both vessels. Ward concealed his joy when he informed Washington that the examiners considered neither vessel "fit for the service." Knowing His Excellency might ask why, Ward cited several armed vessels in the bay that were "larger than our privateers." By asking for a vessel of "sufficient force" to chase them away, Ward implied that neither *Jenny* nor *Little Hannah* would suffice.[11]

Washington reacted with surprise to Ward's reply, as his information had been exactly the opposite. Five days later he learned of Manley's refusal to go on a cruise without command of a larger vessel.[12] The commodore's resignation rippled through the squadron. Seven officers resigned—Stiles and Ogelbie of *Hancock,* Fettyplace and Salter of *Franklin,* Ryan of *Warren,* Gill of *Lee,* and Tiley of *Lynch*—and with them went most of the crews. Singly and in groups they made their way across the harbor to Salem and, for tidy little bonuses and the promise of better pay, signed on privateers. With Ward at the helm of financial affairs, not one of the crew believed he would be paid. Washington ascribed the resignations to Ward's lack of leadership, but he held Congress equally responsible for foot-dragging.

Ward manifested impatience for any problem brought to his headquarters concerning the schooners, but now he had to pick another commander, replace officers, and recruit new crews. If that were not enough to grind his bladder stones, civilians pooling money to arm privateers hounded him for officers. To Washington he complained, "Frequent applications are made to me to appoint commanders of the privateers, and for other matters which no person here is authorized to transact." Washington ignored most of Ward's complaints and tried to refocus the ailing general's attention on solutions, not problems.

Washington ordered both prizes purchased, but only if they sold for less than their value. *Jenny* went for £1,950, a fair price by Bartlett's calculations, but not so with *Little Hannah*. Washington purchased her for £520 and presented Ward with another vessel to try his patience. Ward disposed of the vessel quickly. Robert Morris, vice chairman of the Marine Committee needed a good sailing vessel to go on a "voyage upon particular business immediately." Ward ordered Bartlett to turn *Little Hannah* over to John Bradford, who would know what to do with her. Bradford subsequently named her *Dispatch* to signify her intended occupation.[13]

On April 17, when Congress selected a commander for the 32-gun frigate *Hancock,* the secretary mistakenly wrote the name "William Manly." Three weeks passed before they caught the mistake and awarded John Manley his commission in the Continental Navy. In May Manley said good-bye to Ward and departed for Newburyport to superintend the completion of his fine new frigate. Whenever time permitted, he traveled to Boston on the matter of prize money. Manley had served his time on Washington's schooners, and served well. Like most patriots who went to sea, Manley's appetite for prize money surpassed his desire for fame. He earned both and had collected the latter. Now he wanted to be paid. Washington's former commodore was a relentless man, and Ward had not seen the last of him.[14]

With Manley gone and the Continental Navy in business, Washington could have turned his schooners over to the Marine Committee and concentrated all his attention on defending New York. With Ward's disinterest in the schooners, the transfer of authority made sense. Why upset the ailing general by saddling him with five small vessels? Washington considered his options. He interviewed Esek Hopkins, commodore of the Continental fleet, but Hopkins did not impress the general as a man of action. On his return from a cruise to the Bahamas, his squadron had clashed ingloriously with HMS *Glasgow* in Long

Island Sound, and the lone British frigate made Hopkins's attack formation look amateurish.

Washington thought Hopkins too preoccupied with small details to think strategically and too willing to make excuses for avoidable delays. In Washington's estimation, Hopkins would find reasons for not cooperating with the army and probably surround himself with a staff of officers who imitated him. Hopkins would not use the schooners to their best advantage, or perhaps not use them at all, which Washington considered an enormous mistake. His Excellency had begun to understand the importance of selecting good subordinates. Until command of the Continental Navy shifted to a more competent officer, he would keep control of the schooners. He instructed Ward to issue warrants for wages due the men and bring an end to their inactivity.[15]

With Manley gone, Ward wanted a commodore appointed to relieve his own workload. Washington preferred to wait. None of the captains had distinguished themselves, and new officers must be recruited to fill resignations. Washington still toyed with the idea of adding more vessels. Choosing a commodore could wait until the overall command crystallized. In the meantime, Ward must become more assertive.

As the war entered its second year, perhaps no one in the colonies understood better than Washington that the defeat of the British depended on the neutralization of their navy. This could not be done with just five schooners, but when Howe withdrew from Boston, Washington knew that the privates of Glover's seafaring regiment had helped throttle the flow of supplies to His Majesty's forces. They were as much a part of the siege of Boston as the men who huddled behind earthworks and skirmished with foraging parties. Because of superior naval power, the British army escaped from Boston. Another British army, five years hence, would not be so lucky.

🏵 17 🏵
The Death of
the Valiant Mugford

ad Ward been less occupied improving Boston's defenses and
more industrious about keeping Washington's fleet active,
many rich prizes may have fallen prey to the schooners.
With the onset of spring, dozens of transports sailed from
England, laden with everything from ordnance and fresh regiments to
provisions and clothing. In his hurried departure from Boston,
Shuldham left too few frigates behind to intercept the broken convoys.
Captain Banks kept three warships in Nantasket Road, safe from rebel
guns emplaced on shore but in sight of any transport working toward the
Boston lighthouse.

For three weeks, Samuel Tucker, now senior captain of
Washington's squadron, attempted to piece together a crew of thirty
from the dissidents still occupying quarters in Bartlett's rented barracks.
Eighteen men agreed to sail, but only after the agent borrowed £35 to
advance their wages.

Tucker added a lieutenant, master, and master's mate to the crew
and transferred his flag to *Hancock*. Twenty-six-year-old Nicholas
Bartlett of Marblehead agreed to serve as lieutenant. In February 1775
Bartlett had been a master on an inbound vessel intercepted by HMS
Lively. When the British had attempted to impress the crew, boats from
Marblehead rowed to their rescue and retrieved all but one man. Bartlett
had a score to settle.[1]

On May 6 Tucker cleared Beverly Harbor and cruised to *Hancock's*
old hunting grounds off Boston Bay. He ranged well to sea, staying out
of sight of the frigates posted in Nantasket Road. The next morning the
watch sighted two brigs standing for Boston. As Tucker suspected, word
of Howe's withdrawal had not reached London in time. With a stiff

easterly blowing, he came about and swung in behind both vessels, scanning them with a practiced eye. Most transports were now armed, and Tucker did not enjoy the prospect of being knocked apart by two vessels twice the size of his schooner. The transports slowed, allowing Tucker to edge closer. A lookout on board one of them spied *Hancock*'s six carriage guns and shouted a warning to the deck. Both vessels crowded on sail, but all too late. Two miles off the Boston lighthouse, a single blast from *Hancock*'s 4-pounder brought the vessels about.[2]

Prize crews took possession of both brigs and sailed into Lynn, seven nautical miles north of the lighthouse. The 120-ton brig *Jane*, James Fulton, master, had sailed from Cork on April 1 laden with provisions and fuel, and covered by insurance amounting to £6,000. Sailing out of St. Michael, the 100-ton brig *William*, Richard Price, master, carried a cargo of wine and fruits from the Azores. Both masters expressed disbelief when they learned the British had been "obliged" to evacuate Boston. When he departed from Cork, Fulton had observed five regiments—including Hessian and Hanoverian units—preparing to embark for America, but at the time none had sailed.

Fulton wrote *Jane*'s owners in England, informing them the vessel had been lost "within two miles of the light-house of Boston, and in sight of four men of war. We are used very well," he added, "and have liberty to walk where we please; but when we shall get home, I cannot tell." Fulton failed to mention the stiff easterly that had prevented Banks's four warships from coming to his rescue. Tucker may not have been so daring had the wind been blowing from the west.[3]

At Marblehead, Jonathan Glover received word of Tucker's prizes, mounted his horse, and jogged to Lynn to take possession of the vessels. As both brigs had insured cargoes, the masters wanted them libeled as quickly as possible. For once, the libeling process moved with uncommon speed. Judge Pickering placed ads on May 20, advising that "the owners of said vessels, or any persons concerned therein, may appear and shew cause, if they have any, why the said vessels, with their cargoes and appertenances, should not be condemned." *Jane* sold at auction at Marblehead on July 4 and *William* on July 17. After nearly a year, the libeling process had achieved an element of routine.[4]

By transferring his flag to *Hancock*, Tucker had left *Franklin* with only one officer, twenty-six-year-old sailing master James Mugford Jr. While other captains muddled with enlistments, Mugford took the ini-

James Mugford Jr. lost his life fighting to save the armed schooner *Franklin*. Lithograph by L. S. Bradford & Co., Boston, 1854. Courtesy Mr. F. S. Hicks and U.S. Naval Historical Center.

tiative and prepared *Franklin* for a cruise. Retaining ten men from the original crew, he obtained six more from Glover's regiment. Mugford exercised his master's warrant and took command of the schooner. Ignoring protocol, he sidestepped Ward, who felt he had no authority to commission officers. Mugford exercised a skipper's privilege and named two Marbleheaders—Thomas Russell and Jeremiah Hibbert—as acting lieutenants. Bartlett advanced a month's wages to the crew, and Mugford sailed from Beverly on May 15. He knew exactly where to look for prizes and set a course for Boston Bay.

On April 10 the 280-ton ship *Hope*, Alexander Lumsdale, master, had sailed from Cork in a convoy of ten vessels escorted by the 28-gun HMS *Greyhound*, Capt. Archibald Dickson. Three more convoys sailed shortly afterward, bringing the total number of vessels bound for Boston to ninety-three. In *Greyhound*'s convoy, *Hope* was one of four large store-ships laden with ordnance. Just before she sailed, the Admiralty discovered fifteen hundred barrels of powder on board. They considered the ladening a mistake, since *Hope*'s owners had not been licensed to carry powder. Because the convoy was scheduled to sail that day, the Admiralty simply noted the error.[5]

During the crossing, Shuldham's frigates intercepted most of the transports and diverted them to Halifax, where *Greyhound* arrived on May 16 with all of her convoy but *Hope*. Heavily laden, *Hope* fell behind, and in a fog on May 10 Lumsdale lost contact with the convoy. In accordance with his orders, he stayed on course for Boston.[6]

A week later Mugford observed *Hope* wallowing through swells seven leagues east of the lighthouse. A steady breeze from the northeast filled her sails, but to Mugford she seemed laboriously slow, acting like a decoy dragging an anchor to entice a privateer. He approached the vessel cautiously, counting gunports, three on each side, but he could not see the 4s and 6s behind them or the dozen swivels swinging on their pivots. Mugford followed her almost to the lighthouse, posting a lookout to keep a close eye on the spars visible in Nantasket Road. With an easterly beating into the harbor, *Renown* and her consorts could not come out, but breezes could change without warning.

Mugford brought *Franklin* abeam of *Hope* and, in a swift, unexpected move, grappled onto her stern quarter. After sailing side by side for two or three leagues, Lumsdale had relaxed. The schooner behaved like a friendly pilot boat. When Mugford's pistol-brandishing marines clambered on deck, Lumsdale realized his error and ordered his men to quarters. Eighteen hands armed only with knives climbed topside, and Lumsdale, with one eye on the idle *Renown* and the other on Mugford, ordered his men to cut the rigging. Mugford warned them off, vowing to shoot the first man who put a knife to the ropes. Knives skittered to the deck. Lumsdale swallowed hard and surrendered. Not a shot had been fired by either vessel, although the carriage guns on *Hope* had been double-shotted with grape.

Mugford, grasping the importance of *Hope*'s cargo, needed to speed the prize to a place of safety. Lieutenant Dawson, in another *Hope*, had already started to tack out of the Road with all fourteen guns loaded.[7] Mugford chose Boston, but to avoid crossing paths with the Royal Navy he steered toward Deer Island, keeping well out of *Renown*'s range. With the wind holding from the east, he led *Hope* into Pulling Point Gut, a narrow, winding fisherman's channel running between Shirley Point and Deer Island. Had Mugford consulted his tide tables, he may have chosen a different route. He had been through the winding gut many times before, but with the ebb running full the heavily laden *Hope* struck bottom as she entered.[8]

News of *Hope's* grounding reached Marblehead about noon. Jonathan Glover threw a saddle on his fastest horse and rode down the shore road to Pulling Point Gut. The Gut was well named. *Hope* was not the first vessel to need a little pulling, but for a ship her size a little pulling would not get the job done. She had to be lightened.

On this particular Friday, a day designated by Congress for observing the Continental fast, worshipers from Boston were filing out of Christ Church when someone spotted *Franklin* leading her prize inshore. They stood on the hill and watched *Hope* ease into Pulling Point Gut. Someone in the crowd cried out, "Look! She's aground!" Dozens of churchgoers rushed to their boats and sailed out to help.

Glover enlisted hundreds of small craft, and by dusk they had carried off twelve hundred barrels of powder, weighing roughly seventy-five tons. He sent an express to Ward asking for at least 150 guards, as he expected to be attacked after dark. Another express returned with "the best pilot in Boston." Glover wanted the prize moved that night with the flood tide, but the pilot refused to try the channel in the dark, arguing it was too crooked and "he could not see the marks." Glover insisted. With a cargo containing a thousand carbines and bayonets, cartridge boxes, five gun carriages, thousands of pieces of hardware, and *Hope's* six guns, he wanted the vessel moved to Boston before daylight.[9]

Glover offered to light the channel by using small boats with lanterns, and the pilot agreed to try. At midnight lanterns dotted the channel, marking off shoals. The tide was up, and a fair breeze blew off the bay. Glover made short sail, and, with many hands on board, the pilot snaked the vessel through the Gut, followed by Mugford in *Franklin*. At daylight both vessels bumped against Hancock's wharf. "I ceased not till with vast labour and fatigue the whole cargo was secured," Glover reported. "On account of this business, for four days and three nights I did not pull off my cloths, and scarcely slept at all."[10]

Ward, who had missed the excitement, dutifully informed His Excellency, "Captain Mugford this day took and brought into this harbour . . . a very valuable prize." From the invoice, Ward could appreciate its value to the Continental Army, but three days passed before Glover finished the full inventory. He estimated the value of the cargo at between £40,000 and £50,000. With a nice commission pending for his trouble and a fresh supply of money to placate the crew, Glover attempted to expedite the libeling process and notified Judge Pickering of his wishes.[11]

Word of *Hope*'s capture did not reach Halifax for several days, but even before the bad news arrived Captain Dickson of *Greyhound* shared his apprehensions with Shuldham. Before departing from England, Dickson had received an anonymous letter intimating that Lumsdale "was disaffectedly inclined." As a precaution Dickson put a petty officer and two marines on board, with orders "to attend very particularly to the conduct of the Master, and if he suspected him of any design to separate from the convoy, or to put the ship in the way of being taken by the Rebel Privateers, to confine him and take command of her." When the ship fell behind the convoy, neither Lumsdale nor the royal spies believed sailing to Boston violated the Admiralty's instructions. Why Lumsdale and his naval observers made no effort to defend the vessel can be explained by Mugford's deception as a friendly pilot. Lumsdale's order to his men to cut down the rigging came too late. There is no evidence other than Dickson's statement to suggest Lumsdale hoped to be captured. Dickson's explanation to Shuldham, however, provided the admiral with an excuse for losing *Hope*.

Three weeks later Shuldham obtained confirmation from Banks that *Hope* had been snatched by a "privateer." Using his current line of reasoning, the admiral suggested that all "masters of merchant ships and persons of little property or consideration are easily . . . bribed. Their treachery may be productive of the most fatal consequences." In the future, he suggested, military supplies should be transported in warships under the command of a king's officer.[12] Instigating such a practice may have made sense to Shuldham, but in a navy where promotion depended on patronage and fighting, aspiring officers on British warships would resent such service.

Before leaving Hancock's wharf, Mugford detached four men to guard *Hope,* thereby reducing his complement to seventeen. He planned to make a quick trip to Beverly to obtain more hands, but on his way out the ebb tide carried him onto a bar. Before departing he had spoken with Joseph Cunningham, commander of *Lady Washington,* a small privateer schooner, and encouraged him to tag along. Cunningham's crew numbered seven, and Mugford promised the skipper he would find a dozen or so recruits at Salem or Beverly. Cunningham needed more than a crew. He also needed a set of carriage guns, as his schooner carried only a few swivels, and Mugford thought Glover might be able to furnish a pair.

When *Franklin* ran aground, Cunningham anchored *Lady Washington* nearby. Mugford, forced to wait for the tide, anticipated a night attack and ordered the men to ram musket balls into the carriage guns and load the swivels. Leaving little to chance, he brought every musket on deck, armed the crew with cutlasses, spears, and pistols, and shouted to Cunningham to do the same.

Banks had a score to settle with *Franklin*, and when Mugford shoved off Hancock's wharf lookouts in *Renown*'s tops reported her movements. Cunningham followed Mugford about an hour later, but no one on board *Renown* gave particular notice to the diminutive *Lady*. Banks came topside when an officer reported *Franklin* aground off Pulling Point Gut. He saw his opportunity to eliminate a pestiferous privateer and sent an order to *Experiment* to prepare the boats for a night attack.

At 8:00 P.M. five boats—three from *Experiment* and two from *Renown*, all under the command of Lt. Josiah Harris—shoved off, and as the sun began to set on Boston Bay an odd assortment of barges, pinnaces, and cutters, mere shadows on the still water, slithered across the harbor. One hundred men bearing muskets, pistols, and cutlasses filled the boats, half of them marines and the other half seamen. In addition to Harris, an officer commanded each boat. From the deck of *Renown* the mission looked fairly routine, but somehow the watch had not noticed or attached any importance to the presence of *Lady Washington*.

Harris had timed his trip across the harbor about right. Darkness settled in around the boats as the men doubled the Gut and spotted the silhouette of *Franklin*, her broadside bearing directly toward them. Harris's barge led the attack, her outline distinct against the backdrop of a starlit sky. In an effort to stay clear of the schooner's guns, Harris motioned for the boats to come up behind her.

Mugford watched from the steerage as the boats drew near, waiting for them to range up closer to his carriage guns. He ordered the gunners to concentrate their fire on the barge, as she obviously carried the officer in charge. Mugford had little fear of firing on a friend, but he hailed the barge, demanding she identify herself.

"From Boston," came the reply, but Mugford could see boats behind the barge and knew they belonged to British warships. He warned them off, threatening to open fire.

"For God's sake," an English voice replied, "Don't fire. We just want permission to come on board."

Mugford believed not a word, leveled his musket on a tall figure in the barge, and pulled the trigger. Instantly, every hand on *Franklin* and *Lady Washington* opened fire.

Shouts mixed with groans came from the advancing boats. Mugford cut the cable, and *Franklin* swung about. With her broadside facing the boats, the carriage guns opened with grape. Before Mugford's men could reload, two or three boats bumped alongside, each carrying more men than the entire crew of the schooner. Balls whipped across *Franklin's* deck, answered by every swivel, musket, and pistol on board the schooner. When the initial firing slackened, no one had time to reload. Mugford and his men grabbed cutlasses, spears, and musket stocks and spread out along the bulwarks.

For half an hour the men of *Franklin* stood their ground, slashing in the darkness at any head that popped up over the rail. In the turmoil *Renown's* barge capsized, dumping Harris's body and twenty others into the cold water of the bay. Those who could swim clung to the sides of the boats still engaged, but their weapons had gone over the side. Those overboard stayed in the water. It was safer there.

Mugford's men fought valiantly. Not one enemy set foot on the deck of the schooner. The British made a final assault, this time armed with lances. Mugford rallied the men, cutlass in hand. A few feet away a British marine climbed the rail. Mugford swung at his head and felt the blade bite deep, but just before the blow struck home the marine drove a spear into Mugford's body. The lancer slumped into the water, his head sliced open, but blood poured from Mugford's chest. He called for Russell. "I'm a dead man," Mugford groaned, blood running between his lips. "Don't give up the vessel! You will be able to beat them off!" As he spoke his last words, the four remaining boats drew away. The fight was over, but James Mugford, *Franklin's* lone casualty, lay dead on the deck.

A hundred feet away, two boats attacked *Lady Washington.* In the darkness they mistook her for a brig four times her actual size. With seven men, Cunningham blasted away with swivels and blunderbusses, holding the boats at bay. The boarders had not been warned of a second vessel. Her presence rattled them, and they made no attempt to board her. She also alarmed the boats attacking *Franklin.* The *Lady Washington,* an unexpected adversary with unknown firepower, played an important role in repulsing the attack.

After news of the fight reached shore, Ward blustered a few words of praise to Washington. Writing lavishly, he reported that Cunningham had been attacked by five boats containing one hundred men, who, after repeated efforts to board, were "beaten off by the intrepidity and exertions of the little company who gloriously defended the *Lady* against the brutal ravishers of liberty."

This epistle, as usual, came from a man who seldom had his facts straight. Ward had earlier informed the general that Mugford had been attacked and killed by "twelve or thirteen boats full of men." He credited Mugford with sinking several boats and killing sixty or seventy of the enemy before he died. Ward's version of the fight became public knowledge. A week after the fight Abigail Adams sent her husband the same garbled account. By then, Ward's report had become a matter of public record, ultimately finding its way into Mugford's funeral eulogy.[13]

The British account, taken from the journals of *Renown* and *Experiment,* had the flavor of conventional naval brevity. During the early part of the fight, after Harris had been killed, no one took charge of the attack. In less than half an hour the boats drew back to regroup. Some men were missing, others wounded, but in the darkness no one could count casualties. They feared the worst. When the barge swamped, an officer claimed all her men had been lost and advised against resuming the attack.

The night attack had been unexpectedly bloody for Banks's boarding party. With their shot-up sails and splintered oars, the sailors headed back for the squadron, arriving on board the flagship at 11:30 P.M. Banks counted heads and found but five missing. He left no record of the number wounded. Capt. Alexander Scott of *Experiment* reported two missing and several wounded and blamed the hurried retreat of his sailors on the unexpected arrival of "an armed brig."[14]

The late-night tide carried *Franklin* to sea. In light morning breezes, Russell rounded Nahant for Marblehead, Mugford's home. People gathered on Marblehead Neck to watch the vessel come in, and as she tacked up the harbor they followed quietly, some on foot and others in carriages, their heads bent in mourning. The entire town converged at the wharf. Women held their children, men their hats. Cunningham had carried the dreadful news of Mugford's death back to Boston, and early that morning Glover had sent an express to Marblehead.

On May 22 a long procession of friends and admirers gathered outside the church to escort Mugford's body to its final resting place in Marblehead's "Old Burying Ground." John Glover, with a detachment from his regiment, led the group from the church to the grave site as bells tolled a solemn dirge. A soft breeze blew off the ocean. Gulls circled overhead. Women dabbed their eyes and silently prayed as they watched the coffin of "their James" lowered into the freshly dug grave. The colonel raised his sword, the soldiers their muskets, and a volley roared across the harbor. The gulls flew away, and the people returned to their homes, more determined than ever to win their war for independence.

Many eulogies followed Mugford's death. A reporter for the *New England Chronicle* wrote that Mugford had "left this honour to embalm his memory, that he made as brave and vigorous a stand in defence of American liberty as any among the living can boast of. His funeral was attended with suitable military honours, by a detachment of the 14th regiment." A broadside printed in Salem contained a heroic poem immortalizing the fallen skipper. Even in far-off Baltimore, the shipping firm of Woolsey & Salmon lamented the loss, writing, "The loss of Capt. Mugford is irreparable to his country, however he died nobly, and left such a character behind that we should endeavor to [emulate], and though we are sorry for the death of such a man, yet the cause he died in makes us believe that he must be happy." Whether Mugford was happy for his early grave is questionable. He died as the only skipper of Washington's schooners who never received a commission.[15]

Mugford had fought his last battle, but two skirmishes followed over *Hope*'s spoils. Thomas Cushing, who chaired Boston's War

Committee, eyed the ship's manifest and dispatched a plea to Hancock. He claimed that when Washington departed from Boston, he forced the town to raise two regiments, which, Cushing declared, had no arms or entrenching tools to defend the city. Therefore, he argued, all the carbines, shovels, and at least ten tons of gunpowder should remain with the town for use by the regiments. Cushing's request failed to draw a response from Hancock. Washington had interceded with Congress and obtained a resolution reserving for the army all "arms, ammunition, and military stores" taken by armed vessels "in the pay of the United Colonies." Details loaded the ordnance onto carts for transfer to Providence, where a correspondent for the *Gazette* observed them bound for New York on June 5.[16]

The other skirmish involved Jonathan Glover and John Bradford, who had recently been appointed by Congress as prize agent for the state of Massachusetts. Bradford, a Bostonian and member of the Secret Committee, was a staunch supporter and crony of Hancock, and the president of the Continental Congress looked after his friends. Without Washington's knowledge, Hancock deposed all the agents in Massachusetts, who themselves had only recently attained a measure of administrative efficiency, by giving the job to Bradford. Although Bradford had the power to appoint deputies, Hancock failed to clarify financial details.[17]

Weeks later, when knowledge of Bradford's unexplained appointment reached Marblehead, an angry Jonathan Glover rode to Boston and asked questions Bradford could not answer. Bradford disliked underlings accosting his character, but he could not produce his commission or explain his authority to deputize subagents. Glover considered Bradford's appointment irregular unless his intended role was to "superintend over the whole," in which case the agents could continue to act as before. Bradford, however, remained in doubt. Hancock had simply empowered a friend to collect commissions without informing Washington's agents their services had ended. For months, Bradford remained confused.

Before departing from Boston, Glover spoke with Ward, who knew nothing of Bradford's appointment. Ward told Glover not to worry, promising the matter would soon be clarified. Glover rode back to Marblehead convinced his agency had not been disturbed and resumed his duties.[18]

Eventually, avarice penetrated Bradford's consciousness. Hancock's letter had reached him prior to the capture of *Hope*. Two and one-half percent of the value of her cargo would place a nice sum in the rightful agent's pocket. But Glover, acting as agent, had already libeled the vessel, and the trial had been set by Judge Pickering for June 21.[19]

Disregarding the matter of who deserved the commission, Bradford conspired to obtain it for himself, and who could help him better than John Hancock? On July 1 he wrote his honorable friend a long letter, casting Glover as a shady character who could not be trusted. As an aside, Bradford mentioned that *Hope* and two brigs had been captured after his appointment, which dated from April 23. He felt entitled to the commission and asked Hancock to intercede on his behalf.[20]

Glover learned of Bradford's attempt to rob him of his commissions and on July 20 appealed to Washington. In a rather long letter, he explained how he hurried down from Marblehead the moment he received word of *Hope*'s capture and attended to the prize. After securing the cargo and initiating libels, "nothing now remains to be done," Glover declared. "In this stage of the business, Mr. John Bradford of Boston steps in and . . . claims a commission. As I have received no intimation of this from your Excellency, who appointed me an agent, nor from any person under the authority of Congress, and as Mr. Bradford's commission has not arrived, and perhaps never may, I thought it my duty to . . . continue acting in that capacity [respecting] those vessels that come into my hands." Glover asked Washington to refer the matter to the Marine Committee, hoping they "may settle this matter as in justice it ought to be."[21]

Washington sent a copy of Glover's letter to Hancock, asking that the dispute between the two agents be resolved by Congress. The general excused himself from the problem, saying he had neither the authority nor "the smallest inclination to interfere" in the matter. "I will only observe," Washington added, "that Mr. Glover was recommended to me as a proper person for an agent when we first fitted out the armed vessels . . . and so far as I know, discharged his office with fidelity and industry."[22]

In a letter to Washington, Bradford carefully avoided any mention of his dispute with Glover, but his letters to Hancock seldom failed to mention the matter of his commissions. When he heard nothing from Hancock, he wrote Robert Morris, another friend in Congress and vice chairman of the Marine Committee, declaring that his monetary woes would be resolved if Congress would graciously forward his promised commission as agent for Massachusetts.[23] He could then force "the late agents," who showed him no regard, to provide him with all the Continental funds secreted in their possession. "It's marvelous to me," Bradford wrote sarcastically, "that Glover and Bartlett should not have money in their hands belonging to the Continent as they've had so many valuable prizes." Bradford ignored the fact that Washington had authorized his agents to borrow money on their own account to pay crews and provision the schooners. He conveniently forgot most transactions were on paper, not in hard money, and that many cargoes had been taken by the army. By August, Bradford found himself in similar trouble. "I have been under the necessity of borrowing money," he wrote, warning he would be obliged to borrow more.

Without credentials, Bradford could exercise no control over Glover or Bartlett, and more prizes came into Marblehead. Finally, on August 8, he received his official commission. With the precious paper in his hands, he rushed copies for publication in bold print to all Massachusetts papers, and with the genuine article tucked in a pouch, he set off for Marblehead and Beverly to wave it the faces of his archrivals. Bradford, who had been deducting his commission from the sale of all prizes brought to Boston, now anticipated deducting his commission from surplus funds in the possession of Glover and Bartlett. To Bradford's chagrin, the deposed agents informed him their accounts indicated a balance due them, as Washington had carted most of the cargoes to army headquarters.

Another shock also hit Bradford in the pocketbook. Glover examined Bradford's commission and handed it back to him with a smile. The commission dated from July 30, 1776, not April 23, as Bradford claimed. *Hope* belonged to Glover, along with three other prizes Bradford attempted to claim.[24]

Bradford's ascendancy to the role of agent later led to many difficulties with Washington. Agents appointed by the general kept careful records of transactions because their commissions were tied directly to receipts and disbursements. Like Bradford, they were motivated by money, but unlike Bradford, they reported to Washington and responded to his needs before considering their own. As time passed, Bradford became unscrupulously divisive and, out of pure avarice, a great hindrance in providing for the needs of the army.

Why Washington never interceded when he learned of Bradford's appointment has never been explained. He probably saw it for what it was—an outright political appointment by Hancock, a man in power passing favors to his henchman. Washington never said anything to his agents, because Hancock failed to inform him. Congress created the mess, and Washington chose not to interfere. In its own way, Congress rectified part of the injustice by not retrodating Bradford's commission. Perhaps Hancock learned something about granting favors to friends through use of a public office, since Bradford would eventually demonstrate, by his actions, a flagrant misuse of friendship.

18

Greeting the Royal Highlanders

*C*apture of the powder ship *Hope* revitalized Washington's skippers, but Mugford's death created a new reality—the routine cat-and-mouse game had turned deadly. Strength lay in numbers, but five armed schooners sailing together were no match for the heavy 9-pounders of a 28-gun frigate. A few days before *Franklin* limped into Marblehead bearing Mugford's body, the captains met at Beverly and agreed to work together, sharing equally in their prizes, and by mid-May the schooners were ready to sail.

Ayres worked *Lynch* up the coast to Portsmouth, and Waters took *Lee* to Gloucester, both in search of a few more hands. Burke remained at Beverly waiting for Tucker, who had gone to Marblehead to raise more men. Tucker attended Mugford's funeral and sent word back from Marblehead for Burke to sail without him. *Franklin* needed a captain, and when *Hope*'s prisoners confirmed the convoy was still at sea, Tucker remained behind to find one.

For much of May, two British frigates—*Lively* and *Milford*—ranged off Beverly and Cape Ann, keeping a close watch for rebel privateers. Having added more hands, Ayres sailed out of Portsmouth on May 13 and set a course for Beverly. With a fair wind at his back, he stayed close inshore, passing inside Thatcher's Island. The watch reported a frigate off the port beam and closing fast. Ayres stretched his sails, rounding Eastern Point just ahead of *Milford.* The frigate fired twice, came about, and stood to sea, cruising slowly back and forth off Cape Ann. Three hours later Ayres tried again, only to find *Milford* offshore and waiting. Fifteen shots plunged into the water, driving Ayres back up the harbor. At nightfall, both *Lee* and *Lynch* cleared Cape Ann and sailed to Beverly.[1]

At dawn on the 17th, *Lee, Lynch,* and *Warren* cleared the harbor and headed into Massachusetts Bay. *Milford* sighted the trio and beat north, driving them back to Marblehead. With two fast frigates on the bay, the schooners could not afford fouled bottoms. Tucker put *Hancock* and *Franklin* on Beverly's graving dock and set the crews to work scraping the hulls.[2]

Banks, intending to end the depredations of privateers, kept three warships cruising between the Boston and Cape Ann. On the 24th, HM sloop *Hope* sighted *Lee, Lynch,* and *Warren* standing off the lighthouse and chased them into Marblehead. Three days later, sailing eight leagues off Cape Ann in thick weather, *Milford* sighted the same trio and drove them into Cape Ann.[3]

After being constantly harassed by Banks's patrols, Ayres, Burke, and Waters returned to Beverly to talk with Tucker. Perhaps their cruising days were over. Perhaps the run of British shipping along the coast had ended. Four men from *Warren* thought so and deserted. Glover posted a reward for their capture, offering three dollars for each.[4]

Neither *Hancock* nor *Franklin* was ready, but Tucker told Ayres, Burke, and Waters to fill their water casks and larders and get back to sea. The three vessels cleared the harbor on June 5, but this time, instead of cruising off Cape Ann, they set a course for deep water.[5]

ON APRIL 4, Capt. John Brisbane of the HMS *Flora,* 32, received orders from the Admiralty to convoy thirty-five transports carrying the 42nd and 71st Royal Highlanders to Boston. The reinforcements would give Howe the strength he needed to breach Washington's lines. The Admiralty's orders carried a tone of urgency. Brisbane must put to sea "with the first opportunity of wind and weather & proceed . . . without a moment's loss of time." Two weeks later Brisbane arrived at Grennock and found about half of the transports ready to sail. Maj. Gen. Simon Frazer's 71st Highlanders filed into Grennock a week late without their ammunition or equipment, delaying the departure of the convoy until April 29. News of Howe's evacuation of Boston reached London about four days later.[6]

A fierce storm struck the convoy a week out of Scotland, scattering the transports. Brisbane fell back, herded together what strays he could find, and resumed the journey to Boston. During the storm the 223-ton transport *Anne* leaped ahead of the convoy, and by the time the storm passed she was far out of sight. John Dennison, her skipper, had been stretching his canvas to catch up with the convoy, unaware the others had fallen behind. *Anne*, the first transport to appear on the American coast, made the crossing in five weeks, and Dennison had not seen another sail since the storm. As he approached land three sail blossomed to starboard. He raised his glass and studied the trio. They had the cut of three small schooners coming on fast from hard astern.[7]

Capt. John Maxwell, brother of the Duchess of Gordon, paced the quarterdeck, warning Dennison to avoid the schooners, as they were neither from the convoy nor from His Majesty's Royal Navy. Maxwell's Highlanders, dressed in red uniforms, leaned over the rail, waiting for the captain to order out the muskets. Six 6s, mounted on carriages, lay behind the bulwarks, three on each side, but no one thought to load them. The schooners were still far back, and when Dennison crowded on more sail, *Anne* began to pull away.

Dennison lost the wind at nightfall but took comfort in seeing the lighthouse dead ahead. He dropped anchor knowing the schooners, a good league off, had also lost the wind. As a precaution he doubled the watch, but the night passed quietly. Dennison wanted an early start and caught a few winks himself.

The same calm immobilizing *Anne* stopped Ayres, Burke, and Waters. They had seen the red-coated soldiers on the deck of the British vessel and knew what she was, a transport and a fine sailing ship. If the morning wind came again from the east, they would not reach her before she fell in with Banks. The three skippers came abeam, talked briefly, and agreed to try for her. Marines manned the sweeps and rowed quietly toward the lighthouse. In the false dawn they lay off *Anne*, a gray shadow against the backdrop of Lovell Island. Two of the schooners rowed around to her stern quarter and the other took station off her bow, carefully avoiding *Anne*'s carriage guns. The muzzles of six 4s poked through the gunports of the schooners as Waters ordered Dennison to haul down his colors. Maxwell called a council of war, but Dennison convinced him to surrender. He could not bring his guns to bear, and Maxwell's muskets could not compete against the schooners' firepower. Before enough daylight flooded the bay for Banks to observe the capture off the lighthouse, Washington's skippers transferred 110 Highlanders to the schooners and sent the prize off to Marblehead. Ayres separated from the squadron and headed for Plymouth with twenty-five of the prisoners. Burke and Waters stayed with the prize and at 8:00 A.M. sighted *Milford* bowling out of the southeast in chase. The frigate gained slowly but sheered off to chase a nearby brig. At 11:30 A.M. Burke and Waters anchored their prize in Marblehead Harbor.[8]

Jonathan Glover took possession of the prize and turned the prisoners over to his brother, who still had part of the 14th Regiment stationed near Marblehead. *Anne* carried forty small cannon—4s and 6s—a hefty cargo for a transport. Even more astounding, Glover uncovered boxes filled with checked and striped linens, shirts, trousers, stockings, shoes, hats, and writing paper—a strange lading for a military vessel. Either Dennison or the owner had stowed a small cargo for his own account and enjoyed a little free transportation at the expense of the Admiralty. Glover also uncovered a box of broadswords, a weapon better suited for the knights of King Arthur's round table.[9]

News of *Anne*'s capture did not reach London until September. Maxwell concocted a brave story for the readers of the *Public Advertiser.* A writer for the *Glasgow Journal* called Maxwell's account a whitewash of the facts and derided the Highlanders for allowing *Anne*'s capture "without firing a gun, notwithstanding she had six carriage guns aboard." Responding to the writer's criticism, Maxwell denied any lack of courage on the part of his regiment. He downgraded *Anne*'s armament to two carriage guns, not six, and two swivels, put on "for show." From such accounts is the history of the American Revolution written.[10]

When Washington learned of *Anne*'s capture, he extended his compliments to Ward but nudged him to be more attentive to the schooners. "Keep a good lookout," he added sharply, "as the whole [British] fleet are bound to Boston . . . and more of them will fall into our hands." Prior to *Anne*'s capture, the schooners had been idle for a month, and Washington suspected Ward's inertia to be the cause. An occasional word of encouragement served as a reminder to Ward that his scope of responsibility extended beyond the streets of Boston.[11] He might have sent Ward another compliment had he known that Tucker, with help from Bartlett and Glover, had all five schooners ready for sea.

Tucker, who had spent four weeks repairing *Hancock,* used his time ashore well. To replace the fallen Mugford he recruited John Skimmer, a Boston master he had known through past association. Skimmer, a respected and knowledgeable seaman, sought an opportunity to command a privateer, and when *Franklin* became available he asked for a commission. Tucker pestered Ward for two weeks before the general issued a brevet. Mugford had sailed with only master's papers, but Tucker refused to let Skimmer take the same risk. Ward declared he had "no power to commission" and no doubt felt duress in granting the brevet, but a brevet provided Skimmer better protection from His Majesty's yardarm than master's papers. Quite by accident, Ward made one of his better decisions by brevetting Skimmer.[12]

On June 7 Tucker sailed from Beverly, leaving instructions for the squadron to join him at Cape Ann. For a few days he cruised off the cape, ranging in the track of Boston-bound vessels. On June 11 the watch sighted two transports beating against southwesterlies. Tucker scanned the pair carefully, wishing he had another schooner to support him.

Remembering the 6s on *Anne,* Tucker closed slowly, posing as a pilot vessel. Taking station off the vessel's bow, he signaled them to follow. Instead of heading for Boston, he sailed for Cape Ann. The watch reported another sail, and from her cut Tucker recognized her. *Hancock* was no match for HM sloop *Hope,* so Tucker ordered all sail and beat toward the cape, the two transports trimming their sheets to follow. As Tucker sailed into Cape Ann, *Hope* overhauled the transports and turned them about. Eight shots from the sloop splashed a few yards from *Hancock.* Another hour and both transports would have sailed right into Tucker's well-laid trap.[13]

On June 8, sailing side by side, Waters and Burke had a similar unhappy experience. After sighting two transports tracking toward Boston, Burke signaled Waters to pursue. *Mayflower* contained a company of the 71st Royal Highlanders, Capt. Aeneas M'Intosh, who later reported engaging two armed schooners for three and one-half hours before being rescued by a British warship. According to Bradford, who seldom had anything favorable to report on the subject of Washington's schooners, Burke lost both prizes because Waters stood off and failed to engage. After conferring with Burke, Bradford made no effort to hear Waters's version of the fight. As two prizes were at stake, not one, Waters had probably engaged the second vessel. Bradford sent his complaints to Hancock, writing, "The unhappy disputes among those captains has been the means of losing two transports owing to a dispute between Capts. Waters and Burke, who were vulgar enough to quarrel on the Sabbath morning in hearing of their boats' crews on a wharf at

Marblehead, and would have got to blows had the people not prevented it." Bradford never included Washington in his private correspondence to Hancock. Perhaps he preferred to have no formal investigation into his complaints.[14]

If friction existed between the captains, Tucker attempted to end it by consolidating the fleet under his command. For well over a week the schooners had been chased up and down the bay by Banks's warships, which had become especially active in their efforts to locate the transports. Tucker had no intention of tangling with *Milford*, but if *Hope* gave them trouble he would give some back.

On June 12 Tucker took the squadron a few leagues off the Boston lighthouse and waited for a prize. At 3:00 P.M. *Hope* ranged into sight and sheered as if to engage. Tucker decided the time had come to rid the bay of a perpetual nuisance and signaled the squadron to quarters. Four schooners came about and stood in chase. Dawson recognized *Hancock*, heeled to starboard, and beat safely into Nantasket Road.[15]

If Tucker wondered why Ward passively permitted Banks the use of the Road for his royal warships, the answer to this question erupted with a roar at daybreak on June 14. Col. Thomas Crafts, with five hundred men from the Colony Train, had spent the night emplacing two batteries of heavy guns on Long Island in Boston Harbor. At 5:00 A.M. he opened on *Renown* and *Hope* with telling effect. Banks piped the men to quarters and fired fifty shots at the batteries. Unable to dislodge the guns, he signaled the fleet to weigh anchor and assemble off the lighthouse. One shot knocked down a yard, and several others punched holes through *Renown*'s hull.

Thirteen British vessels lay in Nantasket Road, including eight transports carrying about eight hundred Highlanders, and three prizes. On his way to sea Banks underscored his retreat by emptying a defiant broadside into the town of Nantasket. *Hope* stopped at George's Island to cover the embarkation of the sick while hospital staff carried patients to transports.

At 9:00 A.M. Banks anchored in five fathoms off the Boston lighthouse and waited for the other vessels to pass out of the Road. Thinking he was out of range, Banks sent a detail with two barrels of powder to blow up the lighthouse. While the demolition crew set the charge, Capt. Joshua Swan shifted his guns into position on Quaker Hill and opened from a battery on Nantasket Head, scattering several shots around

Renown. Banks replied with forty rounds but with no effect. At 10:00 A.M. the lighthouse exploded, telegraphing a message to jubilant Continental gunners—they had driven the Royal Navy out of Boston Harbor.

An hour later the British squadron stood out to sea but with light, variable breezes made no headway. Banks, still under fire from shore batteries, ordered out boats, sweeps, and towing lines. The transports limped behind, nudged along by *Hope.* At noon *Renown* passed out of range, and Banks signaled for the masters of the transports to come to the flagship for orders. The sea was calm, the atmosphere hazy. *Milford* ranged in sight, guiding three more transports. Banks waited for the frigate to arrive before issuing sailing orders, but he had already decided to evacuate Boston Harbor.

When Captain Burr of *Milford* came on board, he reported sighting "5 sail of privateers" off Marblehead. He knew what they were—Tucker's armed schooners, roving like a hungry wolf pack and waiting for the transports to be flushed out of the harbor. Banks ordered a tight sailing formation, slotting each vessel under a protective wing of a warship. At 8:00 P.M. they would sail for Halifax. Once at sea *Renown* would fire a gun every hour as a signal for the convoy to hold or change headings. *Milford* and *Hope* would flank the convoy, keeping it in good sailing order.[16]

No more than half a dozen well-placed Continental guns had forced Banks out of Nantasket Road. The retreat was ridiculous, and Banks made a second mistake in not leaving a warship off the lighthouse. With a thousand armed Highlanders camped on transports, he had sufficient means to take the Colony Train. In his hurried abandonment of Boston, Banks left no instructions for his command operating to the south. The only evidence of his departure was the ruined lighthouse, which could have been destroyed by the rebels. The unexpected attack had jarred Banks's nerves and clouded his judgment.

Even Ward seemed surprised by Banks's hasty departure. Sniffing an unexpected opportunity, he dashed off a message to the Massachusetts Council suggesting that a large vessel "with a broad pennant as a decoy" be anchored in Nantasket Road to lure incoming transports. He had a prize to fit the purpose well. He also sent a message to Washington asking approval of his plan. Apparently, Ward did not feel sufficiently empowered to make the simplest of decisions. Washington approved the idea, as it served the Continental Army's interest to prevent the Highlanders from joining the British army—wherever Howe chose to take it.[17]

From the firing of the first gun on Long Island to the departure of the convoy at sunset, Washington's schooners observed Banks's withdrawal. Tucker could only guess at the cause of the cannon fire, but with the emergence of the fleet from the Road and the demolition of the lighthouse, he edged closer to the harbor. At dusk, when *Renown* eased to sea with the convoy clustered around her, Tucker trailed behind, hoping to fall in among the stragglers at dark. But there were no gales to upset the formation and no contrary winds to separate the poor sailers from the pack. Tucker dogged the convoy until dawn, breaking off pursuit east of Cape Ann. He counted eleven transports, and if the balance of the convoy had not been diverted to Halifax he expected to find them still on course for Boston. Tucker brought the schooners about and dropped back down the coast for Boston Bay. As they passed Marblehead, he slipped into Beverly for a minor repair. He could not see the two British transports whose sails lay buried below the eastern horizon.

The 220-ton ship *George*, Archibald Bog, master, and the 180-ton brig *Annabella*, Hugh Walter, master, had been sailing together since the storm dismantled the convoy a few days out of Scotland. Unlike *Anne*, *George* and *Annabella* had fallen far astern the main convoy. They had not seen a vessel for seven weeks—at least none with the latest news from Boston. Each vessel carried a company of the 71st Royal Highlanders, *George* with 119 of the second battalion and *Annabella* with 87 of the first battalion. Col. Archibald Campbell and Major Menzies made the crossing on *George*, Capt. George M'Kenzie on *Annabella*.

After passing Cape Ann the transports swung toward Boston, tacking back and forth in light winds. At dusk on June 15, Waters observed the pair standing for the harbor. He pursued but lost sight of them at nightfall. Doubting the enemy would attempt an entrance before daylight, and expecting them to keep a league or two to sea, he worked the schooners through the night, slowly closing. At 4:00 A.M. Waters sighted both vessels nearby and positioned *Lee* off *George*'s bow. Skimmer, in *Franklin*, stood off *Annabella*, waiting for Burke and Ayers to come up.

Before the schooners ranged within speaking distance, a discussion between Campbell, Menzies, and Bog took place on *George*'s quarterdeck. They decided the vessels had to be His Majesty's pilot boats "in the service of his Majesty." Still cautious, however, Campbell kept *George*'s guns charged, but *Annabella* carried only a pair of swivels. Waters observed soldiers on board and stayed beyond musket range.

When Burke and Ayers closed, Waters hailed *George* and ordered her to strike, but Campbell refused. Waters and Skimmer opened with their 4s; Campbell replied with a broadside from his 6s. *Lee* and *Franklin* engaged *George* at close range, mixing their shots with grape. *Warren* and *Lynch* lay farther off and hammered *Annabella* with shot from long range. Campbell returned the fire, and the action evolved into a running battle as the transports filled for Boston Harbor.

Perhaps the big pennant flying from the peak of Ward's decoy gave Campbell and his Highlanders a false sense of security. The same pennant may have given Waters misgivings. If Banks had returned to the Road, Waters did not want to lead the squadron inside where it could be blown to pieces.

Early in the afternoon, Waters broke off the engagement and started for Plymouth to replenish ammunition. *George* and *Annabella* beat for Boston Harbor, making little progress against the westerlies. Campbell tallied his casualties—three men mortally wounded and one killed on *George,* another wounded on *Annabella.* Puzzled by the absence of the Royal Navy, Campbell "pushed forward into the harbour, not doubting that I should receive protection from a fort or some ship of force stationed there for the security of our fleet."[18]

On the way to Plymouth, Waters hailed the Connecticut brig *Defence,* Capt. Seth Harding, who had heard the firing and was on his way to investigate the cause. Waters explained they had been engaged most of the day but withdrew because the firing was too hot. Harding asked about casualties, and to his surprise Waters replied, "Not one." Waters mentioned he had seen a warship flying a pennant inside the Road, but she had not moved since the fight began. Harding wanted a closer look. Waters brought the squadron about and followed *Defence* back to Boston Bay.

Defence carried an arsenal of sixteen 6s and twenty swivels and a complement of 117 men. By the time Harding and the schooners reached Alderton Point, the sun lay low in the western sky. Both transports stood off the Point, and from the north another schooner was making her way slowly toward them in the dying westerlies. It was Tucker, back for the finale in *Hancock.*

George eased by the Point, followed by *Annabella*. Soldiers crowded the decks and stared shoreward, perhaps wondering why the harbor seemed so desolate. They searched but could find no British vessel to greet them and no banner aloft on any hill—just the dim outline of a large vessel flying a big, bright pennant. They could not see the 18-pounder mounted on the Point or the gunners hidden at their stations and waiting for the rearmost vessel to cross their sights. All was quiet. *Annabella* tacked to gather in the light offshore and grounded on Alderton shoal, right under the muzzle of the Colony Train's gun.

Captain Swan ordered the Continental gunners to wait until both vessels passed the Point, and then he hailed, ordering *Annabella* to strike. M'Kenzie refused, suspecting a bluff voiced by a few harmless rebels armed with blunderbusses. The 18-pounder opened with a round of grape, spraying the deck of the brig with deadly metal. Hugh Walter, the brig's master, observed men fall. Having no means of defense, he struck. M'Kenzie came ashore and surrendered his company, and for the next hour boats shuttled back and forth from the brig, hauling Highlanders to the beach. Swan did not wait for the formality of M'Kenzie's surrender to shift the gun and fire a few rounds in the direction of *George*. When darkness engulfed the harbor, the gunners at the Point congratulated themselves on the probability she had surrendered, too.

The stark reality of the ship's predicament finally struck Campbell between the ears. "As we stood up for Nantasket road," he wrote, "an American battery opened upon us, which was the first serious proof we had that there could scarcely be any friends of ours at Boston; and we were too far embayed to retreat, especially as the wind had died away, and the tide of flood not half expended." Bog maneuvered the ship to George's Island and dropped anchor, not expecting trouble before morning. Nonetheless, gunners checked the loads in their 6s, men rested on their arms, and a double watch scanned the islands lying in the harbor in anticipation of a night attack.[19]

At 11:00 P.M. Tucker's squadron and *Defence* formed around *George*—four schooners off her bow, one off her stern, and the armed brig about two hundred yards off her starboard. Harding's voice boomed from the quarterdeck of *Defence*, asking, "Where from is that vessel?"

"From Great Britain," came the answer.

"Then I order you to strike your colours to America."

"Who is it that demands we strike?"

"The Connecticut Navy brig *Defence,*" Harding replied. "I do not want to kill your men, but the ship I have will do it."

While Bog parleyed with Harding, Campbell called a council of war. "Although the mate of our ship, and every sailor on board (the captain only excepted) refused . . . to fight any longer," Campbell claimed, "there was not an officer, non-commissioned officer, or private man of the seventy-first, but what stood to their quarters with a ready and cheerful obedience."

Harding, impatient, again ordered *George* to strike.

"Yes," came the reply, "I'll strike," but the words became lost in the flash and roar of *George's* broadsides.

Defence replied, followed by a crisp blast of 4s from the schooners. Harding worked in close, carrying the action with his heavier guns. Tucker lay off the bow and raked her with his 4s. The other schooners stood off her stern but seldom fired. The fight lasted an hour and a half, the enemy losing eight killed and thirteen wounded. The Highlanders served their guns well, wounding eight on *Defence* and four on the schooners before running out of ammunition. The firing from *George* went high, knocking down spars and tearing up *Defence's* rigging. The deck of *George,* however, became a gory pile of human parts and jagged, blood-stained splinters.

"Hemmed in as we were [by] six privateers in the middle of the enemy's harbour, beset with a dead calm, without the power of escaping, or . . . the most distant hope of relief," Campbell wrote, "I thought it became my duty not to sacrifice the lives of our gallant men wantonly in the arduous attempt of an evident impossibility."[20]

At the time Campbell surrendered *George,* high tide lifted *Annabella* off Alderton shoal. Her crew and a number of Highlanders were still on board. They quietly made sail and worked back into the channel, keeping to the northward. A short time later they ran hard onto Black Rock off Lovell's Island and bilged. The schooners found her there in the morning and took off the remaining prisoners.

While the body of Major Menzies received the honors of war, hosted by Ward and his military staff from the steps of the statehouse, details conveyed the dead from *Annabella* and *George* to an outer island for burial. Tucker came ashore and attended the services, aware for the first time of the large number of wives and children who had accompanied their men to Boston. Highlanders played an ancient dirge, and women wept. Tucker, "who had a musical soul," picked up the melody and could be heard whistling the plaintive notes as he returned to his ship.

Campbell's report to Howe must have made the general's stomach turn. Howe blamed Shuldham for Banks's decision to desert Boston. The admiral, Howe complained, manifested remarkable similarities to his predecessor's indifference when it came to matters concerning the welfare of the army. Howe thought he had a solution to the problem and wrote to London. His brother, Lord Richard, or "Black Dick," as the sailor's called him, was an admiral with superb credentials. Replace Shuldham, the general declared, and the Howe brothers would bring an end to the war and restore the colonies to the Crown. Howe doubted whether anyone in power would listen. The family's Whiggish antecedents had left both brothers in a sea of political nebulousness. Oddly enough, the Admiralty had already decided the job in America required a man of greater ability, and "Black Dick" was on his way with another flotilla of warships.[21]

On the afternoon of June 18, following Menzies's burial, another transport tacked slowly into Boston Harbor. Her master, Robert Park, observed the brig *Annabella* lodged on Black Rock. Ahead to starboard lay the scattered ruins of the lighthouse. He worked the 200-ton ship *Lord Howe* closer to the island for a better look. Capt. Lawrence Campbell, 71st Grenadiers, stood on the quarterdeck with Park, discussing what to do. They, like all the other transports bending toward Boston, expected to be greeted by friends. When Harding sailed *Defence* out to meet them, followed by Tucker's schooners, Park and Campbell saw no British banners flying from their mastheads. Unlike *George, Lord Howe* carried no guns. When Harding demanded her surrender, Park struck.

Harding and Tucker brought the transport into Boston and tied her up beside *George,* adding another 112 Highlanders to Ward's prisoner trove. Park, without knowing the true status of the convoy, admitted more transports were on the way.

Bradford was already counting his commissions and, with more prizes in the offing, asked Harding to remain at Boston. Harding agreed to stay until his brig was repaired. He was ill and welcomed a few days' rest at Bradford's home, but when ten sail and two frigates appeared off the harbor on June 22, Harding bounded out of bed and hastened down to his ship.

Tucker, ready with four schooners, met Harding at the wharf. Once out of the harbor, the two captains took a closer look at the frigates guarding the convoy and turned back. Bradford grumbled when *Defence* returned to Boston empty-handed. *Hancock* and *Warren* sailed back to Marblehead, *Lee* and *Lynch* returned to Boston, and *Franklin* sailed for Cape Ann.[22]

Tucker stopped at Marblehead to enlist Jonathan Glover's assistance in claiming prize money for capturing *George, Annabella,* and *Lord Howe.* Glover and Bartlett had mutually agreed to yield to Bradford's central agency on all vessels captured after *Anne* and sent Tucker and Burke back to Boston to present their claims. Bradford had assured Harding that he and his crew would "share in the emoluments" but remained unclear as to the amount. When Harding learned Tucker had claimed all three prizes, he libeled for three-fourths of *George* and *Annabella* and a proportionate share of *Lord Howe.* The other claimants were the gunners in the Colony Train, who had captured *Annabella* but failed to hold her. Since she was bilged and on the rocks, no one showed interest in securing whatever valuables lay in her hold.

The dispute devolved on Bradford, who never anticipated being asked to referee prize shares or perform the more onerous tasks of sorting cargoes or itemizing and tracking inventories. Unlike Glover and Bartlett, he knew very little about managing prizes, although he had quickly mastered the simple process of tallying commissions. Without bothering to look, Bradford believed all three transports contained nothing but Highlanders, their arms, and personal baggage. Two weeks later, men rummaging through the holds uncovered a wealth of small arms, bullets, camping equipment, blankets, clothing, shoes, rum, provisions, and dozens of articles needed by Washington's army. Burke helped himself to four pairs of shoes and a drum but could not locate a fife to add to his complement of musical instruments.[23]

Bradford conceived a unique method for dealing with the bothersome schooners, but he felt insecure acting on his own. Soliciting Hancock's approval, he suggested sending "two or three of them [on] a month's cruise to the southward in pursuit of Jamaica ships." With the British gone from Boston, Bradford felt the schooners would give him nothing but trouble if they loitered in the harbor. However, by doubling their crews and sending them to the West Indies, every prize sent back to Boston would benefit the Continent and enhance his commissions. Hancock never responded, perhaps surmising Washington would not consider the scheme in keeping with the schooners' original mission.

Without resolving the division of prize shares, Bradford libeled the transports for trial on July 23. In the interim, much of the inventory taken from the vessels mysteriously disappeared. Annoyed by Bradford's failure to forward war material, Washington ordered Ward to seize all military supplies, but nothing had been itemized and Bradford refused to release them.

A week later, Howe's transports began to appear off Sandy Hook, and Washington sent another urgent message to Ward ordering him to commandeer all war material and ship it immediately. Bradford still dallied, finding numerous excuses for retaining the arms. On July 4 Washington wrote again. The British had landed on Staten Island—he must have the arms now! Militia joining his Continental forces at New York arrived without muskets, but Washington's demands failed to elicit a response from either Ward or Bradford. In desperation he appealed to Hancock, who directed his henchman to "send the arms taken out of the Scotch transports to Genl Washington in New York." Three weeks passed before Bradford complied, explaining that he had given a local company "seventy muskets and fifteen fuzees" and apologizing for the large number "embezell'd" by none other, he claimed, than the men of Washington's schooners. He neglected to mention that every article removed by the marines had been inventoried, right down to Burke's drum and "one old ensign."[24]

Bradford's appointment as Continental agent had a deleterious effect on Washington's skippers, as well as on the ailing Ward. Older captains like Tucker, Waters, and Ayres had established good working relationships with Glover and Bartlett. Between them existed a feeling of mutual trust and mutual benefit. With Bradford they lost trust, and from Ward they received no support, as he had neither the stamina nor the will to contend with the wily Bradford. Unable to curb the hostility growing between Bradford and the schooner commanders, Ward asked "to be relieved as soon as possible," but with British troops landing on Long Island, Washington had no time to devote to Ward's problems. As useless as Ward had become, he remained in command.

Abigail Adams, who always spoke her mind, declared that Ward must be removed and blamed Congress "for not appointing us a General." But Ward stayed on as commander, and the schooner captains drifted through the summer of 1776 without a word of encouragement or any sense of direction.[25]

Of thirty-three Scotch transports sailing from Clyde River late in April, all but six reached Halifax safely. Of the six, Washington's schooners captured four.[26] With Howe moving his army to New York, another opportunity to pick up strays gave Tucker and his men a timely incentive to replenish their ammunition and get back to sea.

✺ 19 ✺
Summer of Dissension

*T*he concentration of Howe's forces on Staten Island preoccupied Washington. He seldom gave his schooners a thought. Aside from short messages pressing Ward for supplies, the only lengthy letter he sent contained a copy of the Declaration of Independence, which, on July 4, formally "dissolved the connection between the American Colonies and Great Britain, and declared them *free and independent States*." Washington asked Ward to "cause this Declaration to be immediately proclaimed at the head of the Continental regiments in Massachusetts Bay." The general failed to mention that the document should also be read to the members of his personal navy; however, he did remember to remind Ward he was still waiting for the shipment of arms taken from the Scotch transports.[1]

Lord Howe's fleet first appeared off Sandy Hook on June 29. Shuldham had been expecting the admiral since March, agreeing to cheerfully "resign that command to his Lordship in the consciousness of having discharged my duty to His Majesty, and with the diligence and attention the importance of the service required." The Admiralty let Shuldham down easily, placing the Howe brothers together to act in the capacity of peacemakers but with military clout if the colonists refused to throw down their arms. Howe did not catch up to his fleet for another two weeks, arriving well after the ink had dried on the Declaration of Independence. He probably threw the document aside, his peacekeeping mission emasculated by a piece of paper demanding the only concession the Howe brothers could not grant—independence.[2]

Once British troops began to disembark at Staten Island, Washington sent Ward no further instructions on the flotilla. Ward had not resigned his commission, but he had asked to be relieved. While he waited for his replacement to arrive, he stayed away from Bradford and

189

ignored the schooners. Ward could not have guessed how many months would pass before Washington found time to consider his resignation.

Although Tucker attempted to assume the role of senior commander of the squadron, neither Washington nor Ward had given him such authority. But without a senior commander, cruising agendas depended too much on the cooperation of the captains. The dispute over prize money between Glover, Bradford, and Harding destroyed some of the cohesiveness Manley had achieved when Washington was at Cambridge. Tucker could not hold the captains together, and they went their separate ways.

After the capture of *Lord Howe,* more than a month passed before another prize was taken, this one by Tucker and Skimmer cruising in *Hancock* and *Franklin.* The two captains, one the longest in grade and the other the youngest in age, preferred sailing together. Not expecting any more transports, Tucker and Skimmer loaded with provisions and sailed far to the east, cruising to the southward off Cape Sable. On July 27 they surrounded the 240-ton ship *Peggy,* James Kennedy, master, which carried eight guns but surrendered without a fight.

Peggy produced interesting antecedents. Sailing as *Charming Peggy* in 1775, she had cleared Philadelphia with a cargo of flour for Lisbon early in July. On the 25th HMS *Glasgow* captured her and sent her into Boston, where her cargo was dispersed to the British army.[3] When Shuldham evacuated Boston, he used the vessel to carry soldiers and Loyalists to Halifax, where her ownership and register were changed to Glasgow and her name shortened to *Peggy.* The same Loyalists who fled to Halifax now hoped to establish homes among friends in New York. Aside from personal belongings, *Peggy'*s cargo consisted of a large assortment of liquid intoxicants, tons of provisions from Scotland, boxes of cloth and clothing, and enough goods to stock a merchant's storehouse. *Peggy* sailed from Halifax on July 4 in a convoy escorted by *Renown* and *Flora* but straggled far behind the others.[4]

Several Tories, including the "pious" merchant Benjamin Davis, anticipated Howe's capture of New York and wished to be among the first to profit from the town's occupation. Davis owned most of the merchandise on *Peggy,* valued at £1,500, and carried another £500 in gold in a chest. The prize crew broke open the chest and helped themselves to a bagful of coins. Davis complained to Tucker, who found half of the money still in the bag and some loose in the hold. Tucker recovered most of it, returned it to the bag, and carried it to his cabin.

Tucker and Skimmer, still befuddled over the matter of agency, carried the prize to Marblehead and turned her over to Glover, who initiated the libel as a favor to the two captains, both of whom distrusted Bradford. Glover quartered the women at Marblehead but placed the men on a schooner and sent them to Boston. Upon their arrival at Long Wharf, Bradford learned of *Peggy*'s capture and relibeled the ship in Boston. Glover calmly withdrew from the libeling contest. Nonetheless, he completed the inventory and forwarded the information to Ward.[5]

When Ward reported the capture to Washington, he neglected to mention the inventory but included in his dispatch an old, soiled newspaper found on *Peggy*. It contained an article confirming a rumor the general apprehended with deep despair. German mercenaries, recruited by George III, were in the convoy standing off Staten Island. The presence of Hessians gave Washington grave concern. The king had decided to quash the rebellion by sending a force powerful enough to whip the Continental Army—or so he thought.[6]

The first shots fired by Hessians, however, occurred at sea. Burke, sailing off Cape Sable in *Warren* early in July, engaged His Majesty's transport *Unity*, Captain Morgan, bound for New York. As most enemy transports mounted carriage guns, Burke's solo cruising invited disaster. For six hours he trailed *Unity*, wary of those guns and unable to decide what action to take.

From *Unity*'s quarterdeck Morgan studied the schooner's antics. She showed no colors and trailed half a mile astern. He kept a company of Hessians out of sight below the quarterdeck and shifted four carriage guns abaft. He waited and watched, ready to sail in company with a friend or defend against a foe. Burke finally sent a shot across *Unity*'s bow, and Morgan came about. "We were surprised at this," Morgan wrote, "and could therefore hardly think she was one of our . . . schooners, as the officer would certainly know his duty better."

Burke ran in close under *Unity*'s stern and trumpeted orders to surrender "to the Congress." Morgan replied with two blasts from his stern guns. Burke, not expecting to find guns abaft, fell away and reapproached off *Unity*'s bow. He observed only a half dozen hands on the brig's deck and had his own men standing by with grappling hooks when armed Hessians surged topside and lined up along the bulwarks. "Our soldiers immediately went forward," Morgan recalled, "and gave them such a discharge of small arms, that she found she had caught a Tartar." Morgan believed the first volley killed at least five men on *Warren*.

Burke, taken completely by surprise, eased off and stood out of musket range. One of his gunners, attempting to reload a 4-pounder, mishandled the powder and blew up the quarterdeck, killing three men and wounding seven. Smoke filled the schooner. Burke did well to withdraw from the fight without being captured. After assessing his damage, he sailed to Marblehead. In his report to Ward, Burke claimed he had fought two vessels, the other a schooner, and stated both were on the verge of surrender when the accident occurred. Morgan, however, claimed the Hessians were prepared to extend the fight indefinitely. He made no mention of a second vessel because none was there.[7]

Unlike Ayres and Waters, whose activities had not been reported for over a month, Tucker and Skimmer headed back to sea a day after delivering *Peggy* to Marblehead. This time they stood southeast, cruising in the lanes of West Indies traffic. On August 4, after five days of hard sailing, Skimmer overhauled the 140-ton brig *Perkins*, William Jenkins, master. Tucker ranged a short distance off, letting Skimmer manage the capture on his own. The cargo, as shabby as the old brig, consisted of 3,600 uncured deer skins and 6,840 pounds of indigo. Skimmer put a prize crew on board and ordered her into Marblehead. Tucker and Skimmer still felt no obligation to send their prizes to Bradford, who was now the only person in Massachusetts with authority to libel vessels in the name of the captors.[8]

Tucker and Skimmer held their position off the Virginia capes and on August 6 sighted a large vessel tracking northeasterly. The quarry bristled with firepower. Through his glass Tucker counted eighteen guns, but only a half dozen men bobbed about the deck. Tucker smelled a bluff and approached cautiously, sensing something disingenuous about all those guns. *Hancock* and *Franklin* ranged in closer, one schooner off the bow, the other aft. When Tucker ordered the vessel to strike, she luffed into the wind. As she came about Tucker half expected to be stung by a heavy broadside, but not a gun fired. Marines from *Hancock* leaped on board and circled about the vessel. Of her eighteen guns, twelve had been carved from wood, and the other six were 2s and 3s.

The 305-ton ship *Nelly Frigate*, Lyonel Bradstreet, master, had sailed from Honduras Bay ten weeks earlier for London, laden with 126,000 feet of mahogany, 40 tons of logwood, and a cargo of turtle. Contrary winds drove the prize crew into Portsmouth, where the ship came to anchor to wait out the night. Joshua Wentworth, who had retained his commission as agent for New Hampshire, spotted the vessel in the harbor, ordered her up to town, libeled her, and advised Washington he would "pursue to trial."

Wentworth also notified Washington that *Elizabeth*, captured by Manley on April 2 and laden with merchandise looted by Boston Tories, had been acquitted by the jury. Wentworth considered the acquittal incomprehensible and "directly contrary to the resolves of Congress & the law of this Colony." He had already initiated an appeal but asked Washington's advice before proceeding further. Assuming *Elizabeth* would be condemned, he had removed the cargo. The claimants had agreed to compromise with the captors by offering them "their full quota of salvage," being one-third of half the value of the vessel and the cargo. "Should Your Excellency recommend my compromising with those claimants," Wentworth inquired, "I shall comport with it."[9]

As Wentworth was writing Washington for advice, Bradford heard *Nelly Frigate* had been libeled at Portsmouth, thereby denying him the commission. He penned a hurried complaint to Hancock, arguing that if other agents had the authority to apprehend prizes that went "into the mouth of their harbour for a night's anchorage, no more Continental prizes may be expected in this port." Bradford did not consider himself the reason prizemasters avoided Boston; he attributed this problem to the forthcoming storms of winter or to flight from British cruisers. Referring to Wentworth, Bradford thought it "extraordinary for them gentlemen who have no care or trouble in fitting out the schooners to receive the emolument." Bradford, however, overlooked his own machinations to obtain emoluments at the expense of agents such as Glover and Bartlett.[10]

Hancock provided no direction on the matter, despite Bradford's promise to send him some of the fine wines taken from *Peggy*. Wentworth's appeal to Washington drew only a brief comment. The general excused himself from the matter, being too far removed "and involved in a great multiplicity of important business." The Continentals had just evacuated Long Island, and the general was attempting to reconcentrate his forces to defend the town of New York. He concurred with Wentworth on the appeal of *Elizabeth*'s verdict but suggested the matter be referred to the Marine Committee if the "laws prescribed by Congress" had not been upheld.[11]

Washington's reference to the Marine Committee resulted from action taken by Congress to demote Commodore Esek Hopkins for mismanaging the Continental fleet. On August 5 Congress passed a resolution empowering the Marine Committee "to order the ships and armed vessels belonging to the Continent, out on such cruises as they think proper." Perhaps only Washington realized the resolution also encompassed his schooners, as they, too, had been fitted out at Continental expense. The Marine Committee, however, had exercised no jurisdiction over the schooners in the past and probably did not consider them part of their responsibility.[12]

Bradford, receiving no reply from Hancock, penned a letter to the Marine Committee, hoping Robert Morris would intercede on his behalf and strip Wentworth of *Nelly Frigate*. He claimed cargoes would sell for half what he could raise for them in Boston, implying that the Marine Committee would be wise to direct all prizes into Boston. Morris understood the request for what it was—an appeal to collect a commission. Like Hancock, Morris chose not to respond.[13]

For the first time in several weeks, all five schooners were at sea. *Hancock* and *Franklin* cruised off the Virginia capes; *Warren*, with a new quarterdeck, sailed with *Lee* for Nova Scotia; and *Lynch*, which had been on a long, unproductive cruise, reprovisioned at Boston on the 16th and sailed for Cape Sable. They all stayed clear of New York. Lord Howe's fleet, now greatly enhanced by the addition of several more warships, cruised the coast. HMS *Milford* had returned to her station in the bay, this time with a twin sister, the 28-gun *Liverpool*, Capt. Henry Bellew.

Once again the British navy exercised its dominance of coastal America. On August 1 *Liverpool* captured a sloop and a brig. Two days later she recaptured a vessel taken by a privateer, then headed to Halifax with her prizes. On August 19 *Milford* took a fishing schooner off Cape Cod, two days later another off Cape Ann, a third on the 22nd, and two more the following day, making a total of five in five days. Off Thatcher's Island on the 24th she chased the 400-ton *Isaac*, prize of a

Massachusetts privateer, so close into Marblehead that gunners on Marblehead Neck opened and drove the frigate back to sea. *Milford* compensated the following day by capturing a brig and a sloop, thereby keeping her average for the week at one prize a day.[14]

After depositing *Liverpool*'s prizes at Halifax, Bellew returned to Massachusetts Bay. On August 26 the watch reported two schooners well to windward. With a stiff wind blowing from the east, Bellew knew he had them trapped, set his studding sails, and went in chase. Burke and Ayres observed *Liverpool* sheer toward them and came abeam for a quick conference. They agreed to separate, one beating to the north, the other south. Bellew picked *Warren* and closed quickly, firing several shots, but Burke forced the chase, enabling Ayres to sail out of range. When *Warren* struck, Bellew hurried a boat over to the schooner, but he saw she carried guns and stood off to protect his boarders, all the time watching *Lynch* as she bore away. A gale struck shortly after noon, followed by rain, and by the time the weather cleared, *Lynch* was out of sight.

Bellew kept *Warren* as an armed tender and manned her from the frigate. On September 4 the watch on *Liverpool* sighted four sail. Both vessels cleared for action and went in chase, only to overhaul *Milford* bowling along with three prizes. Bellew then disarmed *Warren* and sent her to Halifax. Late in the day, *Milford* captured the sloop *Betsey*, laden with wood. Burr turned the vessel over to a prize crew and ordered her to Halifax, but the sloop never made it.[15]

Ayres returned to Boston and reported *Warren*'s capture to Ward, but he said nothing to Bradford, who discovered the loss quite by accident. Ayres's disregard of Bradford's authority stemmed from his personal dislike of the agent's flagrant grubbing for commissions. Waters ignored Bradford completely. Neither captain had captured a prize for over two months, but their expenses continued to accumulate on Bradford's tab. Trouble between the dissident captains and Bradford was heating to the boiling point.[16]

Quite by accident, Waters brought in a prize. *Lee*, cruising off the tip of Nova Scotia, ran low on provisions and Waters steered for Boston. On September 2 he recaptured the 60-ton sloop *Betsey* off Cape Sable, complete with her cordwood and *Milford*'s prize crew. He carried her into Boston and deposited the vessel with Bradford, who failed to file the libel. This sparked heated words from Waters. Bradford countered by penning one of his complaining letters to Hancock, condemning Waters for having an "obstinate, perverse temper" and for not taking advantage of the "best officered and manned [crew] of any vessel in the service." In his lengthy letter, Bradford mentioned nothing about Waters's capture of *Betsey*. Perhaps he considered his commission on a recapture inconsequential and refused to pay Waters, who annoyed him, a compliment.

What Bradford expected to accomplish by dragging Hancock into his squabble with Waters remains a mystery. If Bradford wanted Waters dismissed without jeopardizing his already weak relationship with Washington, he had access to the Marine Committee. Hancock and Washington were both too absorbed in the British invasion of New York to listen to Bradford's complaints. Bradford, however, seemed oblivious to any problem outside his own interests.

Waters refused to tolerate interference from Bradford and flourished a copy of Washington's instructions he still loyally followed. His directions had not changed since receiving his captain's commission, and, in Waters's opinion, Bradford could not give him orders. Bradford complained to Hancock, "I humbly presume if conduct like this passes with impunity the little Navy will rather be a clog than a service to the public." Once again, neither Hancock nor the Marine Committee replied.

Washington's schooners, now numbering four, cleared Boston Harbor in mid-September and sailed east. Tucker and Skimmer, who had returned to Boston early in the month to replace their spars, set sail on the 16th for the sea lanes of West Indies commerce; Ayres and Waters returned to Nova Scotia. Bradford rejoiced. The bothersome skippers were back at sea. Without prizes there could be no commissions.[17]

Halfway to Nova Scotia, Waters changed his mind and informed Ayres he would cruise off the coast of Maine. Ayres followed what he considered his orders from Bradford and took station south off Cape Sable, staying well to sea and working to the east. Where Waters cruised during his four-week absence is anyone's guess. Bradford believed the "indolent" captain was in the track of the Jamaica ships "after wasting a whole month in harbours." Waters preferred the hospitality of Maine's small ports to the rugged waters of the high seas. From time to time he cruised as far north as the Bay of Fundy, and perhaps as far east as Cape

Sable, but he seldom ventured far from the coast. After consuming most of the ship's provisions, he set a course for Boston.

If Waters was a cautious man, he was also very lucky. Homeward bound on October 3, he captured the 90-ton schooner *Sally*, Joseph Noble, master, bound from Halifax for New York. Noble readily admitted his cargo of fish and lumber was intended for the British army. On October 5 Waters sailed into Boston with his prize. Despite his purported indolence, Waters had captured the only two prizes taken by Washington's schooners during the past two months.

Bradford may not have considered *Lee's* small prize worthy of recognition, but a Boston reporter thanked Waters rather effusively for capturing a cargo intended for "those very Blood-Hounds of Britain ... whose hellish cry continually is Havoc, Blood, Murder, and Plunder. Tis really a pity," the correspondent lamented, that "some method could not be found to banish those Sons of Tyranny, Oppression, and Slavery, out of this free (determined to be) Western American Empire."[18]

Any euphoria Bradford experienced from Waters's capture of *Sally* collapsed a day later when he learned that Ayres had sailed into Salem without his guns. Without knowing the facts, Bradford condemned Ayres for wantonly jettisoning his cannon.

At daylight on September 27, Ayres stood about 1,000 miles east of Long Island when the watch sighted a huge convoy bearing for New York and carrying Gen. John Burgoyne's cavalry—horses and all. Ayres never took time to count all forty-nine vessels, but he spotted five frigates and three towering triple-deckers dispersed among the convoy. With the wind slightly in his favor, he came about and headed for the American coast, doubtful whether he could outrun the 28-gun frigate *Unicorn*, Capt. John Ford, who was on his heels.

Ford came on fast, his guns charged with musket ball, but Ayres stayed out of range by exercising superb seamanship. Cutting his carriage guns loose, he heaved them overboard and trimmed the schooner as best he could. With *Unicorn* still gaining, he stove in the water casks. When Ford closed to a mile, Ayres started to empty his larder, and when that failed to lighten the vessel sufficiently he ordered up saws and cut down the upper works. The chase lasted until 11:30 P.M. With a gale blowing out of the northeast, Ayres lost the frigate in the darkness. Having little food and water and no way of defending himself, he caught a favorable wind and hastened for home.[19]

The stripped-down, cut-up *Lynch* looked a sorry wreck as she sailed into Boston. Bradford ordered her hauled up and set aside. He would not put another penny into her without Hancock's approval, but he kept Ayres and the crew on full pay while he waited for an answer. Bradford, of course, collected a commission on every cent spent to hold, house, and board the crew. Perhaps Hancock enjoyed having a few friends he could ignore but who still wrote him servile letters. "Your friends are great[ly] disappointed," Bradford penned, "in the happiness they promised themselves in seeing you this Fall, but none more than your most humble servant."[20]

Nothing had been heard from Tucker or Skimmer for six weeks, or from Waters for two. The summer had been hard on the schooners, and now there were only three.

❦ 20 ❦
The Autumn of '76

he capture of Warren and the dismantling of *Lynch* could have discouraged Washington from maintaining command of his fleet, had he not already decided to relinquish the schooners to the Marine Committee. He had no influence over political appointee Bradford, who had snatched control of the squadron from Ward. The acquisitive agent exercised far more energy than the ailing general, who seemed content to abdicate his naval responsibilities to the younger man. Washington never reacted publicly to Bradford's appointment as agent. The deposed agents, however, persisted in applying to Washington for a settlement of their grievances against Bradford.[1]

Agent Wentworth of New Hampshire had not been usurped by Bradford, and when the Portsmouth court acquitted the prize brig *Elizabeth* and restored her cargo, Wentworth asked Washington's advice. And when *Nelly Frigate* stopped on her way to Boston and Wentworth libeled her, precipitating another flurry of correspondence between Bradford and Hancock, the general had no time to arbitrate commissions or to interfere in the rulings of the court, regardless of whether he agreed with the judgment.[2] With help from Colonel Glover's regiment, he had rescued his army from destruction on Long Island. Now he had to decide whether to defend New York or to cross the Hudson River and escape with his remaining force. He referred Wentworth to the Marine Committee and, by doing so, ratified his relinquishment of the schooners.[3]

Congress preferred to have the commander in chief's attention focused on military affairs, but it never asked him to give up his navy. When he did, Congress rushed through a resolution empowering the Marine Committee with responsibility for the schooners.[4]

The committee wasted no time issuing instructions to all agents, past and present, demanding a full accounting. They had thirteen frigates under construction and no money to pay for them. Bradford's letters accused the general's agents of holding proceeds from the sale of prizes and converting them for their own use. Imagining some golden nest egg secreted in the agents' coffers, the Marine Committee ordered Bartlett, Watson, Wentworth, Sargent, Jonathan Glover, and—last, but not least—Bradford to send in all their accounts, court decrees, and "the Continental share" to Ebenezer Hancock (John Hancock's brother), the Continental paymaster at Boston.[5]

The amount of detail demanded by the Marine Committee stunned the agents. They kept simple ledgers. Any loose money they might have forwarded to Paymaster Hancock they now held, skeptical of how their accounts would look after restructuring them to meet the committee's new criteria. Bradford had his own bookkeeping problems but temporarily escaped notice by placing the onus of shabby records on Washington's agents. Glover's, Bartlett's, and Sargent's accounts were complicated by partnership agreements to share jointly in the proceeds from prizes. Another problem involved Washington's commissary and quartermaster, who had stripped ordnance from *Nancy,* coal from *Jenny,* and clothing from *Concord* without placing a value on the goods. Bartlett asked Washington for assistance in obtaining valuations. The general had not given the matter three minutes' thought for the past nine months, but he may have felt responsible for Bartlett's loss of self-esteem. The deposed agent wrote sorrowfully, "The reflection joined to the impeachment which is generally implied . . . by a dismission from any office under government has I must confess given me sensible pain."[6]

Neither the Marine Committee nor Bradford comprehended the extent to which both Glover and Bartlett had advanced funds and borrowed heavily to keep the fleet at sea. Both agents wanted their accounts settled. The government owed them money. The agents knew it but needed documentation to support their claims. Bradford, who had assured the Marine Committee that the devilish agents held a veritable pot of gold, now suspected the truth. He resorted to a diversion by reporting that "the prizes taken prior to the three Scotch transports were under the direction of other agents [Bradford still hoped to collect a commission on two transports taken into Marblehead], who by a former order from Congress I have repeatedly called on to exhibit their accounts for a settlement . . . tho' Mr. Watson assures me in a fortnight he will be ready to come to a settlement. But I despair of doing anything with Bartlett and Glover—the latter bawls out of the unreasonableness of calling on him, when he is in advance for the Continent."

Robert Morris knew Bradford well enough to understand the workings of the agent's mind. He suggested that all agents be monitored on a regular basis, thereby forcing them to keep auditable records. Bradford received instructions from the committee requiring a quarterly accounting, "crediting therein the Continental share of every prize whose accounts can be settled and included within that quarter of the year, and that you add thereto a schedule containing an exact account of all the prizes that then remain in your care whose accounts are unsettled." The committee demanded its share as quickly as Bradford collected it.[7]

Bradford's ledgers were in no better condition than Glover's or Bartlett's—perhaps worse, as he had skimmed off commissions with regularity. The committee wisely expanded reporting requirements for Bradford, who promised to give "very close attention" to settling the accounts of prizes falling into his hands but groaned over the inconvenience and cost of keeping so many records. The job, a seemingly rich endowment from his friend Hancock, now looked too much like work. The silver platter on which his appointment had been delivered showed visible signs of tarnish.[8]

While Bradford muddled over his accounts, Washington's three remaining schooners returned to sea. Once again Tucker and Skimmer teamed together, taking *Hancock* and *Franklin* around Cape Sable and deep into the Atlantic. Waters wanted no company and returned with *Lee* to the coast of Maine and worked across the Bay of Fundy. Autumn storms had begun to blow, and, to placate an argumentative crew, Waters stayed in reach of a friendly port.

The distance one sailed from Boston to take a prize made little difference. Off Cape Sable on November 7, *Lee* captured the 130-ton brig *Elizabeth,* Thomas Edwards, master, with a cargo of fifty thousand oak staves and loose lumber bound from Halifax to Jamaica. This was Waters's second *Elizabeth,* the first having been captured with the help of Manley and Ayres in April. Waters escorted the vessel back to Boston.

The *Boston Gazette* congratulated the crew of *Lee,* but Bradford treated Waters's premature return as an opportunity to "acquaint" the Marine Committee with the surly captain's past transgressions. Of

Washington's captains, Bradford had developed the greatest partiality toward Skimmer and Burke, although Burke won the agent's praise not by his acts but by his subservience. Tucker distrusted Bradford, but not overtly. The agent sensed Tucker's avoidance but could not decide whether to consider him hostile or diffident. Bradford's antipathy toward Waters and Ayres sparked when both captains ignored his instructions. Since Ayres no longer had a vessel, Bradford could concentrate his invectives solely on Waters. Instead of complimenting Waters for bringing in *Elizabeth*, he condemned him for "refusing to joyn Capt. Burke in attacking two vessels off Marblehead who was a good deal shattered by them while he [Waters] remained ashore & was only a spectator." By now, this story was six months old.

Bradford never witnessed this purported act of cowardice; he probably concocted the story from a conversation he had pried from Burke. If the Marine Committee kept a blacklist, the allegation might have barred Waters from service in the Continental Navy. Bradford resorted to tall tales to rid himself of Waters, even though the recalcitrant captain had carried into Boston the only three prizes taken in the past three months. For a man who counted his commissions before he went to bed each night, John Bradford sure had a keen dislike for Captain Waters.[9]

Bradford's opportunity to sack Waters occurred soon after *Lee* came in with her prize. The clever agent was a patient man, at times coming close to outwitting himself. Surrounded by servile employees, he enjoyed no direct supervision of his own activities, and Waters's future began to unravel with the return of *Hancock* and *Franklin*.

Tucker and Skimmer, gone for two months, captured the 130-ton brig *Triton*, Thomas Brinton, master, before Waters took *Elizabeth*. Because *Hancock* and *Franklin* were deep in the Atlantic, the prize did not reach Boston for two weeks, tying up at Long Wharf soon after Waters arrived. Laden with 426 tierces of salmon and 420 quintals of dried fish, *Triton* had sailed from Newfoundland for the Mediterranean. Ignoring Waters's haul of oak staves, Bradford voiced high praise for Tucker's and Skimmer's brigload of fish.

Six days later, November 13, Tucker and Skimmer arrived with a much richer prize, the sleek 150-ton brig *Lively*, Nicholas Martindale, master, captured off Newfoundland and laden with a huge cargo of winter clothing for Howe's army. Bradford, who rarely communicated with

Washington, broke tradition and wrote effusively, "I have the honour to congratulate Your Excellency on the acquisition lately made by . . . *Franklin* & *Hancock* of a brig bound from Scotland to [New] York with a cargo calculated to make the winter's campaign more comfortable for your army." Ward had been given an inventory of the cargo to send to headquarters, Bradford stated, and in an expression of good fellowship added, "If your Excellency should have occasion for any of the liqours I shall esteem it an honor to receive orders to forward them." Bradford's euphoria stemmed from scanning the vessel's invoice, which totaled a stunning £25,000.[10]

Bradford sent a lengthier letter of congratulation to Hancock, this time taking the trouble to include a copy of *Lively*'s inventory. Bradford assured Hancock he had sent a copy of the manifest to Washington, although he had lent it to Ward to transcribe. Ward neglected to copy the manifest, and Congress began scouring the country to locate clothing for Washington's freezing regiments.

Three weeks later, Ward recalled the manifest of *Lively*, confirmed the clothing was still on board, and began removing 17,000 suits, 30,000 shirts, 30,000 pairs of stockings, and 30,000 pairs of shoes. On December 6, twelve wagons with thirty-nine bales of clothing began their overland trip to "the Army at or near New York." Ward failed to advise Washington the clothing was on the way until December 23. By then, the general and his army were neither at nor near New York but mustering on the western shore of the Delaware River for a surprise attack on Trenton. Bradford failed to appraise the clothing before Ward shipped it, but he agreed to accept the quartermaster's inventory and assign a valuation later. No record of the inventory ever surfaced, drawing Tucker into a heated dispute with Bradford over prize money.

Much merchandise remained in the hold of *Lively*, items such as women's shoes, silk stockings, diaper cloth, nightcaps, wine, porter, and tons of household goods. Merchant Abraham Livingston of Boston had been sent to Dartmouth by Bradford to obtain part of the cargo of the Continental prize *Mellish*. After purchasing some goods for the army, he returned to Boston, where he met fellow merchant William Turnbull of Baltimore. They read a notice in the local papers offering the balance of *Lively*'s cargo for sale on January 8 and visited Bradford to determine whether any of the articles in the auction could be of use to the army.

After scanning the inventory, both merchants recognized how marvelous their shelves would look if stocked with *Lively*'s merchandise. However, they needed a strategy for acquiring the goods at the best price.

Bradford suggested that the surest way to prevent competitive bids from running up the price was for Livingston and Turnbull to present themselves as agents buying clothing for the army. Bradford did not allow bidders to inspect the contents of the crates beforehand. Had they done so, they would have found nothing suitable for military wear. Whether the sheriff participated in the deceit is not known. On the day of the auction, the public withdrew from the bidding. They had sons and relatives in the Continental Army, and warm clothes would give their boys comfort and perhaps spare them from disease and frostbite.

The absence of fair bidding enraged Tucker's crew, who had scattered themselves among the crowd. Witnessing their prize money diminishing to nearly nothing, they pooled their scant resources, but their attempt to bid up the merchandise failed. Tempers flared as bidding came to an end. Several of the crew overheard a merchant offer Turnbull twice what he had paid for part of his purchase. Bradford found himself further alienated from the men when he could not produce an accounting showing the value of the goods Ward transferred to the army. The crew stormed away from the auction, accusing the agent of collusion. A few days later word spread from Newburyport to New Bedford—Bradford could not be trusted. No prize was safe in his hands.

As news of Bradford's deception rippled through Massachusetts, the Marine Committee suddenly experienced grave difficulties in obtaining men to serve on their brand-new frigates. Fearing an investigation, Bradford attempted to explain the misunderstanding to his friends on the Secret Committee. After summarizing the events of the auction with unstained innocence, Bradford admitted, "It happens to be very unlucky that this should happen just at a time when the two frigates are getting their hands, for the sailors [of *Hancock* and *Franklin*] propagate it that the Continental prizes were given away for half price. It seems at the close of the second day's sale a gentleman offered Mr. Turnbull a hundred per cent on his purchase. This got among the Tarrs [sailors] & created great bickerings & uneasiness. . . ." Bradford assured the committee he had resolved the matter with the "Tarrs" and would distribute prize money as soon as he received Ward's valuation. A month had passed since Ward shipped the clothing to the army. Bradford must by then have suspected the inventory had never been taken. His influence with Hancock and the Secret Committee, however, preserved his reputation at the levels of government making him rich.[11]

After purchasing *Lively*'s cargo for £8,000, the merchants paid for it with drafts in the name of Robert Morris, leaving Bradford with negotiable paper but no money to settle with the prize crew. Bradford appealed to Morris for funds. "When I first had the honour of coming into office," he wrote, and "after advancing all my own money, I borrowed a considerable sum of those who were warm in the great Cause, and the credit of the Continent was not injured. I hope I shall not be obliged to do like again. At present we have no prospects of any prizes, as I know not of a single Continental cruiser out."[12]

Bradford's explanation and appeal for funds passed gently through the Secret Committee to the Marine Committee. No one in Congress accused their honest agent in Boston of duplicity. Having no funds themselves, they remained silent on the matter. Morris, however, told Bradford to "inform Mr. Turnbull that altho the Congress wish[es] by all means to procure the Public stores on the most reasonable terms possible, yet they cannot desire to injure one part of the Public service for the sake of another, and that the Honest Tars ought to have fair play in the sales of their prizes." Morris warned Bradford to "guard against monopolizers, forestallers and combinations of that kind," perhaps not realizing he was speaking to the proverbial fox in the henhouse.[13]

Bradford possessed an ability to capitalize on opportunities to rid his life of critics. He decommissioned the gunless *Lynch*, idling Ayres, thereby elevating Waters to the top of his list of expendable captains. Waters had frustrated Bradford's plans by bringing in three prizes while Tucker and Skimmer chalked up three months of hard cruising without taking one. This all had changed the day Tucker and Skimmer sent in *Triton* and *Lively*.

Bradford also envisioned Tucker as a potential problem and, in the manner of a well-trained politician, fished about for something to humiliate him. In a discussion with Stiles, *Hancock*'s first lieutenant, Bradford learned that Tucker had removed a number of articles from a prize, sold them, and pocketed the money. Bradford questioned Bartlett on the matter, who reported Tucker had "acknowledged it," but he ignored Bartlett's claim that Tucker also "accounted for it." Martindale, master of *Lively*, deposed a different story. According to him, Tucker treated the crew of *Lively* "with all manner of civilities and good usage," retrieved the crew's personal belongings, and, for those articles not found, "generously paid the full price from out of his own pocket." Tucker did not sound like a man who sold public property for his own profit, but Bradford, a master of chicanery himself, possessed a well-trained mind for altering the truth.[14] Tucker had earned the respect and support of Bradford's associates, but the agent tried to cast him in the role of troublemaker, as he had with Ayres and Waters.

When Tucker and Skimmer returned from their last cruise, *Hancock* and *Franklin* required a complete overhaul. Bradford assessed the damage and made his report to Morris. Refitting the vessels would cost more than they were worth. Despite his animosity toward Tucker, Bradford asked Hancock for permission to shift Tucker to *Lee*—thereby dispensing with Waters—and Skimmer to the laid-up *Lynch*. To Bradford's way of thinking, *Lynch* was not worth repairing for Ayres but good enough for Skimmer. Having no schooners at sea to send in prizes disrupted Bradford's cash flow, but with no reply from Hancock the issue remained unresolved.[15]

With the arrival of winter, none of the schooners sailed. On December 17 the Massachusetts Board of War asked Bradford to send his schooners on a mission to intercept the ship *Mellish*, which had sailed for Newport without knowing the port had fallen to the British. Ayres needed a new mast, and neither Waters nor Skimmer could locate their crews. Two weeks later the Massachusetts Council asked Ayres and Waters to take *Lynch* and *Lee* to New York as cartels in a prisoner exchange. Both captains refused, claiming a "refractory disposition of the men." The crews believed that once they arrived off New York they would be captured and impressed into the Royal Navy. Ayres finally agreed to march the prisoners to Providence and obtain a better vessel before proceeding to New York, but Waters flatly refused, even though *Lee* remained in good sailing condition.[16]

As 1776 came to an end, both Tucker and Waters found employment in the Continental Navy. For several months, Ayres occupied his time sailing back and forth on Continental cartels. Skimmer, however, had a ship but no commission. Bradford reminded Hancock that "he runs the risque of being ill treated if he should be taken. I think he is worthy of a commission & won't dishonour it."[17]

Bradford excelled at helping people he liked and used excellent judgment in favoring Skimmer. The same did not apply to his other favorite, William Burke, who remained a prisoner in New York Harbor. Bradford appealed to Washington for Burke's release and, when that failed, penned a note to Hancock. "I need not urge the matter to a gentleman of your benevolent mind," he scribbled with customary fealty. "I wrote to the amiable General under the 9th of November to let him know that Capt. Burke was sailed from Halifax to be exchanged, but his [Washington's] mind is so engaged that no provision is made to release poor Burke. He is a brave man and I could have wished him better fate."[18]

Despite a year of confusion, Washington's schooners had taken twenty-two vessels. Unlike Broughton's and Selman's prizes, they were mostly large vessels carrying arms, troops, provisions, and supplies. Overall, the schooners had better commanders, among them John Manley, promoted to the command of the Continental frigate *Hancock,* and Samuel Tucker, whose promotion came later. But the heyday of the schooners fell rapidly into decline, hurried in part by the building of the Continental Navy, and hurried in a more noxious way by the petty manipulations of an agent who could not detach himself from the flunky system. All this would play itself out in the months to come, but not before John Skimmer added his name to the list of valor.

🏵 21 🏵
Winter of Unrest

*T*he *first day of 1777* broke gray and blustery along the coast of New England. People warmed themselves by their firesides, and John Bradford sat in his counting house to assess his prospects for the coming spring. Two Continental frigates, *Hancock* and *Boston*, would soon be ready for sea. Other Continental ships had been commissioned, and the number of privateers operating out of Massachusetts continued to grow. Even without Washington's schooners, Bradford anticipated plenty of prizes to keep him prosperous and busy with work.

He now had three unemployed captains—Tucker, Skimmer, and Ayres—still on the Continental payroll, and if "poor Burke" returned from captivity he would have no vessel to command. Waters balked at taking *Lee* on a winter cruise, but he refused to give up the vessel. With reluctance, Bradford returned the battered *Hancock* and disabled *Franklin* to Thomas Grant and Archibald Selman, their respective owners. *Lynch* had no guns and needed a mast, and Ayres refused to sail without replacements. He also demanded twenty hands to dignify his rank. All Bradford's captains had more time in grade than Skimmer. If Tucker so chose, he could transfer his flag to *Lee*, leaving Ayres or Waters with *Lynch*. Bradford wanted to be rid of Tucker, Waters, and Ayres, thereby saving the last two schooners for Skimmer and Burke.[1]

Tucker and Waters solved part of Bradford's dilemma by seeking commissions in the Continental Navy. Bradford rejoiced, but his enmity toward the pair surpassed his willingness to see them dignified by Congressional commissions. Bradford could not forget how Tucker and his men had challenged the bidding at the auction of *Lively*'s cargo. He had escaped censure, but only because of his friends in Congress. As for Waters, Bradford simply disliked him, and the feeling was mutual.

John Langdon had been building the frigates *Raleigh* and *Ranger* at Portsmouth. In early January, Tucker and Waters, perhaps at Manley's suggestion, rode to the shipyard and offered their services. *Raleigh* had been ready for sea for several months but had not sailed for want of guns. *Ranger*'s captain, John Roche, who had previously been the first lieutenant on *Lynch,* had just started to build his frigate when winter brought work to a standstill. Langdon had no assignment for either Tucker or Waters and sent them to Congress, attesting to "their known good character" and promising that "the services they have done the States in taking so many valuable prizes, no doubt will meet the approbation of the Honbl Marine Committee."[2]

Thomas Cushing, agent for building *Boston* and *Hancock,* also interviewed the pair and issued another favorable recommendation to Congress. Both captains told Cushing they had some "uncertainty about their orders," or from whom they should receive them, as neither Bradford nor Ward provided any. Cushing capitalized on this bit of news and suggested to Hancock that, in the future, prizes captured by Continental cruisers should be libeled through his office rather than Bradford's. In Cushing's view, Bradford failed to find time to provide Washington's schooners with proper instructions because he had too many prizes to manage. If Bradford had kept Tucker and Waters busy, Cushing implied, the two men would not be looking for employment elsewhere.[3] Hancock considered it imprudent to give a man as busy as Cushing responsibility for prizes, but he may have been amused by the prospect of hearing Bradford's screams if the emolument went to another agent.

With two letters of recommendation tucked in their pockets, Tucker and Waters notified Bradford they were off to Congress. Bradford scribbled his own note to Hancock, sealed it, and handed it to Waters for delivery. Langdon and Cushing did not share with Bradford their private conversations with Tucker and Waters, but the politically astute agent was wily enough to anticipate problems. Bradford's letter contained a summary of all the complaints he had registered with Hancock in the past and represented his final, futile condemnation of Tucker and Waters. In closing he wrote, "I assure you, sir, it gives me pain to characterize [them] in so disagreeable a light. But I can with great truth say it is from an ardent wish that such persons only may be employ'd that will do honour to our growing navy. . . ."[4]

Tucker and Waters found the Marine Committee frustrated by long delays in getting their frigates to sea and studying an inventory of vessels laid up in ports along Massachusetts Bay. Prizes could be armed and fitted out much faster than new frigates. To sail they needed a few guns, an experienced commander, and a willing crew. The Marine Committee asked Congress for funds to purchase three such vessels. They also recommended that Tucker and Waters be appointed captains, and on March 15 Congress passed a resolution transferring the pair to the Continental Navy. Hancock signed the transfer, and Bradford had no choice but to accept the resolutions of Congress.[5]

After granting Tucker and Waters commissions, the committee, perhaps with a little irony, directed Bradford to purchase vessels for the pair to command. Tucker and Waters returned to Boston, camped on the agent's doorstep, and demanded action. Bradford moved at his own pace—deliberately slow, complaining all the while that he had no money. Waters finally agreed to sail as first lieutenant on *Hancock*, Manley's frigate. Tucker held out for his own command.[6]

Bradford purchased several prizes for the Marine Committee, among them *Triton* and *Lively*, fine brigs that had been captured by Tucker and Skimmer. However, neither vessel had been built to serve as a warship. Without Glover or Bartlett to help him, Bradford inherited the task of arming the vessels and ladening them with trade goods. The Continental Navy had commissioned and armed "letter of marque" vessels with charters to carry and exchange goods for ordnance and, if the skipper happened on the enemy, to take a prize or two. Tucker declined. He wanted to be on a fighting ship.[7]

Waters's reappointment to *Hancock* solved one of Bradford's problems, and he assigned Skimmer to *Lee*. Ayres remained in command of *Lynch*, although he had all but abandoned the vessel, and "poor Burke" remained in confinement on board a prison ship. Ayres spent most of the winter running cartels back and forth between Boston, Newport, and New York, but on none of these exchanges did he obtain Burke.[8]

In mid-February Bradford received an urgent request from the Secret Committee to send *Lynch* to France with important papers for

Benjamin Franklin and Silas Deane. He notified Ayres of the mission and asked him to be ready on a moment's notice. Ayres declined. He planned to seek a commission in the Continental Navy. This suited Bradford. He now had a vessel for Burke. "The schooner *Lynch* goes on this errand," Bradford wrote Morris. He added, referring to Ayres, "We are luckily rid of him. I have got a man who will answer the purpose exactly. I'll be bound by his abilities and vigilance. Why should Ayres, like a rotten limb be supported, by the useful members. . . . I leave you to judge, sir, if that man is deserving a commission who the counsel did not choose to trust a paquet by. He is beyond dispute the most bashfull [unassertive] man on earth." Bradford used his office to try to dissuade the Marine Committee from granting the "rotten limb" a commission. When he disliked a person, there seemed to be no end to his malice.[9]

Bradford penned a similar message to Hancock, and like a good henchman, he replaced Ayres not with Burke but with Capt. John Adams (not *the* John Adams), formerly a skipper in the service of Hancock's mercantile interests. Bradford knew Hancock would be pleased with the selection. "I know him to be as smart and as capable a man as any in the state," Bradford wrote, adding, "if he performs the voyage I hope it may introduce him to the notice of the Congress and I am well assured he would not dishonor a commission." If Bradford's attempt to secure a commission for Adams was intended to deny one for Ayres, the ploy failed. Ayres continued in the Continental service and spent the next year shuttling prisoners back and forth on the cartel *Two Polly*.[10]

On March 3, after waiting for a bout of frigid weather to pass, Adams sailed for France with letters "of very great Consequence to the Public." Bradford provided Adams with instructions, ordering him to "imbrace the first fair wind and make your way to the port of Nant[e]s ... carefully avoiding coming near any vessels at sea. You are to keep your dispatches from Congress with all your private letters, slung with a proper weight, and be in readiness to sink them at a moment's warning. But bare in mind not to be surprised into such an act before you are well assured that [you] are really in the power of your enemy, and cannot make your escape." Once safely in France, Adams was to ride to Paris and deliver the letters to the commissioners, namely, "Honorable Doctor Franklin," Silas Deane, and Arthur Lee.[11]

Bradford could not resist the opportunity to ingratiate himself with the "Honorable Doctor" by showering him with a few servile words. "The agreeable news of your arrival at the Court of France diffused a joy throughout this Continent. May it please the indulgent providence to confirm your health, that you may in the eve of life render your country as important services, as you have rendered the world. . . ."[12]

With his friend Adams on a mission to France, Bradford conspired to convert the voyage into an opportunity to make money. Shortly before *Lynch* sailed, the Marine Committee instructed Bradford to laden her with potash, oil, and commodities marketable in France and to deliver the cargo to Pliarne, Penet and Company in Nantes. On such short notice, Bradford failed to fill the vessel with the types of articles wanted in France but made up a cargo by shipping a ton of potash, about three tons of currier's oil, and one hundred tierces of pickled salmon from the prize brig *Triton*. The cargo would be for the credit of the Continent, but Bradford donned his merchant's hat and suggested to Pliarne and Penet, "If you have any inclination to speculate in the article of Bohea [a black Chinese] tea, and have any goods at market, if you ship twelve chests by Capt. Adams and interest me one half, I make no doubt it will give a hundred [percent] profit."[13]

Adams made a fast, uneventful passage. Landing at Nantes on April 3, he placed the cargo in the care of Pliarne and Penet and hired a coach to Paris. He found Franklin and Deane in their chambers (Lee had gone to Spain) and delivered the messages. The commissioners handed him a packet of correspondence and ordered him to return to Boston as soon as he obtained a cargo. Franklin encouraged Adams to sail "with all expedition" and ordered him to "enclose the dispatches in a box with lead, & have it always ready to sink, should you be in unavoidable danger of falling into the enemies hands." Upon reaching the American coast, Adams must head for the nearest harbor and express the dispatches to Congress.[14]

Adams returned to Nantes on April 11 and found agent Jonathan Williams Jr. working feverishly but making little progress assembling a cargo of arms for *Lynch*.[15] Adams blamed delays on the "backwardness of the agents." A rider on a lathered horse brought a message from Deane asking Adams to wait for another packet of dispatches coming in a day or two. Adams warned Williams that when the letters came he would sail in ballast if the arms were not on board. Another agent informed Adams he had "no right to expect any goods, as he bro't no cargo." Williams made an advance against the receipt of a future cargo and on April 29 loaded *Lynch* with thirty cases containing 525 carbines and 450 pistols. Pliarne and Penet evidently declined Bradford's proposition, as no Bohea tea appeared on the lading.[16]

Watered and provisioned, Adams dropped down the Loire on May 19 and set sail for the northeastern coast of America. With a fair wind, he passed Saint-Nazaire and headed into the Bay of Biscay. A few miles offshore the watch reported a large man-of-war standing south of Belle Island. Moments later the warship filled and, under a full press of sail, made for *Lynch*. Adams came about and headed for the island, hoping to ground in shallow water, but the 80-gun HMS *Foudroyant*, Capt. John Jervis, cut *Lynch* off and forced her surrender. Adams dropped the correspondence overboard and waited for his captors to send over a boat.

Jervis thought he had captured a simple merchantman and escorted *Lynch* into Plymouth, England. When the Admiralty inspectors opened the crates and discovered "arms and cloathing for the use of the rebel army," Jervis felt better rewarded for his trouble, as the smell of pickled salmon had not left the hold. Adams, who had been discharged at Plymouth, enjoyed about three hours of freedom before being arrested for smuggling arms and marched back on board *Foudroyant*. Jervis released him a few days later, and Adams eventually made his way back to Nantes, where he obtained passage to Boston.[17]

With *Lynch* a prize of the Royal Navy, Bradford no longer had a schooner for either Adams or "poor Burke," and with Ayres in the employ of the Marine Committee, Skimmer took command of *Lee*.

On March 3, 1777, the incapacitated Ward, after waiting nearly nine months, finally got his wish. Washington replaced him with Maj. Gen. William Heath, another Bostonian whom His Excellency could not use on the front lines of his army. His only instructions to Heath regarding the armed schooners involved a supply of powder borrowed by the army from the state of Massachusetts. Washington authorized its return, provided the powder had not been lent "since my departure from Boston." He asked Heath to review the matter with Ward and, if the powder had not been returned, to determine "by what means it was neglected." The general probably knew the answer to his own question.[18]

By the spring of 1777, the only vestige of what had once been a formative part of Washington's squadron was the schooner *Lee*. John Skimmer, her new skipper, had not been a member of His Excellency's command, just as Bradford had not been one of the general's appointed agents. Bradford, either through negligence or out of maliciousness toward the schooners' commanders, had let the squadron deteriorate. His attempts to retain *Lee* for Skimmer and salvage *Lynch* for Burke had been solely for the purpose of rewarding those who patronized him, and patronage had little to do with competence. Burke had not demonstrated strong leadership as a skipper, and the balance of his wartime career showed little change. Skimmer's cruises had been in company with Tucker, and he benefited from the relationship. Had Bradford chosen Skimmer for reasons other than patronage, he would have deserved credit for making a fine decision. Skimmer possessed ability, far more than even Bradford suspected.

☙ 22 ☙
The Last Schooner

arly in 1777, Bradford prodded the Marine Committee for direction on the use or disposition of Washington's two remaining schooners. At the time, *Lynch* was at Boston but without guns, and only *Lee* remained serviceable for duty. Morris gave the matter little thought until February, when he needed *Lynch* as a dispatch vessel to France. "If any of the rest of them are good vessels, suitable for cruisers," Morris declared, "I should think it best to buy them and continue them in the service, especially as . . . some of the commanders and officers have merit to deserve a continuation in the service." If the owners refused to sell, Morris added, the schooners must then be "paid off and dismissed."[1]

Bradford, after asking Morris for direction, ignored it and retained *Lee* under the original lease agreement. Because of his close relationship with Hancock, he felt free to do as he pleased, although he often asked his superiors for the very instructions he wanted to follow. In the matter of *Lee,* he considered Skimmer deserving of "a continuation in the service," which appears to be the only phrase in Morris's letter Bradford read.[2]

Since Morris never legitimized Skimmer's occupation by granting him a commission in the navy, Bradford petitioned the Massachusetts Council. On March 10, 1777, the court delivered a letter of marque to Skimmer, thereby providing him with a privateer's commission, a necessary credential in the event of his capture. For nine months the young skipper had sailed with only a master's brevet.[3]

With provisions for a two-month cruise, Skimmer sailed from Boston on March 20 with fifty-four officers and men, ten carriage guns, eighteen swivels, and four cohorns—a huge arsenal for a small vessel like *Lee.* He headed for Bermuda, a frequent stopping place for West Indies traders. During the first two weeks, the only vessel he chased was the armed American ship *Success,* James Anderson, master, with a cargo of arms from Nantes to Philadelphia. After the vessels parted, Skimmer worked slowly to the north, keeping within the sea lanes of West Indies commerce.

On April 13 Skimmer captured the 70-ton schooner *Hawke,* Daniel Collins, master. *Hawke,* several days out of Canso, carried a hefty cargo of dried fish and oil for Barbados. Skimmer transferred the prisoners to *Lee* and ordered the prize into Boston. On the 21st, facing contrary winds, *Hawke* anchored at Marblehead. Jonathan Glover looked at the cargo but refused to libel the prize. Instead, he advised a friend to buy the fish for a shipment being loaded for Bilbao. Bradford considered the capture of little value but on May 8 libeled the prize on Skimmer's behalf.[4]

Skimmer, satisfied his crew had performed well in taking their first prize, kept *Lee* at sea. Abandoning the deserted West Indies sea lanes, he steered for the Grand Banks of Newfoundland to help initiate the spring fishing season. He expected to find vessels from Europe, among them many from Great Britain.

On May 3 the watch reported a sloop drifting along with barely a sail aloft but manifesting the telltale markings of a fisherman. Skimmer came abeam and asked her identity. Nathaniel Horrick, master, replied the sloop was *Betsey,* from London. Skimmer ordered her surrender and brought Horrick over to *Lee* with his papers.

Betsey must have been a popular name for English vessels, as she was the third by that name captured by Washington's schooners. Horrick had been at sea for fifty-three days and had five thousand green fish and forty hogsheads of pure salt stowed below. The fourteen-year-old, 58-ton *Betsey* had seen hard use. She would not bring much at the auction block, but because of the fish in her hold Skimmer sent her off to Bradford. The court condemned the vessel on June 24, to be auctioned on July 3 in company with "two Negro men and one Negro woman" to be sold into servitude for a period of seven years, "at the expiration of which term they are to be free'd by the purchaser." The sale of both vessel and servants took place at Hancock's wharf.[5]

Skimmer stayed at sea and on May 11 captured the brig *Charles,* Jeffery Tapley, master, of Waterford, Ireland. The brig, another old fisherman but much larger than *Betsey,* had been peaceably at anchor. Her crew of ten swelled the number of prisoners already on board the cramped *Lee.* Nonetheless, Skimmer refilled his diminishing larder with provisions from *Charles* and sent her to Boston under the command of William Hooper, his sailing master. Bradford never had the opportunity to complain about the rickety old fishing brig. Twelve days later the prize stumbled into the path of HMS *Mermaid,* and on June 16 Hooper and three sailors reached Halifax and spent the rest of the summer on a prison ship. The local admiralty court returned the vessel to her owners, but her master, Jeffery Tapley, remained a prisoner of *Lee* until he reached Boston.[6]

Skimmer cruised off the Grand Banks for another twenty days before running low on provisions. As he turned toward home, the watch reported two brigs drift fishing within speaking distance of each other. Skimmer roved alongside and ordered them to surrender. The 110-ton *Capling,* John Coulrick, master, and the 80-ton *Industry,* John Browne, master, had sailed from the Island of Jersey a few weeks earlier and had barely wetted their lines when *Lee* came abeam. Skimmer could not send off two prize crews without the risk of being overwhelmed by his trove of prisoners. Instead of cramming them into *Lee's* hold, he divided the prisoners among the three vessels, locked them below, distributed his marines among the vessels, and sailed for the closest American port. The holds of *Capling* and *Industry* contained seventy hogsheads of salt but only "a trifle of green fish."

Skimmer attempted to carry his prizes to Boston, but British cruisers forced him to keep close to shore along the coast of Maine. He reached Falmouth (Portland, Maine) on June 10 and turned both vessels over to Simeon Mayo, Bradford's deputy. Skimmer reported seeing British warships between Townsend (Boothbay) and Piscataqua and felt certain of capture had he tried for Boston. At the time, Lord Howe had ten warships posted between Halifax and Boston. With two slow sailers and a shorthanded crew, Skimmer did well to reach Falmouth safely.

Mayo libeled the prizes at Falmouth, and on June 25 Skimmer carried the inventories to Boston and presented them to Bradford. Instead of showing a little gratitude for his favorite skipper's long cruise, Bradford grumbled that the prizes should have been brought around to Boston, where they would sell for a higher price. Skimmer explained his reasons, hoping to soothe the disgruntled agent. Bradford finally agreed to let the proceeds from the sale at Falmouth determine whether it would have been worth running "the risque of getting them to Boston." He wrote Mayo a hurried letter asking that the two prizes be sold and settled without delay, as he "was pressed for the want of money."[7] Bradford's appetite for a few extra dollars later led to consequences for Skimmer and his crew.

Bradford, pressed for medicines, discovered that Skimmer had thoughtfully removed a handsome supply from each of his five prizes. Richard Stiles, formerly the first lieutenant on the armed schooner *Hancock,* now held letters of marque for the Massachusetts privateer *True Blue,* owned in part by Jonathan Glover. Stiles obtained nine items from *Lee's* medicine chest, and Bradford tallied £2 10s. 4d. in favor of Skimmer's account.[8] Bradford used the cash to reprovision *Lee.* With William Addiscot, a new master's mate to replace Hooper, Skimmer sailed on July 11 and set a heading for Newfoundland's banks. Six weeks passed and Bradford heard nothing from Skimmer.

In the meantime, the Continental Navy's new 28-gun frigate *Boston* and 32-gun frigate *Hancock*—the latter commanded by John Manley— engaged three British warships—the 44-gun *Rainbow,* the 32-gun *Flora,* and the 10-gun brig *Victor.* Bradford had helped provision both frigates, and their absence bothered him as much as no word from Skimmer. When he learned that *Hancock* had been captured, Bradford reacted by applying his usual hindsight. He confided to Hancock that if Skimmer had commanded the frigate instead of Manley, she would not have been taken. "I look on him [Skimmer] to be equal in judgment & spirit to any man in the Northern Department. He carries a strict command and his men merely idolize him." Bradford, however, suspected Skimmer had also been captured. If so, he wanted his favorite skipper on record as a brave man whose potential had never been recognized.[9]

Bradford's discomfort over Skimmer's long absence ended on September 23 when a prize crew from *Lee* sailed into Boston with the 160-ton *Industrious Bee,* John Biddecombe, master. Skimmer had been cruising east of St. John's, Newfoundland, hoping to intercept a stray merchantman. Finding nothing but neutral fishing vessels, he shifted to the lower latitudes and on August 29 sighted a westbound brig bounding over the waves with a full spread of canvas. Skimmer ordered pursuit and overhauled her after a chase that began at daybreak and ended late afternoon. *Industrious Bee* carried five hundred hogsheads of "LaMalt Salt" from the Straits of Gibraltar for St. John's fisheries. "The brig is a fine vessel," Bradford informed the Marine Committee, "sails remarkably fast, and has been off the stocks but ten months." Bradford thought she would make an excellent addition to the Continental Navy. To Morris he added a few good words on Skimmer's behalf, asking for Congress to promote the young skipper, although Bradford admitted he did not know whether Skimmer wanted a transfer to the Continental Navy.[10]

On August 30, the day after *Lee* captured *Industrious Bee*, Skimmer intercepted the brig *Lively*, John Carter, master, from Bristol, England, to Halifax with a cargo of rice and staves. Like *Bee*, the vessel was virtually new. Not believing misfortune could strike twice, Skimmer placed his new master, William Addiscot, on board as prizemaster with instructions to take her into Boston. Fifteen leagues off the harbor Addiscot fell in with HMS *Diamond*. Skimmer not only lost his prize, he lost another master.

To placate Bradford, Skimmer had ordered the prize to Boston. Had Addiscot worked down the coast, he could easily have reached Falmouth or Portsmouth. Portsmouth, however, was Wentworth's territory, and Bradford would not have collected a commission. As it turned out, no one collected a cent. For the pittance of a 2.5 percent commission are such decisions made.

Addiscot and his prize crew landed in Halifax, where they joined more than three hundred prisoners in a "large brick building, barricaded by a very high fence, under the care of the provost guard." Prison ships in the harbor were already filled with Americans. His Majesty's warships had begun to exact a heavy toll on America's navy and an even heavier toll on her privateers. Addiscot watched British officers apply to the provost guards for seamen, and those refusing to serve the king "were kicked and banged, and hauled forcibly away." One day the guard grabbed Addiscot. He resisted, got "kicked and banged," and was dragged off to a warship. Several months later he reached England and from there escaped to Cherbourg, where he found friends who helped him home.[11]

After capturing *Lively*, Skimmer stayed at sea, cruising to the southward until his provisions ran low. At the end of September he sailed for home, disappointed he had nothing to show for another hard month at sea. On October 1 his luck changed when the watch reported a distant sail dead ahead. The ancient vessel wallowed in light swells, and the speedy *Lee* swiftly overhauled her. The 120-ton brig *Dolphin,* John Shields, master, bound from Barbados for Newfoundland with rum and sugar, proved to be old and leaky. She carried a small crew and too few provisions to bolster *Lee's* dwindling larder. Skimmer placed a prize crew on board and, keeping her close, set a heading for Boston. As he approached the coast of New England, a typical autumn storm whipped across Massachusetts Bay and drove both vessels into Marblehead. On October 26 Skimmer touched land for the first time in three months. His had been the longest continuous cruise of all of Washington's schooners—and the last.[12]

On October 30 Bradford wrote the Marine Committee, asking "whether to keep the *Lee* in pay or discharge her." He also reminded the committee that Skimmer deserved a Continental commission. Four months had elapsed without a reply to his last request. Without waiting for the committee to respond on the disposition of the schooner, Bradford returned the schooner to her owner, Thomas Stevens, and settled the account. A few days later a privateer brought a prize worth £12,000 into Portsmouth and reported a large fleet of English transports off Massachusetts Bay—the first of the fall convoys bringing winter provisions to General Howe's army. Bradford damned his bad luck for having discharged *Lee.*[13]

In December the Marine Committee authorized the Navy Board of the Eastern Department—a district office created on June 26 by Congress—to grant Skimmer his long-sought commission. He now had credentials but no ship. Bradford purchased *Industrious Bee,* and the Naval Board converted the brig to a sloop of war with fourteen 4s and renamed her *General Gates* in honor of the victor at Saratoga.[14] Skimmer sailed from Marblehead on May 24, 1778, with a crew of one hundred, and three days later departed from Cape Ann in company with the 12-gun privateer brig *Hawk,* Jonathan Oakes, commander.[15]

In early July, the first two prizes taken by Skimmer and Oakes arrived at Boston. The 300-ton ship *Jenny,* James Cummings, master, had beaten off *Hawk* when Skimmer came up and forced her to strike. The 180-ton brig *Thomas,* John Robenson, master, surrendered without a fight. Skimmer and Oakes sent both vessels homeward and remained at sea.[16]

General Gates and *Hawk* separated after sending their third prize, the 100-ton brig *Nancy*, into Boston at the end of July. *Nancy*'s cargo of 2,070 quintals of fish convinced Skimmer a trip to the Grand Banks might pay good dividends.[17] A few days later *General Gates* overhauled the 80-ton schooner *Polly*, Benjamin Marston, master, and sent another 106 hogsheads of fish back to Bradford.[18]

On August 3 Skimmer overhauled the fast brig *Montague*, armed with fourteen double-fortified 3s and manned by a crew of forty. *Montague*'s Scottish commander, William Nelson, whose family resided in New York, held no commission but behaved much like any other sloop of war in the act of privateering. The lack of a commission made Nelson a pirate, compelling him to fight Skimmer, which he did "with ferocity rather than bravery." Long after Nelson had any hope of saving his vessel, and with his shot all expended, he charged his guns with crowbars, knives, and whatever metal scraps he could find. *General Gates* lay alongside, riddling the vessel with broadsides. Skimmer stood on the quarterdeck demanding she strike, but the battle raged for two and a half hours. A double-headed shot from *General Gates* landed in Nelson's cabin, and a boy picked it up and brought it to the deck. Nelson loaded it into a 3-pounder and fired it back. The shot struck a swivel on *General Gates* and broke in two, and one of the pieces struck Skimmer in the head. He died instantly.[19]

Lt. William Dennis took command of *General Gates*, but another hour passed before Nelson finally struck. Despite severe damage to *Montague*, Dennis brought her to Boston with her cargo and with a deck filled with wounded. As *General Gates* entered the harbor on August 31, Dennis fired half-minute guns, signaling "the death of the worthy commander."[20]

While commanding an armed schooner, no skipper captured more prizes than John Skimmer—not even Manley. Cruising with Tucker and Burke, Skimmer participated in eight captures. While cruising on his own he took eight more, bringing his total to sixteen. Manley's fourteen prizes were more valuable, but he never sailed as far as Skimmer to find them. Manley camped off the Boston lighthouse and waited for transports and victuallers to come to him, but Skimmer sailed the arc from Newfoundland to Bermuda to Cape Hatteras in search of his. No one worked harder than Skimmer. His final cruise on *Lee* lasted longer than the combined time spent at sea by men like Waters, Burke, Broughton, Ayres, and Coit during the siege of Boston.

During the short careers of Washington's sailing captains, many precedents were established and written into naval policy. Skimmer's death created another. On September 3 Bradford wrote Morris: "The Publick have lost one of their best men. He has left a distress'd family, a Widow with eleven children & she is near going to bed again. Only two of the children are capable of providing for themselves. I should be extremely happy if the Congress shou'd see fit to order me to present the Widow with a present. Under your influence, sir, such a thing might be brought about."[21]

With the Marine Committee's recommendation, Congress passed a resolution on September 23, 1778, directing the Naval Board of the Eastern Department to pay one hundred dollars quarterly for the support of Skimmer's widow and nine of their children for a period of three years.[22]

Two men, James Mugford and John Skimmer, both captains who began their careers on Washington's schooners, heroically gave their lives to the American cause. But what about the others who lived to fight another day? Did they, like the schooners they skippered, drift back into obscurity, or did Washington, when he created his flotilla, select men capable of serving with distinction in the Continental Navy?

There was still a war to fight—a very long war—and men like Daniel Waters, William Burke, Samuel Tucker, and John Manley had not seen the end of it.

📧 23 📧
Fighters to the End

hen General Gates limped into Boston with the prize brig *Montague* and the body of John Skimmer, the Navy Board looked about for a new commander. Without hesitation they selected another of Washington's skippers, Daniel Waters, the man who annoyed Bradford by his insolence. Waters sailed on November 14, 1778, in company with the 28-gun sloop *Providence*, John Peck Rathbun, commander.[1]

The two vessels cruised off Canso and on December 4 captured the schooner *Friendship*, Quebec to England with flour. Waters manned her with a prize crew from *General Gates* and placed Lt. John Kerr on board as prizemaster. Two days later a storm separated the three vessels. *Providence* arrived in New Bedford on January 11, 1779, with four prizes, but no word had been heard from either Waters or Kerr.[2]

Another month passed and Bradford decided *General Gates* and her prize had been lost for good. To his surprise, the schooner *General Leslie* arrived in Boston on February 24 manned by hands from *General Gates*. Waters had captured her off Bermuda early in February. She was carrying a cargo of raisins, wines, and lemons for New York, with a quarter cask of wine specially marked for the table of Sir Henry Clinton, "to Cheer the Heart of our Amiable General." Bradford felt better after talking to the prizemaster, but the disappearance of *Friendship* remained a mystery.[3]

Blown southward by storms, Waters sailed into Martinique on February 10 "to stop his leaks." He had not taken a prize since capturing *General Leslie* but in writing to the Navy Board promised to "make the Utmost haste in refitting his Vessell & proceed on a cruise."[4] He lost a month waiting for repairs, running up charges the Marine Committee considered "very extravagent." They ordered the Navy Board to itemize any superfluous items and deduct them from Waters's pay.[5]

Repaired and reprovisioned, *General Gates* sailed from Martinique on March 13 with the Massachusetts brig *Hazard*, John Foster Williams, commander. *Hazard* also carried sixteen 4s, and since both vessels sailed for Boston, a fleet of homeward-bound merchantmen tagged along, appointing Waters acting commodore "by right of seniority."

Once under way, Waters discovered that expensive repairs had not improved the sailing qualities of his ship. Three days out of Martinique, *Hazard* captured the British privateer brig *Active*, Capt. William Sims, after a bloody thirty-five-minute engagement during which the enemy lost half her complement of 120 men. *Active* struck before Waters reached the fight.[6] A few days later Waters participated in the capture of the 120-ton brig *Union*, John Campbell, master, from Halifax to the West Indies with a cargo of fish. After ordering *Union* to Boston, *General Gates* and *Hazard* separated, but Waters kept company with the prize. *Gates* became unseaworthy and Waters feared she would sink. She limped into Boston on April 13, and there she stayed. The Navy Board inspected the vessel and decommissioned her.[7]

The Marine Committee showed confidence in Waters by transferring his command to *Thorn*, a British sloop of war recently captured by Samuel Tucker.[8] Fitted out as a privateer, *Thorn* carried eighteen 6s and sailed on her first cruise in December 1779. In his previous correspondence with Hancock and the Marine Committee, Bradford had condemned Waters as a skulker and a coward. Waters was nothing of the sort, and his first cruise on *Thorn* provided evidence of his bravery.

At 4:00 P.M. on December 24, *Thorn* closed on two brigs, but night fell before she could engage them. The wind died, the sea became calm, and Waters stood off and waited for daylight. Throughout the night all three vessels cleared for action, sanded their decks, and prepared for battle at dawn. The brigs facing Waters were both Loyalist privateers out of New York. The 16-gun *Governor Tryon*, Captain Stebbins, carried 4s, 6s, and 12s and eighty-six men. The 18-gun *Sir William Erskine*, Captain Hamilton, carried 4s and 6s and eighty-five men. Either vessel matched well against *Thorn*'s eighteen 6s, but Waters attacked them both.

One brig moved into position off *Thorn*'s weather quarter while the other stood off the weather bow. Both opened with broadsides, and shot whistled through *Thorn*'s tops. Waters came about and fired well-aimed broadsides into both vessels. Two hours into the fight, with blood running through her scuppers, *Sir William Erskine* struck. *Governor Tryon* disengaged and attempted to escape. Waters had been wounded in the knee, but the pain only made him madder. He put a prize crew on board *Erskine* and ordered both vessels after *Governor Tryon*. At 3:00 P.M. Waters overhauled the brig and, in fifteen minutes of sharp fighting, forced her to strike. In the darkness he tried to keep her abeam, but at 8:00 P.M. the breeze freshened, clouds thickened, rain fell, and *Governor Tryon* disappeared into the night.

Despite a painful wound, Waters continued to cruise off Long Island with *Sir William Erskine*, now manned by marines from *Thorn*. Off Boston on January 13, he fell in with the 18-gun privateer *Spartan*, Liverpool to New York, with a complement of ninety-seven men. After a forty-minute battle, *Spartan* struck. Waters now had two prizes and about 170 prisoners. He had lost eighteen killed and wounded in the first engagement and one killed and two wounded in the second. When he sailed into Nantasket Road on February 17, 1780, newspapers gave him broad coverage. Bradford, in reading the account, may have wondered if the Daniel Waters praised in local accounts could have been someone else by the same name—but he surely knew better.[9]

As 1777 came to a close, the Marine Committee's bright hopes of floating a navy of thirteen frigates had been upset by the Royal Navy and by Howe's occupation of Philadelphia. *Hancock* had been captured, *Delaware* was lost in the river of her name, *Congress* and *Montgomery* had been destroyed in the Hudson, and *Washington* and *Effingham* were about to suffer similar fates. British warships had effectively blockaded four other Continental frigates—*Warren* and *Providence* in Narragansett Bay, *Virginia* in the Chesapeake, and the heavy *Trumbull*, which could not get over a bar in the Connecticut River. Of all the frigates planned, only *Boston*, *Raleigh*, and *Randolph* were at sea, along with a few lesser vessels, one being *Resistance*, Burke's new command.

If Bradford's assessment of Waters's ability had been erroneous, then how accurate was his glowing opinion of "poor Capt. Burke?" In June 1777 the Marine Committee purchased a 180-ton brig, named her *Resistance*, and armed her with fourteen 4s and twelve swivels. The committee gave command of the brig to Samuel Chew, who lost his life in the West Indies on March 4, 1778, during an encounter with a 20-gun letter of marque. *Resistance* limped into port for repairs, and Burke, who had returned from captivity in June 1778, became her new commander.[10]

On May 30, 1778, Capt. John Barry took command of the frigate *Raleigh* and in August received orders to sail south in company with *Resistance*. Burke, now fully recovered from his long imprisonment, had ascended to the command of the armed brig by having two credentials: he had been a captain on Washington's schooners, and he had Bradford's highest recommendation. A few days before Barry sailed, the Marine Committee sent Burke to sea to meet the French fleet, under Admiral le Comte D'Estaing, whose arrival off the coast was expected hourly. Burke missed the French fleet but fell in with the Royal Navy. Finding himself among the enemy, Burke surrendered and resumed his former role as a rebel prisoner.[11] No record exists of Bradford's reaction when news of Burke's capture reached Boston. He probably lamented, "Poor Burke. He is in gaol again."

Burke returned from captivity to command the 16-gun *Sky Rocket,* which he lost during the mismanaged campaign to oust a small British force from Penobscot Bay. After abandoning the vessel and taking to the woods, he returned to Boston to command the 12-gun *Henry.* Burke's experiences on *Henry* are obscure, but four months later he commanded the 16-gun *General Greene,* formerly of the Pennsylvania navy. As the Royal Navy destroyed or captured nearly every vessel commissioned by the Marine Committee, Waters and Burke ended their careers commanding privateers.

Tucker, whom Bradford called "the most volatile empty body I ever met," took command of the 30-gun frigate *Boston* in the autumn of 1777.[12] On February 15, 1778, he sailed from Boston with two distinguished passengers, John Adams and his son, John Quincy Adams. The senior Adams had been appointed commissioner to France, replacing Silas Deane. Five days out a storm struck. "A clap of thunder with sharp lightning broke upon the mainmast just above the upper moulding, which burnt several of the men on deck. A most terrible night," Adams wrote. "The captain of the mainmast was struck with the lightning, which burnt a place on the top of his head about the bigness of a quarter dollar—he lived three days and died raving mad." In addition to a damaged mainmast, Tucker discovered a British frigate on his heels. Instructed by Congress not to risk the vessel in a way that might endanger Adams, Tucker crowded on all the sail she could carry and sped away.

With *Boston* in mid-ocean on March 10, the watch reported a ship to windward and closing. She showed no colors, and Tucker ordered his men to quarters. The vessel ranged alongside and fired three guns, one shot carrying away a mizzen yard. Tucker lofted the American flag and replied with a well-aimed broadside. She struck, but with a squall brewing the prize crew almost lost the enemy's mail packet, which had been tossed overboard but failed to sink. The prize ship *Martha* carried sixteen 9s and was bound from London for New York. Before sending her to Boston, Tucker examined the invoice. *Martha* carried a cargo worth £97,000. "I hope to pay for the *Boston*," Tucker wrote the Marine Committee, "as I told your honours before sailing. I am but poorly manned to my sorrow. I dare not attack a 20 gun ship." But capturing his first prize since October 1776 revived his appetite for striking the enemy.[13]

On March 31 *Boston* anchored in the Garonne River, and the next day Tucker took her up to Bordeaux. With damage to her upper works and barnacles on her hull, French workers spent two months getting the frigate ready for sea again.

Tucker enlisted a number of Frenchmen and on June 6 sailed in company with a French frigate and a fleet of merchantmen. During a four-week cruise, *Boston* captured four prizes in the Bay of Biscay, but because of friction among the crew Tucker returned to L'Orient. He released forty-seven hands to the local French general, sent one of his four prizes to Boston, and sold the other three at L'Orient before sailing to Saint-Nazaire. On August 22, joined by the frigates *Providence,* Capt. Abraham Whipple, and *Ranger,* Capt. John Paul Jones, he sailed for America, arriving at Portsmouth on October 15 with three more prizes.[14]

In 1779 Tucker sailed with the frigate *Confederacy,* commanded by the same Seth Harding who had participated in the capture of three Scotch transports three years earlier. The Marine Committee put Tucker in charge and directed the two captains to "cruize upon this coast from the latitude of forty to thirty-five degrees and to take, burn, sink or destroy as many of the enemy's ships or vessels of every kind as may be in [your] power." Tucker's cruise lasted a month. He captured several prizes, among them the 24-gun British privateer *Pole.*[15]

On July 29, *Boston* and *Deane* sailed out of Chesapeake Bay with two ships of the Virginia navy and a convoy of merchantmen. Once at sea, *Boston* and *Deane* separated from the convoy and cruised until September 6, capturing eight prizes, including four New York privateers, and 250 prisoners. The prizes included the packet *Sandwich*, 16, and two privateers, *Glencairn*, 20, and *Thorn*, 18. The Marine Committee bought *Thorn*, a fine sailing ship, and fitted her out for Daniel Waters.[16]

To protect Charleston, South Carolina, from an expected attack by the British, the Marine Committee sent Commodore Whipple to Charleston Bay with the frigates *Providence, Boston,* and *Ranger.* Unfortunately, the Royal Navy arrived at the same time. In May 1780 Whipple lost his entire fleet, including Tucker's *Boston*. Whipple failed to issue orders for the destruction of the Continental frigates, and *Boston* became the property of the enemy, who renamed her *Charleston.*

Shortly after Tucker's capture, the British exchanged him for Captain Wardlaw. Ironically, when Tucker captured *Thorn* in August 1779, Wardlaw had been her commander. Tucker passed through Philadelphia on his way back to Boston. With Waters wounded, the Marine Committee reassigned Tucker to *Thorn*.[17]

In 1781, HMS *Hind* caught up with *Thorn*, recaptured Tucker, and sent him under guard to the Island of Saint John. Tucker made his escape, reporting exceptionally kind treatment while imprisoned there. By then the inhabitants of the island had forgotten the depredations of Broughton and Selman, perhaps not realizing the old sea dog in their custody had once been a captain sailing the same schooner (*Hancock*) under the same orders as the ruffians who had kidnapped their officials in the fall of 1775.

For a brief period of time, Tucker also commanded the privateer *Live Oak*.[18] No one will ever know exactly how many prizes Tucker captured before the war finally came to an end, but one thing is certain—he was not the "volatile empty body" Bradford claimed. Of all the captains sailing under the new American flag, he stood among the best.

The captain from Washington's ranks who deserved highest distinction was Manley, whose capture of the ordnance ship *Nancy* early in the war earned the general's praise and congressional recognition. By a resolution of Congress on October 10, 1776, the Marine Committee placed Manley second on the list of the first twenty-four captains commissioned into the Continental Navy, ranked only by James Nicholson.[19] Assigned command of the 32-gun *Hancock*, Manley sailed on May 21, 1777, in company with *Boston*, Capt. Hector McNeill. Unfortunately, bad blood existed between the two commanders.

HMS *Milford* still cruised off Cape Ann and had taken several prizes in Ipswich Bay. The Massachusetts Court suggested that *Hancock* and *Boston* "ought immediately to put to sea in pursuit of said vessel or any other that may be infesting this coast."[20] Manley sailed on May 27 with a squadron of privateers, but they soon separated from *Hancock* and *Boston* and went their own way. Rev. Samuel Cooper of Boston had observed trouble brewing between Manley and McNeill and wrote John Adams, "Manly and McNeil do not agree. It is not, I believe, the fault of the first. . . . If they are not united, infinite damage may accrue."[21] Cooper's prediction came too late to save *Hancock*.

On June 6, Manley and McNeill captured the Dartmouth brig *Patty*, Thomas Hardy, master, peacefully fishing off the coast of Nova Scotia. Manley removed the prisoners and every article of value and, in obedience to orders, torched the vessel.[22] No longer were captains compelled to carry prizes into port. If neither the prize nor its cargo belonged to a neutral nation, the captain could retain her; if he considered her of no value, he could destroy her. Because Continental warships were undermanned, commanders could not afford to deplete their crews to send prizes of little value to home ports.

The following day Manley fell in with the 28-gun frigate HMS *Fox*, Capt. Patrick Fotheringham, and ordered her to strike. Otherwise, he trumpeted, "I will fire into you."

"If you are ready," Fotheringham replied, "fire away."

After the first broadside, Fotheringham moved off. For two hours a running fight ensued, in which *Boston* took no part. McNeill stood by, holding out of range, but as soon as *Fox* struck he came alongside and opened with a broadside. Fotheringham's account read differently, claiming McNeill engaged just prior to *Fox*'s surrender. Either way, McNeill stayed out of the fight until the end.[23]

Hancock sustained serious damage, and for several days the crew replaced yards. McNeill suggested all three vessels sail to Charleston where they could be properly repaired, but Manley wanted to settle his old score with *Milford* and insisted on cruising off Cape Sable. He placed Lt. Stephen Hills on *Fox* with orders to fight the ship as he would *Hancock*. Hills discovered he did not get along any better with McNeill's men than Manley did.[24]

For four weeks *Hancock*, *Boston*, and *Fox* cruised off Nova Scotia, capturing three prizes. Manley had a small sloop in tow when the watch reported two ships and then a third, the last approaching from a different direction. As night fell Manley could not identify the vessels, one being the double-decked 44-gun *Rainbow*, Commodore Sir George

Collier, the other the 10-gun brig *Victor,* Lt. Michael Hyndman. The third vessel was another old adversary, the frigate *Flora,* Capt. John Brisbane. Neither Collier nor Manley could identify *Flora,* and Collier erroneously assumed she was another rebel. McNeill claimed all three were enemy warships, but Manley ordered him to stand by. He would fight them in the morning—his three ships against theirs. Encumbered by the sloop, Manley set her on fire, cast her loose, and cleared for action.

Collier stood off until morning, not wanting to bring on an engagement until he knew whom he was fighting. At dawn, much to his surprise, *Flora* attacked *Fox,* the furthermost of the rebel vessels. Encouraged by *Flora's* presence, Collier sent his men to quarters and closed on Manley and McNeill, who had just passed *Flora,* exchanging broadsides. *Hancock* and *Boston* sailed for *Rainbow,* leaving *Fox* with a crew of one hundred to battle *Flora.* As Manley and McNeill passed *Rainbow,* both discharged broadsides.

For the first time, Manley realized he had not taken on a frigate but a big double-decker. Manley and Collier squared around to do battle, but McNeill stood off, claiming he could not wear ship until he repaired damage. Manley waited, and when he thought McNeill was ready he came about to attack, but McNeill sheered off and made sail to the north. By the time Manley realized his partner had deserted him, he was feeling the superior firepower of *Rainbow.* Mistaking *Rainbow* for the 64-gun *Raisonable,* Manley felt heavily outmatched and, with *Boston* in full flight, he came about and attempted to escape. With *Hancock* out of the action, *Fox* surrendered to *Flora,* and Collier chased *Hancock* as a hound would a rabbit. One of Collier's sailors had been a prisoner in Boston and told him she was Manley's frigate. Manley held a top slot on the Admiralty's "ten most wanted" list, and the entire British squadron off the northeastern coast had been looking for him.

Hancock was fast but out of trim. She had been damaged in the battle with *Fox* and cut up in her exchange with *Rainbow.* McNeill, now well to the north, had fled out of harm's way, so Collier kept *Rainbow* on *Hancock's* heels. Thirty-nine hours later, riddled by grape, Manley surrendered.[25]

Instead of returning to Boston, McNeill put into a remote port in Maine and left a vague account of his cruise. As fragments of the affair drifted into Bradford's office, he considered it peculiar that McNeill could not explain *Hancock*'s whereabouts. During the battle, McNeill claimed Manley had signaled "to . . . take care of themselves." Bradford was skeptical, writing the Marine Committee, "We are much at a loss to know why Capt. McNeill has not wrote to any of his friends here." His suspicions magnified when a messenger burst into his chamber with news that Hills was a prisoner on *Fox* and that the last Hills had seen of *Hancock* had been her flight from *Rainbow*. Daniel Waters, the messenger reported, lost part of his hand in the fight.[26]

Up to this time, Manley's reputation as a fighter stood high among friend and foe. Collier rejoiced when he learned whom he had captured. He wrote Lord Germain, "We have all long wished to get this man into our possession, from his talents and intrepidity, and fortunate it is that we have done so, as he was beginning to shew the Americans what they had not been accustomed to, the seeing of one of his Majesty's ships in their possession, for he had just taken the *Fox* of 28 guns. . . . Everybody here is overjoyed at the capture of Mr. Manley, esteeming him more capable of doing mischief to the King's subjects than General [Charles] Lee was."[27]

The Marine Committee considered the loss of *Hancock* a calamity. A week later McNeill sailed into Boston to face a hostile reception. The public accused him of not supporting Manley, thereby causing *Hancock*'s capture. The Marine Committee listened to testimony from eyewitnesses and agreed with the public. In November 1777 they suspended McNeill, pending Manley's return.[28]

The British sent Manley to New York, where he remained a prisoner until exchanged. Returning to Boston on April 21, 1778, Manley requested a court of inquiry. McNeill, suspended since November, presented his case during the trial. The court acquitted Manley and dismissed McNeill from the service.[29]

With the Continental Navy bereft of vessels, Manley took command of a Boston privateer, the 20-gun ship *Cumberland*.[30] In December 1778 he sailed for the West Indies, but after a short cruise fell in with the British frigate *Pomona*. Captured again by a superior vessel, he was imprisoned at Barbados and harshly treated. He organized an escape, bribed the jailer, seized a British tender, and sailed to friendly Martinique, arriving back in Boston in April 1779.[31]

In June he took command of the privateer ship *Jason*, fitted out with eighteen 6s and 120 men. After a few days at sea, the lookout reported two sail ahead. Manley took his glass to the foretop and told the first officer that they looked like an American privateer and her prize. The first officer climbed aloft and disagreed. One, he said, was a frigate and the other a brig. Manley edged closer for a better view, and when neither of the vessels changed course he put about to see if they would chase. When both did, Manley ordered sail and headed for the Isle of Shoals off Portsmouth. The frigate closed almost within range when a squall struck, dismasted *Jason*, and drove the British vessels out to sea.

During the cleanup the crew found one of their own men caught under the downed fore-topsail and drowned. They ceased working and huddled. Manley had lost too many ships. Now, barely two days out, he had wrecked *Jason*. The dead sailor confirmed their fears. The captain brought bad luck. Manley refused their demand to take the vessel into port. He knew they wanted off the ship. Instead, he quelled the mutiny by putting them to work, and thirty-six hours later had the vessel ready to sail.

When the watch reported another pair of vessels off Sandy Hook on July 23, the crew envisioned a reenactment of their last calamity. The vessels were two British privateers, *Hazard* from Liverpool and *Adventurer* from Glasgow, both 18-gun brigs. They ranged in close to give *Jason* their broadsides. Manley ordered the sailing master to hurl the bower anchor into the fore shrouds of *Hazard* and hook onto her. The anchor caught in the rigging, swinging the brig alongside *Jason*. The maneuver took *Hazard* by surprise. Her crew ran below and the captain surrendered.

Adventurer came about and showed her heels. Manley ordered *Hazard*'s fore rigging cut away and sailed after her. He overhauled her and fired a few rounds from his bow guns, and the brig struck. Three men had been wounded on *Jason*, and the sailing master who first sighted the two prizes died from a shot in the head. British casualties were heavy, with thirty killed or wounded. Manley escorted his prizes to Boston, but by then the crew had changed their mind. They no longer wanted to mutiny.

On September 30, after capturing a brig off Newfoundland, Manley's luck again soured, propagated by those among his crew who preferred the safety of His Majesty's prisons to another pitched battle against a superior vessel. Stranded by a morning calm off St. John's, a large vessel ranged off *Jason*'s starboard beam. The first light breeze filled the sails of the 28-gun HMS *Surprize,* Capt. Robert Linzee, one of the fastest vessels in His Majesty's navy. Manley caught what wind he could and sped away, keeping out of range throughout the day.

At 11:00 P.M. *Surprize* got under *Jason*'s port quarter and fired a broadside. Manley held his fire, letting the frigate edge closer. A second broadside ripped through the tops, chasing *Jason*'s men to the deck. Then Manley opened. "We gave them a broadside which silenced two of her bow guns," wrote boy Joshua Davis. "The next we gave her cut away her maintopsail and drove her maintop-men out of it. Both sides continued to fire until one o'clock. Our studding sails and booms, our sails, rigging, yards &c. were so cut away that they were useless. Lanterns were hung at the ship's side, between the guns, on nails, but they soon fell on deck at the shaking of the guns; which made it so dark that the men could not see to load the guns. They broke the fore hatches open and ran below." With the gun deck deserted, Manley struck, but in the fight *Surprize* lost fifteen killed and thirty wounded, *Jason* five killed and a dozen wounded.[32]

Once again the British had Manley. This time they sent him to England's Mill Prison, a dungeonlike structure from which few escaped. Manley tried three times and failed. Exchanged in January 1782, he went to France. By April he was back in Boston seeking a command. Because he took risks, investors hesitated to provide him with a privateer, but the Continental Navy was glad to have him back. Given command of the frigate *Hague* (formerly *Deane*), Manley sailed to the West Indies, only to be chased by four British warships, one with seventy-four guns, another with fifty. He grounded on a bar off Guadalupe and for two days withstood the cannonading of all four vessels, returning in kind whenever he could. On the third day he floated free, fired thirteen guns—one for each colony—in farewell defiance, and escaped.[33]

Manley returned to Boston in May 1783 and paid off his crew. To the people of that town, he had been a hero from the day he captured *Nancy,* the first significant prize of the war. By a singular coincidence, he also captured the last valuable prize of the war, the 340-ton ship *Baille,* laden with sixteen hundred barrels of provisions.[34]

Manley remained in the service of his country until his death on February 12, 1793, but little is known of his life after the war. Fate played the same trick on all the commanders of George Washington's schooners. They each faded into obscurity, forgotten men who once fought for their country, and—for courageous men like Mugford and Skimmer—died for it.

Epilogue

O n *March 21, 1777*, the Marine Committee appointed Isaac Smith, Ebenezer Storer, and William Phillips to settle the accounts of the Continental agents appointed by Washington.[1] Ten months had passed since Bradford became sole agent for the state of Massachusetts, and the committee had not been able to close the old accounts. Instead, the business of settling with Washington's mariners had worsened. Bradford had ignored the committee's instructions by applying them exclusively to Washington's deposed agents. If Bradford believed his relationship with Hancock shielded him from criticism, or from the need to keep good records, the Marine Committee minced no words expressing their dissatisfaction. To Bradford they wrote:[2]

> We find complaints are made by the officers and seamen concerned in the capture of prizes that have fallen into your hands . . . for want of distribution of prize money, and it is urged by Mr. [Jonathan] Glover, their agent, that you neglect or refuse to settle the accounts or to pay him the share appertaining to the captors, which puts it totally out of his power to make distribution. . . . In consequence of these delays, the Maritime service of the Continent suffers exceedingly. In short, it is owing to unhappy circumstances of this kind that the Navy cannot be manned and we now must press your immediate attention and utmost exertion to settle the accounts of every prize. . . .

Before replying, Bradford appealed to Hancock for instructions, perhaps hoping that his patron would sidetrack the committee's three commissioners by offering inadvertent direction. He also attempted, once more, to recover the proceeds from four prizes libeled by others and asked Hancock to intercede on his behalf.[3] A careful examination of

Bradford's correspondence leads one to wonder whether the president of Congress secretly participated in the agent's profits.

Perhaps realizing Hancock might forward his letter to the Marine Committee, Bradford begged "leave to exculpate" himself from any impression of practicing procrastination and promised to lose no more time in settling his accounts. He blamed delays on "a pressure of business." Bradford made the mistake of telling the committee he had too much to do.[4]

On July 10, 1777, the Marine Committee solved part of Bradford's woes by creating the Continental Navy Board of the Eastern Department, which encompassed all of Bradford's domain. Hereafter, the board would superintend and fit for sea all armed vessels of the United States, thereby relieving Bradford of much work, some of his commissions, and most of his excuse for not having his accounts in order.[5]

With Bradford shunted aside, Washington's agents worked with the Navy Board and closed their accounts. Two of the agents—Wentworth of Portsmouth and Watson of Plymouth—owed small balances and paid them. The other three—Glover, Bartlett, and Sargent—all held balances in their favor. Because these three had worked together with mutual side agreements, their accounts required considerable reconciliation. Bradford had never accepted Glover's or Bartlett's accounts because they included four prizes to which he felt entitled. He also would not admit that either of the agents were in advance to the Continent. The Navy Board felt differently and sent an express to the Marine Committee on July 28 to pay Bartlett the sum of $15,013 and Glover $55,091, plus some change, as they were "in great want of the money in order to settle with the captors." Sargent carried the smallest balance due, $3,180. On August 11 the Continental Congress approved the sum, and the loan office paid it.[6]

Bradford's accounts were a colossal mess, partly because the ship *Peggy*, his very first prize, had not been settled. The commissioners did not expect to become involved in reconciling Bradford's records, as they considered him an experienced businessman. In early 1777 Bradford had blamed delays on Washington's agents, but the commissioners eliminated that excuse in August. December came and went. To use Bradford's own words, the accounts were still "ripening," whatever that meant. On March 25, 1778, they fully ripened, but he claimed his clerk was ill. In April he sent the commissioners his records for all but *Peggy*, which remained unsettled. *Peggy*'s case survived the war, not docketed to be heard in the Court of Appeals until June 1783. By then Bradford had grown tired of waiting, and in the summer of 1782 he sold the vessel without the court's approval.[7]

Bradford never cleared all the accounts of Washington's schooners. After the war ended, he lost much of his fortune because of lawsuits initiated by those who felt cheated. In 1784 a few loose ends still awaited congressional action. They were stuffed into File No. 5 in the Library of Congress, to be "referred to the consideration of the next Congress." Some are still there.[8]

In the early days of the war, Washington's schooners contributed to the discomfort of the British. Never an overpowering force, they nibbled away at supply lines, frustrated His Majesty's navy by playing a deadly cat-and-mouse game, and accelerated Howe's decision to evacuate Boston. As heavily armed privateers took to sea, followed by the frigates of the Continental Navy, Washington's schooners declined in importance, but during their twenty-six months of activity they performed a remarkable service to thirteen colonies that had formulated no naval policy.

More important than the schooners were the men who sailed them. From Nicholson Broughton, who carried *Unity* into Cape Ann on September 7, 1775, to John Skimmer, who brought the rum-laden brig *Dolphin* into Marblehead on October 26, 1777, an American naval policy slowly emerged. Washington introduced that policy when he issued his first sailing instructions to Broughton, on September 2, 1775.[9]

Broughton may have been Washington's worst commander. If so, he and his sailing companion, John Selman, entered the general's navy at the right time. Thereafter, Washington's selection process improved, but, like the Continental Navy, never reached perfection. Washington returned Broughton's and Selman's eight prizes to their owners. In defense of the two captains, five of those prizes would have been libeled had they been taken three months later. At the time, Congress fought a half-war concentrated mainly in New England. Colonists still loved their king but hated his ministers. As long as this peculiar détente existed, Washington's skippers did not have the authority to interdict vessels of the king's subjects unless they happened to be in the service of the king's ministers. Broughton and Selman never had an opportunity to demonstrate their abilities after the rules changed.

William Coit—whom Washington came to call "mere blubber"—
and Sion Martindale were the only two captains to sail out of Plymouth.
Coit took four prizes, Martindale one. Coit's conquests amounted to little, but he had the distinction of capturing the first two legitimate prizes,
and later a third, the fourth being returned to her owner. He probably
sailed in the oldest and feeblest of Washington's schooners, but not
Martindale. He rerigged his schooner to a brig, spent lavishly to fit out
and arm the largest vessel in the fleet, and added such useless pomp as a
fifer and a drummer to his crew. With his grand vessel he captured only
a small sloop carrying wood and hay, which Washington returned to her
Beverly owners. On Martindale's next outing he and his brig surrendered
to HMS *Fowey* without firing a shot.[10] Martindale lacked resourceful-
ness, and losing him was far less serious than the loss of his brig.

Winborn Adams, first skipper of *Warren,* captured three vessels, one
a fair prize but the others reverted to their owners. Washington considered Adams an inactive skipper, categorizing his skills with the likes of
Coit and Martindale. In this regard the general may have done Adams
an injustice, as his vessel had been armed with defective guns.
Washington, however, had become slightly prejudiced. Manley had gone
to sea in *Lee* and in the same span of time captured nine vessels, including the ordnance brig *Nancy.*

Despite Washington's disappointment with some of his commanders, they captured twenty-five vessels late in 1775. As the war entered
the year 1776 and the armed schooners resumed their cruises, the sole
remaining commander, John Manley, became commodore of the fleet.

During 1776, the combined efforts of Manley, Tucker, Ayres,
Waters, Mugford, Burke, and Skimmer netted another twenty-two
prizes. In contrast to 1775, all the prizes were legitimate; however, the
Gloucester Committee of Safety released the 60-ton sloop *Rainbow* by
mistake, and the 240-ton ship *Peggy* languished in the court system for
seven years. Because none of Washington's commanders kept logs and
few bothered to write reports, it is not possible to determine the number
of vessels stopped and released that inexperienced captains like
Broughton and Selman might have shuttled into port.

By 1777, all of Washington's active commanders but Skimmer had
accepted some form of employment with the Marine Committee, either
on frigates of the Continental Navy or on vessels under its purview. The

exception was James Mugford, who lost his life repulsing an attack on *Franklin*. For most of 1777 Skimmer commanded the last armed schooner in commission as a cruiser and captured eight vessels—all fair prizes—although two were recaptured before they reached port. By then the cruising grounds had expanded to the mid-Atlantic. Skimmer demonstrated the same toughness and determination as Manley, Tucker, and Mugford, but, like Mugford, lost his life fighting his ship.

When John Bradford decommissioned *Lee* in the fall of 1777, the eight original schooners fitted out at Continental expense by Washington had captured fifty-five vessels. Twelve commanders participated in a naval campaign initiated by the Continental Army. To rank them may be an injustice to some whose records are less complete than others, but it is difficult to deprive Manley of the top slot. To visualize a 70-ton schooner facing off against a 400-ton ship like *Jenny* and forcing her surrender reminds one of David fighting Goliath. Manley captured or participated in the capture of fourteen prizes, totaling about twenty-four hundred tons burden. Taken together, Washington's investment in eight small schooners paid rich dividends.

In the early stages of the American War for Independence, the man least likely to understand the importance of sea power was perhaps the one who understood it best. George Washington had never been to sea, not even as a novice sailor, but when there was no navy, he created one. When he needed agents to buy, fit, arm, and provision his vessels and to pay the men and care for their prizes, he appointed them. When he needed captains to command the schooners, he commissioned them. If he needed sailors and marines, he took them from his regiments and assigned them to the sea. When he needed admiralty courts to libel his prizes, he demanded them. And if he needed rules and regulations for his commanders, he issued them. By the time Congress got around to organizing what eventually became the Marine Committee, Washington had much of the administrative work done—all this while successfully conducting the siege of Boston.

George Washington, a military man, not only fathered the country. He gave birth to the American Navy.

APPENDIX
Prizes Captured by Washington's Schooners

Date	Schooner/Captain	Prize[a]	Tons	Master
1775				
Sept. 7	*Hannah*/Broughton	*Unity* (ship)	260	Flagg
Oct. 29	*Hancock*/Broughton *Franklin*/Selman	*Prince William* (schooner)	—	Standley
Oct. 29	*Hancock*/Broughton *Franklin*/Selman	*Mary* (schooner)	—	Russell
Oct. 31	*Hancock*/Broughton *Franklin*/Selman	*Phoebe* (sloop)	—	Hawkins
Nov. 5	*Hancock*/Broughton *Franklin*/Selman	*Warren* (sloop)	—	Denny
Nov. 5	*Harrison*/Coit	*Polly* (sloop)	75	White
Nov. 5	*Harrison*/Coit	*Industry* (schooner)	85	Coffin
Nov. 6	*Warren*/Adams	— (sloop)	—	—
Nov. 7	*Lee*/Manley	*Ranger* (sloop)	—	McGlathry
Nov. 8	*Lee*/Manley	*Two Sisters* (schooner)	80	Robbins
Nov. 10	*Lee*/Manley	— (schooner)	40	—
Nov. 13	*Hancock*/Broughton *Franklin*/Selman	*Speedwell* (sloop)	—	Corey
Nov. 20	*Hancock*/Broughton *Franklin*/Selman	— (schooner)	170	Higgins
Nov. 25	*Warren*/Adams	*Rainbow* (schooner)	45	McMonagle
Nov. 26	*Hancock*/Broughton *Franklin*/Selman	*Kingston Packet* (brig)	—	Ingersoll
Nov. 27	*Washington*/Martindale	*Britannia* (sloop)	80	Hall
Nov. 28	*Lee*/Manley	*Polly* (sloop)	80	Smith
Nov. 28	*Lee*/Manley	*Nancy* (brig)	250	Hunter
Nov. 29	*Harrison*/Coit	*Thomas* (schooner)	—	—
Nov. 29	*Harrison*/Coit	— (schooner)	15	Downey
Dec. 3	*Lee*/Manley	*Concord* (ship)	300	Lowrie
Dec. 8	*Lee*/Manley	*Jenny* (ship)	400	Foster
Dec. 8	*Lee*/Manley	*Little Hannah* (brig)	140	Adams
Dec. 17	*Lee*/Manley	*Betsey* (sloop)	60	Atkinson
Dec. 24	*Warren*/Adams	*Sally* (sloop)	70	Emburgh

Date	Schooner/Captain	Prize[a]	Tons	Master
1776				
Jan. 25	*Hancock*/Manley	*Happy Return* (ship)	130	Hall
Jan. 25	*Hancock*/Manley	*Norfolk* (ship)	120	Grendal
Jan. 29	*Franklin*/Tucker *Lee*/Waters	*Henry and Esther* (brig)	300	Nellis
Jan. 29	*Franklin*/Tucker *Lee*/Waters	*Rainbow* (sloop)	60	Perkins
Mar. 6	*Hancock*/Manley *Franklin*/Tucker	*Susannah* (ship)	300	Frazer
Mar. 10	*Lee*/Waters *Lynch*/Ayres	*Stakesby* (ship)	300	Watts
Apr. 2	*Hancock*/Manley *Lee*/Waters *Lynch*/Ayres	*Elizabeth* (brig)	—	Ramsey
May 7	*Hancock*/Tucker	*Jane* (brig)	120	Fulton
May 7	*Hancock*/Tucker	*William* (brig)	100	Price
May 17	*Franklin*/Mugford	*Hope* (ship)	280	Lumsdale
June 6	*Lee*/Waters *Warren*/Burke *Lynch*/Ayres	*Anne* (ship)	223	Dennison
June 16	*Hancock*/Tucker *Lee*/Waters	*George* (ship)	220	Bog
June 16	*Warren*/Burke *Franklin*/Skimmer	*Annabella* (brig)	180	Walter
June 18	*Lynch*/Ayres	*Lord Howe* (ship)	200	Park
July 27	*Hancock*/Tucker *Franklin*/Skimmer	*Peggy* (ship)	240	Kennedy
Aug. 4	*Hancock*/Tucker *Franklin*/Skimmer	*Perkins* (brig)	140	Jenkins
Aug. 6	*Hancock*/Tucker *Franklin*/Skimmer	*Nelly Frigate* (ship)	305	Bradstreet
Sept. 2	*Lee*/Waters	*Betsey* (sloop)	60	—
Oct. 3	*Lee*/Waters	*Sally* (schooner)	90	Noble
Oct. ?	*Hancock*/Tucker *Franklin*/Skimmer	*Triton* (brig)	130	Brinton
Oct. ?	*Lee*/Waters	*Elizabeth* (brig)	130	Edwards
Oct. 29	*Hancock*/Tucker	*Lively* (brig)	150	Martindale
1777				
Apr. 13	*Lee*/Skimmer	*Hawke* (schooner)	70	Collins
May 3	*Lee*/Skimmer	*Betsey* (sloop)	58	Horrick
May 11	*Lee*/Skimmer	*Charles* (brig)	—	Tapley
May 31	*Lee*/Skimmer	*Capling* (brig)	110	Coulrick
May 31	*Lee*/Skimmer	*Industry* (brig)	80	Browne
Aug. 29	*Lee*/Skimmer	*Industrious Bee* (brig)	160	Biddecomb
Aug. 30	*Lee*/Skimmer	*Lively* (brig)	—	Carter
Oct. 1	*Lee*/Skimmer	*Dolphin* (brig)	129	Shields

[a]Of the 55 vessels captured, 18 were brigs, 11 schooners, 13 ships, and 13 sloops.
Source: "Prizes and Captures," LC

Notes

ABBREVIATIONS

APS	American Philosophical Society
BM	British Museum
BHS	Beverly Historical Society
CHS	Chicago Historical Society
ConnHS	Connecticut Historical Society
ConnSL	Connecticut State Library
EI	Essex Institute
HUL	Harvard University Library
JCC	*Journal of the Continental Congress* (Ford et al., eds.)
LC	Library of Congress
MHS	Marblehead Historical Society
MassArch	Massachusetts Archives
MassHS	Massachusetts Historical Society
MM	Mariner's Museum
NA	National Archives
NDAR	*Naval Documents of the American Revolution* (Clark et al., eds.)
NYHS	New York Historical Society
NYPL	New York Public Library
PCC	Papers of the Continental Congress
PMHS	*Proceedings of the Massachusetts Historical Society*
PRO/ADM	Public Records Office, Admiralty
PRO/COL	Public Records Office, Colonial Office
RIHC	*Rhode Island Historical Collections*
YUL	Yale University Library

CHAPTER 1

1. *JCC,* 2:90–91, 96–98.
2. Fitzpatrick, *Writings of George Washington,* 3:308; Force, *American Archives,* Ser. 4, 2:1625, 1629; French, *First Year,* 321.
3. Fitzpatrick, *Writings of George Washington,* 3:320–29.
4. Ford, *Warren-Adams Letters,* 1:81, 82; Clark, *George Washington's Navy,* 3.
5. Billias, *General John Glover,* 17–20.
6. Howe, *Beverly Privateers,* 318–20.
7. Ibid., 49–66 passim.
8. Bowen Day Book, June 6, 1887, MHS; Lincoln, *Journals,* 411–12.
9. Billias, *General John Glover,* 68; Glover Colony Ledger, MHS. Both Glover and Manley have been credited with suggesting the use of armed vessels to Washington.
10. Howe, *Beverly Privateers,* 318–20; Log of *Nautilus,* PRO/ADM, 51/629.
11. Beattie and Collins, *Washington's New England Fleet,* 4; Billias, *General John Glover,* 74; Moylan and Glover to Washington, Oct. 9, 1775, *NDAR,* 2:368.
12. Glover endorsement, July 1781, PCC, 41, 1:349, NA.
13. Fitzpatrick, *Writings of George Washington,* 3:467–69; *NDAR,* 1:1287–89.
14. Journals of the Massachusetts House of Representatives, Oct. 6, 9, 14, 17, 18, 19, 27, Nov. 1, 1775, Massachusetts State Library; *JCC,* Nov. 25, 1775, 3:370–76.
15. Holyoke, "Familiar Letters," 211.

CHAPTER 2

1. Broughton to Washington, Sept. 7, 1775, *NDAR,* 2:36; Journal of *Lively,* Sept. 5, 1775, PRO/ADM, 51/968. Piscataqua is near Portsmouth, N.H.
2. Broughton to Washington, Sept. 9, 1775, *NDAR,* 2:56; *Boston Gazette,* Sept. 11, 1775.
3. Broughton to Washington, Sept. 9, 1775, *NDAR,* 2:56–57; *Boston Gazette,* Sept. 11, 1775.
4. *New England Chronicle,* Sept. 14, 1775; Washington to Langdon, Sept. 21, 1775, Langdon Papers, HUL.
5. Cleaves Diary, Sept. 14, 1775, MassHS.
6. Washington to Langdon, Sept. 21, 1775, Langdon Papers, HUL.
7. "Journal of Private Phineas Ingalls," 87. Ingalls was in Benjamin Farnum's company from Andover, Massachusetts; Fitzpatrick, *Writings of George Washington,* 3:514, 515.

8. Graves, *Conduct,* 1:141–43, BM.

9. John White Almanac, Oct. 10, 1775, *Essex Institute Historical Collections,* 49:92.

10. Collins to Graves, Oct. 12, 1775, and Journal of *Nautilus,* PRO/ADM, 51/629; Graves, *Conduct,* 1:97–98, appendix, 141–43, 149, BM; Stone, *History of Beverly,* 64–66.

11. *New England Chronicle,* Oct. 12, 1775.

12. Glover to Washington, Oct. 15, 1775, *NDAR,* 2:459–60.

CHAPTER 3

1. Cooke to Whipple, Sept. 12, 1775, *NDAR,* 2:77–78; Graves to Bruere, Sept. 28, 1775, Graves, *Conduct,* appendix, 95, BM.

2. Washington to Arnold, Sept. 14, 1775, *NDAR,* 2:94.

3. Hancock to Washington, Oct. 5, 1775, *NDAR,* 2:311.

4. Fitzpatrick, *Writings of George Washington,* 4:4–6, 9–13.

5. Stevens to Washington, Sept. 28, 1775, MassArch, 206:383.

6. Inventory of schooner *Industry, NDAR,* 2:248–50, 300; Journal of the Massachusetts House of Representatives, MassArch, 206:384, 292:692.

7. Reed to committees, and Reed to Glover, Oct. 4, 1775, *NDAR,* 2:279, 289–90.

8. Hancock to Massachusetts Council, Oct. 4, 1775, *NDAR,* 2:312.

9. Fitzpatrick, *Writings of George Washington,* 4:6–7.

10. Moylan and Glover to Washington, Oct. 9, 1775, *NDAR,* 3:368.

11. Glover to Washington, Oct. 15, Reed to Glover, Oct. 17, 1775, *NDAR,* 2:459–61, 490.

12. Moylan to Reed, Oct. 24, 1775, *NDAR,* 2:589–90.

13. Billias, *General John Glover,* 81.

14. Reed to Broughton, Oct. 12, Glover to Washington, Oct. 15, 1775, *NDAR,* 2:416, 459–61; appraisal of schooner *Franklin,* PCC, "Prizes and Captures," 13, LC.

15. Washington to Broughton (and Selman), Oct. 16, 1775, Fitzpatrick, *Writings of George Washington,* 4:33–34.

16. Reed to Glover and Moylan, Oct. 16, 1775, *NDAR,* 2:472, 565; Selman's Narrative, *Salem Gazette,* July 22, 1856.

17. PCC, "Prizes and Captures," 29, 31, 33, 35, LC.

18. Selman's Narrative, *Salem Gazette,* July 22, 1856.

19. Ibid.; list of items removed from *Mary* and *Prince William,* Bartlett Papers, 5516, 5517, BHS.

20. Moylan to Bartlett, Dec. 2, 1775, *NDAR,* 2:1229; Broughton to Washington, Broughton to Doak, Nov. 2, 1775, *NDAR,* 2:850; John Bartlett to

Washington, Nov. 8, 1775, *NDAR,* 2:928; list of items taken by Broughton and Selman, Bartlett Papers, 5516, 5517, BHS.

21. Broughton and Selman to Washington, Nov. 6, 1775, *NDAR,* 2:899–900; items taken by Broughton, Bartlett Papers, 5517, BHS; Selman's Narrative, *Salem Gazette,* July 22, 1856.

22. Items taken by Broughton and Selman, Bartlett Papers, 5516, 5517, BHS; Sargent to Washington, Dec. 29, 1775, *NDAR,* 3:290.

23. *London Chronicle,* Jan. 4–6, 1776; Selman's Narrative, *Salem Gazette,* July 22, 1856; Minutes of Executive Council of Nova Scotia, Feb. 8, 1776, *NDAR,* 3:479, 1167–77; Innes, *Diary of Simeon Perkins,* 109.

CHAPTER 4

1. *London Chronicle,* Jan. 4–6, 1776; Selman's Narrative, *Salem Gazette,* July 22, 1856; Clark, *George Washington's Navy,* 50–51.

2. Broughton's raid has been reconstructed from the following sources: Selman's Narrative, *Salem Gazette,* July 22, 1856; Lord Budd to Lord Dartmouth, Nov. 25, 1775, Wright to Lord Dartmouth, Dec. 15, 1775, Callbeck to Lord Dartmouth, Jan. 5, 1776, PRO/COL, 226/6; Minutes of the Royal Council of Nova Scotia, Nov. 30, Petition of Callbeck and Wright, Dec. 7, 1775, *NDAR,* 2:1198, 1319–22, 3:626.

3. Arbuthnot to Graves, Dec. 1, 1775, PRO/ADM, 1/485; Wentworth to Moylan, Dec. 3, 1775, *NDAR,* 2:1244; *New Hampshire Gazette,* Dec. 5, 1775.

4. Spence to Dartmouth, Nov. 23, 1775, PRO/COL, 226/6.

5. Arbuthnot to Graves, Dec. 1, 1775, PRO/ADM, 1/485; Wentworth to Moylan, Dec. 3, Moylan to Salem Committee of Safety, Dec. 5, Pickering to Moylan, Dec. 7, 1775, *NDAR,* 2:1244, 1284, 1316–17.

6. Wentworth to Moylan, Dec. 3, 1775, *NDAR,* 2:1244; *New Hampshire Gazette,* Dec. 5, 1775.

7. Broughton to Washington, Nov. 6, Moylan to Jonathan Glover, Nov. 9, Dec. 19, 1775, *NDAR,* 2:900, 944–45; 3:165.

8. Cooke to Washington, Nov. 30, Moylan to Bartlett, Dec. 2, Washington to Cooke, Dec. 6, 1775, *NDAR,* 2:1204, 1229, 1302–3.

9. Harrison to Bartlett, Dec. 4, 1775, *NDAR,* 2:1259.

10. Washington to Hancock, Dec. 4, 1775, *NDAR,* 2:1259.

11. Moylan to Salem Committee of Safety, Dec. 5, Pickering to Moylan, Derby to Moylan, Dec. 7, 1775, *NDAR,* 2:1284, 1316–17.

12. Moylan to Glover, Dec. 8, 1775, *NDAR,* 3:6.

13. Derby to Salem Committee of Safety, Dec. 9, 1775, Pickering Papers, MassHS, 39:126.

14. Petition of Callbeck and Wright, Dec. 7, Callbeck to Washington, Dec. 24, 1775, *NDAR,* 2:1319–22, 3:223–24; Legge to Dartmouth, Dec. 29, 1775, PRO/COL, 217/52.

15. Denison to Washington, Jan. 8, 1776, *NDAR,* 3:679.

16. *Salem Gazette,* July 26, 1856; Waite, *Extracts,* 27.

17. Washington to Hancock, Dec. 7, 1775, *NDAR,* 2:1322.

18. Reed, *Life and Correspondence,* 1:137–40.

19. Clark, *George Washington's Navy,* 78.

20. Graves, *Conduct,* 2:24, BM; Callbeck to Shuldham, Jan. 10, 1776, PRO/ADM, 1/484.

CHAPTER 5

1. Congressional delegates' meeting, Oct. 23, 1775, *NDAR,* 2:575–76. *Hannah* had been decommissioned and was not in this count.

2. Reed to Moylan and Glover, Oct. 11, Reed to Moylan, Oct. 15, Reed to Glover, Oct. 17, 1775, *NDAR,* 2:398, 461, 490.

3. Reed's report, Oct. 29, 1775, *NDAR,* 2:637–38.

4. Reed to Bowen, Oct. 13, 1775, *NDAR,* 2:436–37; Reed to Watson, Oct. 17, 1775, *NDAR,* 2:492–94; Journal of Ephraim Bowen, Oct. 15, 17, 1775, *NDAR,* 2:462, 475–76, 490–91; Journal of the Massachusetts House of Representatives, Nov. 2, 1775, MassArch; agreement of Bartlett and Glover to serve as agents, PCC, "Prizes and Captures," 385, 389, LC.

5. Bowen's Journal, Oct. 18, Bowen to Reed, Oct. 19, 1775, *NDAR,* 2:504, 519–20.

6. Reed to Bowen, Oct. 17, 1775, *NDAR,* 2:491.

7. Bowen to Reed, Oct. 19, 1775, *NDAR,* 2:520.

8. Reed to Bowen, Oct. 17, 1775, *NDAR,* 2:491.

9. Charter agreement for *Harrison,* PCC, "Prizes and Captures," 75, LC; Bowen to Reed, Oct. 19, 1775, *NDAR,* 2:519.

10. Bowen to Reed, Oct. 19, Reed to Bowen, Oct. 20, 1775, *NDAR,* 2:519–20, 536.

11. Bowen to Reed, Oct. 22, Martindale to Reed, Nov. 2, 1775, *NDAR,* 2:571–722, 859.

12. Reed to Bowen, Oct. 20, 1775, *NDAR,* 2:537.

13. Ibid.

14. Bowen's Journal, Oct. 25, 26, 27, 28, Nov. 1, 1775, *NDAR,* 2:605, 611, 620, 626, 841; Cooke to Washington, Oct. 28, 1775, *NDAR,* 2:625; Bowen to Reed, Oct. 29, 1775, *NDAR,* 2:639; Potter to Bowen, Oct. 28, 1775, PCC, "Prizes and Captures," 283, LC.

15. Martindale to Reed, Nov. 2, Moylan to Watson, Nov. 6, 1775, *NDAR,* 2:859, 902.

16. Bowen to Reed, Nov. 3, 16, 1775, *NDAR,* 2:870, 1043, 1368–72; Accounts of William Watson, PCC, "Prizes and Captures," 373, 375, LC.

17. Clark, *George Washington's Navy,* 22.

18. Reed's report, Oct. 29, 1775, *NDAR,* 2:638.

19. Webb, *Reminiscences,* 155–56.

20. Reed to Glover and Moylan, Oct. 20, 1775, *NDAR,* 2:538; Accounts of William Watson, *NDAR,* 2:1368, 1372.

21. Moylan to Watson, Nov. 6, 1775, *NDAR,* 2:902.

22. Charter for *Washington,* Nov. 3, 1775, *NDAR,* 2:871.

23. Reed to Bowen, Oct. 29, 1775, *NDAR,* 2:636.

CHAPTER 6

1. Fitzpatrick, *Writings of George Washington,* 4:37–39; Webb, *Reminiscences,* 155–56.

2. Reed to Coit, Oct. 29, 1775, *NDAR,* 2:636.

3. Bowen to Reed, Nov. 3, Watson to Washington, Nov. 3, 6, 1775, *NDAR,* 2:870, 871, 903.

4. Bowen to Washington, Nov. 6, 1775, *NDAR,* 2:903, 904; *Pennsylvania Journal,* Nov. 29, 1775.

5. Webb, *Reminiscences,* 155–56; Williams to Coit, Nov. 9, 1775, Lane Collection, YUL.

6. Moylan to Warren, Nov. 10, Moylan to Watson, Nov. 16, 1775, *NDAR,* 2:965, 1042; Diary of Ezekiel Price, Nov. 11, 1775, *PMHS,* Ser. 1, 7:213.

7. Reed, *Life and Correspondence,* 1:126–27; Watson to Moylan, Dec. 4, 1775, *NDAR,* 2:1268; MassArch, 164:192, 193, 194.

8. Bowen to Washington, Nov. 6, 1775, *NDAR,* 2:903; Washington to Hancock, Nov. 8, 1775, Hancock Papers, vol. 2, LC.

9. Bowen's Journal, Nov. 13, Moylan to Watson, Nov. 17, Watson to Moylan, Nov. 23, 1775, *NDAR,* 2:1010, 1056, 1107.

10. Muster role of *Washington,* Dec. 5, 1775, PRO/ADM, 36/7506.

11. Washington to Martindale, Oct. 8, Reed to Bowen, Oct. 29, 1775, *NDAR,* 2:354–55, 637; Manvide's Journal, PRO/ADM, 1/485.

12. Watson to Moylan, Nov. 23, 1775, *NDAR,* 2:1107.

13. Journal of *Raven,* PRO/ADM, 51/771, and Manvide's Journal, PRO/ADM, 1/485.

14. "The Kemble Papers," *Collections of the New York Historical Society,* 1:62; Journals of *Raven* and *Phoenix,* Nov. 24, 1775, PRO/ADM, 51/771, 793; Graves, *Conduct,* 1:170–73, BM; *Pennsylvania Evening Post,* Dec. 21, 1775; *London Evening Post and British Chronicle,* Jan. 1–3, 1776.

15. Journal of *Raven*, Nov. 25, 1775, PRO/ADM 51/771; Watson to Moylan, Dec. 4, 1775, *NDAR*, 2:1268; Diary of Ezekiel Price, *PMHS*, Ser. 1, 7:216.

16. Moylan to Watson, Dec. 1, 1776, *NDAR*, 2:1218.

17. Manvide's Journal, Nov. 25, 26, 1775, PRO/ADM, 1/485.

18. Ibid., Nov. 27, 28, 1775.

19. Log of *Nautilus*, Nov. 26, 1775, PRO/ADM, 52/1884; *Boston Gazette*, Dec. 4, 1775.

20. Manvide's Journal, Nov. 29, 30, Dec. 1, 1775, PRO/ADM, 1/485.

21. Moylan to Watson, Dec. 5, 1775, *NDAR*, 2:1284–85.

22. Accounts of William Watson, Dec. 8, 1775, PCC, "Prizes and Captures," 121, LC; commitment of George Price, Dec. 9, 1775, MassArch, 104:213; libel of fishing schooner, *Boston Gazette*, Mar. 25, 1776.

23. Moylan to Watson, Dec. 1, Watson to Moylan, Dec. 4, 1775, *NDAR*, 2:1218, 1268.

24. Watson to Washington, Nov. 29, 1775, *NDAR*, 2:1189–90.

25. Moylan to Watson, Dec. 1, 1775, *NDAR*, 2:1218.

26. Watson to Moylan, Dec. 4, 1775, *NDAR*, 2:1268.

27. Hoadly, *Public Records of the Colony of Connecticut*, 15:475, 476.

28. Hoadly, *Public Records of the State of Connecticut*, 1:216; Trumbull to Coit, Apr. 11, 1777, Jonathan Trumbull Papers, ConnSL.

CHAPTER 7

1. Watson to Moylan, Dec. 4, 1775, *NDAR*, 2:1268.

2. Journal of *Fowey*, Dec. 4, 5, 1775, PRO/ADM, 51/375; muster role of *Washington*, PRO/ADM, 36/7506.

3. Howe to Dartmouth, Dec. 14, 1775, PRO/COL, 5/93.

4. Washington to Hancock, Dec. 31, 1775, PCC (Letters of Washington), 152, 1:381–86, NA.

5. Diary of Ezekiel Price, *PMHS*, Ser. 1, 7:220.

6. Cooke to Rhode Island delegates, Dec. 17, 1775, Cooke Papers, Rhode Island Historical Society.

7. Graves's order for and carpenters' survey of *Washington*, Dec. 8, 1775, PRO/ADM, 51/720; Graves to Stephens, Dec. 15, 1775, PRO/ADM, 1/485; Franklin Papers, APS, 13:123; *Massachusetts Gazette*, Dec. 14, 1775.

8. Martindale's statement, Dec. 12, and Graves to Stephens, Dec. 15, 1775, PRO/ADM, 1/485; Howe to Dartmouth, Dec. 13, 1775, PRO/COL, 5/93.

9. Potter, *Life*, 18, 19.

10. Barnes and Owen, *Private Papers*, 1:96–97.

11. Palliser to Sandwich, Jan. 6, 1776, PRO/COL, 5/123, 9; Lords Commissioners to Germain, Jan. 6, and to Douglas, Jan. 10, 1776, PRO/COL, 5/259, 2–3, and PRO/ADM, 2/100, 349.

12. *Connecticut Courant*, Apr. 29, 1776; *London Chronicle*, Jan. 9–11, 1776.

13. Commissioners to Germain, Jan. 15, 17, 1776, PRO/COL, 5/259, 13–14, 15; Commissioners to Germain, Jan. 30, 1776, PRO/COL, 5/123, 44a, 44b; Douglas to Stephens, Jan. 16, 1776, PRO/COL, 5/123, 26b; Jackson to Douglas, Jan. 17, 1776, PRO/ADM, 2/551, 14; *London Chronicle*, Jan. 23–25, 25–27, 1776.

14. Franklin Papers, APS, 13:123.

15. Potter, *Life*, 107–8; *London Chronicle*, Jan. 25–27, 1776.

16. *London Chronicle*, Jan. 25–27, 1776; Potter, *Life*, 20, 107–8, *Public Advertiser*, Feb. 6, 1776.

17. Germain to Keith, Jan. 24, 1776, PRO/COL, 137/71, part 1; Potter, *Life*, 20.

18. Lords Commissioners to Douglas, Feb. 3, 1776, PRO/ADM, 2/100, 384; Jackson to Douglas, Feb. 6, 1776, PRO/ADM, 2/551, 73–74.

19. *Newport Mercury*, July 1, 1776; *New England Chronicle*, July 4, 1776; *The Freeman's Journal*, July 27, 1776; *Connecticut Courant*, Sept. 16, 1776.

20. Watson to Washington, Aug. 8, 1776, *NDAR*, 6:115; Washington to Hancock, Sept. 7, 1776, PCC (Letters of Washington), 152, 2:523, NA.

21. Watson to Washington, Dec. 23, Washington memo to Watson, Dec. 26, 1775, *NDAR*, 3:214–15, 253.

22. Washington to Howe, Dec. 18, 1775, PCC (Letters of Washington), 153, 1:394, NA.

23. *JCC*, 3:395–402, 4:345–46, 347, 5:495, 460, 463, 6:102; Force, *American Archives*, Ser. 4, 6:1150–51; Washington to Admiral Howe, Aug. 17, and Admiral Howe to Washington, Aug. 19, 1776, *NDAR*, 6:219, 235.

24. Howland to Massachusetts Council, Jan. 9, Loring to Howland, Feb. 1, 1977, *NDAR*, 7:904, 1081.

25. Reed, *Life and Correspondence*, 1:137–40.

CHAPTER 8

1. *NDAR*, 9:273, n. 3.

2. Peabody, "Naval Career," 5; Greenwood, *Captain John Manley*, 1–8.

3. Bartlett Papers, BHS, 5483; Moylan and Glover to Washington, Oct. 9, 1775, *NDAR*, 2:368; appraisal of *Two Brothers* and *Hawk*, PCC, "Prizes and Captures," 141, 267, LC; Force, *American Archives*, Ser. 4, 3:1251.

4. Reed to Moylan, Oct. 15, 1775, *NDAR*, 2:461.

5. Moylan and Glover to Reed, Oct. 22, 1775, Force, *American Archives*, Ser. 4, 3:1134.

6. Reed to Glover and Moylan, Oct. 16, 1775, *NDAR,* 2:472.

7. Moylan to Reed, Oct. 27, 1775, *NDAR,* 2:617–19.

8. Moylan and Glover to Reed, Oct. 28, 1775, *NDAR,* 2:622.

9. Reed to Glover and Moylan, Oct. 25, 1775, *NDAR,* 2:601.

10. Moylan and Glover to Reed, Oct. 28, 1775, *NDAR,* 2:622.

11. Peabody, "Naval Career," 6–7; Force, *American Archives,* Ser. 4, 3:1126, 1208, 1251, Ser. 5, 3:1068, 1134; Reed's report, Oct. 29, 1775, *NDAR,* 2:637.

12. Moylan to Reed, Oct. 27, 1775, *NDAR,* 2:619.

13. Bouton, *Provincial Papers,* 7:632–34.

14. Journal of *Charming Nancy,* Sept. 8, 1775, NYHS.

15. Graves to Graeme, Nov. 9, 1775, Graves, *Conduct,* appendix, 105, BM.

16. Journal of *Charming Nancy,* Nov. 8, 9, 1775; Graves, *Conduct,* 1:161, 162, 165–66, 169, and appendix, 106, 107, BM.

CHAPTER 9

1. Bowen to Reed, Nov. 3, 1775, *NDAR,* 2:870.

2. Watson to Washington, Nov. 3, 1775, *NDAR,* 2:870–71.

3. Journal of *Cerberus,* Nov. 5, 1775, PRO/ADM, 51/181.

4. Letter from Roxbury, Nov. 10, 1775, *Pennsylvania Journal,* Nov. 25, 1775.

5. Moylan to Glover, Nov. 9, 27, 1775, *NDAR,* 2:945, 1154.

6. Washington to Hancock, Nov. 11, 1775, Hancock Papers, 2, LC; Glover to Washington, Nov. 22, 1775, *NDAR,* 2:1098–1100; Pickering Papers, MassHS, 33:139.

7. Bartlett to Washington, Nov. 9, 1775, *NDAR,* 2:944.

8. George III proclamation, Aug. 23, 1775, *NDAR,* 2:685; Washington to Hancock, Nov. 11, 1775, Hancock Papers, 2, LC; Warren to Samuel Adams, Nov. 12, 1775, Ford, *Warren-Adams Letters,* 2:425–27.

9. Moylan to Bartlett, Nov. 11, 1775, *NDAR,* 2:980.

10. Journal of *Lively,* Nov. 8, 9, 1775, PRO/ADM, 51/546.

11. Glover to Washington, Nov. 10, 1775, *NDAR,* 2:965; *Boston Gazette,* Nov. 13, 1775.

12. Moylan to Glover, Nov. 11, 1775, *NDAR,* 2:981.

13. Glover-Bartlett agreement, Nov. 14, 1775, Bartlett Papers, 5481, BHS.

14. Robbins's bond, Nov. 14, 1775, *NDAR,* 2:1019.

15. Washington to Hancock, Nov. 30, 1775, PCC (Letters of Washington), 152, 1:301, NA; *Boston Gazette,* Feb. 26, 1776. The first *Polly* was captured by Coit on Nov. 5, 1775.

16. Graves to Stephens, Nov. 30, 1775, Graves, *Conduct,* 2:6, BM.

17. Moylan to Bartlett, Nov. 26, 1775, Bartlett Papers, 5484, BHS: Fitzpatrick, *Writings of George Washington,* 4:22–25.

18. Symons to Graves, Nov. 26, 1775, Graves, *Conduct,* 1:170–71, BM.

19. Journal of *Mercury,* Nov. 27, 1775, PRO/ADM, 51/600.

20. Washington to Hancock, Nov. 30, 1775, PCC (Letters of Washington), 152, 1:301, NA; *London Chronicle,* Dec. 30–Jan. 2, Feb. 24–27, 1776; *Pennsylvania Journal,* Dec. 13, 1775; Peabody, "Naval Career," 8.

21. Quoted in Miller, *Sea of Glory,* 71–72.

22. Peabody, "Naval Career," 9; accounts for expenses relative to *Nancy,* PCC, "Prizes and Captures," in Bartlett's accounts, odd numbers in 169–209, LC; Palfrey to Washington, Dec. 5, 1775, *NDAR,* 2:1282–83; *Essex Gazette,* Dec. 7, 1775; Reed, *Life and Correspondence,* 1:133.

23. *Diary of Samuel Richards,* 24–27; manifest of stores, *Pennsylvania Evening Post,* Dec. 12, 1775; Washington to Reed, May 7, 1776, Washington Papers, LC; *New York Journal,* Dec. 7, 1775.

24. Edward Green to Joshua Green, Dec. 3, 1775, Green Papers, MassHS; Howe to Dartmouth, Dec. 3, 1775, PRO/COL, 5/92; Cooper to Knox, Jan. 2, 1776, *NDAR,* 3:470.

25. Graves to Howe, Nov. 26, 1775, Graves, *Conduct,* 1:171–72, BM.

26. Force, *American Archives,* Ser. 4, 4:710–12.

27. John Prince to friend in London, Emmet Autograph Collection, NYPL.

28. Moylan to Bartlett, Moylan to Glover, Dec. 2, 1775, *NDAR,* 2:1229; Sandwich to Germain, Dec. 28, 1775, *NDAR,* 3:460; Sandwich to correspondent, Dec. 30, 1775, Lord Sandwich Papers, Duke University Library.

29. Graves to Stephens, Dec. 4, 1775, Graves, *Conduct,* 2:10–12, BM.

30. Peabody, "Naval Career," 9.

CHAPTER 10

1. Moylan to Watson, Dec. 1, 1775, *NDAR,* 2:1218.

2. *London Chronicle,* Jan. 20–23, 1776.

3. Palfrey to Washington, Dec. 5, 1775, *NDAR,* 2:1283.

4. Glover to Washington, Dec. 3, Moylan to Glover and Bartlett, Dec. 4, 1775, *NDAR,* 2:1244, 1260; Tudor to Adams, Dec. 3, 1775, Adams Papers, MassHS.

5. Washington to Hancock, Dec. 4, 1775, Fitzpatrick, *Writings of George Washington,* 4:141–45, 200–202; *London Chronicle,* Jan. 23–25, 1776, valued *Concord*'s cargo at £5,000.

6. Reed, *Life and Correspondence,* 1:133, 134; *Boston Gazette,* Dec. 11, 1775.

7. *JCC,* Dec. 19, 1775, 3:436–37.

8. Bartlett to Washington, Dec. 20, 1775, articles delivered from *Concord* by Bartlett, *NDAR,* 3:181, 192, 4:347.

9. Harrison to Bartlett, Jan. 17, 1776, *NDAR,* 3:833.

10. Robinson to Foster, Oct. 19, 1775, PCC (Intercepted Letters), 51, 2:157, NA.

11. Callbeck to Shuldham, Jan. 10, 1776, PRO/ADM, 1/484.

12. Bartlett to Washington, Dec. 9, 1775, *NDAR,* 3:17.

13. Moylan to Bartlett, Dec. 10, 1775, *NDAR,* 3:35; *Essex Gazette,* Dec. 14, 1775; *Boston Gazette,* Dec. 11, 1776.

14. Bartlett to Washington, Dec. 14, 1775, *NDAR,* 3:93–94.

15. Moylan to Bartlett, Dec. 15, 1775, *NDAR,* 3:110.

16. Moylan to Bartlett, Dec. 10, 15, 1775, *NDAR,* 3:35–36, 110.

17. Gates to Massachusetts House of Representatives, Jan. 4, 1776, MassArch, 194:182–84.

18. Washington to Hancock, Dec. 18, 31, 1775, PCC (Letters of Washington), 152, 1:351–55, 381–86, NA; Letter from Beverly, Dec. 18, 1775, *Pennsylvania Packet,* Jan. 8, 1776; PCC, "Prizes and Captures," 205, LC.

19. Smith Diary, Dec. 30, 1775, LC; *Pennsylvania Evening Post,* Jan. 18, 1776.

20. Washington to Hancock, Dec. 31, 1775, PCC (Letters of Washington), 152, 1:381–86, NA; *JCC,* 3:465–67.

21. Extract of a letter from Boston, Dec. 13, 1775, *Public Advertiser,* Jan. 10, 1776; *Morning Post and Daily Advertiser,* Jan. 17, 1776.

22. Graves, *Conduct,* Dec. 12, 1775, 2:17–18, BM.

23. Barnes and Owens, *Private Papers,* 1:70–72.

24. Sewall to Winslow, Jan. 10, 1776, *NDAR,* 3:495–96. Before going to England, Sewall had been an intimate friend of John Adams.

25. Graves, *Conduct,* 2:24, 39–40, 40–41, BM; Sewall to Winslow, Jan. 10, 1776, *NDAR,* 3:496; Graves to Stephens, Jan. 29, Feb. 1, 1776, Graves, *Conduct,* 2:39–40, 40–41, BM; Hansard, *Parliamentary History,* 18:841–46.

26. Barnes and Owens, *Private Papers,* Jan. 13, 1776, 1:104–5.

27. Moylan to Watson, Dec. 13, 1775, *NDAR,* 3:81; Moylan to Reed, Jan. 2, 1776, Reed, *Life and Correspondence,* 1:137–40.

CHAPTER 11

1. Reed's report, Oct. 29, and Wentworth to Moylan, Nov. 27, 1775, *NDAR,* 2:637, 1153.

2. Bartlett to Washington, Nov. 4, 1775, *NDAR,* 2:879.

3. Washington to Hancock, Nov. 28, 1775, PCC (Letters of Washington), 152, 1:292, NA; Bouton, *Provincial Papers,* 7: 640, 641.

4. Wentworth to Moylan, Nov. 27, 1775, *NDAR,* 2:1152–53.

5. Washington to Hancock, Nov. 30, 1775, PCC (Letters of Washington), 152, 1:301, NA.

6. Moylan to Wentworth, Dec. 1, 14, 1775, *NDAR*, 2:1217, 3:95.

7. Wentworth to Moylan, Dec. 3, Moylan to Bartlett, Dec. 10, 1775, *NDAR*, 2:1244, 3:36.

8. *New England Chronicle*, Nov. 24–30, 1775.

9. Journal of *Niger*, Dec. 2, 3, 1775, PRO/ADM, 51/637.

10. Washington to Hancock, Dec. 31, 1775, PCC (Letters of Washington), 152, 1:385–86, NA; *Boston Gazette*, Feb. 26, 1776.

11. Washington to Glover, Dec. 26, 1775, *NDAR*, 3:253.

12. Lowrey to Hancock, Jan. 25, 1776, PCC (Letters to Congress), 78, 14:59, NA; *JCC*, 4:104–6; libel of *Sally*, Apr. 23, 1776, *NDAR*, 4:1214.

13. Washington to Bartlett, Dec. 28, 1775, *NDAR*, 3:274; Moylan to Reed, Jan. 2, 1776, Reed, *Life and Correspondence*, 1:137–40.

14. George III's speech to Parliament, Oct. 26, 1775, Hansard, *Parliamentary History*, 18:695–97.

15. Washington to Hancock, Dec. 31, 1775, Jan. 4, 1776, PCC (Letters of Washington), 152, 1:381–86, 407–9, NA.

16. Moylan to Reed, Jan. 2, 1776, Reed, *Life and Correspondence*, 1:137–40.

CHAPTER 12

1. Manley's memo of sundries, Jan. 1, 1776, Bartlett Papers, 5708, BHS.

2. Hutcheson to Haldimand, Dec. 25, 1775, Haldimand Papers, BM; Log of *Fowey*, Dec. 27–29, 1775, PRO/ADM, 51/375.

3. *JCC*, 3:436–37, 438–40.

4. Washington to agents, Jan. 4, 1776, *NDAR*, 3:599.

5. *New England Chronicle*, Dec. 21–28, 1776.

6. Sargent to Washington, Dec. 29, 1775, *NDAR*, 3:290.

7. Washington to Sargent, Jan. 1, 1776, *NDAR*, 3:553–54.

8. Force, *American Archives*, Ser. 4, 4:90; Washington's commission (as typical of all), *NDAR*, 3:553.

9. Force, *American Archives*, Ser. 4, 4:563; advance pay to crew of *Hancock*, Jan. 1, Moylan to Bartlett, Jan. 10, 1776, *NDAR*, 3:552, 713.

10. Bartlett to Moylan, Jan. 5, Moylan to Bartlett, Jan. 8, 10, 1776, *NDAR*, 3:631, 675, 713.

11. Moylan to Reed, Jan. 2, 1776, Reed, *Life and Correspondence*, 1:137–40; Wentworth to Washington and Moylan, Jan. 10, Harrison to Moylan, Jan. 20, 1776, *NDAR*, 3:711, 873–74; *Essex Journal*, Jan. 12, 1776.

12. Hanson to Moylan, Jan. 20, 1776, *NDAR*, 3:873–74.

13. Fettyplace receipt for cartridges, Bartlett Papers, 5753, BHS; officers of Washington's vessels, Feb. 1, Washington to captains, Jan. 20, 1776, *NDAR*, 3:871–73, 1077.

14. *JCC*, 4:300, 301; Pickering Papers, MassArch, 194:176–77.

15. Sheppard, *Life of Samuel Tucker,* 32–35.

16. Log of *Halifax,* Jan. 20, 21, 22, 1776, PRO/ADM, 52/1775; Graves, *Conduct,* Jan. 27, 1776, 2:33–35, BM; officers of armed vessels, *NDAR,* 3:1077.

17. Ayres commission, Feb. 1, 1776, *NDAR,* 3:553, 871–73.

18. Brown Orderly Book, Feb. 3, 1776, BHS.

19. Journal of *Fowey,* Feb. 7, 1776, PRO/ADM, 51/375.

20. Record of Armed Vessels, 1775–76, 1:5500, BHS; Glover to White, Feb. 29, 1776, *New-England Historical and Genealogical Register* 30 (1876): 332; cost of *Lynch,* PCC, "Prizes and Captures," nos. 211–63 passim, LC.

21. Moylan to Watson, Jan. 7, 1776, *NDAR,* 3:669.

22. Washington to Dyar, Jan. 20, 1776, *NDAR,* 3:871–73.

23. Repairs to the Harrison, Dec. 13, 1775, PCC, "Prizes and Captures," 129, 377, LC; Harrison to Watson, Jan. 20, 1776, *NDAR,* 3:870–71.

24. Watson to Washington, Jan. 23, and Moylan to Watson, Jan. 25, 1776, *NDAR,* 3:937, 966.

25. Watson to Washington, Jan. 29, 1776, *NDAR,* 3:1033.

26. Washington to captains, Jan. 20, Washington to Manley, Jan. 28, 1776, *NDAR,* 3:872–73, 1023–24.

CHAPTER 13

1. Wentworth to Washington and Moylan, Jan. 10, 1776, *NDAR,* 3:711.

2. Graves, *Conduct,* Jan. 5, 1776, 2:27, 30, BM.

3. Ibid., 2:30.

4. Master's log of *Hope,* Jan. 27, 1776, PRO/ADM, 52/1823.

5. *New England Chronicle,* Feb. 1, 1776; *Boston Gazette,* Feb. 5, 1776; Fitzpatrick, *Writings of George Washington,* 4:299–301; Watson to Washington, Jan. 26, 1776, and Extract of a letter from Whitehaven, June 18, 1775, *NDAR,* 3:995–96n, 1132–33.

6. Disposition of British fleet on Jan. 27, 1776, Graves, *Conduct,* 2:36–37, BM.

7. Washington to Manley, Jan. 28, 1776, *NDAR,* 3:1023–24.

8. Moylan to Watson, Feb. 1, 1776, Watson Papers, Pilgrim Society; Watson to Washington, Jan. 29, 1776, *NDAR,* 3:1031–33.

9. Graves, *Conduct,* Dec. 28, 1775, Jan. 26, 1776, 2:22–23, 33, BM.

10. Graves, *Conduct,* Feb. 1, 1776, 2:40–41; Log of *Hope,* Jan. 27, 30, 31, PRO/ADM, 52/1823.

11. Ward to Hancock, Feb. 3, 1776, PCC, 159:352, NA.

12. Hutcheson to Haldimand, Feb. 2, 1776, Haldimand Papers, BM; *Providence Gazette,* Feb. 3, 1776; *New England Chronicle,* Feb. 1–8, 1776.

13. *Boston Gazette,* Mar. 26, 1776; *Providence Gazette,* Apr. 20, 1776; *London Chronicle,* June 15 to June 18, 1776; Fitzpatrick, *Writings of George Washington,* 5:25–26; Watson to Moylan, Apr. 20, 1776, *NDAR,* 4:1174–75.

14. Watson to Washington, Feb. 22, 1776, *NDAR,* 4:36.

15. Harrison to Watson, Feb. 24, 1776, *NDAR,* 4:64.

16. Corban Barnes's bond, MassArch, 139:118.

17. Master's log of *Hope,* Feb. 23, 1776, PRO/ADM, 52/1823; Watson to Trumbull, Feb. 26, 1776, Joseph Trumbull Papers, ConnHS.

18. Inventory of *Harrison,* Mar. 8, 1776, "Prizes and Captures," no. 139, LC.

19. Watson to Moylan, Mar. 18, 1776, *NDAR,* 4:391.

CHAPTER 14

1. Graves, *Conduct,* Jan. 27, 1776, 2:34, BM; Journal of *Fowey,* Jan. 30, 1776, PRO/ADM, 51/375.

2. Report of Salem Committee on *Rainbow,* MassArch, 194:255–56 1/2; Sheppard, *Life of Samuel Tucker,* 337–38.

3. Journal of *Fowey,* Feb. 2, 1776, PRO/ADM, 51/375.

4. Ibid., Feb. 3, 1776.

5. Passport for *Rainbow,* MassArch, 194:254.

6. Libel of *Henry and Esther, Boston Gazette,* Feb. 26, 1776; Report of Salem Committee, Feb. 19, Ayres to Ward, Apr. 20, 1776, MassArch, 194:255–56 1/2, 263, 264, 265.

7. Glover to Tucker, Feb. 3, 1776, *NDAR,* 3:1108; *Boston Gazette,* Feb. 26, Mar. 11, 1776; Sheppard, *Life of Samuel Tucker,* 337–38.

8. Ward to Bartlett, Apr. 26, 1776, Bartlett Papers, BHS; *Providence Gazette,* Apr. 20, 1776.

9. Bartlett to Moylan, Feb. 3, 1776, *NDAR,* 3:1108.

10. Moylan to Bartlett, Feb. 12, 1776, *NDAR,* 3:1226.

11. Bartlett Papers, no. 5692, BHS; Moylan to Bartlett, Mar. 11, 1776, *NDAR,* 4:295.

12. "Prizes and Captures," 12, LC; Bartlett's accounts are summarized from documents nos. 211–73, Bartlett Account Book, no. 5515, BHS.

13. Washington to Hancock, Feb. 26, 1776, PCC (Letters of Washington), 152, 1:505–7, NA; Gates to John Adams, Mar. 8, 1776, Silliman Papers, YUL.

14. Washington to Hancock, Mar. 7, 1776, PCC (Letters of Washington), 152, 1:509–12, NA.

15. *Diary of Samuel Richards,* 24–27.

16. Washington to Hancock, Mar. 9, 1776, PCC (Letters of Washington), 152, 1:512–16.

CHAPTER 15

1. Master's log of *Nautilus,* Feb. 21, 22, 1776, PRO/ADM, 52/1884; Journal of *Fowey,* Mar. 2, 1776, *NDAR,* 51/375.

2. *Pennsylvania Packet,* Mar. 11, 1776; Journal of *Fowey,* Mar. 2, 1776, PRO/ADM, 51/375; Smith Diary, Mar. 6, 1776, LC.

3. Diary of John Rowe, *PMHS,* Ser. 2, 10:95; Log of *Hope,* Mar. 3, 1776, PRO/ADM, 52/1823.

4. Shuldham to Stephens, Mar. 8, 1775, PRO/ADM, 1/484; Journal of *Nautilus,* Mar. 7, 8, 1776, PRO/ADM, 51/529.

5. Morgan to Washington, Apr. 22, 1776, *NDAR,* 4:1190.

6. Washington to Hancock, Mar. 9, 1776, PCC (Letters of Washington), 152, 1:515–16; *Pennsylvania Packet,* Mar. 18, 1776; *Boston Gazette,* Mar. 11, 18, 1776.

7. Harrison to Wentworth, Mar. 25, 1776, *NDAR,* 4:496.

8. *Essex Journal,* Mar. 15, 1776; Smith Diary, Mar. 15, 1776, LC.

9. *Boston Gazette,* Mar. 11, 1776; Sargent to Washington, Mar. 12, 14, 26, Apr. 7, 1776, *NDAR,* 4:307–8, 330, 520.

10. Master's log of *Hope,* Mar. 13, 1776, PRO/ADM 52/1823; Sargent to Washington, Mar. 14, 26, 1776, *NDAR,* 4:330, 520.

11. Washington to Hancock, Mar. 9, 1776, PCC (Letters of Washington), 152, 1:515–16.

12. Disposition of Shuldham's vessels, Mar. 22, and Shuldham to Stephens, Mar. 23, 1776, PRO/ADM 1/484; Shuldham to Banks, Mar. 27, 1776, PRO/ADM, 1/487.

13. Howe to Germain, Apr. 25, 1776, PRO/COL 5/93; Williams to Coit, Mar. 21, 1776, Trumbull Papers, YUL; Washington to Hancock, Mar. 24, 1776, PCC (Letters of Washington), 152, 1:541–44, NA.

14. "The Kemble Papers," *Collections of the New York Historical Society,* 1:74; Journal of *Diligent,* Mar. 21, 1776, PRO/ADM, 51/4109.

15. Sarah Sever's account, Mar. 23, 1776, *PMHS,* Ser. 2, 2:158–59.

16. Hutcheson to Haldimand, Mar. 24, 1776, Haldimand Papers, BM.

17. Bartlett's returns, Apr. 1, 1776, *NDAR,* 4:608.

18. Sargent to Washington, Mar. 26, and Quincy to Washington, Mar. 26, 1776, *NDAR,* 4:520, 521.

19. Brush to Robertson, Mar. 25, and to Howe, Mar. 26, *NDAR,* 4:501–3, 522–23.

20. Journals of *Chatham* and *Centurion,* Mar. 27, 1776, PRO/ADM, 51/192, 51/177; Shuldham to Stephens, Apr. 16, 1776, PRO/ADM, 1/484.

21. Journal of *Niger,* Mar. 27–31, 1776, PRO/ADM, 51/637.

22. *Pennsylvania Gazette,* Apr. 17, 1776.

23. Sargent to Washington, Apr. 7, 1776, *NDAR,* 4:694.

24. Wentworth to Moylan, Apr. 15, 1776, *NDAR,* 4:828–30; Howe to Germain, Apr. 25, 1776, PRO/COL, 5/93, 279–82.

25. Diary of John Rowe, Apr. 6, 1776, *PMHS,* Ser. 2, 10:98; Glover to Massachusetts Council, Apr. 9, 1776, and subsequent resolutions of . . . , MassArch, 34:753, 758, 803; 164:313, 316; 194:334; 208:393; Journal of the Massachusetts Council, Apr. 12, 13, 17, 24, 1776, MassArch, 18:87, 34:752–53, 757, 758, 803, and *New England Chronicle,* Apr. 25, 1776.

26. Shuldham to Stephens, Mar. 27, 1776, PRO/ADM, 1/484; Log of *Milford,* Apr. 3, 1776, PRO/ADM, 52/1865; *London Chronicle,* Apr. 6–9, 1776; Clark, *George Washington's Navy,* 129–30.

27. Ward to Bartlett, Apr. 15, 1776, Ward Orderly Book, Joseph Ward Papers, CHS; Ward to Washington, May 3, 1776, *NDAR,* 4:1391.

CHAPTER 16

1. Washington to Hancock, Mar. 19, 24, 27, 1776, PCC (Letters of Washington), 152, 1:537–38, 541–44, 563–65; Washington to Ward, Apr. 4, 1776, *NDAR,* 4:659.

2. Martyn, *Life of Artemus Ward,* 91; French, *First Year,* 49, 83.

3. Washington to Hancock, Apr. 15, 1776, PCC (Letters of Washington), 152, 1:587–89, NA; Washington to Ward, Apr. 4, 1776, *NDAR,* 4:659.

4. Wentworth to Moylan, Apr. 15, 1776, *NDAR,* 4:828–30.

5. Washington to Hancock, Apr. 15, 25, 1776, PCC (Letters of Washington), 152, 1:619–25, NA; Ward to Washington, Apr. 11, 1776, *NDAR,* 4:766–67; Fitzpatrick, *Writings of George Washington,* 4:490; Ward to Bartlett, Apr. 26, 1776, Bartlett Papers, BHS.

6. Ward to Bartlett, Apr. 16, 17, 18, 23, 1776, Bartlett Papers, BHS; *Boston Gazette,* Mar. 25, 1776; *Providence Gazette,* Apr. 20, 1776; Watson to Moylan, Apr. 20, 1776, *NDAR,* 4:1174.

7. John Adams to Joseph Ward, Apr. 16, 1776, Ward Papers, Force Transcripts, LC.

8. *JCC,* 4:289–91.

9. Washington to Hancock, Apr. 25, 1776, PCC (Letters of Washington), 152, 1:619–25, NA.

10. Ward to Bartlett, Apr. 26, 1776, Bartlett Papers, BHS.

11. Fitzpatrick, *Writings of George Washington,* 4:490; Ward to Washington, Apr. 28, 1776, *NDAR,* 4:1294–95.

12. Ward to Washington, May 3, 1776, *NDAR,* 4:1391.

13. Fitzpatrick, *Writings of George Washington,* 5:25–26; Bartlett to Ward, May 25, 1776, Ward Papers, MassHS; Ward Orderly Book, May 27, 1776, Joseph Ward Papers, CHS; Ward to Washington, May 27, Bartlett to Washington, June 7, 1776, *NDAR,* 5:267, 470.

14. *JCC,* 4:289–91.

15. Fitzpatrick, *Writings of George Washington,* 4:490; PCC, 78, 11:33–35, NA; Huntington to Trumbull, Apr. 8, 1776, Jonathan Trumbull Papers, 5:24a, ConnSL.

CHAPTER 17

1. Bowen Diary, Feb. 6, 1776, EI; Appleton to Smith, Feb. 7, 1776, *PMHS,* 59:111–12.

2. Ward to Washington, May 9, 1776, *NDAR,* 5:6; *New England Chronicle,* May 9, 1776.

3. Almon, *Remembrancer,* 3:139; *Public Advertiser,* July 3, 1776.

4. Glover to Pickering, May 11, 1776, Pickering Papers, MassHS, 56:82; *Boston Gazette,* May 20, 1776; *New England Chronicle,* June 13, July 4, 1776.

5. Jackson to Pownall, Apr. 10, 1776, PRO/COL, 5/259; Stephens to Shuldham, Apr. 18, 1776, PRO/ADM, 2/551, 457–65.

6. Journal of HMS *Rose,* May 16, 1776, PRO/ADM, 51/805.

7. Master's log of *Hope,* May 17, 1776, PRO/ADM, 52/1794; Palmer to Cushing, May 17, 1776, MassArch, 195:1.

8. Ingraham to Savage, May 18, 1776, *PMHS,* 44:689.

9. Devens to John Adams, May 17, 1776, Adams Papers, MassHS; Ward to Washington, May 17, 1776, *NDAR,* 5:134–35.

10. Glover to Washington, July 20, 1776, *NDAR,* 5:1152–53.

11. Ibid.; *New England Chronicle,* May 23, 1776; *Boston Gazette,* June 3, 1776.

12. Shuldham to Stephens, May 20, June 8, 1776, PRO/ADM, 1/484.

13. Abigail Adams to John Adams, May 27, 1776, Butterfield, *Adams Papers,* Ser. 2, 1:415–18; Ward to Washington, May 20, 27, 1776, *NDAR,* 5:161–62, 267.

14. Journals of *Renown* and *Experiment,* May 19, 1776, PRO/ADM, 51/776, 51/331; *New England Chronicle,* May 23, 1776.

15. *New England Chronicle,* May 30, 1776; Woolsey and Salmon to Pringle, June 1, 1776, Woolsey and Salmon Letter Book, LC; Funeral elegy for James Mugford, *NDAR,* 5:163.

16. *Providence Gazette,* June 8, 1776; *JCC,* 4:390, 393, 394, 395–60; Cushing to Hancock, May 17, 1776, *NDAR,* 5:135.

17. Bradford to Hancock, May 15, 1776, *NDAR,* 5:102.

18. Glover's receipts, June 18, 1776, Bartlett Papers, 5726, BHS.

19. *Boston Gazette,* June 3, 1776.

20. Bradford to Hancock, July 1, 1776, Don Collection, SI.

21. Glover to Washington, July 20, 1776, *NDAR,* 5:1152–53.

22. Washington to Hancock, Aug. 7, 1776, Fitzpatrick, *Writings of George Washington*, 5:379–81.

23. Bradford to Morris, July 14, 1776, Morris Papers, Accession 1805, LC.

24. Bradford to Hancock, Aug. 5, 1776, Don Collection, SI; Bradford to Morris, Aug. 8, 1776, Morris Papers, Accession 1805, LC.

CHAPTER 18

1. Log of *Milford*, May 14, 1776, PRO/ADM, 52/1865.

2. Ibid.

3. Ibid., May 27, 1776; Master's log of *Hope*, May 24, 1776, PRO/ADM, 52/1794.

4. Advertisement for deserters from *Warren*, June 6, 1776, *New England Chronicle*.

5. Glover Colony Ledger, June 4, 5, 1776, MHS.

6. Admiralty to Brisbane, Apr. 4, Stephens to Shuldham, Apr. 18, Erskine and Campbell to Brisbane, Apr. 26, 1776, PRO/ADM, 2/101, 8–9, 2/551, 459–60, 5/124, 37c; *London Chronicle*, Apr. 23–25, May 7–9, 1776; *Public Advertiser*, Sept. 16, 1776.

7. Shuldham to Stephens, June 8, 1776, PRO/ADM, 1/484.

8. Master's log of *Milford*, June 8, 1776, PRO/ADM, 52/1865; Glover to Ward, June 8, 1776, Ward Papers, MassHS; *Pennsylvania Evening Post*, July 4, 1776; *Public Advertiser*, Sept. 23, 1776; Ward to Washington, June 9, 1776, *NDAR*, 5:436.

9. *Boston Gazette*, June 10, 1776; *Continental Journal*, June 13, 1776: Webb to Ward, July 18, 1776, *NDAR*, 5:1125.

10. *Public Advertiser*, Sept. 11, 23, 1776.

11. Fitzpatrick, *Writings of George Washington*, 5:143–44, 145.

12. Bradford to Hancock, July 1, 1776, Don Collection, SI.

13. Master's log of *Hope*, June 9, 1776, PRO/ADM, 52/1794.

14. *Public Advertiser*, Aug. 20, 1776; Bradford to Hancock, July 1, 1776, Don Collection, SI.

15. Master's log of *Hope*, June 12, 1776, PRO/ADM, 52/1794.

16. Journals of *Renown*, *Hope*, and *Milford*, June 14, 1776, PRO/ADM, 51/776, 52/1794, 52/1865; Letter from an officer in the colony train at Nantasket, *Connecticut Courant*, June 24, 1776; Joseph Ward to John Adams, June 16, 1776, Adams Papers, MassHS.

17. Ward to Massachusetts Council, June 15, 1776, MassArch, 195:44–44a; Washington to Ward, June 23, 1776, *NDAR*, 5:697.

18. Campbell to Howe, June 19, 1776, *Pennsylvania Evening Post*, July 4, 1776.

19. Ibid.; Journal of Archibald Bog, June 16, 1776, PRO/ADM, 30/715.

20. Campbell to Howe, June 19, 1776, *Pennsylvania Evening Post*, July 4, 1776.

21. Harding to Trumbull, June 19, Smedley to Trumbull, June 28, 1776, Jonathan Trumbull Papers, 5:239, 240, ConnSL; Bradford to Hancock, June 17, 1776, Don Collection, SI; Diary of Ezekiel Price, *PMHS*, Ser. 1, 7:258; Sheppard, *Life of Samuel Tucker*, 59.

22. Harding to Trumbull, June 19, Bradford to Trumbull, June 23, 1776, Jonathan Trumbull Papers, 5:95a, 240, ConnSL; Campbell to Howe, June 19, 1776, *Pennsylvania Evening Post*, July 4, 1776; Glover to Ward, June 23, 1776, Green Papers, MassHS; Ward to Washington, June 23, 1776, *NDAR*, 5:696.

23. Force, *American Archives*, Ser. 4, 5:209–10, 217, 6:1113–14.

24. Bradford to Hancock, July 1, 1776, Don Collection, SI; Hancock to Bradford, July 6, 1776, PCC, 12A, NA; Bradford to Hancock, June 20, Washington to Ward, June 23, July 1, Bradford to Washington, July 29, 1776, *NDAR*, 5:635–36, 697, 1269.

25. Abigail Adams to John Adams, July 14, 1776, Butterfield, *Adams Papers*, Ser. 2, 2:46, 47; Ward to Washington, June 9, 1776, *NDAR*, 5:436.

26. *Public Advertiser*, Sept. 16, 1776.

CHAPTER 19

1. Washington to Ward, July 9, 1776, Fitzpatrick, *Writings of George Washington*, 5:242, 243. The Declaration of Independence was first printed in the *Pennsylvania Evening Post*, July 6, 1776.

2. Shuldham to Jackson, May 12, 1776, PRO/ADM, 1/484; Journal of Capt. Henry Duncan, *NDAR*, 5:1038.

3. Journal of *Glasgow*, July 25, 1775, PRO/ADM, 51/398; *Pennsylvania Packet*, July 3, 1775.

4. Bill of sale and register of *Peggy*, June 26, 1776, Revolutionary War Prize Cases, Court of Appeals, 1776–87, NA.

5. *New England Chronicle*, Aug. 2, 15, 1776; Cobb to Paine, Aug. 5, 1776, Paine Papers, MassHS; Ward to Washington, and libel of *Peggy*, July 29, Aug. 15, 1776, *NDAR*, 5:1268, 1269.

6. Washington to Hancock, Aug. 5, 1776, Fitzpatrick, *Writings of George Washington*, 5:370–72.

7. *New England Chronicle*, Aug. 2, 1776; *Public Advertiser*, Aug. 30, 1776; Washington to Hancock, Aug. 5, 1776, Fitzpatrick, *Writings of George Washington*, 5:370–72.

8. Minutes of the Boston Committe of Correspondence, August 15, 1776, *New-England Historical and Genealogical Register*, 33:23, 24; Cobb to Paine, Aug. 19, 1776, Paine Papers, MassHS; *New England Chronicle*, Aug. 22, 1776; Bradford to Hancock, Aug. 18, 1776, *NDAR*, 6:222.

9. *The Freeman's Journal,* Aug. 24, 1776; Wentworth to Washington, Aug. 26, 1776, *NDAR,* 6:301–2.

10. Bradford to Hancock, Aug. 29, 1776, Don Collection, SI.

11. Ibid., Aug. 12, 1776; Harrison to Wentworth, Sept. 10, 1776, *NDAR,* 6:772.

12. *JCC,* 5:630, 631.

13. Bradford to Morris, Sept. 5, 1776, Morris Papers, Accession 1805, LC.

14. Journal of *Liverpool,* Aug. 1, 3, 1776, PRO/ADM, 51/548; Master's log of *Milford,* Aug. 19, 21, 22, 23, 24, PRO/ADM, 52/1865; William Knox to Henry Knox, Aug. 25, 1776, Knox Papers, MassHS.

15. Journal of *Liverpool,* Aug. 26, Sept. 4, 1776, PRO/ADM, 51/548; Master's log of *Milford,* Sept. 4, 1776, PRO/ADM, 52/1865; muster roll of *Warren,* PRO/ADM, 36/7736.

16. Bradford to Hancock, Sept. 16, 1776, Don Papers, SI; Ward to Washington, Sept. 1, 1776, *NDAR,* 6:638.

17. *New England Chronicle,* Sept. 5, 12, 1776; *Independent Chronicle,* Sept. 26, 1776; Bradford to Hancock, Don Collection, SI.

18. Bradford to Hancock, Sept. 30, Oct. 7, 1776, Society Collection, PHS; *Independent Chronicle,* Oct. 10, 1776.

19. *London Chronicle,* June 29–July 2, 1776; *Boston Gazette,* Oct. 7, 1776; *Independent Chronicle,* Oct. 10, 1776; Richard Derby Jr. to Massachusetts Council, Oct. 3, 1776, *NDAR,* 6:1112–13.

20. Bradford to Hancock, Oct. 21, 1776, Bradford Letter Book, LC.

CHAPTER 20

1. Bradford to Hancock, Aug. 29, 1776, Don Collection, SI; Bradford to Morris, Sept. 5, 1776, Morris Papers, Accession 1805, LC.

2. Wentworth to Washington, Aug. 26, 1776, *NDAR,* 6:301–2, 346.

3. Hanson to Wentworth, Sept. 10, 1776, *NDAR,* 6:772.

4. *JCC,* Oct. 16, 1776, 6:879, 881–83.

5. Marine Committee to agents, Oct. 18, 1776, Marine Committee Letter Book, 37–38, NA.

6. Bartlett to Washington, Oct. 10, 1776, *NDAR,* 6:1194–95.

7. Marine Committee to agents, Oct. 18, 1776, Marine Committee Letter Book, 35–36, NA.

8. Bradford to Marine Committee, Nov. 11, 1776, Bradford Letter Book, LC.

9. Ibid.; *Boston Gazette,* Nov. 11, 1776; *Independent Chronicle,* Nov. 14, 1776.

10. Bradford to Marine Committee, Nov. 11, Bradford to Washington, Nov. 14, 1776, Bradford Letter Book, LC; *Boston Gazette,* Nov. 11, 1776;

Independent Chronicle, Nov. 14, 1776; Petition of Thompson to Massachusetts General Court, Jan. 3, 1777, MassArch, 182:16–17.

11. Bradford to Hancock, Nov. 14, Bradford to Marine Committee, Dec. 21, 1776, Bradford to Secret Committee of Congress, Jan. 17, 1777, Bradford Letter Book, LC; Ward to Hancock, Dec. 23, 1776, PCC, 78, 23:335, NA.

12. Bradford to Morris, Jan. 22, 1777, Bradford Letter Book, LC.

13. Morris to Bradford, Feb. 7, 1777, Marine Committee Letter Book, 59–60, NA.

14. Deposition of Martindale and McCree, *NDAR,* 7:333; Bradford to Hancock, Jan. 27, 1777, Bradford Letter Book, LC.

15. Bradford to Hancock, Nov. 28, 1776, Bradford Letter Book, LC.

16. Minutes of the Massachusetts Board of War, Dec. 17, 1776, Journal of the Massachusetts Council, Jan. 3, 4, 1777, MassArch, 20:149, 150–51, 152, 153–54, 148:52–57.

17. Bradford to Hancock, Nov. 14, 1776, Bradford Letter Book, LC.

18. Bradford to Washington, Nov. 9, Bradford to Hancock, Dec. 2, 1776, Bradford Letter Book, LC.

CHAPTER 21

1. Bradford to Hancock, Nov. 28, 1776, Bradford Letter Book, LC.

2. Langdon to Hancock, Jan. 22, 1777, Langdon Letter Book, Stone Collection.

3. Cushing to Hancock, Jan. 26, 1777, Don Collection, SI.

4. Bradford to Hancock, Jan. 27, 1777, Bradford Letter Book, LC.

5. *JCC,* Mar. 15, 1777, 7:180, 182–83.

6. Bradford to Marine Committee, May 7, 1777, Bradford Letter Book, LC.

7. Bradford to Hancock, Apr. 9, Bradford to Morris, Feb. 17, May 7, 1777, Bradford Letter Book, LC.

8. Ayres's assignments to a cartel can be traced through *NDAR,* 7:851–1189 passim.

9. Bradford to Morris, Feb. 17, 1777, Bradford Letter Book, LC.

10. Bradford to Hancock, Feb. 20, 1777, Bradford Letter Book, LC.

11. Bradford to Adams, Feb. 26, 1777, Bradford Letter Book, LC.

12. Bradford to Franklin, Feb. 25, 1777, Franklin Papers, APS.

13. Bradford to Pilarne, Penet and Company, Feb. 25, and to Secret Committee, Mar. 4, 1777, Bradford Letter Book, LC.

14. American Commissioners to Capt. John Adams, Apr. 11, 1777, Franklin Papers, Ser. 2, 25:2147, LC; Lupton (Van Zandt) to Eden, Apr. 10, 1777, *NDAR,* 8:759.

15. Williams to Deane, Apr. 19, 1777, Williams Letter Book, YUL; Lupton (Van Zandt) to Eden, Apr. 10, 1777, *NDAR*, 8:759.

16. Johnson to Commissioners, Apr. 25, 1777, Deane Papers, ConnHS; Williams to Bradford, Apr. 29, 1777, Williams Letter Book, YUL.

17. *London Chronicle*, May 24, 1777; Porter to Franklin, June 6, 1777, Franklin Papers, vol. 6, pt. 1, p. 50, APS; Narrative of John Porter, June 10, 1777, Williams Letter Book, YUL; Deane to Joseph-Matthias Gerard de Rayneval, June 2, 1777, *NDAR*, 9:373–74.

18. Washington to Heath, Apr. 10, 1777, *NDAR*, 8:315.

CHAPTER 22

1. Morris to Bradford, Feb. 7, 1777, Marine Committee Letter Book, 59–60, NA.

2. Bradford to Morris, Jan. 22, Feb. 17, 1777, Bradford Letter Book, LC.

3. Bradford to Hancock, Nov. 14, 1776, Bradford Letter Book, LC; Bradford to Massachusetts Council, Mar. 10, and Skimmer's bond, Mar. 12, 1777, MassArch, 6:216, 166:327.

4. Glover to Savage, Apr. 22, trial of brig *Charles*, June 4, 1777, *NDAR*, 8:397–98, 9:40; Bradford to Hancock, Mar. 27, and to Marine Committee, Apr. 22, 1777, Bradford Letter Book, LC; *Independent Chronicle*, May 8, 1777.

5. Libel of *Betsey*, *Independent Chronicle*, June 5, 26, 1777; trial of *Betsey*, June 24, 1777, MassArch, 159:108–11.

6. Trial of brig *Charles*, June 4, 6, 1777, *NDAR*, 9:40–41; muster roll of *Mermaid*, June 16, 1777, PRO/ADM, 36/7761.

7. Bradford to Leonard Jarvis, June 18, and to Simeon Mayo, June 25, 1777, Bradford Letter Book, LC; dispositions of Howe's fleet, June 5, 1777, PRO/ADM, 1/487, 388–89; Bartlett to Savage, June 11, 1777, MassArch, 152:251; *Independent Chronicle*, June 19, 1777.

8. Account of medicine for *True Blue*, June 13, 1777, *True Blue* Accounts, MHS.

9. Bradford to Marine Committee, July 10, and Bradford to Hancock, Aug. 22, 1777, Bradford Letter Book, LC. For the engagement of *Hancock* and *Boston* with three British warships, see chapter 23; *London Chronicle*, Aug. 26, 1777; *Boston Gazette*, July 28, Aug. 11, 18, 1777.

10. Bradford to Morris, Sept. 24, and to Marine Committee, Sept. 25, 1777, Bradford Letter Book, LC.

11. Muster role of *Diamond*, Sept. 22, 1777, PRO/ADM, 36:7761; *Independent Chronicle*, Feb. 5, 1778.

12. *Independent Chronicle*, Nov. 6, 1777.

13. Bradford to Marine Committee, Oct. 30, 1777, Bradford Letter Book, LC.

14. Marine Committee to Naval Board of Eastern Department, June 26, 1777, Marine Committee Letter Book, 98–99, NA; Bradford to Morris, Dec. 17, and Bradford to Marine Committee, Dec. 19, 1977, Bradford Letter Book, LC.

15. Bradford to Morris, Feb. 16, May 25, Bradford to Marine Committee, Mar. 25, and Bradford to Commercial Committee, July 1, 1778, Bradford Letter Book, LC.

16. Bradford to Marine Committee, July 2, 1778, Bradford Letter Book, LC; *Independent Chronicle,* July 16, 1778; *Public Advertiser,* Nov. 4, 1778.

17. Bradford to Marine Committee, July 30, 1778, Bradford Letter Book, LC.

18. Bradford to Marine Committee, Sept. 2, 1778, Bradford Letter Book, LC; *Independent Chronicle,* July 16, 1778.

19. Bradford to Marine Committee, Sept. 2, 1778, Bradford Letter Book, LC; *Continental Journal,* Sept. 3, 1778; *Independent Ledger,* Sept. 7, 1778.

20. *Independent Ledger,* Sept. 7, 1778.

21. Bradford to Morris, Sept. 7, 1778, Bradford Letter Book, LC.

22. *JCC,* 12:946.

CHAPTER 23

1. Navy Board Eastern Department to Marine Committee, Dec. 9, 1778, Navy Board Letter Book, NYPL.

2. Navy Board to Marine Committee, Jan. 15, 1779, Navy Board Letter Book, NYPL; Bradford to Commercial Committee, July 27, 1779, Bradford Letter Book, LC.

3. Bradford to Commercial Committee, Feb. 26, 27, and to Richard Peters, Feb. 27, 1779, Bradford Letter Book, LC; *Independent Chronicle,* Mar. 4, 1779.

4. Navy Board to Marine Committee, Mar. 9, 1779, Navy Board Letter Book, NYPL.

5. Paullin, *Out-Letters,* 1:179.

6. Narrative of John Foster Williams, Revolutionary Papers, Pennsylvania Historical Society.

7. Navy Board to Marine Committee, Apr. 17, May 12, 18, and June 24, 1779, Navy Board Letter Book, NYPL; *Continental Journal,* Apr. 8, 1779; *Independent Chronicle,* Apr. 29, 1779: *Publications of the Rhode Island Historical Society,* 8:259; Marine Committee Letter Book, Apr. 19, June 7, 1779, NA.

8. *Boston Post,* Sept. 11, 1779; *Boston Gazette,* Sept. 13, 1779.

9. *Boston Post,* Feb. 19, 1780; *Boston Gazette,* Feb. 21, 1780; Allen, *Naval History,* 2:414–18.

10. Marine Committee to Chew and to John Deshon, June 17, 1777, Marine Committee Letter Book, 93–94, 94–95, NA; Chew to Shaw, Aug. 26, 1777, *NDAR*, 9:820; *Independent Chronicle*, July 10, 1777.

11. Marine Committee to Barry and Burke, May 8, 9, 30, Aug. 24, 28, Sept. 14, 28, 1778, Marine Committee Letter Book, 147–48, 153–54, 173, 174, 175, 179a, NA; *RIHC*, 8:255.

12. Bradford to Hancock, Jan. 27, 1777, Bradford Letter Book, LC; Marine Committee to McNeill, Nov. 12, 1777, Apr. 28, and May 8, 1778, Marine Committee Letter Book, 109, 143, 147, 165, NA; *Massachusetts Spy*, Apr. 30, 1778.

13. Allen, *Naval History*, 1:352–53.

14. Tucker Papers, July 3, 7, 12, 13, Aug. 24, Sept. 15, 1778, HUL; Marine Committee Letter Book, June 10, 19, 1778, 157, 159, NA; *Boston Gazette*, Oct. 5, Nov. 2, 1778; *Boston Post*, Oct. 24, 1778.

15. Marine Committee to Tucker, Apr. 27, to Tucker and Harding, June 2, to Nicholson, June 12, 1779, Marine Committee Letter Book, 211, 218, 219, 221, NA; Tucker Papers, June 28, 1779, HUL; *Boston Gazette*, July 5, 1779; *Boston Post*, May 8, 1779.

16. Marine Committee to Navy Board, Sept. 18, to Nicholson, Sept. 19, 1779, Marine Committee Letter Book, 237, 238, NA; *Boston Post*, Sept. 11, 1779; *Boston Gazette*, Sept. 13, 1779; *Pennsylvania Gazette*, Sept. 22, 1779.

17. Arbuthnot to Germain, May 15, 1780, *Report on the Manuscripts of Mrs. Stopford-Sackville*, 2:162; *Boston Gazette*, July 10, 1780; "Journal of Lieutenant Jennison," *Pennsylvania Magazine of History*, Apr. 1891; Sheppard, *Life of Samuel Tucker*, chapter 7.

18. Sheppard, *Life of Samuel Tucker*, 163.

19. *JCC*, 6:860, 861.

20. "Journal of Hector McNeill," May 21, 1777, MM; Resolves of Massachusetts General Court, Apr. 24, 1777, *NDAR*, 8:416, 885, 1007 n. 2.

21. Cooper to Adams, Apr. 3, 1777, Adams Papers, MassHS.

22. PRO/ADM, 1/471, 118–20.

23. Deposition of Capt. Thomas Hardy, PRO/ADM, 1/471, 118–20; McNeill to Marine Committee, July 16, 1777, McNeill Letter Book, MassHS; PRO/ADM, Courts Martial, 5309.

24. "Journal of Hector McNeill," June 12, 1777, MM; Manley to McNeill, June 27, 1777, *NDAR*, 9:180–81.

25. *London Chronicle*, Aug. 26, 1777; Journal of *Rainbow*, July 6, 7, 8, 1777, and Collier to Stephens, July 12, 1777, PRO/ADM, 51/762 and 1/1611, 26, 61–63; *Boston Gazette*, July 28, Aug. 11, 18, 1777; Conners Journal, July 7, 1777, MM; Crowninshield Journal, July 6, 1777, MassHS; Jennison Diary, July

5, 6, 7, 1777, LC; McNeill to Thompson, July 21, 1777, McNeill Letter Book, MassHS.

26. Bradford to Marine Committee, July 24, 1777, Bradford Letter Book, LC.

27. *Report on the Manuscripts of Mrs. Stopford-Sackville,* 2:70. General Lee had been taken prisoner by the British several months earlier.

28. Marine Committee to McNeill, Nov. 12, 1777, Marine Committee Letter Book, 109, NA.

29. *RIHC,* 9:246, 247; *Massachusetts Spy,* Apr. 30, 1778; Marine Committee Letter Book, Apr. 28, May 8, July 24, 1778, 143, 147, 165, NA.

30. MassArch, 169:367.

31. *Independent Chronicle,* Apr. 15, 1779.

32. Russell Journal (Russell was Manley's clerk), June 19–Oct. 12, 1779, EI; Davis, *Narrative of Joshua Davis,* 4–12; *Independent Chronicle,* Sept. 23, 1779. Accounts also can be found in Allen's *Naval History,* 2:408–11, and Maclay, *History of American Privateers,* 192–204.

33. *Independent Chronicle,* Sept. 26, 1782, Feb. 27, 1783; John Manley's letter is printed in the *Salem Gazette,* Feb. 27, 1783.

34. *Boston Gazette,* Jan. 27, Feb. 3, Mar. 3, 1783; *Salem Gazette,* Feb. 27, 1783.

EPILOGUE

1. Marine Committee to Smith, Storer, Phillips, and agents for Washington's fleet, Mar. 21, 1777, Marine Committee Letter Book, 61–62, NA.

2. Marine Committee to Bradford, Oct. 18, 1776, and Mar. 21, 1777, Marine Committee Letter Book, 35–36, 63, NA.

3. Bradford to Hancock, Apr. 7, 1777, Bradford Letter Book, LC.

4. Bradford to Marine Committee, Apr. 9, 1777, Bradford Letter Book, LC.

5. Marine Committee to Warren, Vernon, and Deshon, June 26, 1777, Marine Committee Letter Book, 98–99, NA; Marine Committee to Navy Board of Eastern Department, July 10, 1777, Vernon Papers, Newport Historical Society.

6. *JCC,* 8:628–29; United States of America in account with William Bartlett, May, 1777, Bartlett Papers, BHS.

7. All correspondence regarding Bradford's travail in settling his accounts is contained in his Letter Book.

8. Petition of officers and mariners of the armed schooner *Franklin,* and report of Agent of Marine, Apr. 23 and May 3, and Congressional Committee report, May 17, 1784, PCC, 5:42, 6:23, 93, 199, 541, NA.

9. Washington to Broughton, Sept. 2, 1775, Fitzpatrick, *Writings of George Washington,* 3:467–69.

10. Journal of *Fowey,* Dec. 5, 1775, PRO/ADM, 51/375.

Bibliography

DOCUMENTS AND MANUSCRIPTS

American Philosophical Society (APS), Philadelphia, Pa.
  Franklin (Benjamin) Papers
Beverly Historical Society (BHS), Beverly, Mass.
  Bartlett (William) Account Book
  Bartlett (William) Papers
  Brown (Capt. Moses) 14th Regiment Papers
  Brown (Capt. Moses) Orderly Book
  Minutes of the Pennsylvania Committee of Safety, September 2, 1775
  Record of Armed Vessels, 1775–1776, MS I, item 5481
British Museum (BM), London
  Graves (Vice Adm. Samuel), *The Conduct of Vice Admiral Samuel Graves in North America in 1774, 1775, and January, 1776*
  Haldimand (Maj. Gen. Frederick) Papers
Chicago Historical Society (CHS), Chicago, Ill.
  Ward (Gen. Artemus) Orderly Book, Joseph Ward Papers
Connecticut Historical Society (ConnHS), Hartford, Conn.
  Deane (Silas) Papers
  Trumbull (Joseph) Papers
Connecticut State Library (ConnSL), Hartford, Conn.
  Trumbull (Jonathan) Papers
  Trumbull (Joseph) Papers
Duke University Library (DUL), Durham, N.C.
  Lord Sandwich Papers
Essex Institute (EI), Salem, Mass.
  Bowen (Ashley) Diary
  Russell (William) Journal
Harvard University Library (HUL), Cambridge, Mass.
  Langdon (John) Papers
  Tucker (Samuel) Papers

Library of Congress (LC), Washington, D.C.
  Bradford (John) Letter Book (2 vols.)
  Continental Congress, Papers of
  Franklin (Benjamin) Papers
  Hancock (John) Papers (2 vols.)
  Jennison (William) Diary
  Marine Committee Letter Book
  Morris (Robert) Papers, Accession 1805
  Smith (Richard) Diary
  Ward (Col. Joseph) Papers, Force Transcripts
  Washington (George) Papers
  Woolsey and Salmon Letter Book
Marblehead Historical Society (MHS), Marblehead, Mass.
  Bowen (Ashley) Day Book
  Glover (John) Colony Ledger
  True Blue Accounts
Mariner's Museum (MM), Newport News, Va.
  Conners (Patrick) Journal
  "Journal of Captain Hector McNeill in Frigate *Boston*, 1777 No. 10"
Massachusetts Archives (MassArch), Boston, Mass.
  Pickering (Timothy) Papers
Massachusetts Historical Society (MassHS), Boston, Mass.
  Adams (John) Papers
  Cleaves (Nathaniel) Diary
  Crowninshield (Benjamin) Journal
  Gay Transcripts
  Dane (Nathan) Papers
  Davis (Joshua) Narrative
  Green (Edward and Joshua) Papers
  Knox (Henry) Papers
  McNeill (Capt. Hector) Letter Book
  Paine (Robert Treat) Papers
  Pickering (Timothy) Papers
  Ward (Artemus) Papers
Massachusetts State Library, Boston, Mass.
  Journals of the Massachusetts House of Representatives, 1775–1783
National Archives (NA), Washington, D.C.
  Continental Congress, Papers of
  Marine Committee Letter Book
  Revolutionary War Prize Cases, Court of Appeals
Newport Historical Society, Newport, N.H.
  Vernon (William) Papers

New York Historical Society (NYHS), New York, N.Y.
Journal of a Voyage of the *Charming Nancy*
New York Public Library (NYPL), New York, N.Y.
Eastern Department Navy Board Letter Book
Emmet Autograph Collection
New York State Library (NYSL), Albany, N.Y.
Journals of the New York Committee of Safety
Pennsylvania Historical Society (PHS), Philadelphia, Pa.
Hancock (John) Papers
Narrative of John Foster Williams, Revolutionary Papers
Pilgrim Society, Plymouth, Mass.
Watson (William) Papers
Public Records Office, London
Admiralty (PRO/ADM)
Colonial Office (PRO/COL)
Rhode Island Historical Society (RIHS), Providence, R.I.
Cooke (Nicholas) Papers
Smithsonian Institute (SI), Washington, D.C.
Don (Walter Fuller) Collection
Stone (Capt. J. G. M.) Collection, Annapolis, Md.
Langdon (John) Letter Book
Yale University Library (YUL), New Haven, Conn.
Lane (William Griswold) Collection
Silliman (Col. Gold Selleck) Papers
Trumbull (Jonathan) Papers
Williams (Jonathan, Jr.) Letter Book

NEWSPAPERS

The Boston Gazette and Country Journal
The Boston Post
Connecticut Courant (Hartford)
Continental Journal (Boston)
Essex Gazette
Essex Journal (Newburyport, Mass.)
The Freeman's Journal (Philadelphia)
Independent Chronicle (Boston)
Independent Ledger (Boston)
London Chronicle

London Evening Post and British Chronicle
The Marblehead Messenger
Massachusetts Gazette
Massachusetts Spy
Morning Post and Daily Advertiser (London)
The New England Chronicle (Cambridge)
New-England Historical and Genealogical Register
New Hampshire Gazette (Portsmouth)
Newport Mercury (Rhode Island)
New York Journal
North American Intelligencer (Philadelphia)
Pennsylvania Evening Post (Philadelphia)
Pennsylvania Gazette (Philadelphia)
Pennsylvania Journal and Weekly Advertiser (Philadelphia)
Pennsylvania Packet (Philadelphia)
Providence (New Hampshire) Gazette
Public Advertiser (London)
Salem Evening News
Salem Gazette
Town's Pennsylvania Evening Post

BOOKS AND ARTICLES

Abbot, William J. *Naval History of the United States.* 2 vols. New York: P. F. Collier, 1886.

Adams, John. *The Works of John Adams.* Vol. 3. Boston: Little, Brown, 1851.

Allen, Gardner W. *A Naval History of the American Revolution.* 2 vols. New York: Russell & Russell, 1962.

Almon, John, ed. *The Remembrancer, or, Impartial Repository of Public Events.* 17 vols. London: Published by the author, 1775–84.

Barnes, G. R., and J. H. Owen, eds. *The Private Papers of John, Earl of Sandwich First Lord of the Admiralty, 1771–1782.* 4 vols. Printed for the Navy Records Society, 1932–38 in vols. 69, 71, 75, and 78.

Beattie, Donald W., and J. Richard Collins. *Washington's New England Fleet.* Salem, Mass.: Newcomb & Gauss Co., 1964.

Billias, George Athan. *General John Glover and His Marblehead Mariners.* New York: Holt, Rinehart & Winston, 1960.

Bouton, Nathaniel, ed. *Provincial Papers: Documents and Records Relating to the Province of New Hampshire from 1764 to 1776.* 7 vols. Concord, N.H.: New Hampshire Legislature, 1867–73.

Bowen, Catherine Drinker. *John Adams and the American Revolution.* New York: Grosset & Dunlap, 1950.

Butterfield, Lyman H., et al., eds. *The Adams Papers.* Series 1, *Diary and Autobiography of John Adams.* 4 vols. Cambridge, Mass.: Belknap Press of Harvard University, 1961.

———. *The Adams Papers.* Series 2, *Adams Family Correspondence.* 2 vols. Cambridge, Mass.: Belknap Press of Harvard University, 1963.

Chapelle, Howard I. *History of American Sailing Ships.* New York: Norton, 1935.

———. *History of the American Sailing Navy.* New York: Norton, 1949.

Charnock, James. *History of Marine Architecture.* London: R. Faulder, 1800–1802.

Claghorn, Charles. *Naval Officers of the American Revolution: A Concise Biographical Dictionary.* Metuchen, N.J.: Scarecrow Press, 1988.

Clark, Thomas. *Naval History of the United States.* Philadelphia: H. Maxwell, 1814.

Clark, William Bell. "American Naval Policy 1775–76." *American Neptune* 1 (January 1941): 26–41.

———. *George Washington's Navy.* Baton Rouge: Louisiana State University Press, 1960.

Clark, William Bell, et al., eds. *Naval Documents of the American Revolution.* Vols. 1–9. Washington, D.C.: Government Printing Office, 1964–86.

Coggins, Jack. *Ships and Seamen of the American Revolution.* Harrisburg, Pa.: Stackpole Press, 1969.

Collections of the Maine Historical Society. Vol. 6. April 1895.

Collections of the Massachusetts Historical Society. Cambridge, Mass., etc.: The Massachusetts Historical Society, 1792–.

Collections of the New York Historical Society. New York: New York Historical Society, 1868–.

Colonial Records of Connecticut for 1775–1776. Hartford: Case, Lockwood, & Brainard Co., 1890.

Davis, Joshua. *Narrative of Joshua Davis.* Boston: The Massachusetts Historical Society, 1811.

Diary of Samuel Richards, Captain of Connecticut Line War of the Revolution, 1775–1781. Philadelphia: Leeds & Biddle Co., 1909.

Essex Institute Historical Collections. Salem, Mass.: The Institute, 1859–.

Fitzpatrick, John C., ed. *The Writings of George Washington.* 39 vols. Washington, D.C.: Government Printing Office, 1931–44.

Force, Peter, ed. *American Archives.* Series 4, 6 vols.; Series 5, 3 vols. Washington, D.C.: M. St. Clair Clarke and Peter Force, 1837–53.

Ford, C. Worthington, comp. *Warren-Adams Letters, Being Chiefly a Correspondence among John Adams, Samuel Adams and James Warren.* 2 vols. Boston: Massachusetts Historical Society, 1917, 1925.

———, ed. *Writings of George Washington.* 14 vols. New York: Putnam Publishers, 1889–93.

Ford, C. Worthington, et al., eds. *Journals of the Continental Congress, 1774–1789.* 34 vols. Washington: Government Printing Office, 1904–37.

French, Allen. *First Year of the American Revolution.* Boston: Houghton Mifflin, 1934.

Frothingham, Thomas G. "The Services of Marblehead to the United States Navy." United States Naval Institute *Proceedings* 52, no. 12 (December 1926): 2416–29.

Greenwood, Isaac J. *Captain John Manley.* Boston: C. E. Goodspeed, 1915.

Hansard, Thomas C., ed. *The Parliamentary History of England, from the Earliest Period to the Year 1803.* 36 vols. London: T. C. Hansard, 1806–20.

Haywood, Charles F. *Minutemen and Mariners.* New York: Dodd, Mead & Co., 1963.

Hays, I. Minis, ed. *Calendar of the Papers of Benjamin Franklin in the Library of the American Philosophical Society.* 5 vols. Philadelphia: American Philospohical Society, 1906–8.

Hoadly, Charles J., ed. *The Public Records of the State of Connecticut . . . with the Journal of the Council of Safety, 1776–1781.* 3 vols. Hartford: Case, Lockwood, & Brainard Co., 1894–1922.

Hoadly, Charles J., et al., eds. *The Public Records of the Colony of Connecticut, 1636–1776.* 15 vols. Hartford: Case, Lockwood, & Brainard Co., 1850–1890.

Holyoke, Edward A., "Familiar Letters." In *Essex Institute Historical Collections.* Vol. 13. Salem, Mass.: The Institute, 1877.

Howe, Octavius T. *Beverly Privateers in the American Revolution.* Boston: Colonial Society of Massachusetts, 1923.

Innes, Harold A., et al., eds. *The Diary of Simeon Perkins 1766–1796.* 3 vols. Toronto: The Champlain Society, 1948–61.

James, W. M. *The British Navy in Adversity.* London: Longman's, Green & Co., 1926.

"Journal of Private Phineas Ingalls." *Essex Institute Historical Collections.* Vol. 53. Salem, Mass.: The Institute, 1917.

Lincoln, William. *Journals of Each Provincial Congress of Massachusetts.* Boston: Dutton & Wentworth, 1838.

Maclay, Edgar S. *A History of American Privateers.* New York: D. Appleton, 1899.

————. *History of the United States Navy.* 2 vols. New York: D. Appleton, 1894.

The Magazine of History, with Notes and Queries. 26 vols. New York: W. Abbatt, 1905–22.

Mahan, A. T. *The Influence of Sea Power upon History.* Boston: Little, Brown, 1902.

Martyn, Charles. *The Life of Artemas Ward.* New York: Artemus Ward, 1921.

Massachusetts Soldiers and Sailors of the Revolutionary War. 17 vols. Boston: Wright & Potter Printing Company, 1896–1908.

Miller, Nathan. *Sea of Glory—The Continental Navy Fights for Independence, 1775–1783.* New York: David McKay, 1974.

Morgan, William James. *Captains to the Northward: The New England Captains in the Continental Navy.* Barre, Mass.: Barre Gazette, 1959.

Neeser, Robert Wilden, ed. *The Despatches of Molyneux Shuldham, Vice Admiral of the Blue and Commander-in-Chief of His Britannic Majesty's Ships in North America, January–July 1776.* New York: Naval History Society, 1913.

New-England Historical and Genealogical Register. Boston: S. G. Drake, 1847–.

Newell, Timothy, "A Journal Kept During the Time Boston Was Shut Up in 1775–1776." In *Collections of the Massachusetts Historical Society,* 4:269–80. Boston: Metcalf & Co., 1852.

Papers of William Vernon and the Navy Board. Newport: Rhode Island Historical Society, 1901.

Paullin, Charles O. *Navy of the American Revolution.* 2 vols. Cleveland: Burrows Brothers, 1906.

————, ed., *Out-Letters of the Continental Marine Committee and Board of Admiralty, August 1776–September 1780.* 2 vols. New York: Naval History Society, 1914.

Peabody, Robert, "The Naval Career of Captain John Manley of Marblehead." *Essex Institute Historical Collection* 45, no. 1 (January 1909): 1–27.

Potter, Israel R. *Life and Remarkable Adventures of Israel R. Potter (A Native of Cranston, Rhode-Island,) Who Was a Soldier in the American Revolution.* Providence: Printed by J. Howard for I. R. Potter, 1824.

Proceedings of the Massachusetts Historical Society [Series 1, 1791–1883]. 29 vols. Boston: Massachusetts Historical Society, 1879–84.

Publications of the Rhode Island Historical Society. Vol. 8. Providence: Rhode Island Historical Society, 1900.

Reed, William B. *Life and Correspondence of Joseph Reed, Military Secretary of Washington, at Cambridge; Adjutant-General of the Continental Army.* 2 vols. Philadelphia: Lindsay & Blakiston, 1847.

The Report on the Manuscripts of Mrs. Stopford-Sackville, of Drayton House, Northamptonshire. 2 vols. London: His Majesty's Stationery Office, 1904–1910.

Rhode Island Historical Collections. 8 vols. Providence: The Society, 1827–92.

Roads, Samuel. History and Traditions of Marblehead. Boston: Houghton, Osgood & Co., 1880.

Robinson, C. N. The British Fleet. London: George Bell & Sons, 1894.

Sanborn, Nathan P., Gen. John Glover and His Marblehead Regiment in the Revolutionary War. Marblehead, Mass.: Marblehead Historical Society, 1903.

Sheppard, John H. The Life of Samuel Tucker: Commodore in the American Revolution. Boston: A. Mudge & Son, 1868.

Shuldham, Molyneux. The Dispatches of Molyneux Shuldham, Vice Admiral of the Blue. New York: Naval Historical Society, 1913.

Sparks, Jared. Correspondence of the American Revolution, Being Letters of Eminent Men to George Washington. 4 vols. Boston: Little, Brown, 1853.

Staples, W. R. Annals of Providence. Providence: A. C. Greene & Brothers, 1843.

Stone, Edwin M. History of Beverly, Civil and Ecclesiastical, from Its Settlement in 1630 to 1842. Boston: James Munroe & Co., 1843.

Syrett, David. Shipping and the American War, 1775–83: A Study of British Transport Organization. London: University of London, 1970.

Tilley, John A. The British Navy and the American Revolution. Columbia: University of South Carolina Press, 1987.

Trumbull, J. H., and Charles J. Hoadly, eds. The Public Records of the Colony of Connecticut, 1636–1776. 15 vols. Hartford: Case, Lockwood, & Brainard Co., 1850–90.

Underhill, H. A. Sailing Ship Rigs and Rigging. Glasgow: Brown, Son & Ferguson Ltd., 1938.

Waite, Henry E., comp. Extracts, Relating to the Origin of the American Navy. Boston: New England Historical Genealogical Society, 1890.

Washington, George. Writings of George Washington. 12 vols. Edited by Jared Sparks. Boston: Charles C. Little & James Brown, 1834–37.

Webb, J. Watson. Reminiscences of Gen'l Samuel B. Webb of the Revolutionary Army, by His Son, J. Watson Webb. New York: Globe Stationery & Printing Co., 1882.

Winsor, Justin. Narrative and Critical History of the United States. 8 vols. Boston and New York: Houghton Mifflin & Co., 1884–89.

Index

(Italicized numbers indicate where an illustration of the subject is found.)

Aborn, James, 33, 43
Active (Sims), 224
Adams, Abigail, 168, 187
Adams, Daniel, 49–52, 58
Adams, John, 7, 26, 211, 226, 229
Adams, John (*Lynch*), 211–13
Adams, John Quincy, 226
Adams, Robert (*Little Hannah*), 101
Adams, Winborn, 82, 126; captures
    Rainbow, 110; captures *Sally*, 111–12,
    156; captures unnamed sloop, 109;
    commands *Warren*, 82–85, 238; cruise
    of, 92, 109–13
Addiscot, William, 218–19
Adventurer, prize brig, 232
Air, Capt. (*Clementina*), 35
Allen, Ethan, 71, 73, 77–78
Allen, John, 121
America, privateer (Coit), 69
Anderson, James, 99–100, 216
Annabella, brig (Walter), 181–86
Anne, transport (Dennison), 176–78
Arnold, Benedict, 26, 31, 33, 36
Atkinson, John, 104
Ayres, John: captures *Annabella* and
    George, 181–86; captures *Anne*,
    176–78; and cruise of *Lynch*, 122–23,
    142–43, 145, 174–75, 187, 192, 195,
    196–98, 202, 205–6, 208, 210–11, 213,
    222, 238; and flight from *Unicorn*,
    197–98

Baille, prize ship, 233
Banks, Francis (*Renown*), 146, 160, 161,
    165–67, 168, 175, 179–81, 185
Barberie, Peter, 111–12, 156
Barnes, Corbin (*Yankee*), 133

Barry, John, 1, 226
Bartlett, Nicholas, 160
Bartlett, William, 29, 50, 158, 186, 193;
    money problems of, 139–40, 151, 155;
    prize accounts of, 200–201, 205–6,
    236; and problems with prizes, 34, 43,
    90–91, 100–104; questions retaining
    Warren, 111, 113; refits fleet, 116,
    119–20, 122–23, 148, 157
Basden, Robert (*Sally*), 111
Bellew, Henry (*Liverpool*), 194–95
Betsey, sloop: captured by *Lee*, 195–96
Betsey, sloop (Atkinson), 104–5, 106, 156
Betsey, sloop (Horrick), 216–17
Beverly, Mass., 8–9, 15, 18, 30, 42, 47,
    80–85, 89–90, 120, 122–23; damaged
    by *Nautilus*, 21–24
Biddecombe, John (*Industrious Bee*), 218
Bishop, Thomas (*Lively*), 15, 71
Bog, Archibald (*George*), 181–86
Boston, Continental frigate, 132, 208–9,
    218; commanded by McNeill, 228–31;
    commanded by Tucker, 226–28
Boston, Mass., 1, 2, 5–7, 11, 64, *81;* action
    off, 88–93, 99, 101, 111, 127–29, 147,
    161–65, 175–77, 179–81
Boston Gazette, 201
Bourmaster, John, 63
Bowen, Ephraim, Jr.: fits out *Harrison* and
    Washington, 49–54, 58, 60–61, 72, 88
Bradford, John, 77, 120, 158, 178–79,
    185–87, 198, 201–3, 206–7, 208–14,
    216–22, 224, 225–26, 231; administra-
    tive problems of, 189–91, 193–97, 215;
    appointed agent, 170–73; distrust of,
    204–6; prize accounts of, 199–201,
    235–37, 239
Bradstreet, Lyonel (*Nelly Frigate*), 193

Brinton, Thomas (*Triton*), 202
Brisbane, John (*Flora*), 175, 230
Britannia, sloop (Hall), 65
Bromedge, Hugh (HM sloop *Savage*), 15
Broughton, Nicholson, 10–14, 50, 61; as acting commodore, 30–31; attacked by *Nautilus*, 22–24; captures *Kingston Packet*, 42; captures *Phoebe*, 33–34; captures *Prince William*, 33; captures *Speedwell*, 35; captures *Unity*, 16–18, 237; captures *Warren*, 35; commands *Hancock*, 80, 222; commands *Hannah*, 10–11, 15–25; dismissed by Washington, 46, 113; grubs for prize money, 18, 116; at Gut of Canso, 32–35; raids Charlottetown, 36–41; sailing orders of, 11–13, 31–32
Browne, John (*Industry*), 217
Brush, Crean, 149–51
Budd, John, 38–39
Buddington, ——, 35, 45
Bunker Hill, Mass., 2, 48, 106
Burke, William: captured by *Liverpool*, 195, 207; captures *Annabella* and *George*, 181–86; captures *Anne*, 176–77; commands *Warren*, 117–18, 148, 151, 174–75, 208, 210–11, 213–14, 222, 238; in Continental Navy, 225–26; and fight with *Unity*, 191–92
Burr, John (*Milford*), 151, 180
Butler, Francis (*Industry*), 27

Cabot, Stephen, 102
Callbeck, ——, Mrs., 39
Callbeck, Philip, 37–42, 44–47
Campbell, Archibald, 181–85
Campbell, John (*Union*), 224
Campbell, Lawrence, 185
Canceaux, HMS, 86
Cape Ann, Mass., 15, 17, 27, 47, 66, 70, 84, 89, 95–96, 109–11, 116–17, 143–44, 174–75, 225
Capling, brig (Coulrick), 217
Carter, John (*Lively*), 219
Centaur, guardship, 75
Centurion, HMS, 129, 132, 149
Cerberus, HMS (Symons), 88, 92–93
Champion, Henry, 60–61, 64
Charles, brig (Tapley), 216–17
Charleston, HMS (formerly *Boston*), 228

Charlottetown, Island of St. John, 35–37, 41
Charming Nancy, transport, 86
Charming Peggy, 190
Chatham, HMS (Shuldham), 107, 129, 149
Chevalier, Capt. (*Unity*), 35–36
Chew, Samuel, 225
Childs, James, 61, 71, 76–77
Clark, William Bell, 46
Clementina (Air), 35
Clinton, Sir Henry, 223
Cochran, John, 137
Coffin, Charles (*Industry*), 59, 60
Coit, William, 49, 52, 123–24, 222, 238; captures *Industry* and *Polly*, 59–60; captures *Thomas*, 66–67; captures unnamed schooner, 67; commands *Harrison*, 55–69, 88; dismissed, 68–69
Collier, Sir George (*Rainbow*), 229–30
Collins, Daniel (*Hawke*), 216
Collins, John (HMS *Nautilus*), 21; attacks *Hannah*, 21–25
Concord, ship (Lowrie), 99–101, 119, 121, 156, 200
Confederacy (Harding), 227
Continental Army, 1, 2, 3, 26; Colony Train, 179–88; 14th Regiment, 7, 30. *See also* Glover's regiment
Continental Congress, 1, 77, 187, 203; commissions schooner captains, 210; and concern for South, 105, 236; and Declaration of Independence, 189; and dispute over *Hope*, 170–73; elects Washington commander in chief, 5; names Manley captain, 157–58; policy of, on admiralty courts, 61, 89, 97, 100–101, 112, 116; ——, on George III, 11; ——, on gunpowder, 26–27; ——, on navy, 3, 129; ——, on prisoner exchanges, 78; ——, on privateers, 12–13; ——, on prize money, 155–56
Continental Navy, 1, 3, 118, 206–8, 210–11, 219, 228–29, 237, 238–39
Cooke, Nicholas, 43, 53, 72
Cooper, Samuel, 229
Cooper, Sir Grey, 95
Corey, Frances (*Speedwell*), 35
Coulrick, John (*Capling*), 217
Crafts, Thomas, 179
Cumberland, privateer (Manley), 231
Cummings, James (*Jenny*), 220

Cunningham, Joseph, 165–68
Cushing, Nathan, 117, 156
Cushing, Thomas, 169–70

Dartmouth, Lord, 95
Davis, Benjamin, 190
Davis, Joshua, 233
Dawson, George (*Hope*), 72, 130–33, 143, 145–46, 163, 179
Deane, Silas, 211–12, 226
Deane, William, 104
Deane, Continental frigate, 227, 233
Defence, armed brig (Harding), 182–86
Dennis, William, 221
Dennison, John (*Anne*), 176–77
Denny, John (*Warren*), 34–35, 45
Derby, John, 83, 119, 121
Derby, Richard, 42, 44–45, 66–67, 119
Devereaux, John, 10, 33
Diamond, John, 121
Diamond, HMS, 219
Dickson, Archibald (*Greyhound*), 76, 162, 165
Diligent, HM brig, 147
Dispatch, 158
Doak, Benjamin, 34
Dolphin, brig, 27
Dolphin, brig (Shields), 220, 237
Dorchester Heights, 140–41
Doten, Thomas, 124
Douglas, Sir James, 75
Downey, Jeremiah, 67
Dunmore, Lord, 104–5
Dyar, Charles: commands *Harrison,* 124–25, 132–34

Edwards, Thomas (*Elizabeth*), 201
Eliza, schooner (*Franklin*), 29
Elizabeth, brig (Edwards), 201–2
Elizabeth, brig (Ramsey), 148–51, 154, 156, 194, 199
Empress of Russia (Bourmaster), 63
Endeavor, schooner. See *Washington*
Erving, George, 51
Experiment, HMS (Scott), 166, 168–69

Fellows, Gustavus, 157
Fettyplace, Edward, 82, 120, 135, 157
Fisheries Bill, 9
Flagg, —— (*Unity*), 17, 18
Flora, HMS (Brisbane), 175, 190, 218, 230

Ford, John (*Unicorn*), 197
Fort Amherst, 37
Foster, Robert (*Jenny*), 101, 102
Fotheringham, Patrick (*Fox*), 229
Foudroyant, HMS (Jervis), 213
Fowey, HMS (Montagu), 71–72, 75, 77, 86–87, 116, 120–22, 136–38, 142–43, 146, 238
Fox, HMS (Fotheringham), 229
Franklin, Benjamin, 26, 48, 211–12
Franklin, armed schooner: British attack on, 166–69; captures *Annabella* and *George,* 181–86; captures *Henry and Esther,* 136; captures *Hope,* 163–64; captures *Lively,* 202–3; captures *Mary,* 33; captures *Nelly Frigate,* 193; captures *Peggy,* 190–91; captures *Perkins,* 192; captures *Rainbow,* 135; captures *Triton,* 202; commanded by Mugford, 161, 174–75; commanded by Selman, 29–47, 80; commanded by Skimmer, 194, 201, 202; commanded by Tucker, 135–38, 143, 148, 151, 157; decommissioned, 206, 208
Frazer, John (*Susannah*), 144
Frazer, Simon, 175
Friendship, schooner, 223
Fulton, James (*Jane*), 161

Gage, Thomas, 1–2, 6, 49, 102, 106, 107
Gale, Benjamin, 137
Gates, Horatio, 93
Gefferina, George, 106
General Gage, HM sloop, 128–32
General Gates, armed brig: commanded by Skimmer, 220–21; commanded by Waters, 223–24
General Greene (Burke), 226
General Leslie, schooner, 223
George, ship (Bog), 181–86
George III, 1, 3, 7, 26, 94, 115, 147, 191; declaration of, 114; and *Proclamation,* 90
Germain, Lord George, 74, 150, 231
Gill, John, 121, 157
Glasgow, HMS, 158, 190
Glasgow Journal, 177
Glencairn, prize ship, 228
Gloucester, Mass., 15, 35, 71, 145–47; and Committee of Safety, 17–18, 20, 117, 238; and *Hannah*'s mutiny, 20–21; and protection of *Nancy,* 93–94

Glover, Daniel, 123
Glover, Hannah, 8
Glover, John, 7–8, *8*, 9–10, 13, 14, 44, 49, 104, 169; and capture of *Nancy,* 94; enlists new crews, 117–18, 120–21; fits out *Franklin* and *Hancock,* 29–31; fits out *Hannah,* 11, 14; fits out *Lee* and *Warren,* 48, 59, 80–85; inspects *Dolphin* and *Industry,* 27–28; and prize money, 155–56; selects agents, 29
Glover, John, Jr.: on *Hannah,* 10, 17; on *Lee,* 83, 89
Glover, Jonathan, 102–3, 138, 175, 186, 190–91, 193, 218; accounts of, 199–201, 235–36; as agent, 29, 50, 82, 91; and *Anne,* 177; and *Concord,* 100; and *Hope,* 164–65, 170–72; and *Jane,* 160; prize problems of, 150; and *Ranger,* 89; and *Sally,* 112; and *William,* 161
Glover's regiment, 21st Massachusetts, 7, 10; absent without leave, 14; expects prize money, 18–19; and mutiny on *Hannah,* 19–21; recruited for *Hancock* and *Franklin,* 30
Governor Tryon (Stebbins), 224–25
Graeme, Alexander (*Mercury*), 64, 86
Grant, Thomas, 29, 208
Graves, Thomas, 6, 21, 24, 63, 67; recalled, 105–8, 121, 126, 148; and search for *Nancy,* 86–87, 92, 95–99; on *Washington*'s capture, 71–73
Greene, Jacob, 35, 43
Greene, Nathaniel, 43
Gregory, Joseph, 35
Grendal, Jonathan (*Norfolk*), 127, 132
Greyhound, HMS (Dickson), 76, 162, 165
Groves, William, 20
Gulf of St. Lawrence, 31, 32, 34, 43
Gut of Canso, 32–36, 37, 40

Hague, 233. See also *Deane*
Halifax, Nova Scotia, 20, 32, 46, 76–77, 109, 148, 180
Halifax, HM schooner, 129
Hall, James (*Happy Return*), 127, 132
Hall, Joseph (*Britannia*), 65
Hammet, Lucy, 56, 73
Hancock, Ebenezer, 200
Hancock, John, 27, 28, 43, 46, 61, 77, 89, 90, 104, 110, 170–73, 178–79, 187, 193–94, 196, 200–201, 203, 209, 211, 215, 218, 235–36
Hancock, Continental frigate (Manley), 132, 158, 207–10, 218, 225, 228–31
Hancock, schooner: captures *Elizabeth,* 149–50; captures *Happy Return,* 127; captures *Jane,* 161; captures *Kingston Packet,* 42; captures *Lively* (Higgins), 41; captures *Lively* (Martindale), 202–3; captures *Lord Howe,* 185–86; captures *Nelly Frigate,* 193; captures *Norfolk,* 127; captures *Peggy,* 190–91; captures *Perkins,* 192; captures *Phoebe,* 33–34; captures *Prince William,* 33; captures *Speedwell,* 35; captures *Stakesby,* 145; captures *Susannah,* 144; captures *Triton,* 202; captures *William,* 161; commanded by Broughton, 29–47; commanded by Manley, 126–34, 143, 146, 148, 155, 156–57; commanded by Tucker, 160, 175, 177–79, 194, 201, 202; decommissioned, 206, 208; fitted out for Broughton, 29–31, 80; refit of, 116–17, 120; size and specifications of, 32
Hannah, schooner, 8, 13, *19,* 26, 139; attacked, 22–25; captures *Unity,* 17; decommissioned, 29, 82; fitted out, 10, 14–15; mutiny on, 19–21
Happy Return, ship (Hall), 127, 129, 132, 156
Harding, Seth: commands *Defence,* 182–87, 190; commands *Confederacy,* 227
Hardy, Thomas (*Patty*), 229
Harris, Josiah, 166–68
Harrison, Benjamin, 48
Harrison, Robert Hanson, 101
Harrison, armed schooner, 73; and Coit's cruise, 58–59, 88; and Dyar's cruise, 132–34; fitted out, 48–57, 123–25, 130; laid up, 113, 133–34; mutiny on, 61
Hart, Richard, 150
Hatch, Jabez, 60
Hawk, privateer (Oakes), 220–21
Hawk, schooner. See *Warren*
Hawke, schooner (Collins), 216
Hawkins, James (*Phoebe*), 33–34
Hazard, brig (Williams), 224, 232
Heath, William, 213
Henry (Burke), 226

Henry and Esther, brig (Nellis), 136, 138, 156
Herrick, Henry, 22–23
Hibbert, Jeremiah, 162
Hickman, Martha, 80
Higgins, ——— (*Lively*), 41
Hills, Stephen, 229
Hinchinbrook, HMS, 64, 86
Hind, HMS, 228
Homan, Edward, 33
Hooper, William, 217
Hope, HM sloop (Dawson), 129–33, 142–47, 163–65, 175, 178–80
Hope, ship (Lumsdale), 162–65, 169–72, 174
Hopkins, Esek, 53, 118, 158–59, 194
Horrick, Nathaniel (*Betsey*), 216
Howe, Lord Richard, 78, 185–86, 189, 194, 217
Howe, Sir William, 49, 59–60, 71, 78, 104, 107, 113, 138, 185; evacuates Boston, 140–41, 146–47, 150, 152, 175, 237; at New York, 188, 189, 190, 220, 225; and search for *Nancy,* 86, 95–97
Howland, Consider, 61, 76–78
Hunter, Robert (*Nancy*), 92–93, 97
Hutcheson, Francis, 132, 149
Hutchinson, Thomas, 97
Hyndman, Michael (*Victor*), 230

Industrious Bee (Biddecombe), 218–19, 220
Industry, brig (Browne), 217
Industry, schooner (Butler), 27
Industry, schooner (Coffin), 59, 61, 156
Ingalls, Eleazer, 151
Ingersoll, Samuel (*Kingston Packet*), 42
Intolerable Acts of 1774, 9

Jackson, Samuel, 77
Jackson, William, 150–51
James, Richard, 11
Jane, brig (Fulton), 161
Jason, ship (Manley), 232–33
Jenkins, William (*Perkins*), 192
Jenny, ship (Cummings), 220
Jenny, ship (Foster), 101, 106, 139, 156, 157–58, 200, 239
Jervis, John (*Foudroyant*), 213
Jones, John Paul, 1, 227
Jones, Phineas, 150–51

Juno, brig, 86
Jupiter, transport, 65

Katy, Rhode Island armed sloop, 26
Kennedy, James (*Peggy*), 190–91
Kerr, John, 223
Kingston Packet, brig (Ingersoll), 42, 44
Kirkland, Moses, 104–5
Kissick, William, 121

Lady Washington (Cunningham), 165–68
Langdon, John, 17, 18, 20, 21, 209
Lee, Arthur, 211, 212
Lee, Charles, 48, 231
Lee, Jeremiah, 9, 121
Lee, John, 121–22
Lee, Richard Henry, 48
Lee, armed schooner, 48, 59, 73, 81–83, 110, 111, 143, 148–49, 157, 174–75, 194, 201, 206–8, 210, 214–15, 220, 238–39; captures *Annabella,* 181–86; captures *Betsey* (Atkinson), 104–6; captures *Betsey* (Horrick), 216; captures *Betsey* (Waters), 195–96; captures *Capling,* 217; captures *Charles,* 217; captures *Concord,* 99–100; captures *Dolphin,* 220; captures *Elizabeth,* 201–2; captures *George,* 181–86; captures *Hawke,* 216; captures *Industrious Bee,* 218–19; captures *Jenny,* 101; captures *Little Hannah,* 101–2; captures *Lively,* 219; captures *Nancy,* 92–95; captures *Polly,* 92; captures *Rainbow,* 135–36; captures *Ranger,* 89; captures *Sally,* 197; captures *Two Sisters,* 89–90; refit of, 116, 119–21
Lewis, John, 42, 44
Lewis, Thomas, 121
Linzee, Robert (*Surprize*), 233
Little Hannah, brig (Adams), 101–3, 106, 139, 156–58
Lively, brig (Carter), 219
Lively, brig (Martindale), 202–6, 208, 210
Lively, HMS (Bishop), 15, 20, 71–72, 91, 129, 146, 160, 174
Lively, schooner (Higgins), 41, 45
Live Oak, privateer (Tucker), 228
Liverpool, HMS (Bellew), 194–95
Livingston, Abraham, 203–4
London Chronicle, 35, 74
Lord Howe, ship (Park), 185–86, 190
Loring, John, 78

Lowrie, James, 99
Lumsdale, Alexander (*Hope*), 162–63, 165
Lynch, Thomas, 48, 121
Lynch, armed schooner: arming of,
    121–25; commanded by Adams,
    211–14; commanded by Ayres, 48,
    206–10, 215; cruise of, 142–43, 148,
    149, 157, 174–75, 194–95; and flight
    from *Unicorn,* 197, 198

Manley, John, 59, 80–81, 108, 112–13,
    115, 116, 209; captures *Betsey,* 104–5;
    captures *Concord,* 99–101; captures
    Elizabeth, 148–49; captures *Happy
    Return,* 127; captures *Jenny,* 101–2;
    captures *Little Hannah,* 101–2; cap-
    tures *Nancy,* 91–93, 97–98, 110; cap-
    tures *Norfolk,* 127; captures *Polly,* 92;
    captures *Ranger,* 89; captures *Stakesby,*
    145; captures *Susannah,* 144; captures
    Two Sisters, 89–90; captures unnamed
    schooner, 91; commands *Hancock,* 118,
    120, 141, 142–43, 147–48, 151, 152,
    221, 238; commands *Lee,* 81–85, 87;
    fights *Hope,* 143, 145; joins
    Continental Navy, 157–58, 207, 218,
    228–34, 239; named commodore, 125;
    and problems with prize money,
    154–56
Manvide, John, 62, 65–66, 75
Marblehead, Mass., 3, 7–8, 9, 15, 21, 27,
    33, 47, 80, 95–96, 111, 169; and
    Committee of Safety, 27
Marine Committee, 118, 158, 171, 194,
    196, 199–202, 204, 205, 209–13, 215,
    220, 223–24, 226–28, 231, 235–36,
    238–39
Marston, Benjamin (*Polly*), 221
Martha, prize ship, 227
Martindale, Nicholas (*Lively*), 202, 206
Martindale, Sion, 49, 88; captured by
    Fowey, 71–72, 116; captures *Britannia,*
    65; cruise of, 62–66, 70–79, 238;
    delays sailing, 59, 62; dislikes
    Washington, 51–53, 54–56; imprisoned,
    72–77
Mary, schooner (Thomas Russell), 33, 43
Mason, Christopher (*Nautilus*), 126–27
Massachusetts, 21st Regiment. *See*
    Glover's regiment
Massachusetts Bay, *16*

Massachusetts Provincial Congress
    (Council), 150–51; offers Washington
    ships, 27, 28; and privateering, 12, 45,
    118
Matthews, Thomas, 104–5
Maxwell, John, 176–77
Mayflower, transport, 178
Mayo, Simeon, 217–18
McGlathry, William (*Ranger*), 88–89
McMonagle, John (*Rainbow*), 110
McNeill, Hector (*Boston*), 228–31
Medows, Edward (*Tartar*), 62–63, 73
Mellish, prize, 203, 206
Menzies, ——, 181, 184–85
Mercury, HMS (Graeme), 64, 86, 93
Merlin, HMS, 9
Mermaid, HMS, 217
Milford, HMS (Burr), 151, 174–75, 177,
    179–80, 194–95, 228–29
M'Intosh, Aeneas, 178
M'Kenzie, George, 181–83
Montagu, George (*Fowey*), 71, 74, 121,
    122, 137–38
Montagu, John, 74
Montague, brig (Nelson), 221, 223
Morgan, —— (*Unity*), 191–92
Morgan, Mrs. John, 93
Morris, Robert, 118, 158, 194, 201,
    205–6, 211, 215, 219, 222
Moylan, Stephen, 29, 44, 48–49, 54, 56,
    100, 102–3, 110; background of, 28;
    and opinion of Coit, 60–61, 79; and
    opinion of Manley, 79, 99, 108; and
    opinion of Martindale, 79; and prob-
    lems with agents, 90–92, 139; refits
    fleet, 30, 66–67, 80–85, 115, 116,
    119–21, 123–24
Mugford, James, Jr., 120, *162,* 174, 222,
    238–39; captures *Hope,* 162–69; com-
    mands *Franklin,* 161–68; killed,
    167–69, 234

Nancy, brig, 221
Nancy, brig (Hunter), 86, 92–98, 99, 110,
    119, 155–56, 157, 200, 228, 238
Nantasket Road, 3, 6, 21, 127, 180
Nautilus, HMS (Collins), 21, 29, 64;
    attacks *Hannah,* 21–25; and blockade,
    126–27, 142, 143; casualties on, 24–25;
    and search for *Nancy,* 86, 95
Navy Board of Eastern Dept., 220,
    223–24, 236

Nellis, —— (*Henry and Esther*), 136–37
Nelly Frigate, ship (Bradstreet), 193, 199
Nelson, William (*Montague*), 221
Newell, David, 24
New England Chronicle, 24, 132, 169
Nicholson, James, 228
Niger, HMS, 111, 146, 149
Noble, Joseph (*Sally*), 197
Norfolk, ship (Grendal), 127, 156

Oakes, Jonathan (*Hawk*), 220
Oliver, Peter, Jr., 97
Oliver Cromwell (Coit), 68
Ostrich, 75
Otis, James, 151
Otter, HM sloop, 104

Palfrey, William, 93–94
Palliser, Sir Hugh, 74
Park, Robert (*Lord Howe*), 185–86
Parker, Hyde, Jr. (*Phoenix*), 63, 85–86
Parliament, acts of, 9
Patterson, Walter, 37–38
Patty, brig (Hardy), 229
Peabody, Robert E., 80
Peggy, ship (Kennedy), 190–92, 236–38
Perkins, Samuel (*Rainbow*), 135–37
Perkins, Simeon, 36
Perkins, brig (Jenkins), 192
Peter, brig, 77
Phillips, William, 235
Phoebe, sloop (Hawkins): captured by
    Hancock, 33–34, 43
Phoenix, HMS (Parker), 63, 85
Pickering, John, 44
Pickering, Thomas, Jr., 112, 117
Pickering, Timothy, Jr., 156, 161, 165,
    171
Pliarne, Penet and Co., 212–13
Plymouth, Mass., 29, 49–57, 61–62, 123;
    attack on, 147–48; Committee of
    Correspondence, 50–52, 57
Pole, British privateer, 227
Polly, schooner (Marston), 221
Polly, sloop (Smith), 92, 156
Polly, sloop (White), 59, 156
Pomona, HMS: captures Manley, 231
Poor, Enoch, 111
Porter, Oliver, 104
Portsmouth, England, 74
Portsmouth, N.H., 17, 42, 47, 82, 85, 109,
    209, 227

Potter, Israel, 73–47, 76
Potter, Simeon, 53–54
Preston, HMS, 108, 129
Price, Ezekiel, 72
Price, Richard (*William*), 161
Prince William, schooner (Standley), 33,
    43
Providence, R.I., 51, 52–54
Providence, armed sloop (Rathbun), 223
Providence, Continental frigate, 225,
    227–28
Public Advertiser (London), 76, 106, 177

Quebec City, 26–27, 31, 32, 71

Rainbow, HMS (Collier), 218, 229–31
Rainbow, sloop (McMonagle), 110
Rainbow, sloop (Perkins), 135–38, 238
Raleigh, Continental frigate, 132, 209, 226
Ramsey, Peter (*Elizabeth*), 151–53
Ranger, Continental frigate, 209, 227–28
Ranger, sloop (McGlathry), 88–89
Raven, HM sloop (Stanhope), 63–64
Reed, Joseph, 11, 28, 32, 48–53, 58–59,
    83, 100; criticizes Glover, 29–30
Renown, HMS (Banks), 129, 146, 163,
    166–68, 179–81, 190
Resistance, armed brig (Burke), 225–26
Revere, Paul, 90
Richards, Samuel, 140
Robbins, Robert (*Two Sisters*), 89–91
Robenson, John (*Thomas*), 220
Robinson, William, 104–5
Roche, John, 121–22, 209
Rowe, John, 143
Royal Army Regiments: King's Own, 150;
    42nd Royal Highlanders, 175; 71st
    Grenadiers, 185; 71st Royal
    Highlanders, 175, 181
Royal Oak, HMS, 75
Russell, John. *See* Manley, John
Russell, Thomas (*Franklin*), 162, 167, 169
Russell, Thomas (*Mary*), 33
Rust, Enoch, 33
Ryan, William, 121, 157

Salem, Mass., 7–8, 23–24, 47; and
    Committee of Safety, 44, 89, 138
Sally, schooner (Noble), 197
Sally, sloop (Basden), 111–12, 156
Salter, Francis, 120, 157
Sandwich, Earl of, 74, 96–97, 107

Sandwich, prize packet, 228
Sargent, Winthrop, 117, 136–37, 146,
    148, 199, 236
Savage, HM sloop, 147
Scott, Alexander (*Experiment*), 168
Searle, Joseph, 19–20
Selman, Archibald, 29, 208
Selman, John: captures *Mary,* 33; captures
    Warren, 34; and Charlottetown raid,
    36–40; commands *Franklin,* 30–31,
    32–46, 80, 237; dismissed, 46, 112–13;
    Washington's sailing orders to, 31–32
Sever, Sarah, 147–48
Sewell, Jonathan, 108
Shields, James (*Dolphin*), 220
Shuldham, Molyneux, 46–47, 87; evacu-
    ates Boston, 140–41, 143–44, 145–46,
    148, 152, 154, 160, 163, 165, 185,
    189–90; replaces Graves, 107–8, 113,
    121, 126, 138
Sibles, George, 128
Sims, William (*Active*), 224
Sir William Erskine (Hamilton), 224–25
Skimmer, John: captures *Annabella,*
    181–85; captures *Betsey,* 216; captures
    Capling, 217; captures *Charles,* 216–17;
    captures *Dolphin,* 220, 237; captures
    George, 181–85; captures *Hawke,* 216;
    captures *Industrious Bee,* 218–19; cap-
    tures *Industry,* 217; captures *Lively*
    (Carter), 219; captures *Lively*
    (Martindale), 202–3; captures *Nelly
    Frigate,* 193–94; captures *Peggy,*
    190–92; captures *Perkins,* 192; captures
    Triton, 202; commands *Franklin,*
    177–78, 196, 198, 201, 202, 205–7,
    208; commands *Lee,* 210, 213, 214,
    215–20, 238; killed on *General Gates,*
    221–23, 234, 239
Sky Rocket (Burke), 226
Smith, Isaac, 235
Smith, Richard, 105
Smith, S. (*Polly*), 92
Spartan, privateer, 225
Speedwell, schooner: fitted out as *Hancock,*
    29–30
Speedwell, sloop (Corey), 35, 43, 117
Spence, John Russell, 41
Stakesby, ship (Watt), 145–46, 156
Standley, William (*Prince William*), 33
Stanhope, John (*Raven*), 63–64
Stebbins, —— (*Governor Tryon*), 224–25

Stephens, Thomas, 22
Stevens, Thomas, 81–82, 220
Stiles, Richard, 117–18, 131, 157, 205,
    218
Stonington (Maine) Committee of Safety,
    45
Storer, Ebenezer, 235
Stuart, John, 104
Success, ship (Anderson), 216
Sullivan, James, 117
Sullivan, John, 82, 85
Surprize, HMS (Linzee), 233
Susannah, ship (Frazer), 144–45, 148, 156
Swan, Joshua, 179, 183
Symons, Thomas (*Cerberus*), 88

Tapley, Jeffery (*Charles*), 216
Tartar, HMS (Medows), 62–63, 65, 71,
    73–75
Taylor, Jacob, 61, 76–79
Thomas, brig (Robenson), 220
Thomas, schooner (Derby), 66
Thorn, armed sloop: commanded by
    Tucker, 228; commanded by Waters,
    224–25, 228
Tiley, John, 122, 157
Torrey, John, 57
Triton, brig (Brinton), 202, 205, 210, 212
Triton, schooner. See *Harrison*
True Blue, privateer (Glover), 218
Trumbull, Jonathan, 68
Tucker, Samuel: captures *Annabella,*
    184–86; captures *George,* 184–86; cap-
    tures *Henry and Esther,* 136; captures
    Jane, 161; captures *Lively,* 202; cap-
    tures *Lord Howe,* 185–86; captures
    Nelly Frigate, 193–94; captures *Peggy,*
    190–92; captures *Perkins,* 192; captures
    Rainbow, 135–36; captures *Triton,*
    202; captures *William,* 161; commands
    Franklin, 118, 120–21, 136, 142, 145,
    160, 174–75; commands *Hancock,* 160,
    177–79, 180–81, 187–90, 196, 198,
    201, 202, 205–9, 214, 221–22, 238;
    commissioned in Continental Navy,
    210, 224, 226, 228, 238–39
Turnbull, William, 203–4
Turner, Moses, 61, 64–66, 71, 76–77
Twisden, John, 82
Two Brothers. See *Lee*
Two Polly, cartel (Ayres), 211
Two Sisters, schooner (Robbins), 89–91

Unicorn, HMS (Ford), 197
Union, brig (Campbell), 224
Unity (Chevalier), 35
Unity, ship (Flagg), 17–20, 237
Unity, transport (Morgan), 191
Vail, John, 75
Victor, HM brig (Hyndman), 218, 230

Walkar, John, 75
Walter, Hugh (*Annabella*), 181–85
Ward, Artemus, 132, 151, *153*, 168,
177–78, 180, 184, 195, 199, 209; as
administrator, 154–59, 162, 164,
170–71, 187–91, 203; character of,
152–53; relieved, 213
Ward, Joseph, 156
Ward, William, 152
Warren, James, 48, 50
Warren, John, 7
Warren, armed schooner, 48, 92, 116, 121,
142; and Adams's cruise, 109–12; and
Burke's cruise, 117, 148, 151, 157, 175,
194, 199, 238; captured, 195; captures
Rainbow, 110; captures *Sally*, 111–12;
captures unnamed sloop, 109–10; and
fight with *Unity*, 191
Warren, sloop (Denny), 34, 45
Washington, George, 1, *2*, 7, 144; arms
schooners, 3, 48, 50–55, 67–68,
121–22, 124–25; assigns Moylan to fit
out schooners, 27–29; authorizes
agents, 29; background of, 5–6; and
capture of *Nancy*, 93–94, 110; and capture of *Unity*, 17, 18–19; and concern
for South, 104–5; and concerns for
fleet, 111–15, 118–19; and dispute
over *Hope*, 168, 170, 171–73; expands
fleet, 25, 27; forces Howe out of
Boston, 139–40, 146, 152; and George
III *Proclamation*, 90; increases prize
shares, 31; issues sailing orders, 11–14,
31–32, 58, 120; leases *Hannah*, 10; and
libeling courts, 61, 89, 96, 100, 113,
117, 150; named commander in chief,
5; names Broughton acting commodore, 31; and prisoner exchange,
77–78; and problems with agents, 90,
155–56, 193–94; prods Ward, 177,
180–81, 187–89; promotes Manley,
125, 129; and Quebec expedition,
26–27; reaction of, to Broughton's captures, 43–47; rejects *Dolphin* and

Industry, 28; relieves Ward, 213; relin-
quishes fleet, 199; response of, to
mutinies, 20–21, 61, 64–66, 67–69;
and search for ordnance, 7, 26–27, 31,
92; sets prize shares, 11; summarizes
fleet's accomplishments, 237–39
Washington, Martha, 102–3, 113
Washington, armed schooner, 48–49,
51–52, 56–57, 59, 88; captured by
Fowey, 71, 87, 104; cruise of, 62,
64–66, 70–79; mutiny on, 64–65
Waters, Daniel: captures *Annabella*,
181–86; captures *Anne*, 176–77; captures *Betsey*, 196; captures *Elizabeth*,
201; captures *George*, 181–86; captures
Henry and Esther, 136; captures
Rainbow, 135–37; captures *Sally*, 197;
commands *Lee*, 118, 121, 142, 145,
174–75, 178, 187, 192, 196–97, 206–9,
222, 238; in Continental Navy, 210,
223–25
Watertown (Mass.) Committee of Safety,
60
Watson, William, 50–51, 62, 64–69, 71,
77, 99, 113; fits out *Washington* and
Harrison, 55–57, 58, 60–61; prize
accounts of, 200, 240; refits *Harrison*,
123–24, 129–30, 133
Watt, James (*Stakesby*), 145–46
Webb, Samuel B., 55
Wentworth, Joshua, 42, 109–10, 119, 126,
144, 150, 154, 193–94, 199; prize
accounts of, 200, 236
Wheaton, Caleb, 150–51
Whipple, Abraham, 1, 26, 227–28
White, Gideon, 78
White, Sibeline (*Polly*), 59
Wigglesworth, John, 124
William, brig (Price), 161
Williams, John Foster (*Hazard*), 224
Williams, Jonathan, Jr., 212–13
Williamson, transport, 86
Winter Harbor, Maine, 42, 45
Wormwell, Benjamin, 51–52
Wright, Thomas, 38–42, 44, 46

Yankee (Barnes), 135

ABOUT THE AUTHOR

Chester G. Hearn is the author of three other books, *Gray Raiders of the Sea, Mobile Bay and the Mobile Campaign,* and the forthcoming *The Capture of New Orleans, 1862.* A retired manufacturing executive, he has had an interest in naval warfare since his childhood in Erie, Pennsylvania. Although his attention has been focused on the Civil War, he has been collecting material on George Washington's schooners for the past thirty-five years.

A resident of Potts Grove, Pennsylvania, Hearn is also the author of numerous articles published in *Civil War Times Illustrated, Blue and Gray Magazine,* and *America's Civil War.*

The Naval Institute Press is the book-publishing arm of the U.S. Naval Institute, a private, nonprofit society for sea service professionals and others who share an interest in naval and maritime affairs. Established in 1873 at the U.S. Naval Academy in Annapolis, Maryland, where its offices remain, today the Naval Institute has more than 100,000 members worldwide.

Members of the Naval Institute receive the influential monthly magazine *Proceedings* and discounts on fine nautical prints and on ship and aircraft photos. They also have access to the transcripts of the Institute's Oral History Program and get discounted admission to any of the Institute-sponsored seminars offered around the country.

The Naval Institute also publishes *Naval History* magazine. This colorful bimonthly is filled with entertaining and thought-provoking articles, first-person reminiscences, and dramatic art and photography. Members receive a discount on *Naval History* subscriptions.

The Naval Institute's book-publishing program, begun in 1898 with basic guides to naval practices, has broadened its scope in recent years to include books of more general interest. Now the Naval Institute Press publishes more than seventy titles each year, ranging from how-to books on boating and navigation to battle histories, biographies, ship and aircraft guides, and novels. Institute member receive discounts on the Press's nearly 400 books in print.

For a free catalog describing Naval Institute Press books currently available, and for further information about subscribing to *Naval History* magazine or about joining the U.S. Naval Institute, please write to:

Membership & Communications Department
U.S. Naval Institute
118 Maryland Avenue
Annapolis, Maryland 21402-5035

Or call, toll-free, (800) 233-USNI.